Android™ User Interface Design

Android™ User Interface Design

Implementing Material Design for Developers

Second Edition

Ian G. Clifton

✦✦Addison-Wesley

New York • Boston • Indianapolis • San Francisco
Toronto • Montreal • London • Munich • Paris • Madrid
Cape Town • Sydney • Tokyo • Singapore • Mexico City

For information about buying this title in bulk quantities, or for special sales opportunities (which may include electronic versions; custom cover designs; and content particular to your business, training goals, marketing focus, or branding interests), please contact our corporate sales department at corpsales@pearsoned.com or (800) 382-3419.

For government sales inquiries, please contact governmentsales@pearsoned.com.

For questions about sales outside the U.S., please contact international@pearsoned.com.

Visit us on the Web: informit.com/aw

Library of Congress Control Number: 2015950113

ISBN-13: 978-0-134-19140-9
ISBN-10: 0-134-19140-4

Text printed in the United States on recycled paper at RR Donnelley in Crawfordsville, Indiana.

First printing: November 2015

Editor-in-Chief
Mark Taub

Executive Editor
Laura Lewin

Development Editor
Songlin Qiu

Managing Editor
Kristy Hart

Project Editor
Namita Gahtori

Copy Editor
Cenveo® Publisher Services

Indexer
Cenveo Publisher Services

Proofreader
Cenveo Publisher Services

Technical Reviewers
Cameron Banga
Joshua Jamison
Adam Porter

Editorial Assistant
Olivia Basegio

Cover Designer
Chuti Prastersith

Compositor
Cenveo Publisher Services

Dedicated to those who care about user experience

Contents at a Glance

Contents

PREFACE

Android has evolved at an incredible speed, and keeping up with the changes is a difficult job for any developer. While working to keep up with the latest features and API changes, it can be easy to neglect the design changes Android is undergoing. When Google announced the Material Design guidelines, even designers who had long dismissed Android's visuals started paying attention.

It's more important than ever for Android developers to understand the core aspects of design and the Material Design guidelines go some of the way toward making that possible; however, without years of background in design, it can be difficult to make sense of everything. This book will guide you through the real-world process of design starting from an abstract idea and sketches on paper and working all the way through animations, RenderScript, and custom views. The idea is to touch on each of the core concepts and cover enough so that you can have productive conversations with designers or even create everything yourself.

Design has many purposes, but two of the most important are usability and visual appeal. You want brand-new users to be able to jump into your app and get started without any effort because mobile users are more impatient than users of nearly any other platform. Users need to know exactly what they can interact with, and they need to be able to do so in a hurry while distracted. That also means you have to be mindful of what platform conventions are in order to take advantage of learned behavior.

If you have picked up this book, I probably do not need to go on and on about how important design is. You get it. You want to make the commitment of making beautiful apps that are a pleasure to use.

This book will serve as a tutorial for the entire design and implementation process as well as a handy reference that you can keep using again and again. You will understand how to talk with designers and developers alike to make the best applications possible. You will be able to make apps that are visually appealing while still easy to change when those last-minute design requests inevitably come in.

Ultimately, designers and developers both want their apps to be amazing, and I am excited to teach you how to make that happen.

—Ian G. Clifton

ACKNOWLEDGMENTS

You would think that the second edition of a book would be easier than the first, but when you find yourself rewriting 90 percent of it because both the technology and design trends are changing so rapidly, it helps to have assistance. Executive Editor, Laura Lewin, once again helped keep me on track even as I restructured the book and dove in depth in places I didn't originally expect. Olivia Basegio, the Editorial Assistant, kept track of all the moving pieces, including getting the Rough Cuts online so that interested readers could get a glimpse into the book as it evolved. Songlin Qiu was the Development Editor again and took on the task of making sense of my late-night draft chapters. I am also extremely appreciative of the work done by the technical reviewers, Adam Porter, Cameron Banga, and Joshua Jamison, whose feedback was instrumental in the quality of this book.

ABOUT THE AUTHOR

Ian G. Clifton is a professional Android application developer, user experience advocate, and author. He has worked with many developers and designers, and led Android teams, creating well-known apps such as Saga, CNET News, CBS News, and more.

Ian's love of technology, art, and user experience has led him along a variety of paths. In addition to Android development, he has done platform, web, and desktop development. He served in the U.S. Air Force as a Satellite, Wideband, and Telemetry Systems Journeyman and has also created quite a bit of art with pencil, charcoal, brush, camera, and even wood.

You can follow Ian G. Clifton on Twitter at http://twitter.com/IanGClifton and see his thoughts about mobile development on his blog at http://blog.iangclifton.com. He also published a video series called "The Essentials of Android Application Development LiveLessons, 2nd Edition," available at http://goo.gl/4jr2j0.

INTRODUCTION

Audience for This Book

This book is intended primarily for Android developers who want to better understand user interfaces (UI) in Android. To focus on the important topics of Android UI design, this book makes the assumption that you already have a basic understanding of Android, so if you haven't made a "Hello, World" Android app or set up your computer for development, you should do so before reading this book (the Android developer site is a good place to start: http://developer.android.com/training/basics/firstapp/index.html).

Most developers have limited or no design experience, so this book makes no assumptions that you understand design. Whenever a design topic is important, such as choosing colors, this book will walk you through the basics, so that you can feel confident making your own decisions and understand what goes into those decisions.

Organization of This Book

This book is organized into a few parts. Part I, "The Basics of Android User Interface," provides an overview of the Android UI and trends before diving into the specific classes used to create an interface in Android. It also covers the use of graphics and resources. Part II, "The Full Design and Development Process," mirrors the stages of app development, starting with just ideas and goals, working through wireframes and prototypes, and developing complete apps that include efficient layouts, animations, and more. Part III, "Advanced Topics for Android User Interfaces," explores much more complex topics including troubleshooting UI performance problems with Systrace and creating custom views that handle drawing, scrolling, and state saving.

This book also has two appendices. The first focuses on Google Play assets (and covers the differences to know about when preparing for the Amazon Appstore as well), diving into app icon creation. The second covers a variety of common UI-related tasks that are good to know but don't necessarily fit elsewhere (such as custom view attributes).

The emphasis throughout is on implementation in simple and clear ways. You do not have to worry about pounding your head against complex topics such as 3D matrix transformations in OpenGL; instead, you will learn how to create smooth animations, add PorterDuff compositing into your custom views, and efficiently work with touch events. The little math involved will be broken down, making it simple. In addition, illustrations will make even the most complex examples clear, and every example will be practical.

How to Use This Book

This book starts with a very broad overview before going into more specific and more advanced topics. As such, it is intended to be read in order, but it is also organized to make reference as easy as possible. Even if you're an advanced developer, it is a good idea to read through all the chapters because of the wide range of material covered; however, you can also jump directly to the topics that most interest you. For example, if you really want to focus on creating your own custom views, you can jump right to Chapter 12, "Developing Custom Views."

This Book's Website

You can find the source code for the examples used throughout this book at https://github .com/IanGClifton/auid2 and the publisher's website at http://www.informit.com/store/android-user-interface-design-implementing-material-9780134191409. From there, you can clone the entire repository, download a full ZIP file, and browse through individual files.

Conventions Used in This Book

This book uses typical conventions found in most programming-related books. Code terms such as class names or keywords appear in `monospace font`. When a class is being referred to specifically (e.g., "Your class should extend the `View` class"), then it will be in monospace font. If it's used more generally (e.g., "When developing a view, don't forget to test on a real device"), then it will not be in a special font.

Occasionally when a line of code is too long to fit on a printed line in the book, a code-continuation arrow (➡) is used to mark the continuation.

You will also see some asides from time to time that present useful information that does not fit into flow of the main text.

> note
>
> Notes look like this and are short asides intended to supplement the material in the book with other information you may find useful.

tip

Tips look like this and give you advice on specific topics.

warning

POTENTIAL DATA LOSS OR SECURITY ISSUES   Warnings look like this and are meant to bring to your attention to potential issues you may run into or things you should look out for.

CHAPTER 1

ANDROID UI AND MATERIAL DESIGN

It is a good idea to have an overview of the user interface (UI) as it pertains to Android, so that's the starting point here. You will learn a brief history of Android design to see how it evolved to Material Design before diving into some core design principles. You will also learn some of the high-level components of Android design and some of the changes that have come to Android design as the world's most popular mobile operating system has evolved.

A Brief History of Android Design

Android had a very technical start with a lot of amazing work going on to make it a platform that could run on a variety of devices without most apps having to care too much about the details. That base allowed Android to handle many types of hardware input (trackballs, hardware directional pads, sliding keyboards, touch interface, and so on). It also kept Android largely focused on scalable design, much more closely related to fluid web design than typical mobile design. The underlying code could even handle running on a device that did not have a graphics processing unit (GPU). Unfortunately, all of that also meant that early design for Android was blasé and focused on the lowest common denominator, so embellishments like animations were sparse. Colors were bland and often inconsistent, and most input and visual organization was based on what had been done in the past rather than pushing things forward.

In 2010, Google hired Matias Duarte (most known for his excellent work with WebOS) as the Senior Director of Android User Experience, which made it clear that Google had become serious about the user experience for Android and its related visual design. The Android beta was released way back in 2007, so Matias and his colleagues had a lot of work in front of them. How do you go from a very functional but visually bland UI to one that enhances that functionality by improving the entire design and user experience?

About a year later, the first Android tablets running Honeycomb (Android 3.0) were revealed. These tablets gave Google the opportunity to really experiment with the UI because there was no prior version of Android that had been designed for tablets, and therefore users did not have strong expectations. With the radical new Holo theme, these tablets were a significant departure from the previous Android styles.

By the end of 2011, Google had revealed Android 4.0, Ice Cream Sandwich, which showed how they were able to improve the tablet-only Honeycomb styling to tone down some of the "techieness" and smooth out the user experience. The tablet/phone divide was eliminated and the platform was brought together in a much more cohesive manner, emphasizing interaction, visuals, and simplicity. Even the default system font changed to the newly created Roboto, significantly improving on the previous Droid fonts. Regardless of whether you are the kind of person who gets giddy over straight-sided Grotesk sans serif fonts, you will appreciate the attention to detail this font signifies.

Android 4.1, Jelly Bean, was revealed at Google I/O in 2012. A release focused primarily on usability, Jelly Bean gave Android a much better sense of polish. "Project Butter" brought about a much more fluid user experience with graphics improvements such as triple buffering. Even components of Android that hadn't been touched in years, such as notifications, were updated to improve the user experience. Android 4.2 came just a few months later, with support for multiple users, the "Daydream" feature (essentially, application-provided screensavers with the ability to be interactive), support for photo spheres (panoramas that can cover 360 degrees), and wireless mirroring. Android 4.3 followed with many more features, including OpenGL ES 3.0 support. Android 4.4 finished off the 4.x version with major system improvements, allowing Android to run on devices with as little as 512MB of RAM.

Then, Android undertook a radical change for version 5.0, Lollipop, with the introduction of Material Design. See how the home screen has changed from Android 1.6 to Android 5.0 in Figure 1.1.

Figure 1.1 The home screen for Android 1.6 (top left), 2.3 (top right), 4.2 (bottom left), and 5.0 (bottom right)

Material Design

Although Android 5.0 and Material Design are closely linked, Material Design isn't just a design language for Android 5.0 and beyond. It is meant to be a set of design principles that apply across device types and arbitrary software versions. That means best practices from Material Design should be applied to older versions of Android and even web apps. Google describes it this way:

> A material metaphor is the unifying theory of a rationalized space and a system of motion. The material is grounded in tactile reality, inspired by the study of paper and ink, yet technologically advanced and open to imagination and magic.

If you're like most nondesigners, your immediate reaction is "What?" It is easy to dismiss this type of statement as just "designer fluff" and not appreciate the meaning, but designers have guiding principles that are meant to make their work better and more coherent just like developers (who have principles such as "Don't repeat yourself"). Google's description is saying that Material Design is based on real paper and ink, but it isn't limited to just what those elements can do in the physical world.

General Concepts

In the Material Design world, paper is the primary surface that everything else exists on. It can grow and shrink, unlike paper in the real world. That means a piece of paper can appear in the center of the screen by growing from a single pixel to its full size and it can even change shape. Paper always shows up with some kind of transition (growing or sliding into place); it is never just suddenly there at full size. Pieces of paper can push each other when their edges collide. Pieces of paper can be split into two, and multiple pieces can join to become one. A sheet of paper can never go through another, but one sheet of paper can slide over another.

The fact that paper can slide in front of other paper means that Material Design exists in a 3D environment. The third dimension, plotted on the Z-axis, is how close the object is to the surface of the screen, which affects the shadow it casts and whether it is in front of or behind another piece of paper. Material Design treats the Z-axis as very finite, meaning that there is no significant amount of depth that can be shown (just how many pieces of paper thick is your actual screen?). This limitation means that differences in depth are much more noticeable. Paper is always one density-independent pixel thick (the concept of density-independent pixels, or dips, is covered in detail in Chapter 4, "Adding App Graphics and Resources," but you can simply think of a dip as a unit for now), which means that it does not bend or fold.

Devices don't (yet) have a third dimension to their screens, so this depth is created with the traditional techniques of perspective, obscuring (sometimes called occlusion), and shadow. As shown in Figure 1.2, an object closer to the surface is bigger than the same object at a lower level. An

Figure 1.2 Simple perspective means closer objects are larger, but with that cue alone it is unclear if an object is closer or just larger than the others

object that is in front of another obscures some or all of what it is behind it just like in Figure 1.3. A closer object casts a shadow as demonstrated in Figure 1.4. Combining these simple principles means that you get a much clearer picture of the depth of objects as shown in Figure 1.5.

Shadows in Material Design are created by two light sources: a key light and an ambient light. If you imagine taking a quick photo of someone with your phone, the flash is the key light and all the other light is ambient. The key light is what creates the strong, directional shadows. The

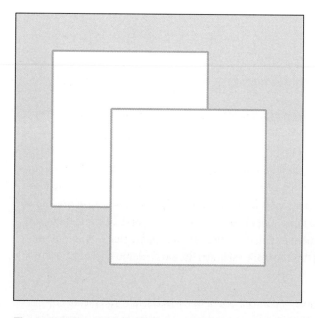

Figure 1.3 Obscuring allows you to show that one object is in front of another, but it doesn't tell you how much in front

Figure 1.4 A simple shadow can indicate that an object is closer, but the lack of a size change (due to perspective) can create confusion

Figure 1.5 When you combine all of these principles, it is much more obvious that the middle item is closer even with the outside pieces of paper being raised from the surface slightly

ambient light creates soft shadows in all directions. The key light is coming from the top center of the screen, casting shadows down from paper; this also means that these bottom shadows are slightly more pronounced for paper that is at the bottom of the screen because the light is at a sharper angle. This sort of subtle visual detail goes almost unnoticed, but it enhances the consistency of the artificial environment and makes the shadows appear that little bit more realistic. To better understand what this means, see Figure 1.6, which demonstrates these concepts in the 3D environment.

In addition to paper, ink is the other major component of Material Design. Ink is what colors paper and creates text on paper. It has no thickness. It can move around on a piece of paper (e.g., a photo can move from the top to the bottom of a piece of paper or grow from a

Figure 1.6 3D rendering of a Material Design app

thumbnail to a larger photo on that paper). It can grow or shrink, and change color or shape. It is generally bold and purposeful. Many apps have been designed with very subdued colors or even just shades of gray, but Material Design calls for a vibrancy to the design. Chapter 7, "Designing the Visuals," discusses color choice in detail.

Interaction and Animation

One of the most important aspects of app design that is often ignored is interaction. What happens when the user touches this button? Sure, it shows a new screen, but what is the process to get there? Does the button grow or shrink or change color? Does the new content slide in or grow from the old content? Material Design puts much more emphasis on interaction and animation than previous design guidelines, which will help make your apps feel well polished.

Touch events in the past were often expressed with a simple background color change. Tapping a row in a list might have caused the background to suddenly go from white to orange or blue. Material Design is about natural transitions, so the typical touch reaction is a ripple. You can imagine dropping a rock in a pond and seeing the water ripples move outward from that point; that is similar to the response of an interactive element in Material Design. In addition, an item's paper can react. If a standalone piece of paper reacts to touch, the whole paper rises up as if eager to meet the finger. This is important to note because it is the opposite of traditional design where objects like buttons are pushed down in an effort to mimic the physical world (called skeuomorphic design).

Animations should be fluid and accelerate or decelerate where appropriate. Just like how a car doesn't start out at its top speed when you press the accelerator, a piece of paper sliding off the screen in response to your touch shouldn't start at its maximum speed. As small as the paper may be, it does have mass. The way an animation changes as it goes from 0% complete to 100% complete is called interpolation. Choosing to have an interpolation that accelerates rather than being linear might seem like an unimportant detail, but it is one of those many little pieces that come together to make your app that much better. In addition, it is actually easy to do (Chapter 9, "Polishing with Animations," explains animations in great detail).

Another important note about animations is that their purpose is not to "wow" the user. It is not to distract the user or arbitrarily make things interesting. The purpose is to help the user understand the transition from what was on the screen to what will be on the screen. Animations guide the user's eyes to the important elements and explain what is changing. When done right, these transitions create some enjoyment for the user and can even lead the user to trigger them again just to watch the animation.

Typography

When Android 4.0 was released, Google also unveiled Roboto. Roboto is a typeface designed specifically for today's mobile devices, making it appear crisp on a variety of densities. For Android 5.0, Roboto has been updated to fix some of its more noticeable quirks, improving some characters (such as the capital "R") and making the dots for punctuation and tittles (the dots above lowercase "i" and "j") the more common circle rather than a harsh square. You can see some of the changes in Figure 1.7.

1679gijRK

1679gijRK

Figure 1.7 Some of the more noticeable differences between the original Roboto font (top) and the revised version (bottom)

The other font used in Material Design that you should know of is Noto. It is actually the default font for Chrome OS as well as languages that Roboto doesn't support on Android. A simple rule to start with is use Roboto for languages that use Latin, Greek, and Cyrillic (commonly used in eastern Europe as well as north and parts of central Asia) scripts and Noto for all others. Typography is covered in much more detail in Chapter 7, "Designing the Visuals."

Metrics and Alignment

Material Design emphasizes a 4dp (or four density-independent pixel) grid. That means every element on the screen is aligned based on a multiple of four. For instance, the left and right sides of the screen are typically indented 16dp on a phone, so thumbnails and text in a list all start 16dp from the left. When images such as thumbnails or icons are shown to the left of a list item, the Material Guidelines say that the text that follows is indented a total of 72dp from the left edge of the screen.

These layout and alignment concepts are covered in detail in Chapter 5, "Starting a New App." They're also used throughout the example implementations in this book.

The Android Design Website

That was quite a bit about Material Design, but there is a lot more to it. Throughout this book, you will be learning more about Material Design, what factors into certain decisions, and how to actually implement it all, but it is also a good idea to look at the Android design website (http://developer.android.com/design/). That site will give very specific details about how Material Design applies to specific Android components. You should also look at the Material Design spec from Google (http://www.google.com/design/spec/material-design/), which has a lot of great video clips for demonstrating things that are hard to understand with just words, such as interaction animations.

You don't need to have the content of either of those sites memorized before you start designing your own app or implementing a design someone else has created, but you should look through them to have an idea of what is there and be ready to come back to them any time you have a question. Note that the Android developer website (including the design portion of it) has a huge number of pages, giving descriptions and tutorials for a variety of topics. That is great because it means you can almost always find some help there, but it also means that many of the pages are not as up-to-date as would be ideal. If you see a page there that seems to disagree with Material Design, it is most likely just outdated (you can often tell by looking at whether the screenshots show an older version of Android such as 4.x with the Holo blue in the status bar), so you should prefer the guidance provided by the Material Design spec. It's also worth noting that the Material Design guidelines are regularly being updated, adding examples and details to further clarify the principles.

Core Principles

It is impossible to come up with a perfect checklist that lets you know that your app is exactly right when everything is checked, but guiding principles can make a big difference. Start with your users' goals to define exactly what your app should do. You might be surprised how many apps do not have a clear user goal in mind before launching, and it is reflected in their design. User goals and product goals are explained in detail in Chapter 5, "Starting a New App," but it's important to look at the core principles first.

Do One Thing and Do It Well

If you ever want to build a mediocre app, a sure way to do so is by trying to make it do everything. The more narrowly focused your app is, the easier it is to make sure that it does what it is supposed to and that it does so well. When you're starting on a new app, list everything you want it to do. Next, start crossing off the least important things in that list until you have narrowed it down to just the absolute essentials. You can always add functionality later, but you can't add a clear focus halfway through making a jack-of-all-trades app. A narrow focus also helps ensure that the desired features and functionality are clear.

You are probably ready when you can answer the question, "Why would someone use this app?" without including conjunctions (such as "and" and "or") and without using a second sentence. Here are two examples:

> **Good:** "Users will use this app to write quick notes to themselves."

> **Bad:** "Users will use this app to write notes to themselves, browse past notes, and share notes with other users on Twitter."

Yes, being able to browse notes can be an important part of the app, but writing the notes is the most important part. Making that decision makes it clear that you should be able to begin a new note in a single touch from the starting screen, probably via a floating action button (or "FAB"). Of course, you could be building an app where organizing those notes is the most important part; in that case, you will emphasize browsing, sorting, and searching.

Consider the Contacts app as an example (see Figure 1.8). It's really just a list of people who can have pictures and various data associated with them. From that app, you can call someone or email someone, but those actions happen outside of the app.

As tempting as it can be to make an app that does many things, such as an email app that can modify photos before adding them as attachments, you need to start with a single focus and make that part of the app excellent before moving on. If the email portion is terrible, no one will download the app just to use the photo manipulation aspect of it.

There are times when your app does have multiple purposes because these features are too intertwined to separate or the requirements are outside of your control. In those cases, you

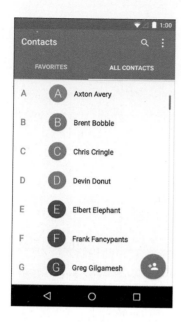

Figure 1.8 The Contacts app is a good example of an app with a singular and obvious focus

should split the functionality in a clear and meaningful way for the user. For instance, consider the Gallery in Android. It allows users to look at their photos and manipulate them in simple ways. It doesn't allow users to draw images or manage the file system, so it has a clear and obvious focus. The Gallery has a quick link to jump to the Camera app, but the Camera also has its own icon that the user can go to from the launcher. Conceptually, the Camera app just takes photos and videos. As complex as the code is to do that well, users don't have to think about it. In fact, users do not need to know that the Camera app and the Gallery app are part of the same app in stock Android (some manufacturers do create separate, custom apps for these features, and Google provides their own replacements). If users want to look at photos, they will go to the Gallery. If users want to take photos, they will go to the Camera app.

Play Nicely with Others

Just because your app does only one thing extremely well doesn't mean it needs to limit the user's experience. One of the best parts about Android is that apps are really just components in the overall user experience. Your app should handle reasonable `Intents`, which is the class Android uses to indicate what the user is trying to do and to find an appropriate app to accomplish that objective. Is it an app for a particular site? Have it handle links for that site. Does it let the user modify images? Handle any `Intent` for working with an image.

Do not waste development time adding in sharing for specific sharing mechanisms such as Twitter and Facebook. If you do, you will have to decide on each and every other service, such

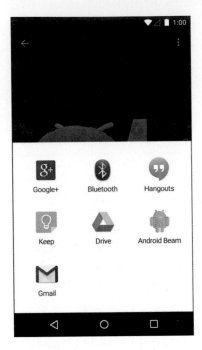

Figure 1.9 Default UI for letting a user share with whichever app he or she chooses

as Google Plus. Do your users care about Google Plus? Why bother finding out when you can just let the user pick whichever apps he or she wants to share with? If Google Plus is important to a user, that user will have the app installed. With just a couple lines of work, you can present a dialog to the user (Figure 1.9), which supports far more services than you'd want to develop code for. By creating specific code for sharing with a given service, you're actually removing support for sharing with every other service the user may want to use. Not only that, but supporting a specific sharing service often requires additional maintenance to update the applicable SDKs, tackle bugs, and handle API changes.

The time you spend implementing sharing for third-party services in your own app is time that could be spent making your app better. Why would you spend a week developing some tolerable sharing tools when you can pass that work off to the user's favorite apps? You can bet that regardless of whichever Twitter client the user is going to share with, the developer of that app spent more time on it than you can afford to for a single feature. You use existing Java classes, so why not use existing Android apps?

This does not just go for sharing either. You can build an amazing alarm app that, from the user perspective, just triggers other apps. That sounds simple, but once you combine it with the system to allow that app to start playing a music app or preload a weather or news app, your clear, easy functionality becomes extremely valuable.

Visuals, Visuals, Visuals

One of the major challenges of mobile applications is that you often have a lot of information to convey, but you have very little screen real estate to do so. Even worse, the user is frequently only taking a quick look at the app. That means it needs to be easy to scan for the exact information desired. Use short text for headers, directions, and dialogs. Make sure that buttons state a real action, such as "Save File" instead of "Okay," so that a button's function is immediately obvious.

Use images to convey meaning quickly. Use consistent visuals to anchor the user. Always include all applicable touch states. At a minimum, anything the user can interact with should have a normal state, a pressed state, and a focused state. The pressed state is shown when the user is actively touching the view, so excluding it means the user is unsure what views can be interacted with and whether the app is even responding. The focused state is shown when a view is selected by means of the directional pad or other method so that the user knows what view will be pressed. It can also be used in touch mode, such as how an `EditText` will highlight to show users where they are entering text. Without a focused state, users cannot effectively use alternate means of navigation.

Visuals are not just limited to images either. Users of your app will quickly learn to recognize repeated words such as headers. If a portion of your app always says "Related Images" in the same font and style, users will learn to recognize the shape of that text without even needing to read it.

Easy but Powerful

People are judgmental. People using an app for the first time are hyperjudgmental, and that means it is critical that your app be easy to use. The primary functions should be clear and obvious. This need ties in with visuals and a recognizable focus. If you jump into that note-taking app and see a big plus icon, you can guess right away that the plus button starts a new note. The powerful side of it comes when pressing that plus button also populates meta-data that the user does not have to care about (at that moment), such as the date the note was started or the user's location at that time. When the note is saved, the app can scan it for important words or names that match the user's contacts. Suddenly the app is able to do useful things such as finding all notes mentioning Susan in the past month without the user having to consider that ability when creating the note.

If your app provides photo filters, do not just say "stretch contrast" or "remove red channel." Instead, show a preview thumbnail so the user can see and understand the effect of the button (see Figure 1.10). When the user scrolls to the bottom of your list of news articles, automatically fetch the next group of articles to add to the list. Simple features like these are intuitive and make the user feel empowered.

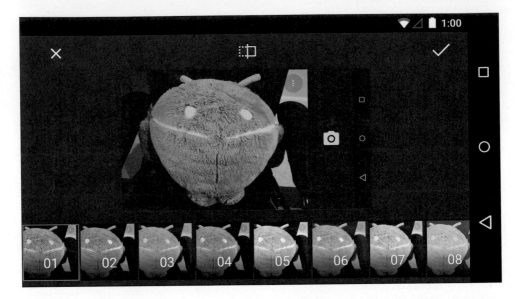

Figure 1.10 Each image-processing technique along the bottom has a simple thumbnail illustrating the effect

One last thing to remember about making your app easy but powerful is that the user is always right, even when making a mistake. When the user presses a "delete" button, in 99% of cases, the user meant to press that button. Don't ask the user "Did you really mean to do that thing you just did?" Assume the user meant to, but make it easy to undo the action. Don't make features difficult to access to keep the user from making a mistake. Make features easy to use, including undo, to encourage the user to explore your app. An app that does this extremely well is Gmail. When you delete an email, you have the option to undo it. The app doesn't ask you whether you meant to delete it because that gets in the way of a good user experience. Of course, if it's not reasonably possible to undo an action (like the extreme case of formatting the device), then a confirmation dialog is a good idea.

Platform Consistency

When in doubt, follow the user experience expectations of the platform. Even when you're not in doubt, you should follow the user experience expectations of the platform. In other words, unless you have an extremely good reason, you should not do things differently from how they are done in the built-in apps. "We want our iOS app and Android app to look/behave similarly" is *not* a good excuse. Your Android users use their Android devices on a daily basis; they rarely (if ever) use iOS devices (or other mobile platforms). These platforms have very different user expectations, and using the behavior or styles of another platform in your Android app will lead to user confusion and frustration.

Other platforms can require navigational buttons such as a back button or an exit button; these do *not* belong in an Android app. The actual Android back button should have an obvious and intuitive function in your app, and adding another element to the UI that does the same thing creates user confusion. There is no need to exit your app, because the user can either back out of it or simply press the home button. Your button is either going to artificially replicate one of these scenarios or, worse, it will truly exit the app and slow down its next startup time. That does not just slow down the user experience; it wastes power rereading assets from disk that might have been able to stay in memory.

Using styling from another platform not only looks out of place, but it is also awkward for the user. For example, Android has a specific sharing icon that looks quite distinct from other platforms such as iOS and Windows Phone. Users are likely to be confused if an icon from another platform is used. Take advantage of what the user has already learned from other apps on Android by being consistent with the platform.

Most Android developers have to deal with a manager or other person at some time who insists on making the user experience worse by copying aspects of the iOS app such as a loading screen. Fight this! Not only is it a waste of your time to develop, making the user experience worse also leads to lower app use and user retention. When your app has an artificial 2-second delay to show a splash screen that's little better than a full-screen branding advertisement and the competitor's app opens in a hundred milliseconds, which is the user going to want? Worse, it's easy to make mistakes implementing something like a splash screen, causing your app to open to the real content after an artificial delay despite the fact that the user switched to another app because the splash screen took too long. Now it feels like the app is being aggressive, trying to force the user to use it, and it is even more likely to be uninstalled and given a low rating.

Bend to the User

One of the great things about Android is that users have a lot of choice right from the beginning. A construction worker might choose a rigid device with a physical keyboard over a more powerful thin device. Someone with larger hands has the option to pick a device with a 6-inch screen over a much smaller screen. Android makes it extremely easy to support these different scenarios. Just because it can be difficult to support landscape and portrait on other platforms does not mean that the support should be dropped for Android as well.

Bending to the user does not just mean adjusting your app to give the best experience on a given device; it also means picking up on user habits. How much you pick up their habits is up to you. The simplest method is just giving preferences that the user can set. Is your app a reading app? It might make sense to offer an option to force a particular orientation for reading while lying down. If your app shows white text on a black background at night, but the user always switches it back to black on white, your app can learn that preference.

Standard Components

Regardless of whether you meticulously sketch your design concepts, quickly rough them out to refine later, or dip your pet's feet in ink and have him walk around on a large piece of paper hoping for something magical to appear, it is important to know the standard components of Android.

System Bars

Android has two system bars: the status bar and the navigation bar. The status bar (shown in Figure 1.11) is at the top of the screen and displays icons for notifications on the left and standard phone status info on the right, such as battery and signal levels. The navigation bar (shown in Figure 1.12) is at the bottom of the screen and consists of back, home, and overview software buttons when hardware buttons are not present. Apps that were built against older versions of Android will also cause a menu button to appear in the navigation bar. Tablet devices had a combined bar that displayed both status and navigation controls for Android 3.x (Honeycomb), but the UI was updated for Android 4.2 to be like phones, with the status bar on top and the navigation bar at the bottom.

Figure 1.11 The standard Android status bar (top) and the status bar colored by an app (bottom)

Figure 1.12 The standard Android navigation bar is typically black but can also be colored

For the most part, these do not need to be considered much during design. You can hide the status bar, but you almost never should. It's acceptable to hide the system bars during video playback and it's fine to hide the status bar when it might interfere with the user experience. Casual games should typically still show the status bar (no reason for the user to have to leave a game of solitaire to see what notifications are pending or what time it is). Nearly all apps should show the status bar. How do you know if yours is an exception? Try your app with the status bar being displayed and see if it interferes with the user experience. If it does not, you should display the status bar. Code examples demonstrating how to show and hide these bars are available in Appendix B, "Common Task Reference."

Notifications

Right from the start, Android was designed with multitasking in mind. A user shouldn't have to stare at a progress bar in an app that is downloading resources, nor should a user have to exit an app to have access to the most important information on his or her device. Notifications are a great feature that many apps do not take advantage of. If your app does something in the background, such as syncing a playlist, it should show a notification while that is happening. If your app has important information the user should be aware of, such as a stock alert that the user has set, it should be displayed as a notification.

Android 4.1 brought about richer notifications that allow notifications to have actions as well as larger displays. For example, an email notification might show just the subject and sender, but the expanded notification could show part of the actual message as well as buttons to reply or archive the email. Notification design is improved for Android 5.0 by changing to a dark on light theme with support for accent colors and much more. See Figure 1.13 to view the new style.

Figure 1.13 The Android 5.0 update for notifications changed to a light background with dark text

The design of notifications is covered in Chapter 7, "Designing the Visuals," and the implementation (including supporting older versions of Android) is in Chapter 8, "Applying the Design."

App Bar

The app bar is the toolbar that sits at the very top of the app, just below the status bar. Previously called the action bar, this toolbar is now able to be implemented just like any other view. This actually fixes some issues with the old action bar (which was implemented as part of the window, which limited its capabilities) and has a few design changes. See Figure 1.14 for an example.

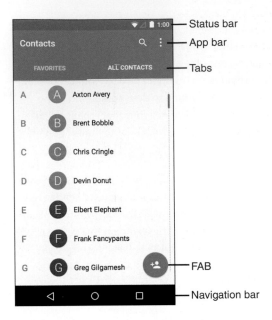

Figure 1.14 The primary components of an Android app

The app icon is typically no longer included in the bar, but navigation still goes on the left (such as "up" navigation, which allows the user to navigate "up" one level in the hierarchy, or the hamburger menu icon, which indicates a sliding drawer) and contextual actions still go on the right. Just like before, infrequently accessed actions and actions that don't fit on the app bar go into an overflow menu that is represented by three vertical dots. Although you can include a logo, it's generally not desirable. You can include any kind of custom view applicable to your app to make the bar work for you. The standard height is now 56dp on mobile devices (the action bar was 48dp), but it can actually be taller if needed and even animate between sizes. Other sheets of paper can push against the app bar, slide behind it, or even go in front of it. You can also have a second toolbar at the bottom of the app, which is typically just referred to as a "bottom toolbar" and not an app bar.

The app bar makes sense for most apps, but you can hide it as needed (such as for an app focused on reading or watching videos). A common behavior in Material Design is for the app bar to slide away as the user is interacting with the content (such as when scrolling down the page) but come back when the user might need it (such as when scrolling back up). You will work with the `Toolbar` class throughout this book. It is a concrete implementation available in the support library that makes an app bar as easy as any view and it has built-in support for creating menus.

Tabs and Navigation Drawer

Tabs have been a common form of navigation since well before PCs, and they continue to be effective. In Android, tabs always go at the top. If there is an app bar, the tabs are the bottom portion of that bar (see Figure 1.14 for an example). As opposed to most other navigation methods, tabs are easily understood and increase the visibility of different sections of your app. When in a fixed position, having two or three tabs is ideal. If you have more tabs, you can make them scrollable, but you should consider another means of navigation, such as a navigation drawer.

The navigation drawer is a navigation mechanism where there are several sections to the app or when navigating from deep in the app to different top-level sections is common. The drawer is accessed either by pressing the hamburger menu icon (the three horizontal lines that are stacked vertically) or by swiping in from the left. It should always take the full height of the screen. That means it goes in front of the app bar and behind the status bar. In the past, navigation drawers were often implemented below the app bar (called the action bar then), but that was an implementation limitation (the action bar was part of the window décor, which makes sliding views in front of it problematic). Any navigation drawer you create now should always be the full screen height.

Both tabs and navigation drawers are covered in more depth in Chapter 6, "Prototyping and Developing the App Foundation."

The FAB

The "FAB" is a fairly iconic piece of Material Design. It is the circular floating action button that is shown in an accent color when there is a primary action for a given page (see Figure 1.14 for an example). This allows the important action to draw more attention and also be in a position that might make more sense (from a layout perspective or from a thumb-reach perspective). Although it stands for floating action button, you can also think of it as the frequently accessed button because it should always be for an action that is very frequently used on a given page. If this is a note-taking app and the user is on the page listing all notes, the FAB would almost definitely be for creating a new note (either with a large plus icon or with an icon that combines a note with a plus). A FAB is not required, so don't force one onto a page where it doesn't make sense. If the user is browsing archived notes and cannot add any, then it's just fine to have no FAB. Never use the FAB for an uncommon action, such as accessing settings.

Supporting Multiple Devices

Although already briefly touched on in the "Bend to the User" section, the importance of supporting multiple devices cannot be overstated. If you're not doing anything with the NDK (and if you don't know what that is, you're not using it, so wipe that sweat off your forehead), it's typically very easy to support a range of devices wider than you even know to exist. In fact, most work that you do to support a variety of devices will be done simply by providing alternate layouts for different devices. You will group UI components into fragments (more on those in Chapter 3, "Creating Full Layouts with View Groups and Fragments") and combine fragments as necessary to provide an ideal experience on each different device. The fragments will typically contain all the logic necessary to load data, handle interactions, and so on, so they can be easily used across different device types. Because your views will use identifiers, your code can say something like "Change the additional info `TextView` to say 'Bacon'" and it does not have to worry about whether that `TextView` is at the top of the screen, the bottom, or is currently invisible.

> ### note
>
> If your curiosity gets the better of you and you want to know what the NDK is, it's the native development kit that allows you to develop Android apps in C/C++. The primary use case is for CPU-intensive code such as game engines and physics simulations. You can read more about it here: http://developer.android.com/tools/sdk/ndk/index.html.

Throughout this book, you will see many different techniques for supporting multiple devices. At this point, it is just important for you to keep in mind the devices that are out there. Best practices go a long way toward making your app usable on devices that you might not have even considered. For example, including a focused state for all of your UI elements allows you to remove the dependence on having a touch screen. That means your app will be usable on Android TV (though you will want to provide a specific set of layouts for that platform), and it will also be more usable for people with impairments who find that a means of navigation other than the touchscreen works better.

Avoiding Painful Mistakes

Following the guidelines for Material Design will make your app great, but there are a few painful mistakes that many designers and developers still make. Two of these come from old Android standards that are outdated: the menu key and the context menu. In addition, there are two other common mistakes that will call negative attention to your design: incorrect notification icons and styles from other platforms.

Menu Button

Before Android 3.x, devices were expected to have a menu key. Unfortunately, this actually led to several problems. For one, the user had no way of knowing if the menu key did anything in a given app. He or she had to press it to see what happened. Because it often did nothing, users would forget to even try pressing it for apps that did make use of it, leading to confusion on how to access certain features.

The menu key was also meant to be contextual to the current screen contents (it was essentially the precursor to the app bar and the overflow menu), but many developers and designers used the menu key in inconsistent ways, even abusing it as a full navigational menu. Fortunately, all you have to know now is that you should not use the menu key. Your apps should target the newest version of Android so that a software "menu button of shame" does not appear.

Long Press

The long press gesture (sometimes called long touch or long click) was used to bring up a context menu, similar to right-clicking on a desktop application. This use of the long press has gone away and should instead be replaced with selection. Long pressing on a given item should select it and then enable a contextual action bar. Selecting one or more items might give you the options to delete, archive, or flag them. If your app does not have the ability to select items, then long press should not do anything. Android 5.0's ripple will slowly expand out without selecting the item, which lets the user know "your touch is recognized but it is treated as a regular touch because there is no long press action on this item."

The long press is also used to display the title of a toolbar item. Thus, you can long press on an unclear icon and have it display the title so that you know what it does. Fortunately, Android will handle this for you as long as you declare titles for your menu items (and you always should as they're also used for accessibility).

Notification Icons

Notification icons have very specific guidelines, and it is particularly important to follow these guidelines because notifications show up in the status bar across apps. Notification icons should have pixels that are fully white or fully transparent. Not red. Not green. Not translucent. They should be white or transparent. This is because Android will use these as masks and they will appear next to other icons that follow these rules. When your icon breaks these rules, it looks bad and it calls attention to the app as not being properly designed for Android.

Styles from Other Platforms

Although already mentioned in the "Platform Consistency" section, it is worth repeating that you should not use styles from other platforms. One of the most common mistakes in the design of Android apps is to take the design from an iOS app and "port" it over to Android. iOS apps follow a different set of design and interaction guidelines, which cause an iOS-style app to look and feel out of place on Android. It tells users that the people responsible for the app do not care about their Android users and made the app just because "release Android app" was on a checklist somewhere. The app won't be featured in Google Play and may actually result in users seeking out a competing app. If you're told by managers or designers to implement it anyway, point out the Material Design guidelines, point out this book, and point out anything you can to change their minds. You want to make something you can be proud of and that users will actually want; don't just make a sloppy port.

Summary

Now that you have finished this chapter, you should have a good idea about what a modern Android app looks like. You now know the standard components (such as the app bar) and the outdated ones that should be avoided (such as the menu button). You understand some high-level goals from the "Core Principles" section that you can apply to future apps, and you may find it useful to come back to this chapter later on once your app has started being designed.

Before continuing on to Chapter 2, be sure to look at the Android design website (at http://developer.android.com/design/) and the Material Design website (http://www.google .com/design/spec/material-design/), if you haven't already. You might also find it beneficial to pick a few apps that work really well and see how they fit in with what you have learned in this chapter. Paying attention to what current apps on the platform do is a great way to ensure that your app behaves in a way that the user expects and is at least as good as what's already available. You might even notice a way that you can improve an app that you previously thought was perfect.

CHAPTER 2

UNDERSTANDING VIEWS— THE UI BUILDING BLOCKS

Sometimes it is best to start with the building blocks before diving into much more complex topics, and that is the goal here. This chapter is all about views, which allow your apps to display their content to your users. You will learn all the major view subclasses and gain a fundamental understanding of key attributes such as view IDs, padding, and margins. If you have already built any apps, most of this will be review for you, so feel free to skim through the chapter as you move toward the heart of the book.

What Is a View?

Views are the most basic component of the UI, and they extend the `View` class. They always occupy a rectangular area (although they can display content of any shape) and can handle both drawing to the screen and events such as being touched. Everything that is displayed on the screen utilizes a view.

There are two primary types of views: those that stand alone, such as for displaying some text or a picture, and those that are meant to group other views. This chapter focuses on those that stand alone, with the exception of some specialized views. Chapter 3, "Creating Full Layouts with View Groups and Fragments," covers the `ViewGroup` class and its subclasses (i.e., views that group together one or more other views).

Android gives you the flexibility of defining how you use your views using Java within the application code and with XML in external files, typically referred to as "layouts." In most cases, you should define your layouts with XML rather than creating them programmatically because it keeps your application logic separate from the visual appearance, thus keeping your code cleaner and easier to maintain. You also get the advantage of resource qualifiers, which are explained in Chapter 4, "Adding App Graphics and Resources."

Views are highly customizable, and the easiest way to make changes to views is by changing XML attributes in your layout files. Fortunately, most XML attributes also have Java methods that can accomplish the same thing at runtime. And, if nothing else, you can always extend an existing view to modify it in some way or extend the `View` class itself to create something completely custom.

See Table 2.1 for a list of the most commonly used attributes for the `View` class. Remember that all other views extend the `View` class, so these attributes apply to all views (though child classes can handle the attributes differently or even ignore them). The API levels refer to the version of the Android SDK where the attributes were introduced. API level 4 was Android 1.6, called "Donut." API level 11 was Android 3.0, or "Honeycomb." API level 16 was Android 4.1, the first version of "Jelly Bean." For a complete list of the API levels, you can see the table at http://developer.android.com/guide/topics/manifest/uses-sdk-element.html#ApiLevels.

Table 2.1   `View`'s Most Commonly Used Attributes

Attribute	Method	API	Description
alpha	setAlpha(float)	11	Defines the alpha level of the view as a floating point from 0 (fully transparent) to 1 (fully opaque). Be aware that an excessive number of views with an alpha between 0 and 1 can cause performance issues.

Attribute	Method	API	Description
background	setBackground(Drawable) setBackgroundColor(int) setBackgroundDrawable ➡(Drawable) setBackground ➡Resource(int)	1	Sets the Drawable to use for the background (drawables are covered in Chapter 4).
content ➡Description	setContent ➡Description ➡(CharSequence)	4	Sets text to be used to briefly describe this view for accessibility (e.g., an ImageButton is not descriptive to someone with a visual impairment, so you can describe it to be the "cancel button" or similar). When defining a view in XML and you know the view provides no content (e.g., a shadow that's only there for aesthetics), use "@null" as the value for contentDescription.
duplicate ➡ParentState	setDuplicateParentState ➡(bolean)	1	Setting this to true in XML means that the view will get its current state (e.g., pressed or focused) from its parent. This is most commonly used when a ViewGroup is acting as a button.
focusable	setFocusable ➡(boolean)	1	Sets whether the view can take focus; this is false by default.
focusable ➡InTouchMode	setFocusableIn ➡TouchMode(boolean)	1	Sets whether the view can take focus while the app is in "touch mode." If it is set to true, then touching the view will cause it to gain focus.
id	setId(int)	1	Defines an ID for the view so that you can find it in code. More on this shortly.
importantFor ➡Accessibility	setImportantFor ➡Accessibility ➡(boolean)	16	Defines whether this view is important to accessibility. If it is, the view will trigger accessibility events and can be queried by accessibility services. Although this was not defined until Jelly Bean, you can still use the XML attribute in apps with a minSdk prior to Jelly Bean, as long as your target is at least 16.
minHeight	setMinimumHeight ➡(int)	1	Defines a minimum height that the view will take up. Explained shortly.
minWidth	setMinimum ➡Width(int)	1	Defines a minimum width that the view will take up. Explained shortly.

Attribute	Method	API	Description
padding	setPadding ➥(int, int, ➥int, int)	1	There are five variants to this attribute: padding, paddingLeft, paddingTop, paddingRight, and paddingBottom, which are all used to specify padding. There are also two variants used to support RTL (right-to-left) languages such as Arabic: paddingStart and paddingEnd.
visibility	setVisibility ➥(int)	1	Sets whether the view is visible (normal case), invisible (not drawn but still takes up space), or gone (neither measured nor drawn).

View IDs

As you might suspect, view IDs are used to identify views. They allow you to define your layouts in XML and then modify them at runtime by easily getting a reference to the view. Defining an ID for a view in XML is done with android:id="@+id/example". The "at" symbol (@) signifies that you're referring to a resource rather than providing a literal value. The plus (+) indicates that you are creating a new resource reference; without it, you're referring to an existing resource reference. Then comes id, defining what type of resource it is (more on this in Chapter 4). Finally, you have the name of the resource, example. These are most commonly defined using lowercase text and underscores (e.g., title_text), but some people use camel case (e.g., titleText). The most important thing is that you're consistent. In Java, you can refer to this value with R.id.example, where R represents the resources class generated for you, id represents the resource type, and example is the resource name. Ultimately, this is just a reference to an int, which makes resource identifiers very efficient.

You can also predefine IDs in a separate file. Typically, this file is called ids.xml and is placed in the values resource folder. The main reasons for defining IDs like this rather than in the layout files directly are to use the IDs programmatically (such as creating a view in code and then setting its ID), to use the IDs as keys in a map, or to use the IDs for tags. The View class has a setTag() method, which allows you to attach any object to that view for later retrieval. Calling that method with a key allows you to attach multiple objects that are internally held with a SparseArray for efficient retrieval later. This is especially handy when using the "View Holder" pattern (covered in Chapter 10, "Using Advanced Techniques") or when the view represents a specific object that it needs access to later.

> **note**
>
> The R class is generated for you as you make changes in Android Studio. By default, this is built for you whenever it needs to be updated. You can also manually force Android Studio to build your project from the Build menu.

> **warning**
>
> **R CLASS VERSUS ANDROID.R CLASS**   Although your `R` class will be generated for you, there is also an `android.R` class. Unfortunately, IDEs will sometimes import this class when you really mean the `R` class that's specific to your app. If you see your resource references not resolving, verify that you have not imported `android.R`.
>
> It is a good idea to always use `R` within your code to reference your own `R` class and `android.R` to reference the Android `R` class explicitly (meaning that `R.id.list` refers to an ID that you have defined called "list" and `android.R.id.list` refers to the Android-defined "list" ID).

Understanding View Dimensions

One of the challenges designers and developers alike often have, when first starting to think about layouts in Android, is the numerous possible screen sizes and densities. Many design specialties (e.g., print and earlier versions of iOS) are based on exact dimensions, but approaching Android from that perspective will lead to frustration and apps that do not look good on specific resolutions or densities.

Instead, Android apps are better approached from a more fluid perspective in which views expand and shrink to accommodate a given device. The two primary means of doing so are the layout parameters `match_parent` (formerly `fill_parent`) and `wrap_content`. When you tell a view to use `match_parent` (by specifying that as a dimension in either the XML layout or by programmatically creating a `LayoutParams` class to assign to a view), you are saying it should have the same dimensions as the parent view or use up whatever space is remaining in that parent. When you tell a view to use `wrap_content`, you are saying it should only be as big as it needs to be in order to display its content. Using `match_parent` is generally more efficient than `wrap_content` because it doesn't require the child view to measure itself, so prefer `match_parent` if possible (such as for the width of most TextViews).

You can specify dimensions in pixel values as well. Because screens have different densities, specifying your layouts in pixels will cause screen elements to appear to shrink the higher the density of the device. For example, specifying 540 pixels high on a 55-inch high-definition TV (which is 27 inches high, because screen sizes are measured diagonally) means the pixels take up 13.5 inches. On a phone with a 5-inch screen, those same pixels are under an inch-and-a-half in landscape orientation.

Instead, you should use density-independent pixels (abbreviated as dp or dip) to have dimensions automatically scale for you based on the device's density. The six densities Android currently specifies based on dots per inch (DPI) are listed in Table 2.2. Since the original Android devices were MDPI devices, everything else is relative to that density (e.g., extra high density is twice as dense along each axis as MDPI). If you specify a line that is 2dp thick, it will be 2 pixels thick on an MDPI device, 3 pixels thick on an HDPI device, and 8 pixels thick on an XXXHDPI device.

Table 2.2   Android Densities

Abbreviation	Name (Dots per Inch)	Density	Scale
LDPI	Low	120	0.75
MDPI	Medium	160	1
HDPI	High	240	1.5
XHDPI	Extra high	320	2
XXHDPI	Extra, extra high	480	3
XXXHDPI	Extra, extra, extra high	640	4

Fortunately, you don't have to create specific layouts for each density. The main consideration with so many densities is the graphical assets. Android will automatically scale images for you, but obviously blowing up a small image will not look as sharp as having an image of the correct size. Graphics assets and other resources are covered in detail in Chapter 4, "Adding App Graphics and Resources."

There are times when you want a view to be at least a certain size but bigger if needed. A good example is for anything that the user can touch and the smallest you want a touchable view is 48dp (roughly 9 mm). In these cases, you can use the `minHeight` and `minWidth` properties. For example, you can define a `minHeight` of 48dp but the `layout_height` as `wrap_content`. That guarantees that the view will be at least tall enough to touch, but it can be larger to accommodate more content.

Two other parts of layouts are important to understand: padding and margins. If you were to set your phone next to another phone and think of each device as a view, you could think of the screens as the actual content, the bevel around the screens as the padding, and the space between the devices as the margins. Visually, it's not always obvious whether spacing is from padding or margins, but conceptually padding is part of the width of a layout and margins are not. See Figure 2.1 for a visual depiction of margins and padding.

Android also supports RTL (right-to-left) languages such as Arabic. Because it is common to indent the leading side of text differently from the trailing side, you can run into layouts where the only difference would be padding or margins for an RTL language compared to an LTR (left-to-right) one. Fortunately, Android solved this by adding new versions of padding and margins to easily accommodate this in Android 4.2. By replacing "left" with "start" and "right" with "end," you can easily have layouts that dynamically adjust based on language orientation. For example, if an LTR language would have a 72dp padding on the left, you would normally specify `paddingLeft="72dp"` in your layout. By adding `paddingStart="72dp"` to that same layout, the padding will automatically apply to the left side in English and the right side in Arabic. If you support older versions of Android, they'll use the padding left values. Any newer versions will use the padding start values. If you aren't supporting older versions of Android, you don't need to specify the padding left value. See Figure 2.2 for an example of what happens to the

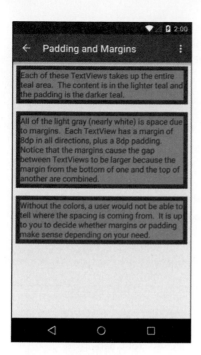

Figure 2.1 A visual demonstration of layouts with padding (dark cyan) and margins (space between the edge and the color)

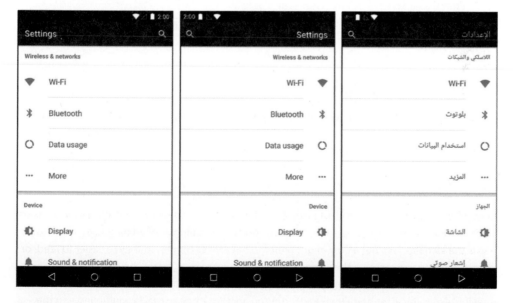

Figure 2.2 Here you can see the Settings screen shown in English both as naturally appearing (left-to-right) on the left and with a forced right-to-left layout in the middle compared to a natural right-to-left language on the right

layout based on the language's layout direction. Notice that the spacing is almost like a mirror image where the LTR layout shows the dividers going all the way to the right with no margin, but the RTL layouts show them going all the way to the left with no layouts and the spacing around the icons is consistent.

---

warning

PROBLEMATIC SAMSUNG DEVICES   Unfortunately, Samsung created their own custom attributes for `paddingStart` and `paddingEnd` by modifying the source code of Android for version 4.1. Their versions of these attributes required integers instead of floats, which means you can get a crash when the layouts are inflated on those specific devices. Fortunately, Android Studio will warn you via lint with a message that says, "Attribute `paddingStart` referenced here can result in a crash on some specific devices older than API 17."

Although that message is not as clear as it could be, the solution is to put the layouts in a layout folder with a resource qualifier (covered in depth in Chapter 4, "Adding App Graphics and Resources") to prevent the layouts from loading on those devices. Most people choose to put the versions of the layouts with these attributes in a `layouts-v17` folder, preventing those layouts from loading on older versions of Android, or `layouts-ldrtl`, preventing the layouts from loading on a device that's not set up to use a layout direction of left to right.

Additional detail about this issue is available at https://code.google.com/p/android/issues/detail?id=60055.

Displaying Text

One of the most fundamental ways in which you will communicate with your users is through text. Android gives you tools both to make displaying text easy and to make handling localization almost no work at all. Resources, covered in depth in Chapter 4, allow you to specify the displayed strings (among other types of content) outside of your layouts, letting the system automatically select the correct strings for a given user's language.

Text sizes are in scale-independent pixels (sp). Think of scale-independent pixels as the same as density-independent pixels but with the user's preferred scaling applied on top. In most cases, 1sp is the same as 1dp, but a user might prefer to have fonts bigger, so they're easier to read, or even smaller to see more on the screen. If you take the size in sp, times the density multiplier in Table 2.2, times the user's preferred scale, you'll get the resulting size. For example, if you specify 14sp (typical for body text) and it runs on an XXHDPI device (a 3× multiplier) and the user has a preferred font size of 10 percent larger, then the result is $14 \times 3 \times 1.1$ or 46 pixels. More important than understanding that formula is knowing that font sizes are in sp and your layouts should always be able to accommodate different font sizes.

TextView

`TextView` is one of the most common views in Android. As its name suggests, it displays text. What its name does not tell you is that it actually supports a wide variety of appearances and content. In fact, you can even specify a `Drawable` (such as an image) to appear to the left, top, right, and/or bottom of a text view. You can add text shadows, change colors, and have portions of text bold and others italicized. You can even have metadata associated with specific portions of text within a text view, allowing for click events on specific words or phrases, for example. Figure 2.3 shows a single text view that uses "spans," which allow the display of a variety of styles and even an inline image. Examples of text views are shown throughout the book, but Chapter 10, "Using Advanced Techniques," shows the specifics about how to accomplish what is shown in Figure 2.3.

Figure 2.3 A single `TextView` showing a variety of spans

Text views are robust but very easy to use. In fact, the majority of views that display text extend the `TextView` class precisely for those reasons. In addition, utilities are available that make some of the more difficult processes easy to do, such as converting portions of the text to links with the `Linkify` class (you can specify whether you want phone numbers to go to the dialer, links to go to a browser, or even custom patterns to do what you'd like) and converting most basic HTML (with the aptly named `Html` class) into styled text that uses the `Spanned` interface.

A wide variety of attributes can be used to make a text view work and look exactly how you want. See Table 2.3 for the most commonly used attributes.

Table 2.3 `TextView`'s Most Commonly Used Attributes

Attribute	Method	API	Description
drawable	setCompound ➥Drawables ➥WithIntrinsic ➥Bounds ➥(int, int, ➥int, int)	1	There are six XML variants of this attribute: `drawableLeft`, `drawableTop`, `drawableRight`, and `drawableBottom` as well as both `drawableStart` and `drawableEnd`. These attributes allow you to specify a resource-based `Drawable` to be displayed along with the text without requiring an additional `View`.
drawable ➥Padding	setCompound ➥Drawable ➥Padding(int)	1	Specifies the padding between the text and the drawable(s) defined with any of the drawable attributes.
ellipsize	setEllipsize ➥(TextUtils. ➥TruncateAt)	1	Setting the `ellipsize` location for a `TextView` lets it end the text with an ellipsis when the text won't all fit within the space available to the view.
fontFamily	setTypeface ➥(Typeface)	1	Sets the font family to be used, defined as a string. The method `setTypeface(Typeface)` can be used with custom fonts.
gravity	setGravity ➥(int)	1	Specifies the alignment of text along the X and/or Y axis. For XML you will primarily use `left` (or `start`), `top`, `right` (or `end`), `bottom`, `center`, `center_vertical`, and `center_horizontal`, though there are others. You can also combine values with a pipe (e.g., `left|bottom`). For the method, see the `Gravity` class for the constants you can use. Keep in mind this is the gravity within the dimensions of the `TextView`.
hint	setHint(int)	1	Mostly used for `EditText`; this defines the text to show when it is empty (giving the user a hint as to what to type in or what format text such as a phone number should be in).
inputType	setRawInputType ➥(int)	1	Mostly used for `EditText`; this defines the type of data being put into the view, allowing the system to better select an input method (such as a keyboard that includes the "at" sign if it's for an email address).

Attribute	Method	API	Description
lineSpacing ➥Extra	setLineSpacing ➥(float, float)	1	Sets extra spacing to include between lines of text, commonly used with custom fonts to give a little more breathing room.
lineSpacing ➥Multiplier	setLineSpacing ➥(float, float)	1	Sets the line spacing multiplier (e.g., 2 is double-spaced).
lines	setLines(int)	1	Sets the exact number of lines of text for this view. If this is 1, it will cut off text that is longer (see ellipsize). If this is 2, the spacing will be reserved for the second line, even if the text is not two lines long.
maxLines	setMaxLines(int)	1	Sets the maximum number of lines that this view can grow to display.
minLines	setMinLines(int)	1	Sets the minimum number of lines worth of spacing that this view reserves.
shadowColor	setShadowLayer ➥(float, float, ➥float, int)	1	Defines the text shadow's color. Use this sparingly, if at all. Shadows can make text more difficult to read and generally don't make sense in Material Design, as ink doesn't have a shadow. Shadows can be used on text that is applied over an image to help set enough contrast to make the text more readable.
shadowDx shadowDy	setShadowLayer ➥(float, float, ➥float, int)	1	Defines the x/y offset of the shadow.
shadowRadius	setShadowLayer ➥(float, float, ➥float, int)	1	Sets how much blur the shadow has; must be defined for the text shadow to appear. Because this is a float, fractional values are allowed (e.g., 0.01) but mostly appear as no blur.
text	setText ➥(CharSequence)	1	Sets the actual text to display. There are several methods for doing this via code.
textColor	setTextColor(int)	1	Sets the color of the text.
textIs ➥Selectable	setTextIsSelectable ➥(boolean)	11	If true, allows the view's text to be selected (e.g., for copying). You should usually set this to true because you never know what content from your app a user might want to share.
textSize	setTextSize ➥(int, float)	1	Sets the size of the text.

Attribute	Method	API	Description
textStyle	setTypeface ➥(Typeface)	1	Sets the style (e.g., bold or italic) of the text.
typeface	setTypeface ➥(Typeface)	1	Sets the Typeface of the text. The attribute can only be normal, sans, serif, or monospace, but the method takes a Typeface object that can be created from a custom font file embedded in your APK.

EditText

EditText is the primary means for allowing the user to input text such as a username or password. Because it extends TextView, the attributes in Table 2.3 are applicable. With EditText, you can specify the type of text the user will input via the inputType attribute or the setRawInputType(int) method. For example, saying that the user will input a phone number allows the keyboard to display numbers and symbols instead of the complete alphabet. You can also provide a hint, which is displayed before the user has entered any text and is a good way of providing context. When a user has entered text that is invalid such as an incorrect username, EditText can easily display error messages as well. See Figure 2.4 for examples of EditText.

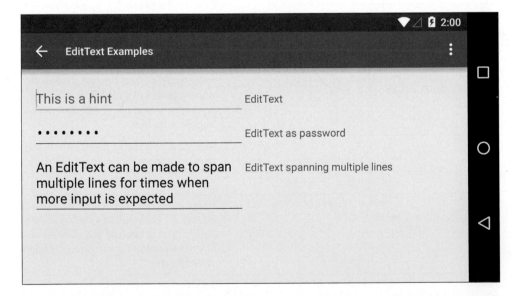

Figure 2.4 Examples of using EditText for different types of input

Button

Like `EditText`, `Button` extends `TextView`. The primary difference is that a button is simply meant to be pressed, but the displayed text lets the user understand what the button will do. In most cases, the fact that `Button` extends `TextView` will be mostly irrelevant. Rarely should you use a mixture of styles in a button or ellipsize it. A button should be obvious with a short string explaining its purpose. A standard button following the Material Design guidelines uses a medium font (which is a font partway between normal and bold), all caps, and 14sp. Additional styling such as bolding a particular word in the button creates a distraction and confuses users. See Figure 2.5 for examples of `Button`.

Figure 2.5 Examples of `buttons` using a raised style and a flat style (the cyan text) as well as an example of what not to do with text shadows

Displaying Images

Although displaying text is vital for nearly any application, an app with text alone is not likely to get everyone screaming with excitement. Fortunately, there are many ways for displaying images and other graphical elements in your apps.

Backgrounds

In many cases, you will be able to apply an image to the background of the view and it will work as expected. One great benefit of doing this is that you do not have to create an extra view, so you save the system a little bit of processing and memory. Unfortunately, you do not have as much control over the backgrounds of views as you do over views that are designed to display images specifically.

In Chapter 4, the various `Drawable` subclasses supported by Android are covered in depth. All of these drawables can be used as the background for views, so they give you a fair amount of control over the display of graphical content for your apps.

ImageView

`ImageView` is the primary class used for displaying images. It supports automatic scaling and even setting custom tinting, for instance. Keep in mind that an image view can also have a background, so you can actually stack images with this one view type. Fortunately, this class has far fewer attributes to consider than the `TextView` class.

The most obvious attribute for an image view is `src`, which defines the source of the image to display. You can also set the image via `setImageBitmap(Bitmap)`, `setImageDrawable(Drawable)`, and `setImageResource(int)` to dynamically set or change the image displayed by this view.

Although later chapters will discuss working with images and the `ImageView` class in much more depth, one more extremely common image view attribute that you should know is `scaleType`, which defines how the view handles displaying an image that is larger or smaller than the view's area. See Table 2.4 for details and Figure 2.6 for a visual example that shows each of the different ways of scaling an image as well as the full-sized image.

Table 2.4   `ScaleType` Values for the `ImageView` class

XML Attribute Value	ScaleType Enum	Description
Matrix	MATRIX	Scales using an image matrix that is set via `setImageMatrix(Matrix)`.
fitXY	FIT_XY	Sets the image's width and height to match those of the view, ignoring aspect ratio.
fitStart	FIT_START	Scales the image down or up, maintaining aspect ratio, and aligns the top left of the image to the top left of the view.
fitCenter	FIT_CENTER	Scales the image down or up, maintaining aspect ratio, so that at least one dimension will be equal to that dimension of the view.
fitEnd	FIT_END	Like `fitStart` but aligns the bottom-right corner.

XML Attribute Value	ScaleType Enum	Description
center	CENTER	Centers the image in the view without scaling.
centerCrop	CENTER_CROP	Scales the image down if needed, maintaining aspect ratio, so that both width and height will be equal to or greater than the size of the view.
centerInside	CENTER_INSIDE	Scales the image down if needed, maintaining aspect ratio, so that both the width and height will be equal to or less than the size of the view.

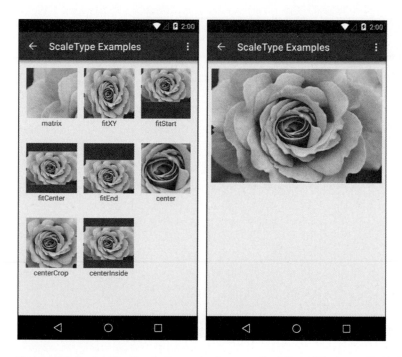

Figure 2.6 Each of the ScaleTypes is shown on the left, and the image that is being scaled is shown on the right

ImageButton

An ImageButton is a class that extends ImageView to display an image on top of a standard button. You set the image the same way as with an image view (typically using the src attribute or any of the setImageBitmap(Bitmap), setImageDrawable(Drawable), or setImageResource(int) methods), and you can change the button by setting the background to something other than the default.

Views for Gathering User Input

You already know about `EditText`, which you can get user input from, as well as both `Button` and `ImageButton` for handling simple touch events, but many more views can be used for collecting user input. Although any view can actually handle user feedback, the following views are specifically designed to do so:

- **`AutoCompleteTextView`**—This is essentially an `EditText` that supplies suggestions as the user is typing.

- **`CalendarView`**—This view lets you easily display dates to users and allow them to select dates. See Figure 2.7 for an example.

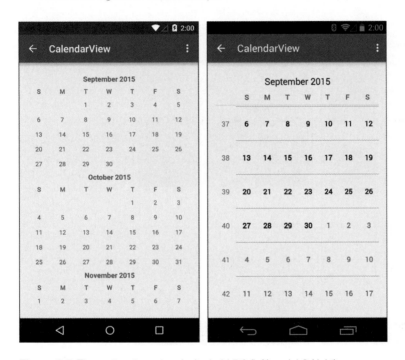

Figure 2.7 The `CalendarView` in Android 5.0 (left) and 4.3 (right)

- **`CheckBox`**—This is your typical check box that has a checked and unchecked state for binary choices. Note that the *B* is capitalized. See Figure 2.8 for an example.

- **`CheckedTextView`**—This is basically a `TextView` that can be checked and is sometimes used in a `ListView` (discussed in the next chapter).

- **`CompoundButton`**—This is an abstract class that is used to implements views that have two states, such as the `CheckBox` class mentioned earlier.

- **`DatePicker`**—This class is used for selecting a date and is sometimes combined with `CalendarView`. See Figure 2.9 for an example.

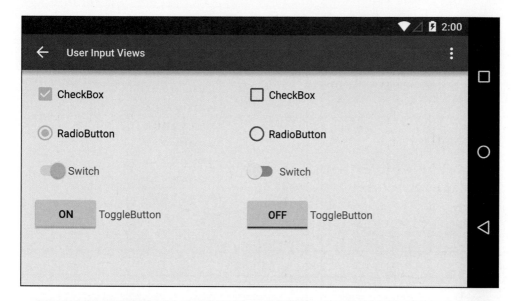

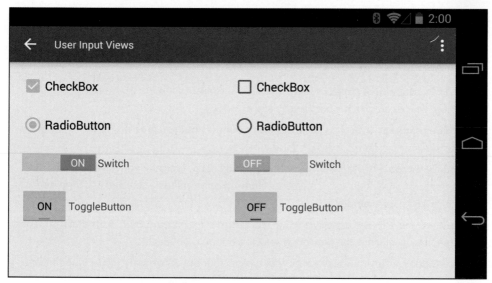

Figure 2.8 An example of `CheckBox`, `RadioButton`, `Switch`, and `ToggleButton` with on (left) and off (right) states; the top image shows Android 5.0's styles and the bottom image shows the same thing on Android 4.3 with an earlier version using the support library

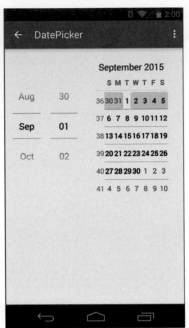

Figure 2.9 The left image is the `DatePicker` on Android 5.0; the right shows the pre-5.0 version

- **MultiAutoCompleteTextView**—This class is similar to `AutoCompleteTextView`, except that it can match a portion of a string.

- **NumberPicker**—This class lets users pick a number, but you probably figured that out already.

- **RadioButton**—This view is used with a `RadioGroup`. Typically, you have several `RadioButton`s within a `RadioGroup`, allowing only one to be selected at a time. See Figure 2.8 for an example.

- **RadioGroup**—This is actually a `ViewGroup` that contains `RadioButton`s that it watches. When one is selected, the previously selected option is deselected.

- **RatingBar**—This view represents your typical "four out of five stars" visual rating indicator, but it is configurable to allow for fractions, different images, and more.

- **SeekBar**—This view is your typical seek bar that has a "thumb" the user can drag to select a value along the bar.

- **Spinner**—This view is commonly called a drop-down or drop-down menu (it's also referred to as a combo box or a picker view). It shows the current option, but when selected, shows the other available options.

- **Switch**—This view is basically a toggle switch, but the user can tap it or drag the thumb. Keep in mind this was introduced in API level 14, but the support library has a `Switch-Compat` class for older versions. See Figure 2.8 for an example.

- `TimePicker`—This view lets users pick a time, but that was pretty obvious, wasn't it? See Figure 2.10 for an example.

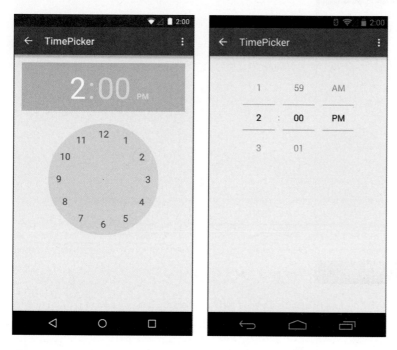

Figure 2.10 Another example where the left side shows the improvements of Android 5.0, in this case for the `TimePicker`, and the right side shows the older style

- `ToggleButton`—This view is conceptually quite similar to a `CheckBox` or a `Switch`, but it is usually displayed as a button with a light that indicates whether or not it is on, and it can have different text to display depending on whether it is on or off. In general, you should prefer a `Switch` over a `ToggleButton`. See Figure 2.8 for an example.

Other Notable Views

Whew, you've made it through the bulk of the chapter, but there are dozens of other views and far more to the views we've discussed so far. Remember that your goal at this point isn't to have every view memorized, but to have some idea of what's out there. If you need to implement a view that does X and you can remember that some view did something pretty similar, you can always jump back here to track it down. For now, it's sufficient to have just a quick explanation of some of the remaining views:

- `AnalogClock`—As you can probably guess, this view displays an analog clock. You are likely to never use it, though it can be a good starting place for a custom analog clock. See Figure 2.11 for an example.

Figure 2.11 An example of the `AnalogClock` on the top and the `DigitalClock` at the center and a `TextClock` at the bottom

- **Chronometer**—This view is basically a simple timer, like on a stopwatch.

- **DigitalClock**—A simple extension of `TextView`, this class displays a digital clock that just triggers a `Runnable` every second to update the display. This class was deprecated in API level 17 in favor of the `TextClock` class. See Figure 2.11 for an example.

- **ExtractEditText**—This is a child class of `EditText` for handling the extracted text. You probably won't directly use this class.

- **GLSurfaceView**—This `SurfaceView` class is for displaying OpenGL ES renders. This is most commonly used in games.

- **KeyboardView**—Another well-named class, this view is for displaying a virtual keyboard. You will probably only ever use this if you make your own keyboard app.

- **MediaRouteButton**—This view was added in Jelly Bean to control the routing of media such as outputting videos or audio to external speakers or another device (such as a Chromecast).

- **QuickContactBadge**—Added in Android 2.0, this class allows you to easily display a contact that can handle various actions when tapped (such as email, text, call, and so on).

- **ProgressBar**—This class can be used for showing progress, including indeterminate progress (i.e., progress for which you don't have a clear sense of where you are in the process, just whether you have started or finished).

- **RSSurfaceView**—This view has been deprecated, but it was for outputting RenderScript.

- **RSTextureView**—This view was deprecated as well; it was also for RenderScript, but API level 16 added a direct replacement, `TextureView`.

- **Space**—This is a simple subclass of `View` that is intended only for spacing and does not draw anything. It is basically a view that is set to invisible, so it handles layouts but not drawing. In most cases, you don't need to use this view because padding and margins can generally give you what you need for positioning. This view is also available in the support library for older versions of Android.

- **SurfaceView**—This view is intended for custom drawing, primarily for content that is frequently changing. Games that are relatively simple can use this view to display the graphics with reasonable efficiency, but most apps won't make use of it. The view is actually behind the `Window` that controls your view hierarchy, so the `SurfaceView` creates a hole to show itself. If you want to draw it on top of other content, you can do so with the `setZOrderOnTop(true)` method with a transparent `SurfaceHolder`, but that causes the GPU to have to do alpha blending with every view change, so it can be inefficient very quickly. In most cases, a `TextureView` is a better solution.

- **TextClock**—This view was added in API level 17 as a replacement for `DigitalClock`.

- **TextureView**—Introduced in Ice Cream Sandwich (API level 14), this view is used for displaying hardware-accelerated content streams such as video or OpenGL.

- **VideoView**—This view is a `SurfaceView` that simplifies displaying video content.

- **WebView**—When you want to display web content (whether remote or local), `WebView` is the class to use.

- **ZoomButton**—This is another class you probably won't use, but it essentially allows the triggering of on-click events in rapid succession, as long as the user is holding down the button (as opposed to just triggering a long-press event).

Listening to Events

You can listen for a number of events simply by registering the appropriate listener (an object that has a method that is triggered when the event happens). Unlike some frameworks, Android's methods for settings listeners take the form of `setOnEventListener` (where "Event" is the event to listen for), meaning that only one of a given listener is registered at a time. Setting a new listener of a given type will replace the old one. This may seem like a limitation, but in practice it rarely is and it helps simplify your code. When you really do need more than one class to listen to a particular event, you can always have one listener act as a relay to trigger other listeners.

One point worth noting is that listeners will return a reference to the view that triggered the event. That means you can have one class handle the events for multiple views, such as having your fragment handle clicks for three different buttons. Most commonly you will determine how to react by switching on the ID of the view with `getId()`, but you can also compare view references or even types. Note that there is a special exception to using a switch when creating a library project due to the IDs not being final; see http://tools.android.com/tips/non-constant-fields for details.

OnClickListener

This is the single most common listener you will use. A "click" event is the default event triggered when a view is tapped or when it has focus and the select key is pressed (such as the d-pad center key or a trackball).

OnLongClickListener

A long-click event is when a click (typically a touch) lasts longer than the value returned by `ViewConfiguration.getLongPressTimeout()`, which is typically 500 milliseconds. This action is now most commonly used for enabling multiselect mode.

OnTouchListener

Although "touch" is a bit misleading, this listener allows you to react to `MotionEvents`, potentially consuming them so that they are not passed on to be handled elsewhere. That means you can react to specific types of motion such as a fling or other gesture. `OnTouchListener` implementations often make use of helper classes such as `GestureDetector` to make it easier to track touches over time. This technique is discussed in Chapter 13, "Handling Input and Scrolling."

Other Listeners

A few other listeners are much less commonly used but are good to know about in case they come in handy. They are as listed here:

- **OnDragListener**—This listener lets you intercept drag events to override a view's default behavior, but it is only available in Honeycomb (API level 11) and newer.
- **OnFocusChangeListener**—This listener is triggered when focus changes for a view so that you can handle when a view gains or loses focus.
- **OnHoverListener**—New in Ice Cream Sandwich (API level 14), this listener allows you to intercept hover events (such as when a cursor is over a view but not clicking that view). Most apps won't use this type of listener.
- **OnGenericMotionListener**—This listener allows you to intercept generic `MotionEvents` as of API level 12.
- **OnKeyListener**—This listener is triggered on hardware key presses.

Summary

Whether you wanted to or not, you now know of the large number of views Android offers you. You also know the most commonly used attributes for the main views, so you can get them to look and behave how you want. At the end of the chapter, you concluded by learning how to handle events for views such as click events. Although not entirely exciting, the details of this chapter are key in breaking down UI concepts into concrete views in Chapter 6, "Prototyping and Developing the App Foundation" and beyond. Much more advanced techniques of using many of these views will also come later on, helping to solidify your knowledge of the Android UI.

CHAPTER 3

CREATING FULL LAYOUTS WITH VIEW GROUPS AND FRAGMENTS

The previous chapter focused on the various views available for you to use. In this chapter you will learn how to bring those views together into one layout and how to use the Fragment class to inflate and interact with those layouts. You will also learn about the variety of view groups available for you to combine views as needed.

Understanding ViewGroup and the Common Implementations

As mentioned in Chapter 2, "Understanding Views—The UI Building Blocks," the `ViewGroup` class is for views that can contain one or more child views. `ViewGroup` provides the standardized methods for these classes to use so that they can perform tasks such as adding, removing, getting, and counting child views. The primary method you will use to find a child is `findViewById(int)`, which is actually defined in the `View` class.

Each child class of `ViewGroup` has a different means of positioning the views it contains, as detailed shortly, but (with very few exceptions) views are drawn in the order they are added to a view group. For example, if you have an XML layout that defines a `TextView`, an `ImageView`, and a `Button`, those views will be drawn in that exact order regardless of their position on the screen. If they are placed at the exact same position, first the `TextView` will be drawn, then the `ImageView` will be drawn on top of it, and finally the `Button` will be drawn on the very top, likely obscuring the lower views. This inefficient drawing of pixels on top of pixels is called overdraw, and reducing overdraw is covered in Chapter 10, "Using Advanced Techniques."

One more useful thing to know is how to iterate through all the views belonging to a given `ViewGroup`. To do so, you will use `getChildCount()` and then a traditional `for` loop with `getChildAt(int)`. See Listing 3.1 for an example.

Listing 3.1   Iterating through a `ViewGroup`'s Children

```
final int childCount = myViewGroup.getChildCount();
for (int i = 0; i < childCount; i++) {
    View v = myViewGroup.getChildAt(i);
    // Do something with the View
}
```

FrameLayout

If you wanted to start off with something easy, this is the view to do it. The `FrameLayout` class just aligns each child view to the top left, drawing each view on top of any previous views. This might seem a bit silly as a way of grouping views, but this class is most commonly used as a placeholder, especially for fragments, which are covered later in the chapter. Instead of trying to figure out where to place a fragment within a view group that has several other views in it already, you can create a `FrameLayout` where you want that fragment to go and easily add it to that view group when needed by searching for its ID. This view group is also sometimes used to add spacing around other views such as in a `ListView`.

LinearLayout

A `LinearLayout` aligns its children one after another, either horizontally or vertically (depending on its `orientation` attribute). You can specify `gravity`, which controls how the layouts are aligned within this view group (e.g., you could have a vertical series of views aligned to the horizontal center of the view group). You can also specify `weight`, a very useful technique for controlling the way views in a `LinearLayout` grow to use the available space. This technique is demonstrated in Listing 3.2, which shows an XML layout that explicitly defines a weight of 0 for each of the views inside the `LinearLayout`. By changing the middle view (the second `TextView`) to have a weight of 1, it is given all the extra vertical space that was not used. See Figure 3.1 for a visual of what this layout looks like.

Listing 3.2   Utilizing `Weight` within a `LinearLayout`

```xml
<?xml version="1.0" encoding="utf-8"?>
<LinearLayout xmlns:android="http://schemas.android.com/apk/res/android"
    android:layout_width="match_parent"
    android:layout_height="match_parent"
    android:paddingLeft="@dimen/activity_horizontal_margin"
    android:paddingRight="@dimen/activity_horizontal_margin"
    android:paddingTop="@dimen/activity_vertical_margin"
    android:paddingBottom="@dimen/activity_vertical_margin"
    android:orientation="vertical" >

    <TextView
        android:layout_width="wrap_content"
        android:layout_height="wrap_content"
        android:layout_marginBottom="@dimen/activity_vertical_margin"
        android:layout_weight="0"
        android:background="@color/accent"
        android:text="TextView 1" />

    <TextView
        android:layout_width="wrap_content"
        android:layout_height="wrap_content"
        android:layout_marginBottom="@dimen/activity_vertical_margin"
        android:layout_weight="1"
        android:background="@color/accent"
        android:text="TextView 2" />

    <Button
        android:layout_width="wrap_content"
        android:layout_height="wrap_content"
        android:layout_gravity="end"
        android:layout_weight="0"
        android:text="Button" />

</LinearLayout>
```

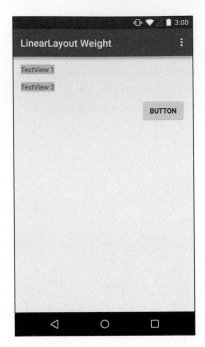 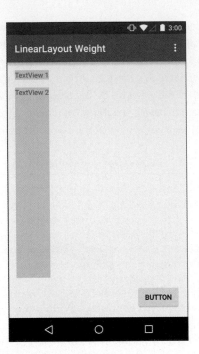

Figure 3.1 The left shows the layouts without weight applied; the right shows a weight of "1" applied to the second `TextView`

Notice that the width of the weighted `TextView` does not change, only the height grows. That is because the `LinearLayout` has a vertical `orientation`. One more thing to note is that weight is taken into account *after* all the views are measured. If you have three views that are 20dp and a total of 90dp of space to put them in, setting a weight of 1 on one of those will make that view take the remaining 30dp of space to be 50dp total. If the views had all been 30dp, the weight of 1 would have made no difference because there would be no extra space to use. Having the weight calculated after the other views are measured means that you can usually optimize cases such as the right layout in Figure 3.1 by supplying a height of 0dp for the view that has a weight specified. Because the weight of the view is going to cause it to take up the remaining space anyway, there is no need to measure it.

If you apply weight to more than one view, each view will grow in proportion to its weight. To calculate the ratio that it grows, you divide the weight of the view by the weight of all children in that `LinearLayout`. For example, if you have a view with a weight of 1 and a second view with a weight of 2 (total weight between the two views is 3), the first view will take up one-third of the available space and the second view will take up two-thirds. You can use whatever values you want for the weight, because they're relative to all the other weights supplied, but most people stick to small values.

RelativeLayout

Learning to use a `RelativeLayout` class effectively is a little tricky at first, but once you are
accustomed to using it, you will find it your go-to view group for a large portion of layouts. As
the name indicates, you specify its children relative to each other or to the `RelativeLayout`
itself. Not only is this an extremely efficient way to create semicomplex layouts that adapt to a
variety of screens, it also allows you to create overlapping views and views that appear to float
on top of others. See Table 3.1 for the `LayoutParams` that can be used with views within a
`RelativeLayout`. Figure 3.2 demonstrates a simple use of a `RelativeLayout` that contains
four `TextView`s. And don't worry; this view will come up again in future chapters where real
use cases make it more understandable.

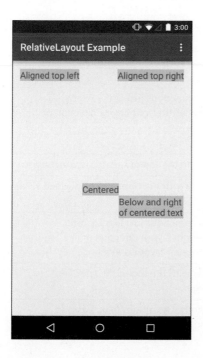

Figure 3.2 An example of positioning four `TextView`s
within a `RelativeLayout`

Table 3.1 `RelativeLayout`'s `LayoutParams` Used for Aligning Views

Attribute	Description
`layout_above`	Aligns the bottom of this view to the top of the specified view (including spacing for the bottom margin of this view and the top margin of the specified view).
`layout_alignBaseline`	Aligns the baseline of this view to the baseline of the specified view. You can think of the baseline as the invisible line that text is written on, so this can be used to make two `TextViews` appear to be written on the same line or make another view appear inline with the text.
`layout_alignBottom`	Aligns the bottom of this view with the bottom of the specified view, accounting for a bottom margin.
`layout_alignEnd`	Added in API level 17, this functions just like `layout_alignRight` for a left-to-right layout direction or like `layout_alignLeft` for a right-to-left layout direction.
`layout_alignLeft`	Aligns the left of this view with the left of the specified view, accounting for a left margin.
`layout_alignParentBottom`	Aligns the bottom of this view to the bottom of the `RelativeLayout`.
`layout_alignParentEnd`	Added in API level 17, this functions just like `layout_alignParentRight` for a left-to-right layout direction or like `layout_alignParentLeft` for a right-to-left layout direction.
`layout_alignParentLeft`	Aligns the left of this view with the left of the `RelativeLayout`.
`layout_alignParentRight`	Aligns the right of this view with the right of the `RelativeLayout`.
`Layout_alignParentStart`	Added in API level 17, this functions just like `layout_alignParentLeft` for a left-to-right layout direction or like `layout_alignParentRight` for a right-to-left layout direction.
`layout_alignParentTop`	Aligns the top of this view to the top of the `RelativeLayout`.
`layout_alignRight`	Aligns the right of this view with the right of the specified view, accounting for a right margin.
`layout_alignStart`	Added in API level 17, this functions just like `layout_alignLeft` for a left-to-right layout direction or like `layout_alignRight` for a right-to-left layout direction.
`layout_alignTop`	Aligns the top of this view with the top of the specified view, accounting for a top margin.
`layout_alignWith` ➡ `ParentIfMissing`	If the layout specified by other attributes (e.g., `layout_alignBottom`) is missing, it will align to the `RelativeLayout`.

Attribute	Description
layout_below	Aligns the top of this view below the bottom of the specified view (including spacing for the top margin of this view and the bottom margin of the specified view).
layout_centerHorizontal	Horizontally centers the view within the RelativeLayout.
layout_centerInParent	Vertically and horizontally centers the view within the RelativeLayout.
layout_centerVertical	Vertically centers the view within the RelativeLayout.
Layout_toEndOf	Added in API level 17, this functions just like layout_toRightOf for a left-to-right layout direction or like layout_toLeftOf for a right-to-left layout direction.
layout_toLeftOf	Aligns the right of this view to the left of the specified view's left edge (including spacing for the right margin of this view and the left margin of the specified view).
layout_toRightOf	Aligns the left of this view to the right of the specified view's right edge (including spacing for the left margin of this view and the right margin of the specified view).
layout_toStartOf	Added in API level 17, this functions just like layout_toLeftOf for a left-to-right layout direction or like layout_toRightOf for a right-to-left layout direction.

AdapterView

Sometimes you have a large data set to work with and creating views for every piece of data is impractical. Other times you simply want an easy and efficient way of creating views for some collection of data. Fortunately, AdapterView was created for these types of scenarios. AdapterView itself is abstract, so you will use one of its subclasses such as ListView, but the overall idea is the same. You have a data set, you throw it at an Adapter, and you end up with views in your layout (see Figure 3.3 for a simple conceptual illustration). Simple, right?

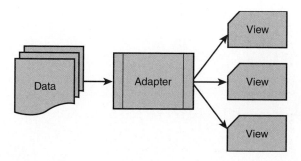

Figure 3.3 Converting a set of data to a usable set of views is what Adapters are made for

ListView

Sometimes concepts are easier to understand with concrete examples, and `ListView` is a great example of `AdapterView`. It presents a vertically scrolling list of views that can be reused. Figure 3.4 illustrates what happens when this view is scrolled. The far left column shows

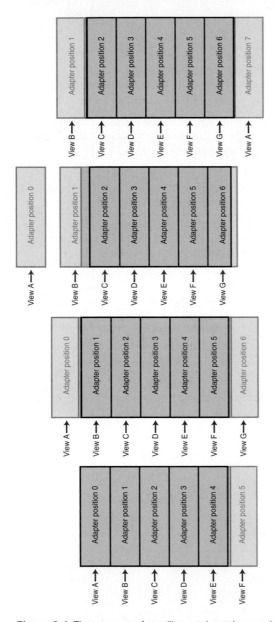

Figure 3.4 The process of scrolling a `ListView` and having the top view recycled

the initial layout, where a view is created for each position that has any content on the screen. The blue outline represents what is visible on the screen; portions of a view that are outside the screen appear faded. The second column shows the user scrolling down. The view that was at the bottom (View F) comes completely onto the screen, and a new view has to be inflated for the data from the adapter's sixth position. The third column shows that as the user continues to scroll down, View A moves completely off the screen and becomes detached. It is no longer part of the view hierarchy, but it isn't garbage collected because a reference to it is retained. The far right column shows that View A is reattached at the bottom and is given the data for the seventh position. In the adapter, this is the `convertView` parameter. This whole process is called "recycling" (as in avoiding garbage collection) and is vital for maintaining a smooth and efficient collection of content.

There is also a special version of `ListView` called `ExpandableListView`, which is used when you have two levels of content. For example, you might list all the countries of the world and then you could expand each country to show its states or provinces. `ExpandableListView` requires an `ExpandableListAdapter`.

GridView

A `GridView` is a two-dimensional grid of views populated by the associated `ListAdapter`. One nice feature is that you can let the number of columns be automatically determined based on size, which makes this view group easy to use. Most commonly, you will see this used for a series of icons or images, although it is not limited to that functionality. See Figure 3.5 for an example.

Figure 3.5 This is a simple example of a `GridView`

Spinner

When you need to give the user an easy way to select from multiple predefined choices, a `Spinner` is often a good solution. This class shows the currently selected choice and, when tapped, presents a drop-down menu of all the choices. A `Spinner` requires a `Spinner-Adapter`, which determines what the drop-down choices look like and what the currently selected item looks like when closed. See Figure 3.6 for an example.

Figure 3.6 When tapping a `Spinner`, a drop-down appears like this one

Gallery

The `Gallery` class provides a way to show horizontally scrolling views backed by an `Adapter`. The original purpose was for, as its name states, displaying a gallery of (center-locked) photos. Each view was an `ImageView`. Because of this, `Gallery` does not recycle any of its views and is extremely inefficient. It also has some problems with scrolling, particularly on tablets where several views might be showing at once. `Gallery` has been deprecated, and you should not use it. It is mentioned here specifically because it comes up frequently as a solution to horizontally scrolling views, so you should be aware of it, but you should avoid using `Gallery` in your own apps. Instead, consider `ViewPager` or `RecyclerView` (both discussed later in this chapter).

Adapter

`Adapter` is the interface that takes a data set and returns views representing that data. The adapter is able to say how many items there are, return an item for a specific position, and return the view associated with a position, among other things. For a `ListView`, you will use the `ListAdapter` interface that extends `Adapter` to add a couple of list-specific methods. Similarly, you will use the `SpinnerAdapter` interface for use in a `Spinner`.

Fortunately, you do not need to implement these from scratch every time. For many cases, you will be using an array of data, so you can use `ArrayAdapter` directly or extend it to meet your needs. If your data is backed by a `Cursor` (a sort of pointer to a result set from a database query), `CursorAdapter` is the class to use. In some cases, you need a bit more control but don't want to implement `ListAdapter` or `SpinnerAdapter` from scratch; fortunately, `BaseAdapter` gives a great starting place to extend.

The most important method of `Adapter` is `getView(int position, View convertView, ViewGroup parent)`. This is where the adapter provides the actual view that represents a given position. The `convertView` parameter is for passing in any existing view of the same type that can be reused, but you *must* handle the case of this being null because the first calls to this method will not have an existing view to reuse and `AdapterView` does not require recycling views when it is extended. The third parameter, `parent`, is the `ViewGroup` that the view you're building will be attached to. You should *not* attach the view yourself; instead, the parent is meant to be used for supplying the appropriate `LayoutParams`.

Interfaces for `AdapterView`

You will commonly use one of these `AdapterView` subclasses to allow each item to be interacted with. Instead of manually assigning event listeners to each view you generate, you can instead set a listener on the `AdapterView`. For example, to listen to clicks, you can create an implementation of the `OnItemClickListener` interface. There are also `OnItemLongClickListener` and `OnItemSelectedListener` interfaces. Each of these interfaces defines a single method that is passed the `AdapterView` itself, the view that the event was triggered on, the position of that view, and the ID for that position. Remember that you can use your `Adapter`'s `getItem(int position)` method within any of those methods when you need the object the view actually represents.

`ViewPager`

Being able to swipe horizontally through full pages of content has been common behavior since before Android, but its prevalence (e.g., the default launcher in each Android version) did not mean that it was supported by a native component. Instead, this pattern, which was originally referred to as "workspaces," was implemented directly without abstraction.

Fortunately, the `ViewPager` was added to the support library (http://developer.android.com/tools/extras/support-library.html), so you can add it to any project that runs Android 1.6 or newer. A common use of this class is in apps that uses tabs for navigation; the user can swipe across each page or tap a tab to jump to a specific page. A `ViewPager` takes a `PageAdapter` that supplies the views, and one of the most common uses is to actually provide fragments via the `FragmentPagerAdapter`. Fragments are covered later in this chapter and throughout the book.

Toolbar

As mentioned in the first chapter, most apps have a toolbar at the top called the app bar. When this concept was introduced into the Android framework in Android 3.0 (referred to as the action bar at that time), its implementation made it part of the window décor, causing it to behave differently from other views and making a lot of desirable features exceedingly difficult to implement. In fact, that implementation caused a very specific problem: a navigation drawer could not slide in front of the app bar.

Android 5.0 introduced the solution: the `Toolbar` class. With this class, you can easily slide a navigation drawer in front of the rest of your app, animate the size of the app bar dynamically, and add whatever features you want. Because `Toolbar` is just another view, it can be included anywhere in your layouts and you have much better control of how you use it. What's even better is that this class is included in the support library, so you can use it for older versions of Android as well.

Other Notable ViewGroups

You would be bored out of your mind if you had to read paragraphs about every single view group available. The fact is, there are many available, and those that were covered previously in the chapter are the main ones you will use. However, it's worth knowing these others to avoid spending the time coding them yourself when they already exist:

- `AbsoluteLayout`—Deprecated layout that was used to position views based on exact pixels. Do not use this layout, but be aware that it exists so that you can shame developers who do use it.

- `AdapterViewAnimator`—Switches among views that are supplied by an `Adapter`, using an animation for the transition. Introduced in API level 11.

- `AdapterViewFlipper`—Similar to `AdapterViewAnimator` but supports automatically changing the view based on a time interval (e.g., for a slideshow). Introduced in API level 11.

- `AppWidgetHostView`—Hosts app widgets, so you will probably only use this if you create a custom launcher.

- `DialerFilter`—Hosts an `EditText` with an ID of `android.R.id.primary` and an `EditText` with an ID of `android.R.id.hint` as well as an optional `ImageView` with an ID of `android.R.id.icon` to provide an easy means of entering phone numbers (including letters that can be converted to numbers). You will probably never use this.

- `FragmentBreadCrumbs`—Simplifies adding "breadcrumbs" (like displaying "Settings > Audio" as the user navigates deeper into content) to the UI, but it was deprecated for Android 5.0. Breadcrumbs are a more common pattern in web apps than mobile apps because most mobile apps should not be particularly deep.

- `GestureOverlayView`—Exists on top of one or more other views to catch gestures on those views.

- `GridLayout`—Organizes its children into a rectangular grid to easily align multiple views. Introduced in API level 14 but exists in the support library.

- `HorizontalScrollView`—Wraps a single child view (usually a `ViewGroup`) to allow it to scroll horizontally when the content is larger than the view's visible dimensions.

- `ImageSwitcher`—Switches between images with an animation (see `ViewSwitcher`).

- `MediaController`—Contains views to control media such as play, pause, fast forward, and a progress indicator.

- `PagerTabStrip`—Provides interactivity to a `PagerTitleStrip`, allowing users to tap on a page title to jump to that page. Included in the support library.

- `PagerTitleStrip`—Indicates the current, previous, and next pages for a `ViewPager` but is designed to display them without interaction. Included in the support library.

- `ScrollView`—Wraps a single child view (usually a `ViewGroup`) to allow it to scroll vertically when the content is larger than the view's visible dimensions.

- `SearchView`—Provides a UI for allowing the user to search with the results coming from a `SearchProvider`. Introduced in API level 11 but also included in the support library.

- `SlidingDrawer`—Holds two views: One is a handle and the other is the content. The handle can be tapped to show or hide the content, and it can also be dragged. This is the original app drawer in Android 1.x and is a very dated view. This class was deprecated in API level 17 and should not be used anymore.

- `StackView`—Stacks multiple views that can be swiped through (so you can get an effect like multiple physical photos in a stack). The views are provided by an `Adapter` and are offset to show when more are below the top view. This is most commonly used as an app widget, and it was introduced in API level 11.

- `TabHost`—Hosts tabs and a single `FrameLayout` for the content of the currently active tab. This was used for most tabbed interfaces prior to Android 3.0; most tabbed interfaces now use tabs in the app bar.

- `TabWidget`—Lives within a `TabHost` and provides the tab event triggers.

- `TableLayout`—Allows you to organize content in a tabular fashion, although you should generally use a `GridLayout` because it is more efficient.

- `TableRow`—Represents a row in a `TableLayout`, although it is essentially just a `LinearLayout`.

- `TextSwitcher`—Animates between two `TextView`s. This is really just a `ViewSwitcher` with a few helper methods.

- `ViewAnimator`—Switches among views, using an animation.

- `ViewFlipper`—Similar to `ViewAnimator` but supports automatically changing the view based on a time interval (e.g., for a slideshow).

- `ViewSwitcher`—Animates between two views, where one is shown at a time.

- `ZoomControls`—Controls zoom. No, really. It provides zoom buttons with callbacks for handling the zoom events.

Encapsulating View Logic with Fragments

One problem that plagued Android a bit early on was that there was no standardized way to encapsulate view logic for use across activities. This was not a major issue because one screen was typically represented by one activity and one layout; however, it started to become a problem when tablets gained popularity. Where you might display a list of news articles on the phone that you can tap to go to a full detail page, you would probably show that list on the left side of the tablet and the details on the right, so they're always both visible. That presented a challenge because your code to populate the list was likely to be living in one activity and the detail page code was in another, but the tablet was only ever showing one activity and needed the logic from both. Enter the `Fragment`.

Like `Activity`, `Context`, and `Intent`, `Fragment` is another one of those classes that is a bit tough to describe up front but quickly makes sense as you use it. Think of a fragment as a *chunk* of your UI, containing the code necessary to inflate or construct a layout as well as handle user interaction with it. The fragment might even load content from the web or other source. A fragment can be simple, such as a full-screen `ImageView`, perhaps with a caption, or it can be complex, such as a series of form elements containing all the logic to validate and submit form responses. In fact, a fragment does not even have to be used for UI; it can be used to encapsulate application behavior needed for activities. But don't worry, this is a book about design, so there's no need to boggle your mind on why you'd do that!

The Fragment Lifecycle

Like activities, fragments have a lifecycle. In fact, activities are closely tied to fragments, and the activity lifecycle influences the lifecycle of the fragment associated with it. First, the fragment runs through this series of lifecycle events in the order they are presented here:

- `onAttach(Activity)` —Indicates that the fragment is associated with an activity; calling `getAcitivity()` from this point on will return the `Activity` that is associated with the fragment.
- `onCreate(Bundle)` —Initializes the fragment.
- `onCreateView(LayoutInflater, ViewGroup, Bundle)` —Returns the view associated with the fragment.
- `onActivityCreated(Bundle)` —Triggered to coincide with the activity's `onCreate()` method.
- `onViewStateRestored(Bundle)` —Triggered to indicate that the state of views (such as the text in an `EditText` instance from another orientation) has been restored.
- `onStart()` —Triggered to coincide with the activity's `onStart()` method and displays the fragment.
- `onResume()` —Triggered to coincide with the activity's `onResume()` method and indicates the fragment can handle interaction.

After the fragment has "resumed," it will stay in that state until a fragment operation modifies that fragment (such as if you are removing the fragment from the screen) or its activity is paused. At that point, it will run through this series of lifecycle events in the order presented:

- `onPause()`—Triggered to coincide with the activity's `onPause()` method or when a fragment operation is modifying it.

- `onStop()`—Triggered to coincide with the activity's `onStop()` method or when a fragment operation is modifying it.

- `onDestroyView()`—Allows the fragment to release any resources associated with its view; you should null out any view references that you have in this method.

- `onDestroy()`—Allows the fragment to release any final resources.

- `onDetach()`—Gives the fragment one last chance to do something before it is disassociated from its activity; at this point `getActivity()` will return null and you should ensure that you do not have any references to the activity.

Giving Fragments Data

One of the great things about fragments is that the system manages them for you. Things like configuration changes (e.g., orientation changes) are easily handled because fragments can save state and restore state. To do so, they must have a default constructor (i.e., a constructor that has no parameters). So, how do you pass data to them if they require a default constructor? The standard way is via a static `newInstance()` method that sets up the fragment's arguments before it is attached to an activity. See Listing 3.3 for a simple example.

Listing 3.3   Passing Arguments to a Fragment and Using Them When Creating the View

```
public class TextViewFragment extends Fragment {

    /**
     * String to use as the key for the "text" argument
     */
    private static final String KEY_TEXT = "text";

    /**
     * Constructs a new TextViewFragment with the specified String
     *
     * @param text String to associated with this TextViewFragment
     * @return TextViewFragment with set arguments
     */
    public static TextViewFragment newInstance(String text) {
        TextViewFragment f = new TextViewFragment();

        Bundle args = new Bundle();
        args.putString(KEY_TEXT, text);
        f.setArguments(args);
```

```java
        return f;
    }
    /**
     * Returns the String set in {@link #newInstance(String)}
     *
     * @return the String set in {@link #newInstance(String)}
     */
    public String getText() {
        return getArguments().getString(KEY_TEXT);
    }


    @Override
    public View onCreateView(LayoutInflater inflater, ViewGroup
➥container, Bundle savedInstanceState) {
        TextView tv = new TextView(getActivity());
        tv.setText(getText());
        return tv;
    }
}
```

You can see that the static `newInstance(String)` method creates the fragment using the default constructor and then it creates a new `Bundle` object, puts the text into that bundle, and assigns that bundle as the fragment's arguments. The bundle is maintained when the fragment is destroyed and will be automatically set for you if it's created again (e.g., when a rotation triggers a configuration change, your fragment is destroyed, but a new one is created and the bundle is assigned to its arguments).

Obviously, using a fragment just for a `TextView` is contrived, but it illustrates how you can set data on a fragment that is retained across configuration changes. In doing this, you can easily separate your data from its presentation. Ideally, `onCreateView(LayoutInflater, View-Group, Bundle)` would inflate an XML layout, which might be different for landscape versus portrait. With your code designed in this way, the orientation change will just work with no extra effort on your part.

Fragments can also be set to be retained across activities with `setRetainInstance(true)`. This allows you to keep data around that isn't configuration-specific and is otherwise hard to put into a `Bundle`. When using this feature, the `onDestroy()` method is not called when the activity is destroyed and the subsequence `onCreate(Bundle)` is not called, because the fragment already exists.

Talking to the Activity

Although fragments can do a lot of things, it's still quite common to need to talk to the activity they are attached to. For instance, you might have a custom `DialogFragment` and you need to tell the activity which button the user pressed. In other situations, you would do this with an interface and a setter method, but the fragment lifecycle makes that problematic. When the user rotates the device, the activity and fragment go away and the new versions are created.

Because the fragment is created with an empty constructor, it no longer has reference to the interface you might have passed in. Instead, you do this by casting the activity. Because blindly casting can easily create bugs, it is a good idea to verify that the activity implements the correct interface in the onAttach(Activity) method and throw an exception if it does not. Listing 3.4 demonstrates both the communication back to the activity and the safety check when the fragment is attached to the activity.

Listing 3.4   Talking to the Activity from a Fragment

```
/**
 * DialogFragment with a simple cancel/confirm dialog and message.
 *
 * Activities using this dialog must implement OnDialogChoiceListener.
 */
public class SampleDialogFragment extends DialogFragment {

    /**
     * Interface for receiving dialog events
     */
    public interface OnDialogChoiceListener {
        /**
         * Triggered when the user presses the cancel button
         */
        public void onDialogCanceled();
        /**
         * Triggered when the user presses the confirm button
         */
        public void onDialogConfirmed();
    }

    private static final String ARG_CONTENT_RESOURCE_ID =
➥ "contentResourceId";
    private static final String ARG_CONFIRM_RESOURCE_ID =
➥ "confirmResourceId";

    private int mContentResourceId;
    private int mConfirmResourceId;

    private OnDialogChoiceListener mListener;

    /**
     * Creates a new instance of the fragment and sets the arguments
     *
     * @param contentResourceId int to use for the content such as
➥ R.string.dialog_text
     * @param confirmResourceId int to use for the confirm button such
➥ as R.string.confirm
     * @return new SampleDialogFragment instance
     */
```

```java
    public static SampleDialogFragment newInstance(int
➥ contentResourceId, int confirmResourceId) {
        SampleDialogFragment fragment = new SampleDialogFragment();
        Bundle args = new Bundle();
        args.putInt(ARG_CONTENT_RESOURCE_ID, contentResourceId);
        args.putInt(ARG_CONFIRM_RESOURCE_ID, confirmResourceId);
        fragment.setArguments(args);
        return fragment;
    }

    public SampleDialogFragment() {
        // Required empty public constructor
    }
    @Override
    public void onCreate(Bundle savedInstanceState) {
        super.onCreate(savedInstanceState);
        final Bundle args = getArguments();
        if (args == null) {
            throw new IllegalStateException("No arguments set, use the"
                    + " newInstance method to construct this fragment");
        }
        mContentResourceId = args.getInt(ARG_CONTENT_RESOURCE_ID);
        mConfirmResourceId = args.getInt(ARG_CONFIRM_RESOURCE_ID);
    }

    @NonNull
    @Override
    public Dialog onCreateDialog(Bundle savedInstanceState) {
        AlertDialog.Builder builder = new AlertDialog.
➥ Builder(getActivity());
        builder.setMessage(mContentResourceId)
            .setPositiveButton(mConfirmResourceId, new DialogInterface.
➥ OnClickListener() {
                public void onClick(DialogInterface dialog, int id) {
                    // Send the positive button event back to the host
➥ activity
                    mListener.onDialogConfirmed();
                }
            })
            .setNegativeButton(R.string.cancel, new DialogInterface.
➥ OnClickListener() {
                public void onClick(DialogInterface dialog, int id) {
                    // Send the negative button event back to the host
➥ activity
                    mListener.onDialogCanceled();
                }
            }
        );
        return builder.create();
    }
```

```
@Override
public void onAttach(Activity activity) {
    super.onAttach(activity);
    try {
        mListener = (OnDialogChoiceListener) activity;
    } catch (ClassCastException e) {
        throw new ClassCastException(activity.toString()
                + " must implement OnFragmentInteractionListener");
    }
}

@Override
public void onDetach() {
    super.onDetach();
    mListener = null;
}
}
```

Fragment Transactions

In many cases, you will not need to worry about fragment transactions directly. You are able to embed fragments in XML, just like views, and `DialogFragments` have a `show()` method that just takes the `FragmentManager` (or `FragmentSupportManager` when using the support library) and a string tag to later find the fragment again. When you do need to add a fragment to the UI programmatically, you use a fragment transaction obtained from the `FragmentManager`'s (or the support version's) `beginTransaction()` method. A fragment transaction can add, detach, hide, remove, replace, and show fragments and a single transaction can include multiple commands. When the transaction is ready, you call either `commit()` or `commitAllowingStateLoss()`. The former is more common but throws an exception if triggered after the activity has saved its state; the latter will not throw an exception, meaning that changes committed after an activity's state has been saved (such as just before an orientation change) could be lost. Finally, a fragment transaction can add itself to the back stack, meaning that pressing the back button will reverse the transaction, by calling `addToBackStack(String)`. See Listing 3.5 for an example of the typical use of a fragment transaction.

Listing 3.5   Typical Use of a Fragment Transaction

```
getSupportFragmentManager().beginTransaction()
        .add(R.id.container, ExampleFragment.newInstance())
        .addToBackStack(null)
        .commit();
```

Controversy

Despite the capabilities that fragments bring to Android, they are not without their problems. The fragment lifecycle is complex, debugging is challenging both due to the underlying source code (particularly due to all the different states) and the asynchronous nature of fragment transactions, and the recreation of fragments using reflection (which means you can't use anonymous classes or any other fragment that doesn't have a default constructor). When making a mistake, it is not uncommon for it to show up later on (either due to a configuration change or an asynchronous transaction), which means the code that actually caused that situation can be very hard to track down.

Although most Android developers use fragments regardless of these issues, there are many other approaches to breaking UI into reusable pieces. Some developers create their own solutions on a case-by-case basis, some create custom view groups as fragment replacements, and some use a variety of third party libraries (such as Flow and Mortar, both developed by Square and available at http://square.github.io/). This book's examples use fragments because they're the most widely used solution to encapsulating reusable UI, but it's a good idea to look at what else is out there once you're familiar with the advantages and disadvantages of fragments.

The Support Library

One of the challenges of Android is that it is an open source operating system used in countless devices. Many of the manufacturers aren't particularly incentivized to provide OS updates after a year or two when you may be looking to upgrade to a new device. One of the ways Google has combated the challenge of developing software for an operating system that evolves extremely rapidly and yet is frequently not up to date on most devices is the support library.

Originally, the support library came out as "Support-V4," meaning that it worked with API level 4 (Android 1.6) and newer, bringing fragments and other features to the majority of Android devices. Google also released other versions such as v13 for Android 3.2 (the last version of Honeycomb), with the idea being that you would pick the support library you needed based on the minimum version you supported (if you didn't support versions older than v13, you could use that library to avoid bringing in features such as fragments that would be natively supported). Later, Google released the ActionBarCompat library for bringing the action bar to older versions of Android.

Since then, the ActionBarCompat library has been renamed to AppCompat and the approach has changed slightly. The idea now is that you will use this library and its components even if the device that the code is running on has fragments or another feature natively supported. This simplifies your code and simplifies the library code because it doesn't have to worry about swapping between native and support versions of classes. Another advantage of this is that XML attributes do not have to be declared twice (you used to have to declare XML attributes for the native code such as `android:actionBarStyle` and then again for the support library such as `actionBarStyle`, which was error prone and caused significant duplication).

The AppCompat library provides a significant amount of simplification that works across Android versions. With it, you can specify just a few colors to have all your app bars colored, the majority of input views such as checkboxes and radio buttons updated to the newer Material Design style, and a lot more. What used to take dozens of image resources for theming now takes just a few lines of XML. The benefits of using this library are such that virtually every app that is developed now should use it and all examples in this book rely on it.

There are eight more libraries that you should know about: CardView, Design, GridLayout, Leanback, MediaRouter, Palette, RecyclerView, and Support Annotations. To use any of them, be sure that you've installed the Android Support Repository via the SDK manager. Listing 3.6 shows the Gradle dependencies for the various libraries. If you're not familiar with Gradle, it is the build system used by Android and it makes including dependencies (i.e., specifying libraries or other projects that your app depends on to build) and configuration details easy. More information about using Gradle for Android builds is available at https://gradle.org/getting-started-android/.

Listing 3.6 Support Library Dependencies for Your Gradle Configuration

```
dependencies {
    // AppCompat - likely in every app you develop
    compile 'com.android.support:appcompat-v7:22.2.1'
    // CardView - for paper with shadows on older versions
    compile 'com.android.support:cardview-v7:22.2.1'
    // Design - for Material Design views and motion
    compile 'com.android.support:design:22.2.1'
    // GridLayout - for laying out views in a grid
    compile 'com.android.support:gridlayout-v7:22.2.1'
    // Leanback - for fragments that simplify TV apps
    compile 'com.android.support:leanback-v17:22.2.1'
    // MediaRouter - for outputting media to various devices
    compile 'com.android.support:mediarouter-v7:22.2.1'
    // Palette - for extracting colors from images
    compile 'com.android.support:palette-v7:22.2.1'
    // RecyclerView - for advanced AdapterView needs
    compile 'com.android.support:recyclerview-v7:22.2.1'
    // Support Annotations - for Java annotations to prevent bugs
    compile 'com.android.support:support-annotations:22.2.1'
    // Support V13 - probably not required in your app
    compile 'com.android.support:support-v13:22.2.1'
    // Support V4 - included by AppCompat, so not necessary to add
    compile 'com.android.support:support-v4:22.2.1'
}
```

The CardView Library

One of the fundamental parts of Material Design is shadows. Unfortunately, this isn't a feature that is easy to support on older versions of Android because of fundamental rendering changes. The CardView library is meant to help with that by providing the `CardView` class, a concrete implementation of a card (a piece of paper) with support for shadows on older versions of Android by using an image. Each card view can hold one child view and give it shadows with support for dynamically changing elevations. See Figure 3.7 for a simple example.

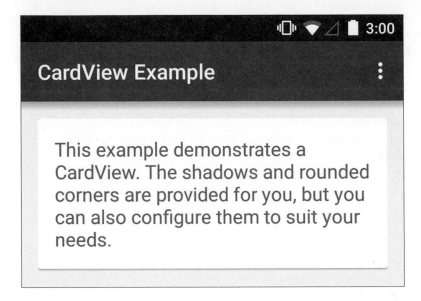

Figure 3.7 The `CardView` class provides a way to create Material Design "paper," complete with shadow, on versions of Android prior to 5.0

Design Library

The design library provides concrete implementations of a variety of Material Design elements such as the FAB (with the `FloatingActionButton` class), snackbars (with the `Snackbar` class), scrollable and fixed tabs (with the `TabLayout` class), the navigation drawer (with the `NavigationView` class), and even floating labels for text entry (with the `TextInputLayout` class). Two other major classes to know in this library are the `CoordinatorLayout` and the `AppBarLayout`. These classes allow you to do things like moving your FAB out of the way when you display a snackbar or scrolling the app bar off the screen while scrolling down a list and back on when scrolling up.

Many of these classes are used in future chapters in this book, but it's a good idea to read the initial announcement of this library so that you can get a feel for what's in it at http://android-developers.blogspot.com/2015/05/android-design-support-library.html.

GridLayout Library

Occasionally you need to align views in a dynamic or complex grid and using relative layouts or nested linear layouts is problematic. In these cases, using the `GridLayout` class can be a good solution. This class was made available in API level 14 (Android 4.0), but this library allows you to use it with older versions of Android

Leanback Library

Apps designed for the TV have fundamentally different design requirements. The so-called 10-foot view necessitates larger fonts and pictures, simple directional navigation, and search. This library provides fragments to simplify implementing browsing rows of content, viewing details, video playback, and search for Android TV apps. For more information about designing for the TV experience, see http://developer.android.com/design/tv/.

MediaRouter Library

Android 4.1 (API level 16) brought about controls for easily routing media. If your app plays music, your users may want to play it from wireless speakers. Similarly, if your app plays video, your users may want to play it from a Chromecast. This library makes doing those things much easier and supports versions of Android as old as API level 7 (Android 2.1).

Palette Library

One common challenge in designing apps is dynamic images. If your app displays a lot of dynamic images, you have to be very careful about what colors you include in the UI around them. It's easy to end up with something that clashes or detracts from the experience. The two main ways designers have gotten around this issue is to either design a UI with limited colors (that's why so many photo apps and websites are white, black, or gray) or to use colors from the images themselves. The second solution is what the `Palette` class provides. It can analyze an image and give you the vibrant and muted colors (plus dark and light versions of each) from the image, allowing you to easily color buttons, chrome, or other UI elements dynamically.

RecyclerView Library

For most lists of content, a `ListView` class works fine. Unfortunately, there are some issues. For instance, you might try animating a view within a list, but scrolling causes that view to be reused while the animation is still going on, leading to a very confusing experience for users. In Android 4.1 (API level 16), `ViewPropertyAnimator`-based animations no longer had this problem issue and the `View` class had another method added called `setHasTransientS tate(boolean)`, specifically designed to tell the adapters that a view was in a transient or temporary state and shouldn't immediately be reused. You also can't create content that is laid on horizontally or in a grid. The `RecyclerView` class is provided by this library to solve these problems and more. It is supported all the way back to API level 7 (Android 2.1) and it can handle custom animations and layouts. The use of this class is covered in detail in Chapter 10, "Using Advanced Techniques."

Support Annotations Library

One of the challenges in writing code is knowing what is allowed or expected. For instance, if you call a method that returns a collection of items, what happens if it has no results?

Depending on the developer, it could return null or it could return an empty collection. What if you have a method that takes a color resource ID and you want to prevent someone from accidentally passing in a raw color `int`? The support annotations solve these problems. You can specify a parameter or return value as `@Nullable` to indicate that it can be null or `@NonNull` to indicate that it can't. You can also declare that a given int is a color resource ID with `@ColorRes` (and there are annotations for each of the types of resources such as `@StringRes`). In addition, there are times in Android when you want to use an enum, but you don't want the performance penalty of full Java classes which Java creates for each enum. Typically these are strings or `ints`, but you have to rely on code comments to get someone to pass in correct values. The annotation library includes `@IntDef` and `@StringDef` for these cases. To learn more, see http://tools.android.com/tech-docs/support-annotations.

Summary

You've survived another dry chapter! Give yourself a pat on the back; you've almost made it to the good stuff. You should now have a solid understanding of how the `ViewGroup` class and its subclasses work as well as how to use fragments to create reusable layouts with display and handling logic contained within. Plus, you're aware of the large number of support libraries that are available to make your life easier. Combine that with the knowledge from Chapter 2 and you know the most important aspects of getting your layouts on the screen exactly where you want them.

Next up, Chapter 4, "Adding App Graphics and Resources," will explain how to add graphics to these views and how to utilize resources in an efficient, reusable manner. That is the last chapter before diving into the real-life process of designing an app.

CHAPTER 4

ADDING APP GRAPHICS AND RESOURCES

As the final chapter of the first part of this book, this chapter teaches you how the resource system works in Android, including the use of graphics. One of the considerations when developing for Android is that there are so many different devices out there. You have to consider displays of various densities, screens of all sizes, whether a device has a hardware keyboard, what orientation it is held in, and even what language should be displayed. Fortunately, Android's resource system makes all this easy.

Introduction to Resources in Android

A solid understanding of Android's resource system is not only essential to developing good apps, it's vital to saving your sanity. If you had to programmatically check every feature of the device every time you did anything, your code would be a mess and you would lose sleep at night (assuming you get any now). To ensure a good user experience, you should generally make adjustments for things such as the size of the screen and the orientation of the device. By using resource "qualifiers," you can let Android take care of this for you.

A qualifier is a portion of a directory's name that marks its contents as being used for a specific situation; this is best illustrated with an example. Your Android project contains a `res` directory (resources) that can contain several other directories for each of the resource types. Your layouts go in a directory called `layout`. If you have a layout specifically for landscape orientation, you can create a directory in `res` called `layout-land`, where "land" designates it as being used for landscape orientations. If you have a layout called `main.xml` in both directories, Android automatically uses the version appropriate to the given device orientation.

Resource Qualifiers

Okay, so you can have a different layout for landscape and portrait orientations, but what else? Actually, there are a *lot* of qualifiers, and they can be applied to any resource directory. That means you can have the images or even strings change based on orientation. It's important to know what folders go in the `res` directory and what content they contain before diving into how that content can differ based on qualifiers. Here's a list of the folder names:

- `animator`—Property animations defined in XML.
- `anim`—View animations defined in XML.
- `color`—State lists of colors defined in XML. State lists are covered later in this chapter.
- `drawable`—Drawable assets that can be defined in XML or image files (PNG, GIF, or JPG).
- `layout`—Layouts defined in XML.
- `menu`—Menus such as the app bar menu defined in XML.
- `mipmap`—Drawable assets just like the `drawable` folder. The difference is that the `drawable` folders for specific densities can be excluded based on your configuration, letting you make density-specific builds, but the `mipmap` folders are always included regardless of density. In practice, you should always put your launcher icons in `mipmap` folders, so that launcher apps can use higher resolution assets when desired. All other images will go in the applicable `drawable` folders.
- `raw`—Any raw files such as audio files and custom bytecode.
- `values`—Various simple values defined in XML, such as strings, floats, and integer colors.
- `xml`—Any XML files you wish to read at runtime (common for configurations such as for app widgets).

By no means are all of these required in any given app. In fact, it is not uncommon to only have `drawable`, `layout`, `mipmap`, and `values` directories in an app, although you will nearly always have multiple `drawable` and `mipmap` folders to accommodate different densities. The various resource folders are generated for you when needed (e.g., creating an XML menu in Android Studio creates the `menu` folder), but you can also create them yourself. For every file in these directories, Android's build tools will automatically create a reference in the R class (short for resources) that is an `int` identifier, which can be used by a variety of methods. That also means your files should be named in all lowercase and underscore separated.

Take a look at Table 4.1 to see the resource qualifiers you can use. These are listed in the order that Android requires, meaning that if you use more than one, you must list them in the same order they appear in this table.

Table 4.1   The Complete List of Resource Qualifiers

Qualifier Type	Examples	Description

Mobile country code
 	
Mobile network code
	`mcc310`
	`mcc440`
	`mcc310-`
	➡ `mnc800`
		The MCC (Mobile Country Code) can be used with or without an accompanying MNC (Mobile Network Code). Typically, you will not use these qualifiers, but they are occasionally used to provide country-specific legal information or carrier-specific data.

		For a list of mobile country codes and mobile network codes, see http://www.itu.int/dms_pub/itu-t/opb/sp/T-SP-E.212B-2011-PDF-E.pdf.

Language
 	
Region
	`en`
	`en-rUS`
	`es`
	`es-rMX`
		The language is specified by two characters and is most commonly used for strings to easily support localization. You might also use the language qualifier for drawables where the text is part of the image. You can specify the region along with the language (but not separately) by using a lowercase *r* and the two-letter code.

		For a list of country codes, see this page: http://www.loc.gov/standards/iso639-2/php/code_list.php.
		For a list of regions, see this page: http://www.iso.org/iso/iso-3166-1_decoding_table.
Language direction	`ldrtl` `ldltr`	This qualifier was added in API level 17. Language direction is either left-to-right (`ldltr`), which is the default, or right-to-left (`ldrtl`), such as for Arabic.

Qualifier Type	Examples	Description
Smallest width	`sw320dp` `sw480dp`	This qualifier was added in API level 13. The smallest width is actually the smallest available dimension, regardless of orientation. For example, a device that is medium density and 320 pixels (px) by 480px has a smallest width of 320dp (density and the difference between px and dp are explained later in this chapter), regardless of whether it is in portrait or landscape orientation. It is also important to note that the system-level UI adjusts this amount. For example, some devices use part of their screen for the system buttons (back, home, and recent apps). The remaining portion of the screen not used for that UI is what determines the smallest width. In other words, the smallest width is the smallest dimension of the screen space available for your app to use.
Available width	`w480dp` `w720dp`	This qualifier was added in API level 13. Available width specifies the minimum available width in the current orientation at which the resource should be used. That means the resources in a given directory might be used while in landscape mode but not portrait mode.
Available height	`h720dp` `h1024dp`	This qualifier was added in API level 13. Available height works the same as available width, but is specific to the height.

Screen size	`small`
	`normal`
	`large`
	`xlarge`
		The screen size qualifier allows you to specify "buckets" for different sizes and has been available since API level 4 (although `xlarge` was added in API level 9). To simplify these sizes, you can think of `small` as being smaller than a normal phone, `normal` as being a typical phone-sized device, `large` as being a 7" tablet, and `xlarge` as being a 10" tablet. More specifically:
		
		`small`—Typically low-density QVGA screens with a minimum size of roughly 320×426dp.
		
		`normal`—Nearly all phone-sized devices; these are usually at least 320×470dp.
		
		`large`—Screens with a minimum size of about 480×640dp.
		
		`xlarge`—Screens with a minimum size of about 720×960dp.
		
		Note that the system will look for resources that have a smaller qualifier but never a larger qualifier. In other words, a device that is large will first look for large, then normal, then small, but it will never look at the xlarge resources. That means specifying only xlarge resources and running the app on a large device will cause it to crash.

Qualifier Type	Examples	Description
Screen aspect	`long` `notlong`	Screen aspect is independent of the device's orientation and specifies whether the device is more square (`notlong`) or rectangular (`long`). For example, a 3:2 or 4:3 device is `notlong` but a 16:9 device is `long`.
Orientation	`port` `land`	Specifies resources for portrait or landscape orientation. Portrait is the default.

UI mode	`car`
	`desk`
	`appliance`
	`television`
	`watch`
		This qualifier was added in API level 8.
		
		`car`—The device is in a car dock (commonly for navigation).
		
		`desk`—The device is in a desk dock.
		
		`appliance`—The device is being used as an appliance without a display.
		
		`television`—The device is displaying on a television (added in API level 13).
		
		`watch`—The device is a wrist watch; typically this means Android Wear (added in API level 20).

Night mode	`night` `notnight`	This qualifier was added in API level 8. Specifies whether the device is in nighttime mode or daytime (`notnight`) mode.

Density	`ldpi`
	`mdpi`
	`hdpi`
	`xhdpi`
	`xxhdpi`
	`xxxhdpi`
	`nodpi`
	`tvdpi`
		Specifies the density of the screen (covered in depth later in the chapter).
		
		`ldpi`—Low density (120dpi).
		
		`mdpi`—Medium density (160dpi).
		
		`hdpi`—High density (240dpi).
		
		`xhdpi`—Extra-high density (320dpi).
		
		`xxhdpi`—Extra-extra-high density (480dpi).
		
		`xxxhdpi`—Extra-extra-extra-high density (640dpi).
		
		`nodpi`—Not density-specific.
		
		`tvdpi`—TV-specific density (roughly 213dpi).
		
		These qualifiers are nearly always used with drawables to provide differently sized assets for different densities.

Touchscreen type	`finger` `notouch`	Specifies whether or not the device has a touchscreen (`finger`).

Qualifier Type	Examples	Description

Keyboard availability	`keysexposed`
	`keyshidden`
	`keyssoft`
		Specifies the status of the keyboard:
		
		`keysexposed`—The device has a keyboard available (i.e., the keys are exposed to the user) whether the keyboard is software or hardware.
		
		`keyshidden`—The device has a hidden hardware keyboard and the software keyboard is not enabled.
		
		`keyssoft`—The device has a software keyboard enabled (regardless of visibility).

Hardware keyboard type	`nokeys`
	`qwerty`
	`12key`
		Specifies the type of hardware keyboard on the device (whether it is extended or not):
		
		`nokeys`—No hardware keyboard.
		
		`qwerty`—A qwerty keyboard exists.
		
		`12key`—A 12-key keyboard exists.

Navigation key availability	`navexposed` `navhidden`	Specifies whether the navigation keys are available (exposed) or hidden.

Primary non-touch navigation method	`nonav`
	`dpad`
	`track-ball`
	`wheel`
		Specifies the type of navigation, other than the touch screen, that the device has:
		
		`nonav`—The device has only the touch screen for navigation.
		
		`dpad`—The device has a directional-pad (D-pad) available.
		
		`trackball`—The device has a trackball available.
		
		`wheel`—The device has one or more directional wheels available.

Platform version	`v8`
	`v14`
	`v23`
		Specifies the minimum platform version of the device. This is most commonly used to have assets blend better with a given platform version (e.g., the notification icons have changed over time, so many apps provide version-specific images). This can also be used to provide strings based on the version such as an explanation of how to add a widget. The device will look for the highest version qualifier that is equal to or less than its version, falling back on qualifiers that aren't version specific.

Regardless of how many or how few qualifiers you use, the R class will only have one reference to a given set of resources. For example, you might have a file at the path `res/drawable-xhdpi/header.png`, and the reference would be `R.drawable.header`. As you can probably see, the format is `R.[resource type without qualifiers].[file name without` extension]. Perhaps this header file also contains text, so you have language-specific versions such as `res/drawable-es-xhdpi/header.png`. Within the Java portion of your app, you will always refer to the resource as `R.drawable.header`. If the device's language is set to Spanish, the reference automatically points to the Spanish version, so you do not have to change anything in your code. If the device is an HDPI device, it would first look in the `drawable-hdpi` directory before the `drawable-xhdpi` directory. When you refer to a resource like `R.drawable.header`, you're asking the system to use whichever header drawable best fits the current device configuration.

> ## warning
>
> **ALWAYS SPECIFY DEFAULTS**   One extremely important thing to note is that you need to specify defaults. With the exception of density qualifiers, all qualifiers are exclusive. For example, you can create a "hello" string. Within `res/values-es/strings.xml`, you define "hello" to be "hola" and within `res/values-en/strings.xml` you define "hello" as "hello." Everything seems good, and you can use that reference in your code as `R.string.hello`.
>
> You test it on your English device, and it works correctly. You test it on your Spanish device, and it works correctly as well. However, when you test it on your Russian device, it crashes. That's because both of those qualifiers exclude Russian. You have not defined a Russian-specific values directory with that string in it, so the system falls back on the values directory with no qualifier. Nothing is there, making the reference invalid.
>
> To avoid this situation, make sure your default directory (i.e., the one without qualifiers) contains all references. The one exception is with density-specific assets, which Android is able to scale for you.

Understanding Density

Although it was covered briefly in Chapter 2, "Understanding Views—The UI Building Blocks," density is one of the most important aspects of an Android device to understand when it comes to design and it's worth covering in detail. Early Android devices had approximately 160 dots per inch (dpi)—and that is considered medium density (MDPI) now. Android 1.6 added support for both low density (LDPI or 120dpi) and high density (HDPI or 240dpi). Android 2.2 added extra high density (XHDPI or 320dpi) to the mix. Continuing the march toward higher and higher densities, Android 4.1 introduced extra, extra high density (XXHDPI or 480dpi) and Android 4.3 brought extra, extra, extra high density (XXXHDPI or 640dpi). These are listed in Table 4.2 for easier reference.

Table 4.2   Android Densities

Abbreviation	Name (Dots per Inch)	Density	Scale
LDPI	Low	120	0.75
MDPI	Medium	160	1
HDPI	High	240	1.5
XHDPI	Extra high	320	2
XXHDPI	Extra, extra high	480	3
XXXHDPI	Extra, extra, extra high	640	4

What do all these letters and numbers mean to you? A given image will appear larger on a screen with a lower density and smaller on a screen with a higher density. If you take a piece of paper and draw a vertical line and a horizontal line, splitting it into four pieces, a single piece (pixel) will take up a quarter of the paper. If you divide each of those quarters into four pieces, then a single piece (pixel) is one fourth of the size that it was. The pixel appears physically smaller even though the total size of the paper (the screen) has not changed.

Fortunately, Android makes handling this easy for you. Instead of specifying dimensions in raw pixels, you will use either density-independent pixels (referred to as dip or dp) or scale-independent pixels (sip or sp). Density-independent pixels are based on MDPI, so 1dp is 1px at medium density. The difference between one sp and one dp is that sp takes into account the user's preferred font size. Therefore, all font sizes should be specified in sp and all other dimensions should be in dp.

There are a lot of numbers and terms to remember, so it can be helpful to break this down more. Most apps can ignore LDPI because it is uncommon (of standard phone sizes and tablet sizes, LDPI represents a fraction of a percent). For the rest of these, you can think of them relative to one another. The ratio from MDPI to XXXHDPI is 2:3:4:6:8. Reading from the right, you might notice that every other density cuts the value in half. An XXXHDPI image of 8 pixels wide would be 4 pixels wide at XHDPI and 2 pixels wide at MDPI. An XXHDPI image of 6 pixels wide would be 3 pixels wide at HDPI. More practically, this means that if you include XHDPI and XXHDPI resources, the system can easily scale those images without ever having to worry about half pixels, so you don't have to export to every single density. The one exception is your launcher icon, which you should have available for every density you support. Table 4.3 shows how this ratio applies to app icons, which are 48dp squares.

Table 4.3 Android Densities Applied to App Icons

Density	Scale	App Icon Size in Pixels
LDPI	0.75	36 × 36
MDPI	1	48 × 48
HDPI	1.5	72 × 72
XHDPI	2	96 × 96
XXHDPI	3	144 × 144
XXXHDPI	4	192 × 192

Supported Image Files

For the longest time, Android supported only "raster" images natively. Raster images are a series of pixels, which makes them efficient for displaying on the screen, but that means they do not resize to arbitrary sizes well. The primary alternative is vectors, which represent images as drawing instructions (e.g., "draw a black line from 0, 0 to 5, 0 that is 2 units thick"). The advantage of vectors is that they are infinitely resizable because all the values are relative. In fact, most icons and logos are designed as vectors and then exported to raster images for specific uses. The disadvantage of vectors is that they are more processor intensive because all the instructions have to be interpreted and turned into the pixels that will be displayed.

One of the many changes announced for Android 5.0 (Lollipop) was native support for vectors. The format supported by Android is a subset of the well-known SVG format, but it will handle most typical uses. The particularly exciting thing about this vector support is that Android also has support for animating between two vectors, which is covered in detail in Chapter 9, "Polishing with Animations."

Raster Images

Android supports JPEGs, PNGs, and GIFs natively. These formats are all "raster" format with red, green, and blue channels (and an alpha channel that represents level of transparency for PNG and GIF images). If you use eight bits (one byte) for each channel, a pixel is 24-bit (without alpha) or 32-bit (with alpha). That means a single 1920×1080 image is over eight megabytes! Fortunately, all of these formats are compressed, so they don't store each individual pixel on disk. JPEGs use lossy compression, meaning that some of the detail is lost to decrease the file size. See Figure 4.1 for an example of heavy JPEG compression compared to no compression. PNGs and GIFs use lossless compression (no detail lost). That means you should use JPEGs for large photographs and any images already saved as JPEGs and PNGs for everything else. Although GIF is supported, PNG is a better file format and should be used instead.

Figure 4.1 Heavy JPEG compression on the left; no compression on the right

> ## Note
>
> **PNG COMPRESSION**   The Android build tools will automatically compress the PNGs by stripping them of all metadata and reducing the bit depth where possible. For example, an image might be converted to an 8-bit PNG with a custom color palette to reduce its file size. This reduces the overall size of your APK, but it does not affect the size of the image once it has been decoded into memory.

Vector Images

Android's vector support that came in Android 5.0 (Lollipop) has been long awaited by designers and developers alike. Devices now are powerful enough to handle typical vector uses (such as for icons in a toolbar) without a problem; however, you still have to be aware of the performance costs. Each vector image is cached as a bitmap representation, which means it can very quickly be drawn and even moved around on the screen, but changing it in any way that invalidates that cache (such as scaling it) causes Android to have to recreate that bitmap. For smaller icons and infrequent animations, this won't be any problem (in fact, animating between vectors is one of the coolest features of Android 5.0), but trying to continuously animate a full-screen vector is going to have a noticeable performance hit. Details are included later in this chapter.

Nine-Patch Images

Oftentimes, you do not know ahead of time how large an image should be. For example, a button will need the ability to be of different sizes to accommodate different languages and text labels. Even if you tell it to be as wide as the screen, there are still many possible widths. It would be a huge amount of work to create an image for every possible width, and your app will look terrible if you hard-code the button to a specific size in pixels. The nine-patch image solves this problem.

If you think of a typical button, there are nine pieces to it: the four corners, the four sides (left, right, top, and bottom), and the center area where the text typically goes. To support a wider button, the top, center, and bottom portions have to be duplicated. For a taller button, the left, center, and right portions would be duplicated. This allows you to preserve the corners and edges while expanding the content area. See Figure 4.2 for an example of how a nine-patch can be resized.

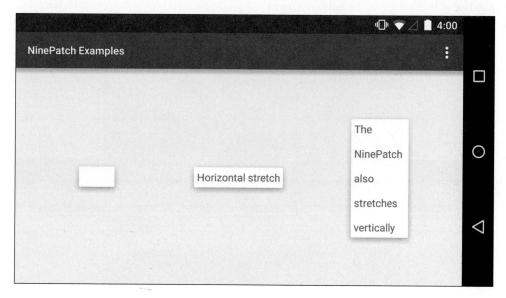

Figure 4.2 An example of a nine-patch accommodating different sizes

A nine-patch is actually just a PNG where the 1px border around the outside of the image consists of pixels that are either fully transparent or fully black. The left and top of the image can contain black pixels to describe how to enlarge the image. Figure 4.3 highlights the "stretchable" area in green.

Figure 4.3 A nine-patch image with the stretchable area highlighted in green

Another feature of nine-patch images is that the right and bottom of the image specify content areas. In the simplest case, you can think of the black part as where content goes and the transparent part as the padding. When you set a view's background to a nine-patch image, the padding of that image will be applied automatically; however, you can still override it. See the purple area in Figure 4.4 to understand where content can go. When the content is larger than this area, the image stretches along the parts that were highlighted green in Figure 4.3.

Figure 4.4 The highlighted purple areas are where content can go, as defined by the right and bottom black pixels

One last thing to note is that you can specify nine-patch images in XML (though it is uncommon). The image itself is still a standard nine-patch PNG, but the XML file allows you to specifically enable or disable dithering, which is a way of adding "noise" to an image to reduce artifacts such as banding, which is caused by low-bitrate displays. See Listing 4.1 for an example of this.

Listing 4.1 Specifying a Nine-Patch with XML

```xml
<?xml version="1.0" encoding="utf-8"?>
<nine-patch xmlns:android="http://schemas.android.com/apk/res/android"
    android:dither="true"
    android:src="@drawable/padding_bg" />
```

XML Drawables

In addition to standard image files, Android supports a variety of XML drawables (the term "drawable" refers simply to something that can be drawn to the screen). Some of these drawables are ways of using multiple image files for one resource; others allow you to actually specify colors within XML. A few you may never need, but some will prove extremely valuable, so it is worth knowing what is available to you.

Each type of drawable that can be defined in XML uses a different root node (which tells Android which class's `inflate` method to call). They are all inflated to specific drawables, but you can interact with them via the abstract `Drawable` class. Drawables that display more than one drawable define each one with the `item` tag. The `item` tag can typically take offsets (`android:left`, `android:top`, `android:right`, and `android:bottom`), which is useful for specific visual effects and for supporting images of different sizes.

Layer List

A layer list is an array of drawables defined in XML that creates a `LayerDrawable` instance when used. Each drawable can be offset on the left, top, right, and/or bottom by a different amount. The drawables are drawn in the order they are declared (just like views) and will be scaled to fit the available space. See Listing 4.2 for a sample layer list.

Listing 4.2   Example of a Simple Layer List

```xml
<?xml version="1.0" encoding="utf-8"?>
<layer-list xmlns:android="http://schemas.android.com/apk/res/android" >

    <item android:drawable="@drawable/example_green_screen"/>
    <item
        android:drawable="@drawable/example_red_screen"
        android:left="64dp"
        android:top="64dp">
    </item>

</layer-list>
```

If you do not want the drawables to be scaled, you can use gravity, like in Listing 4.3. Using gravity allows you to define the anchor point of the drawable. For example, you might be using a drawable as the background of a full screen view. The default behavior is to scale to the size of the view, but you can instead specify a gravity to align the image to a specific location such as the right side of the view. Notice that this requires a separate bitmap node that contains the gravity; the gravity does not go within the `item` tag itself.

Listing 4.3   Example of a Layer List Using Gravity

```xml
<?xml version="1.0" encoding="utf-8"?>
<layer-list xmlns:android="http://schemas.android.com/apk/res/android" >

    <item>
        <bitmap
            android:gravity="center"
            android:src="@drawable/example_green_screen" />
    </item>
```

```
<item
    android:left="64dp"
    android:top="64dp">
    <bitmap
        android:gravity="center"
        android:src="@drawable/example_red_screen" />
</item>

</layer-list>
```

For a comparison of the difference between letting the `LayerListDrawable` scale and keeping its size by the use of gravity, see Figure 4.5. Notice that the device with the green screen on the left is significantly larger than the others due to no offset and no gravity.

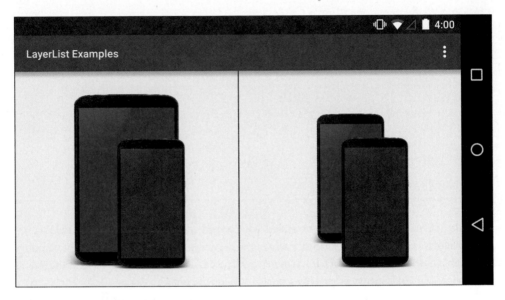

Figure 4.5 The left image is from Listing 4.2; the right is from Listing 4.3

State List

A `StateListDrawable`, defined by the selector XML node, allows you to specify different drawables for different states. For example, a standard button will have different appearances based on whether it is enabled, focused, pressed, and so on. You can specify as few or as many drawables as you like, and you can also combine states (e.g., show a particular drawable only if it is both focused and checked). See Figure 4.6 for an example of different images based on different states. You can use colors in a selector as well. You might decide that your button's text should normally be white but it should be gray when it is disabled.

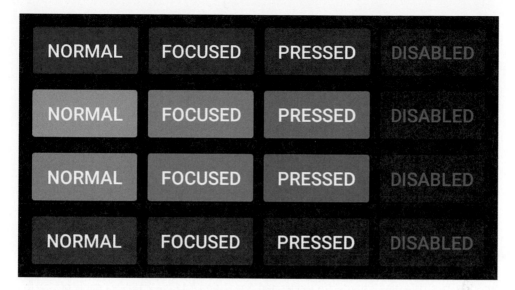

Figure 4.6 Examples of different appearances a drawable might have for each state

It is important to note that the drawable used will be the first that matches, which might not be the best match. For example, if the first item requires a state of pressed and the second item requires both pressed and enabled, the second item will never be used because any image that matches pressed, whether enabled or not, would match the first item immediately. Therefore, you should put the most specific states first and your last state should contain no state requirements.

Here is a list of the most common states:

- `android:state_activated`—Added in API 11, this indicates the item is the activated selection. For example, on a tablet where you have a list of articles on the left and the full article on the right, the list item on the left that represents the article being displayed on the right would be activated. All other items in that list would be false for being activated.

- `android:state_checkable`—Indicates whether the item can be checked. This is really only useful when a view can change between being checkable and not checkable, which is relatively uncommon.

- `android:state_checked`—Indicates whether the item is currently checked.

- `android:state_enabled`—Indicates whether the item is enabled or disabled, which is especially useful with buttons that are only enabled if a certain condition is met (such as a text field being filled out).

- `android:state_focused`—Indicates whether the item is focused. Focus usually happens after an input has been tapped, such as an `EditText`, or after navigating to a given view by means other than touch (e.g., a directional pad or trackball). Drawables that represent a focused state usually have a glow or generally highlighted appearance.

- **android:state_hovered**—Added in API 14, this indicates whether the item is currently being hovered over by the cursor. Typically, this is visually indicated in the same way as focus.

- **android:state_pressed**—Indicates whether the item is being pressed. This state happens when the item is clicked or touched and is usually shown by a visually depressed state (like a button being pushed in) or a brightened/colored appearance.

- **android:state_selected**—Indicates that the item is currently selected. This is very similar to focus but slightly more specific. A particular view group (e.g., `ListView`) can have focus while a specific child is selected.

- **android:state_window_focused**—Indicates whether the app's window is focused. This is generally true unless it is obstructed, like when the notification drawer has been pulled down.

In addition to the common states, there are `state_first`, `state_middle`, and `state_last` states, which are for specifying changes based on position, and `state_accelerated`, which is true if the view is hardware accelerated. See Listing 4.4 for a simple example of how to use a `StateListDrawable` by defining a selector in XML.

Listing 4.4 Example of a Selector (`StateListDrawable`)

```xml
<?xml version="1.0" encoding="utf-8"?>
<selector xmlns:android="http://schemas.android.com/apk/res/android">

    <!-- Shown when enabled but the window is not focused -->
    <item android:drawable="@drawable/btn_default_normal"
        android:state_enabled="true"
        android:state_window_focused="false"
    />

    <!-- Shown when disabled and the window is not focused -->
    <item android:drawable="@drawable/btn_default_disabled"
        android:state_enabled="false"
        android:state_window_focused="false"
    />

    <!-- Shown when pressed -->
    <item android:drawable="@drawable/btn_default_pressed"
        android:state_pressed="true"
    />

    <!-- Shown when enabled and focused -->
    <item android:drawable="@drawable/btn_default_focused"
        android:state_enabled="true"
        android:state_focused="true"
    />
```

```
    <!-- Shown when enabled but not focused -->
    <item android:drawable="@drawable/btn_default_normal"
        android:state_enabled="true"
    />

    <!-- Shown when focused but not enabled -->
    <item android:drawable="@drawable/btn_default_disabled_focused"
        android:state_focused="true"
    />

    <!-- Shown for all other cases -->
    <item android:drawable="@drawable/btn_default_disabled"/>

</selector>
```

Level List

A `LevelListDrawable` manages any number of drawables, assigning each one to a range of integer values. You can set the current level of the `LevelListDrawable` with `Drawable`'s `setLevel(int)` method. Whichever drawable fits in that range will then be used. This is particularly useful for visual indicators where you want to show some difference based on a value but do not want to worry about the exact image to display in your code. The battery indicator is a good example of this. You know that the range is from 0 to 100 percent, but your code does not need to know whether there is a different image for 38 percent versus 39 percent. Instead, you just set the level of the `LevelListDrawable` and the correct drawable will automatically be used. See Listing 4.5 for an example of recreating the typical battery indicator.

Listing 4.5   A Level List for Indicating Battery Level

```
<?xml version="1.0" encoding="utf-8"?>
<level-list xmlns:android="http://schemas.android.com/apk/res/android">
    <item android:maxLevel="4" android:drawable="@drawable/battery_0" />
    <item android:maxLevel="15" android:drawable="@drawable/battery_15" />
    <item android:maxLevel="35" android:drawable="@drawable/battery_28" />
    <item android:maxLevel="49" android:drawable="@drawable/battery_43" />
    <item android:maxLevel="60" android:drawable="@drawable/battery_57" />
    <item android:maxLevel="75" android:drawable="@drawable/battery_71" />
    <item android:maxLevel="90" android:drawable="@drawable/battery_85" />
    <item android:maxLevel="100" android:drawable="@drawable/battery_100" />
</level-list>
```

TransitionDrawable

A `TransitionDrawable` allows you to specify two drawables that you can then crossfade between. Two methods `startTransition(int)` and `reverseTransition(int)` allow you to control the transition between the two drawables. Both methods take an `int`, which defines the duration in milliseconds.

This is not a particularly common drawable because crossfading is often done with views, but it is a fast and efficient way to transition between two drawables and has the advantage of only requiring one view, which means you can combine it with a state list to transition on a specific state. See Listing 4.6 for a simple example of a `TransitionDrawable`.

Listing 4.6   An Example of a Simple `TransitionDrawable`

```xml
<?xml version="1.0" encoding="utf-8"?>
<transition xmlns:android="http://schemas.android.com/apk/res/android" >

    <item android:drawable="@drawable/first_drawable"/>
    <item android:drawable="@drawable/second_drawable"/>

</transition>
```

InsetDrawable

An `InsetDrawable` allows you to inset, or push in, another drawable. It is useful when you have a drawable that you would like to appear smaller than a view or to appear padded. This might seem useless because you could just add transparent pixels to an image to accomplish the same thing, but what if you want to use that same image in one place without that extra spacing and in another with it? See Listing 4.7 for a simple example that insets a drawable by 16dp on all sides.

Listing 4.7   An Example of a Simple `InsetDrawable`

```xml
<?xml version="1.0" encoding="utf-8"?>
<inset
    xmlns:android="http://schemas.android.com/apk/res/android"
    android:drawable="@drawable/padding_bg"
    android:insetTop="16dp"
    android:insetRight="16dp"
    android:insetBottom="16dp"
    android:insetLeft="16dp" />
```

ClipDrawable

A `ClipDrawable` takes a single drawable and clips, or cuts off, that drawable at a point determined by the level. This is most frequently used for progress bars. The drawable that this `Clip-Drawable` wraps would be the full progress bar (what the user would see at 100 percent). By using `setLevel(int)`, your code can reveal more and more of the bar until it is complete. The level is from 0 to 10,000, where 0 does not show the image at all and 10,000 shows it completely without clipping.

You can specify whether the clipping is vertical or horizontal as well as the gravity. For example, a ClipDrawable with gravity set to left and clipOrientation set to horizontal will start drawing from the left side (see Listing 4.8 for an example). By calling setLevel(5000) on this drawable, it will draw the left half of the image.

Listing 4.8 An Example of a Simple ClipDrawable

```xml
<?xml version="1.0" encoding="utf-8"?>
<clip xmlns:android="http://schemas.android.com/apk/res/android"
    android:drawable="@drawable/padding_bg"
    android:clipOrientation="horizontal"
    android:gravity="left" />
```

ScaleDrawable

A ScaleDrawable allows you to use setLevel(int) to scale the drawable at runtime (i.e., while the app is running). This is sometimes also used for progress bars as well as general cases in which you want to scale a drawable based on some other value.

You specify a scaleWidth and a scaleHeight, which is the size of the drawable when the level is 10,000. For example, Listing 4.9 shows a ScaleDrawable with both scale values set to 100 percent. If this drawable has setLevel(5000) called on it, it will display at 50 percent width and 50 percent height.

Listing 4.9 An Example of a Simple ScaleDrawable

```xml
<?xml version="1.0" encoding="utf-8"?>
<scale xmlns:android="http://schemas.android.com/apk/res/android"
    android:drawable="@drawable/ic_launcher"
    android:scaleGravity="center"
    android:scaleHeight="100%"
    android:scaleWidth="100%"
    android:useIntrinsicSizeAsMinimum="true" />
```

ShapeDrawable

A ShapeDrawable is a rectangle, oval, line, or ring that is defined in XML. If it is a rectangle, you can define rounded corners. If it is a ring, you can specify the innerRadius (i.e., the radius of the hole) or innerRadiusRatio (the ratio of the shape's width to the inner radius) and the thickness or thicknessRatio. For all shapes, you can specify a stroke (i.e., the line around the shape), solid fill color, or gradient fill colors, size, and padding.

You can use a variety of attributes to create your `ShapeDrawable`. See Table 4.4 for a complete list of the root node types and the corresponding attributes available.

Table 4.4   Attributes for `ShapeDrawable`

Root Node	Attribute	Description
shape	shape	Specifies the shape of the drawable—one of rectangle, oval, line, or ring.
shape	innerRadius	The radius of the center hole in a ring; ignored for other shape types.
shape	innerRadiusRatio	The radius of the center hole in a ring as a ratio of the shapes width to the inner radius; ignored for other shape types.
shape	thickness	The thickness of the ring; ignored for other shape types.
shape	thicknessRatio	The thickness of the ring as a ratio of the ring's width; ignored for other shape types.
shape	useLevel	When set to `true`, this shape can be used as a level list; you should generally set this to `false` because the level defaults to 0 (meaning the shape will not be shown).
corners	radius	Radius of all the corners of the drawable. This is often specified and then overridden by each of the corner-specific attributes; applicable to rectangles only.
corners	topLeftRadius	Radius of the top-left corner; applicable to rectangles only.
corners	topRightRadius	Radius of the top-right corner; applicable to rectangles only.
corners	bottomLeftRadius	Radius of the bottom-left corner; applicable to rectangles only.
corners	bottomRightRadius	Radius of the bottom-right corner; applicable to rectangles only.
gradient	angle	The angle of the gradient in degrees, where 0 is from left to right and 90 is from bottom to top. Must be a multiple of 45.
gradient	centerX	The relative position for the center of the gradient along the x axis from 0.0 to 1.0. For example, 0.4 represents 40 percent from the left.
gradient	centerY	The relative position for the center of the gradient along the y axis, from 0.0 to 1.0. For example, 0.4 represents 40 percent from the top.
gradient	centerColor	The optional center color of the gradient.
gradient	endColor	The color that the gradient ends with.

Root Node	Attribute	Description
gradient	gradientRadius	The radius of the gradient when using a radial gradient. Note that radial gradients often suffer from significant artifacting on low-quality devices, especially if the display has a low bit depth.
gradient	startColor	The color that the gradient starts with.
gradient	type	Type of gradient—one of linear, radial, and sweep.
padding	left	Left padding. Padding allows you to inset the ShapeDrawable.
padding	top	Top padding.
padding	right	Right padding.
padding	bottom	Bottom padding.
size	height	Height of the shape. Note that when a ShapeDrawable is used as the background of a view, it will scale to fill the view. If you wish it to be exactly the height and width specified, put it in an ImageView with scaleType set to center.
size	width	Width of the shape.
solid	color	Color to completely fill the shape with.
stroke	dashGap	Spacing between each dash (requires dashWidth to be set).
stroke	dashWidth	Width of each dash (requires dashGap to be set).
stroke	color	Color of the stroke line.
stroke	width	Thickness of the stroke line.

note

SPECIFYING ROUNDED CORNERS   If you do specify rounded corners for your rectangle, you must specify all of them as rounded initially. In cases where you only want some of the corners rounded, your code should look like this (assuming you want the bottom corners to not be rounded and the top to have a radius of 8dp):

```
<corners
    android:radius="1dp"
    android:bottomLeftRadius="0dp"
    android:bottomRightRadius="0dp"
    android:topLeftRadius="8dp"
    android:topRightRadius="8dp" />
```

Notice that all corners are initially set to 1dp before being set to 0dp or another value.

As you can see, `ShapeDrawable` has a large number of attributes, which makes it very versatile. It is often a better option than providing multiple density-specific images, with the possible exception of gradients, where a graphics program will give you far more control.

VectorDrawable

A `VectorDrawable` is a drawable that represents an image using vector data. This was introduced in Android 5.0 (Lollipop) and is primarily intended for icons and other small assets. To use a vector in Android, you create an XML file similar to Listing 4.10. The bizarre path data comes from the SVG file format. You'll likely be creating the vector image in a separate app and then copying the values from that file. If you're using Adobe Illustrator, you want to save a copy of your Illustrator file as an SVG (version 1.0). If you're using Inkscape, you want to save a copy as plain SVG (which strips the custom Inkscape values). You can then open the SVG file in a text editor and copy the values needed (e.g., the path data comes from the "d" attribute within a path node).

Note that you must specify a height and a width, which Android will treat as the intrinsic height and width. The height and width should be equivalent to the size that you will use the image at (such as the size of an `ImageView` if used in one). If they're smaller, the drawable will be scaled up, resulting in blur. You will also specify the `viewportWidth` and `viewportHeight`, which tell Android the size of the virtual canvas that the drawable is created on, which gives meaning to the positions specified in the actual path data (e.g., if the path data has a command to draw a line 100 units across, that would be halfway across if the `viewportWidth` is 200 and a quarter of the way if it is 400).

Listing 4.10 An Example of a Simple `VectorDrawable` for a Less-than Sign

```
<?xml version="1.0" encoding="utf-8"?>
<vector xmlns:android="http://schemas.android.com/apk/res/android"
        android:height="72dp"
        android:width="72dp"
        android:viewportHeight="48"
        android:viewportWidth="48" >
    <path
        android:name="line"
        android:strokeColor="#000000"
        android:fillColor="#000000"
        android:pathData="M30.83 32.671-9.17-9.17 9.17-9.17-2.83-2.
➡ 83-12 12 12 12z" />
</vector>
```

A vector is made of groups, paths, and/or clip-paths. A group is a container for any of the three types and it can contain transformation information (i.e., how to rotate, scale, or translate the children). A path is the basic element of a vector, giving info about what to draw. A clip-path is for clipping or constraining another shape. The elements only need names if they are to be animated. The attributes available are listed in Table 4.5.

Table 4.5 Attributes for `VectorDrawable`

Root Node	Attribute	Description
vector	name	Name to apply to the whole drawable; only necessary if animating the full drawable. The name should be unique within the drawable.
vector	width height	Dimensions to use as the intrinsic width and height of the drawable. Think of this as the physical size in pixels this drawable would be if it were a bitmap.
vector	viewportWidth viewportHeight	Dimensions to use for the virtual canvas, giving meaning to the units used in the path(s).
vector	tint	Color to tint the drawable with, if desired.
vector	tintMode	When using a tint, this is the PorterDuff mode to apply the tint with (PorterDuff modes are covered in detail in Chapter 11, "Working with the Canvas and Advanced Drawing").
vector	autoMirrored	If true, the drawable will be mirrored when displayed when the layout direction is right-to-left (such as for the Arabic language).
vector	alpha	Opacity of the drawable as a float (1 being fully opaque).
group	name	Name to apply to the group; only necessary if animating this group. The name should be unique within the drawable.
group	rotation	How much to rotate all of the elements of this group in degrees.
group	pivotX pivotY	The coordinates within the viewport to use for rotating or scaling this group.
group	scaleX scaleY	The amount to scale in the X/Y dimensions.
group	translate translateY	The amount to translate (move) in the X/Y dimension within the viewport.
path	name	Name to apply to the path; only necessary if animating this path. The name should be unique within the drawable.
path	pathData	This is the actual data saying what to draw. If you look at the raw data from an SVG file, this is the same as the "d" attribute.
path	fillApha	Opacity to apply to the `fillColor`.
path	fillColor	Color to fill the path with.

Root Node	Attribute	Description
path	strokeAlpha	Opacity to apply to the strokeColor.
path	strokeColor	Color to apply to the stroke (the outline of the path).
path	strokeWidth	Width of the stroke.
path	strokeLineCap	Defines how the start and end of a stroke looks; one of butt, round, and square.
path	strokeLineJoin	Defines how the part where two strokes touch looks; one of miter, round, bevel.
path	strokeMiterLimit	Defines the ratio limit for two strokes. When two strokes join, the miter can be thicker than the lines and this limits the ratio of how much thicker it can be before being converted to a bevel.
path	trimPathStart	Float saying how much of the path to trim from the start.
path	trimPathEnd	Float saying how much of the path to trim from the end.
path	trimPathOffset	Float saying how much to shift the trimmed region (affecting the start and end).
clip-path	name	Name to apply to the clip-path; only necessary if animating this clip-path. The name should be unique within the drawable.
clip-path	pathData	This is the actual data for the clip-path. If you look at the raw data from an SVG file, this is the same as the "d" attribute.

AnimatedVectorDrawable

Android 5.0 also added AnimatedVectorDrawable, which is a way of easily animating a vector, often by manipulating the path(s) of one vector to become another. You will first define a VectorDrawable, giving a name to any of the elements you want to animate (such as a path). The AnimatedVectorDrawable then has target nodes that specify a name and an animation to apply. That animation is a standard XML object animator, so it can rotate, scale, translate, or even manipulate paths. Listing 4.11 shows a simple example that targets the "line" path from the less-than sign in Listing 4.10 (displayed in Figure 4.7). The animator that is applied to that path is shown in Listing 4.12 (note that you can use string resources to avoid duplicating path data or to simply name path data to make it easier to understand). This animation smoothly animates from a less-than symbol to a greater-than symbol. Figure 4.8 shows some of the frames of this animation to illustrate how Android automatically changes from one path to another when animating a vector.

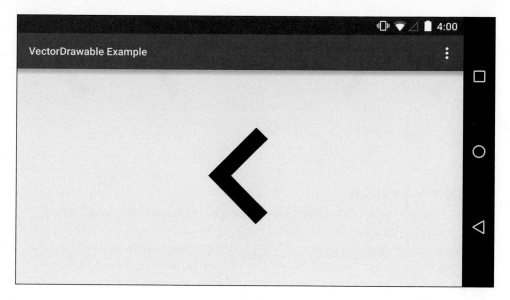

Figure 4.7 This is the `VectorDrawable` from Listing 4.10 but with the height and width increased to make it easier to see here

Listing 4.11 An Example of a Simple `AnimatedVectorDrawable`

```xml
<?xml version="1.0" encoding="utf-8"?>
<animated-vector xmlns:android="http://schemas.android.com/apk/res/android"
    android:drawable="@drawable/less_than_vector">

    <target
        android:animation="@animator/gt_lt_animator"
        android:name="line" />

</animated-vector>
```

Listing 4.12 An Animator Used to Change from One Set of Path Data to Another

```xml
<?xml version="1.0" encoding="utf-8"?>
<objectAnimator xmlns:android="http://schemas.android.com/apk/res/android"
    android:duration="300"
    android:propertyName="pathData"
    android:valueFrom="M30.83 32.67l-9.17-9.17 9.17-9.17-2.83-2.83-12
    12 12 12z"
    android:valueTo="M17.17 32.92l9.17-9.17-9.17-9.17 2.83-2.83 12
    12-12 12z"
    android:valueType="pathType">

</objectAnimator>
```

Figure 4.8 Some of the frames from the `AnimatedVectorDrawable` example

RippleDrawable

One more drawable type that Android 5.0 added is `RippleDrawable`. This is the default drawable used to indicate touch as a growing ripple. When you first touch this drawable, the background appears, expanding out in a circle (which can be drawn using a custom mask that you define) extremely fast. Then, a circle grows slowly, starting from your finger, filling the background. If you tap quickly, that circle expands quickly. If you move your finger away, the drawable fades out. Figure 4.9 shows a simple example.

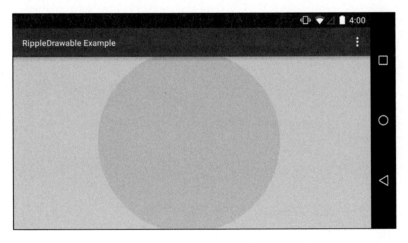

Figure 4.9 A `RippleDrawable` being touched near the center of the screen

This beautiful visual actually required a new thread (called the `RenderThread`) to be created for Android 5.0. Without it, tapping a view would pause the animation of the ripple because the animation and UI work (such as loading a new activity or fragment) were on the same thread. Listing 4.13 demonstrates how you will typically define a `RippleDrawable` in XML, using an inner `item` node, which can refer to a color or other drawable used as a mask. If you leave out the `item` node, the drawable will expand in a circle based on the bounds of the parent view.

Listing 4.13 An Example of a Simple `RippleDrawable`

```xml
<?xml version="1.0" encoding="utf-8"?>
<ripple xmlns:android="http://schemas.android.com/apk/res/android"
    android:color="@color/accent">

    <item android:drawable="@android:color/white" />

</ripple>
```

Other Resources

In addition to visual resources, you can also specify many other resources in XML. You will see these throughout rest of the book, but it's a good idea to overview them now.

Strings

You should specify all user-facing strings in XML. Typically, you put these all in a file called `strings.xml` in `res/values`, although you can call it something else. Putting your strings into an XML file will allow you to easily localize your app at any point, even if you do not intend to in the first version. In addition, it will allow you to keep your vocabulary consistent across the app by reusing strings, which will make your app more accessible to everyone, especially those with a limited understanding of the language that it is in. See Listing 4.14 for a sample `strings` file containing a "hello" string and an "intrograph" string.

Listing 4.14 An Example of a `strings` File

```xml
<?xml version="1.0" encoding="utf-8"?>
<resources>
    <string name="hello">Hello</string>
    <string name="intrograph">Welcome to the greatest app in the
 world!</string>
</resources>
```

At some point, you might decide to support Spanish, so you add a `strings.xml` file in `res/values-es` that looks like Listing 4.15.

Listing 4.15 A Spanish Version of the `strings` File

```xml
<?xml version="1.0" encoding="utf-8"?>
<resources>
    <string name="hello">Hola</string>
    <string name="intrograph">¡Bienvenidos a la mejor aplicación del
 mundo!</string>
</resources>
```

In most cases, you will refer to strings in your layouts, setting the text for a `TextView` in XML, but you can also set it in code. Further, the `Context` class (which `Activity` extends) has a `getString(int)` method, where passing it the resource identifier for the string you desire (e.g., `R.string.hello`) will return the applicable string ("Hello" or "Hola," depending on the device's language). The `getString(int)` method in `Context` is actually just a convenience method for calling `getResources().getString(int)` and there is a similar method in `Fragment`.

These strings also support substitutions. By including `%s` in the string, you can then call the `getString(int, Object...)` method to substitute a string (you can also use any other substitution supported by `String.format()` such as `%d` for a number). For example, if the "hello" string was actually "Hello, %s" then you could call `getString(R.string.hello, "Andy")`, which would give you either "Hello, Andy" or "Hola, Andy" (depending on device's language). You can also include multiple substitutions by numbering them such as "Hello %1$s, do you like %2$s?" and call `getString(R.string.hello, "Andy", "bacon")` to get "Hello Andy, do you like bacon?"

Android also supports plurals across locales. For example, English treats the number one specially (e.g., you would say "word" when referring to a single word but for all other amounts, including zero, you say "words"). There are other languages that treat other numbers in different ways. Using the `plurals` tag, you can easily support these. The supported quantities are `zero`, `one`, `two`, `few`, `many`, and `other`. These quantities are based on grammar requirements. Because English only has a special requirement for single numbers, a case for `zero` or `few` would never be used. See Listing 4.16 for a simple example.

Listing 4.16   A `strings` File Containing a Plural String

```xml
<?xml version="1.0" encoding="utf-8"?>
<resources>
    <plurals name="child_count">
        <item quantity="one">One child</item>
        <item quantity="other">%s children</item>
    </plurals>
</resources>
```

To use the "child_count" string, you would call one of `getQuantityString(int, int)` (for retrieving a string with no substitution), `getQuantityString(int, int, Object...)` (for retrieving a string with substitution), or `getQuantityText(int, int)` (for retrieving a `CharSequence`). For example, you might call `getQuantityString(R.plurals.child_count, 7)` to get "7 children" back. Notice that it is `R.plurals` not `R.string` because of the XML node name.

Arrays

You can define arrays in XML, which is most often helpful for defining sets of data, such as for populating a `Spinner` or a `ListView`. When defining a string array, you use the `string-array` XML node with item child nodes. See Listing 4.17 for an example.

Listing 4.17   A Resources File Containing a String Array

```xml
<?xml version="1.0" encoding="utf-8"?>
<resources>
    <string-array name="sample_array">
        <item>First</item>
        <item>Second</item>
        <item>Third</item>
    </string-array>
</resources>
```

If you want to access the string array in code, you can use the `getStringArray(int)` method of `Resources`. The resource identifier in this case would be `R.array.sample_array`. Android also supports integer arrays (using the `integer-array` node) as well as `TypedArrays` (using the `array` node).

Colors

All of your colors should be specified in XML to ensure consistency and make design changes easy to propagate throughout the app. Colors are specified as alpha, red, green, and blue components in hex with two digits each. Although you can specify your colors as AARRGGBB, RRGGBB, ARGB, or RGB, it is best to be consistent, usually sticking with AARRGGBB. You can also use the `Color` class to use predefined colors and create colors from individual components. To use colors in code, you will typically use the `getColor(int)` method of `Resources`. Usually, you will specify your colors in `res/values/colors.xml`, but the name is a convention. Listing 4.18 shows an example of a simple resource file containing two colors: One refers to a system color and the other is specified in hex. When possible, it's a good idea to use names that are reflective of the intent of the colors. For example, calling a color "accent_color" rather than "bright_blue" means that you can continue to use that name even if the design changes from blue to green. Chapter 7, "Designing the Visuals," goes into detail about making color choices for your app.

Listing 4.18   A `colors.xml` File Containing Two Colors

```xml
<?xml version="1.0" encoding="utf-8"?>
<resources>
    <color name="system_color">@android:color/black</color>
    <color name="primary_color">#FFF43336</color>
</resources>
```

Dimensions

Dimensions are yet another value you can define in XML, and they are far more valuable than they would appear at first glance. For example, you could define three primary font sizes in a `dimens.xml` file that you store in `res/values`. When you test the app on a 10" tablet, you would likely find those font sizes a little small. Instead of having to redefine all the `TextViews`, you could easily just add a new configuration-specific `dimens.xml` file. You can also use these values when using custom views to work with precise dimensions without having to worry about calculating pixels based on density yourself.

You can access these dimensions in your code via the `Resources` class. If you want the exact dimension as a float, you use `getDimensions(int)`. In some cases, you only want the whole portion of the dimension as an integer, dropping off any fractional portion, and that's what `getDimensionPixelOffset(int)` is for. If you want the dimension as an int rounded up to ensure that you don't get any zero values due to fractions, you can use `getDimensionPixelSize(int)`. See Listing 4.19 for a sample `dimens.xml` file.

Listing 4.19 A Simple `dimens.xml` File

```
<?xml version="1.0" encoding="utf-8"?>
<resources>
    <dimen name="default_padding">16dp</dimen>
    <dimen name="text_size_headline">24sp</dimen>
    <dimen name="text_size_title">20sp</dimen>
    <dimen name="text_size_body">14sp</dimen>
    <dimen name="text_size_caption">12sp</dimen>
</resources>
```

Animations

Animations can be specified in XML as well as the resources that have been discussed so far; however, they are not covered here because they are covered in depth in Chapter 9, "Polishing with Animations."

IDs

You'll typically create your IDs in your layout files using the typical `android:id="@+id/name"` format, but you can also specify them like any other XML resource. The convention is to put these in an `ids.xml` file in `res/values`. This is a good practice when you need to programmatically assign an ID to a generated view or change an ID dynamically. It can also be used for the `View.setTag(int, Object)` and `View.getTag(int)` methods. An example of this is shown in Listing 4.20.

Listing 4.20   A Simple `ids.xml` File

```xml
<?xml version="1.0" encoding="utf-8"?>
<resources>
    <item name="tag_view_holder" type="id" />
    <item name="dynamic_view_id" type="id" />
</resources>
```

Menus

Android has supported XML menus since the beginning, but their use shifted in Android 3.0 when they went from being something triggered by a hardware menu key to something displayed in the app bar. Both activities and fragments can contribute to the app bar and you can dynamically change it as needed, including combining multiple menus defined in XML. Each `menu` root node will contain one or more `item` nodes. Each item becomes a `MenuItem` in Java when the menu is inflated and should have an id, icon, `showAsAction`, and title defined at a minimum. The `showAsAction` attribute controls whether the item appears on the app bar or in the overflow menu (the menu represented by three vertical dots on the app bar). If an item is commonly used such as share, you will set `showAsAction` to `ifRoom`, meaning that the item will be displayed as an action icon in the app bar (instead of listed in the overflow menu) if there is room for it. Uncommon actions should never go in the app bar (e.g., items for settings or about pages are unlikely to be pressed by the user most times the app is used, so they should be in the overflow menu). Listing 4.21 shows a simple menu, and menus are covered in more detail later in the book.

Listing 4.21   An Example Menu File

```xml
<?xml version="1.0" encoding="utf-8"?>
<menu xmlns:android="http://schemas.android.com/apk/res/android"
      xmlns:compat="http://schemas.android.com/apk/res-auto">
    <item
        android:id="@+id/menu_share"
        compat:actionProviderClass="android.support.v7.widget.
➡ ShareActionProvider"
        android:icon="@drawable/ic_action_share"
        compat:showAsAction="ifRoom"
        android:title="@string/share"
        android:orderInCategory="50"/>
    <item android:id="@+id/action_settings"
        android:title="@string/action_settings"
        android:orderInCategory="100"
        compat:showAsAction="never"/>
</menu>
```

Summary

The value of understanding Android's resource system cannot be overstated. You should never hard-code any user-facing strings, dimensions, or any other value that can be specified in resources. Even if you never expect to support a language other than your native language or a device other than what you have in your pocket, you should follow the best practices of properly using the resource system; your code will be cleaner for it. What's more, should you decide to support other device configurations, you'll be quite glad you did.

This marks the end of the first part of the book. You now have a strong foundational knowledge of Android's overall design, views, view groups, and the resource system. Next up, it's time to get started on a real-world app with brainstorms, wireframes, and flowcharts.

CHAPTER 5

STARTING A NEW APP

This chapter marks the start of the real process behind designing and developing an app. Here, you will take a user-driven approach, refining every step of the way with user feedback to ensure the ideal experience. This chapter is focused on the user experience (UX) and information hierarchy to provide a solid foundation for the app.

Design Methods

Design is a very loaded term. You can design an algorithm for efficient sorting. You can design a navigational scheme to ensure ease of use. You can design a movie poster to catch people's eyes and convey a sense of what the movie is about.

Before you worry about what your app looks like (graphic design), you need to worry about the deeper requirements. A dresser can have a stunning appearance, but it isn't particularly useful if the drawers can't hold the weight of clothes. That means you first need to figure out your app's requirements. What features should the app have? How is the app organized?

Common Methods

If you're an independent developer, you're probably used to self-design. You think about your own needs and structure the app around best meeting those needs. You might attempt to visualize the needs of other users, but you're often unaware of what the ideal experience is for others. If you're working in a more corporate environment, you may be designing based on features. Someone somewhere (a project manager, a client, a CEO, or even a funder) decided your app needs X feature. A feature specification (or "spec") is probably created, and then you implement the feature.

User-Centered Design

A better method of designing an app is called "User-Centered Design" or UCD (sometimes this is called "Human-Centered Design" to emphasize that some non-users influence the design). The basic idea is that by incorporating users throughout the planning, designing, developing, and even deployment phases, you can provide a better experience. Instead of going through all the phases of the app and finding out that no one likes it *after* releasing; you continually utilize users throughout each phase, focusing on user-centered evaluation.

Key Principles

UCD has six key principles:

1. The design is based on an explicit understanding of users, tasks, and environments.
2. Users are involved throughout design and development.
3. The design is driven and refined by user-centered evaluation.
4. The process is iterative.
5. The design addresses the whole UX.
6. The design team includes multidisciplinary skills and perspectives.

Explicit Understanding

This first principle is core to UCD. Obviously if the design philosophy is called *User*-Centered Design, there will be focus on users; however, it's also important to consider the environment that the users are in. If your app is built for use on a construction site, using an audible chime for important notifications is probably going to be ineffective for workers who have hearing protection. If your app provides real-time transit information, downloading giant images each refresh is going to cause problems because most users won't be on WiFi and may even have a poor cell connection.

This explicit understanding comes from real users. It isn't from reading a study about the "average smartphone user." It isn't from looking at statistics. It is from actually going out to real users, talking to them, and experiencing their characteristics, their tasks, and their environment.

Continuous User Involvement

Quite a bit of software development is done with user involvement at very specific and limited points. Most commonly, the involvement is at or near deployment when changes are most costly. You can spend months or years making this amazing app that checks all the right boxes on the feature list, features excellent design, and is well developed. When it's nearly done you reveal it to users. The reception is so bad that you have to do intensive studies to figure out what is wrong, add features that weren't even thought of, redo the UI, and refactor most of the code. Ouch!

Some software teams try to avoid bad outcomes by involving users early on, helping to answer questions about navigation, feature exposure, and more. They take that initial feedback, make whatever changes are needed, and then develop the app. That process is a lot better than not getting user feedback until after the app is basically ready, but a lot can happen between that initial feedback and the release date. UCD requires continuous user involvement throughout every phase of the product lifecycle. Yes, you should be evaluating your wireframes with users and later evaluating your graphic design with them as well, but you should also have users involved with your error handling (when something is wrong, do they understand how to fix it?) and even your algorithms (is this code that sorts photos based on meta data fast enough?).

User-Centered Evaluation

Every aspect of the app is driven by user-centered evaluation. It doesn't matter if you have 30 years of experience in your field and you're totally confident that your choice is right, it is only right if it works for users. It's also important to isolate what you're testing as much as possible. If you're evaluating the organization of the app, presenting fully completed comps and telling the user to "just ignore the colors" isn't going to work. Every aspect of the experience influences the user's perception of it, so you have to be very conscious of what you are actually evaluating.

Iterate

Fortunately, most mobile app development teams work with an iterative process instead of a traditional waterfall approach. Involve users! You shouldn't just be iterating based on what you finished last week or last sprint, you should be iterating based on user feedback. If you implemented enough of a feature that you could test it out with users, do so. You might find out that it's going in completely the wrong direction, so why write more code to finish the feature as is or spend more time polishing it in Photoshop? Don't think of your designs or code as right or wrong, think of them as hypotheses that you test with users.

Whole User Experience

There are a lot of factors to consider when it comes to users and how they interact with your app. What emotional, cultural, or perceptual issues impact the way users understand or use your app? Is the iconography actually appropriate for all users? Is the hierarchy logical to someone who has a completely different background?

Multidisciplinary Team

It may be tempting to designate one person as the "user advocate" who does all the user interaction and reports the results back, but it is important that you have members across your team interacting with users. The way a project manager perceives user feedback will be different from that of a graphic designer, an API developer, a mobile developer, or a marketer. Discussing those interpretations can lead to a lot of insights. In addition, the more your team interacts with users, the more they will think about users and start considering what the ideal experience is for users. Further, this teamwork encourages transparency in decisions. When a graphic designer understand why a project manager considers a feature important, it's much easier to design it in a way that matches what is actually needed. When a developer understands why a graphic designer created the mockups in a particular way, it's much easier for them to work together if the design isn't feasible.

But, But, But . . .

But it's more work to talk to users. But I don't even know any users. But my boss wants to define the feature set. There are plenty of excuses to use for avoiding UCD, and some are even legitimate, but your app will suffer in one way or another if you don't design it with users. Yes, it is more upfront work, but you create a more precisely honed app without having to redo massive parts as soon as it goes live. Sure, you might not know a lot of users or any users, but working with even just a few can help you catch the majority of UX pitfalls and will ultimately leave you feeling more satisfied. It's unfortunately quite common to have a particular person who wants to dictate the feature set and there are a few ways of dealing with this. You can curl up in a ball, hope the person is a real visionary, and likely end up with a mediocre product. If the person is focused on the business goals (more on goals shortly), you can have that person list out as many business goals as possible and see which ones can be achieved without meeting the needs of actual users. Another option is to try to understand what type of user this person is and actually factor in the feedback. There is more detail about personas later in the chapter, but the general idea is that if you can figure out the type of user this person is, you can better use his or her feedback and/or get that person to realize that his or her needs are different from the needs of other user types.

Defining Goals

What are the goals of the users of the app and what are the goals of the app from a product perspective? A surprising number of apps are designed without strongly defined goals on either side. Typically, this process starts out okay but becomes challenging as specific design decisions are being made. What buttons should be included on a given screen if you do not know the actual goal of the app? Once you have defined the goals, you can much more easily ensure that each decision along the way, especially UX decisions, will cater to those goals. It does not matter how beautifully you have designed and developed an app if it has a lack of focus, leading to user frustration.

User Goals

Starting out with user goals is a great way to get in the mindset of a user and decide what is really important in the app. The challenge is making sure you are defining goals and not tasks. For example, a task for a new Twitter app might be to be able to "read tweets in my time-line," whereas a goal might be to be able to "read all the tweets that I find important." These two sounds similar, but the first makes assumptions that the second does not. Consider the following:

- Does the user's timeline contain all the tweets the user cares about?
- Does the user's timeline consist only of tweets the user cares about?
- Is a chronological order the best for tweets?

By making these goals broad, you keep them separate from the means by which the user accomplishes them. It might just be that a simple, chronological timeline is the best way to read through tweets, but there is a chance that it's not. What if you were to categorize tweets by content or the type of user who is posting them? What if you included tweets from people who might be interesting to the user but aren't being followed? What if the user can give feedback about which tweets are valuable and that can be used to push those types of tweets to the top of the list?

Sometimes it can seem a bit challenging to create meaningful user goals. Maybe you're creating an image manipulation app and all you can come up with is "I want to be able to easily manipulate photos." That is not a very helpful goal, so you can break it down further. First, think of basic navigation requirements: How will users get to the photos? Next, why are they manipulating the photos? Finally, after they've manipulated the photos, what can they do with them? With a bit of brainstorming, your list might look more like this:

- I want to browse all images on my device.
- I want to improve the visual quality of my photos.
- I want to make people in my photos look better.
- I want to share the modified photos.

You can certainly come up with a more exhaustive list than this, but this is a good start. Notice that the photo manipulation goals do not define specific ways they are accomplished. Later, you can define features that allow the user to accomplish these goals. You might decide that the app needs to support easy fixing of blemishes such as pimples and also needs to correct red-eye; both of those features are ways to accomplish the third goal: "I want to make people in my photos look better."

User Personas

An extremely helpful tool in analyzing what your goals mean to your app is the creation of user personas. Personas are represented as individual users, but they are reflective of a group of users with specific behavior and motivations. After learning more about the (potential) users of your app, you will be able to start finding ways of grouping them. If you were creating a photo manipulation app, you might find start to find that there are people who spend thousands of dollars on equipment and are exceedingly picky about the quality of their photos and how the photos are organized. With that knowledge, you might define Susan, an excellent photographer with an eye for perfection. When she is not using her $8,000 digital SLR for photography, she's trying to squeeze every bit of photo quality out of her top-of-the-line phone. She likes to share a few of her photos to Google, but she is very picky about what she shares because her clients might see them. She also mentally organizes her photos by events, such as all the photos from a birthday party or all the photos from a wedding.

Another segment of your users might be more casual. They love cameras on smartphones not because of the quality of photos but because of the immediacy and the ability to share quickly. Now you define Jim, a guy who couldn't care less what SLR stands for and just wants to share good photos with his friends. His phone is fairly average and does not take great photos, but he loves being able to immediately share whatever he is doing with all his social networks. You could explain to him that red-eye happens in photos when the flash is too close to the photo sensor, but he doesn't care. Obviously eyes shouldn't be red, so the device should be able to fix that automatically.

There are more personas that could (and should) be made, such as a younger user who wants to modify pictures in funny ways to get some laughs with friends, but even with just these two users you can easily see the contrasting needs. Consider the previously defined photo manipulation app and how these two users would use the app to accomplish their goals. Susan wants the photos organized by events, whereas Jim wants the newest photos to be first in the list because they are most likely what he wants to share. Susan cares about manually tweaking the white balance, contrast of shadows, and other features that Jim could not care less about; he just wants to easily make the photo look nice. Their requirements around making people in photos look good are similarly different. Susan wants to select a precise skin tone, whereas Jim just wants to be able to tap on that one horrible Friday night pimple and have it disappear. Finally, they both use sharing but in different ways.

Product Goals

Sadly, the reality of app design and development has to hit you at some point and you realize it can't just be all about the users. We would all love for all apps to be free and work on every device, but creating great apps costs money, and supporting all devices takes time. Product goals are the goals that cover monetization, branding, and other considerations that stakehold-ers in the app have. A list of product goals might look like this:

- Reflect company XYZ's branding.
- Release beta version to board members in six weeks.
- Release 1.0 to Google Play in eight weeks.
- Reach 50,000 app downloads within three months of launch.
- Earn $5000 gross within three months of launch.

Notice that these goals are not direct considerations of the users, but they do affect the users. The intent to monetize means the app may cost money, it might have ads, it could have in-app pur-chases, or some other means of making money such as premium account support. The length of time allowed for development controls which features can be included and how refined they can be. These are requirements, but to the best of your ability you should not let them define the app.

Device and Configuration Support

Those who are inexperienced with Android find the question of device support intimidating, often relying on a "wait and see" approach that means the app works well on a typical phone and poorly on everything else. Even if your intent is only to focus on phones early on, it is worth spending some time figuring out how your app would support other devices and other configurations such as landscape. In most cases, a little bit of thinking upfront can make sup-port for a variety of devices and configurations relatively easy, especially because best practices in Android development solve many of the challenges. In short, unless you have an extremely good reason, both the design and development processes should consider the wide variety of Android devices out there.

The other part of device support is determining the minimum version of Android you will support. Ideally, this decision is driven by your target users. If you're building an app for just developers, you might be able to get away with support for Android 4.4 and above. If you're building a chat app for developing nations, targeting only Android 4.4 and above is going to kill any chance you have of success. In most cases, even design that comes from newer versions of Android such as Lollipop can be applied to older versions of Android through the use of the support library, third-party libraries, and even custom solutions. Most apps developed now support version 4.0 (Ice Cream Sandwich) and above or 4.1 (Jelly Bean) and above. If you're not sure what version your users have, then consider targeting one of these versions.

> ## tip
>
> The Android landscape is always changing and it's important to keep up with the trends to understand what devices and device types are most common to make decisions about what you should support. The Android developer dashboard

(http://developer.android.com/about/dashboards/index.html) gives you what percentage of devices run a particular version of Android or have a specific density, which can help make the decision, but remember that your target users may be very different from the general trends.

When it comes to configurations, Android does not have a distinct concept of a "tablet app." Instead, apps can run on any device, unless you specifically set them not to. It is up to you to decide whether you want to provide an experience optimized for a tablet, television, or any other device. It is fine to release an app that does not have a tablet-specific experience in version 1, but users appreciate knowing that upfront, so be sure to let them know in your app description.

note

EXTERNAL LIBRARIES   Although Android is frequently criticized for "fragmentation," the majority of features you will want to use are available in external libraries. For instance, fragments were not available until Android 3.0 (Honeycomb), but they are available through the support library (http://developer.android.com/tools/extras/support-library.html) provided by Google. That library requires version 1.6 of Android and above—that's the version that the original Android phone, the G1 on T-Mobile, can currently run. Even the style used for checkboxes and radio buttons from Android 5.0 and on can be applied with the AppCompat library on versions as old as Android 2.2.

High-Level Flow

The first graphical step to designing a new app is working on the high-level flow and grouping of actions based around meeting the previously established user goals. This is where you decide on the overall structure of the app. Which screen is the main screen? What are the secondary screens? How do you navigate between them? What actions can you take on a given screen?

The high-level flow is very directly tied to the goals you have established for your users. If your primary user goal is "read all the tweets that I find important," then the main screen should facilitate accomplishing that goal. One consideration to keep in mind is that you do not want to overwhelm the user with too many options on any given screen. It's ideal to have a primary action for a screen with a few optional secondary actions.

The main way that people choose to work on high-level flow is with flowcharts. Typically, you represent screens with shapes that have lines or arrows connecting to other screens. This lets you quickly see how easy or difficult it is to navigate through the app. In some cases, people like to create very crude drawings of screens to more easily understand what goes in them. Do whichever works best for you. Plenty of software options are available, such as full desktop solutions like Visio (http://visio.microsoft.com/en-us/pages/default.aspx) for Windows and Omni-Graffle (https://www.omnigroup.com/omnigraffle/) for Mac. There are also open source solutions that work on Linux as well such as yEd (http://www.yworks.com/en/products/yfiles/yed/). If you're looking for a web-based option, Google Drawings (http://www.google.com/drive/start/apps.html#drawings), LucidChart (https://www.lucidchart.com/), and Gliffy (https://www.gliffy.com/uses/flowchart-software/) are worth taking a look at. Whether you're creating the flowchart digitally, on a whiteboard, or on paper, this early planning is exceedingly valuable.

Let's say you are working on an app for new woodworkers. During your initial user research, you found that new woodworkers have a difficult time determining what tools to buy, so your app is going to focus on helping them decide. You brainstorm various ways to organize this and decide on a basic hierarchy with some filters. After some work, you come up with a hand-drawn flowchart that shows the basic app organization (Figure 5.1). You've decided that the hierarchy should be based on power tools with anything else falling under an accessories section. The users will drill into either handheld or stationary for a given category, and then brand, and then a specific tool.

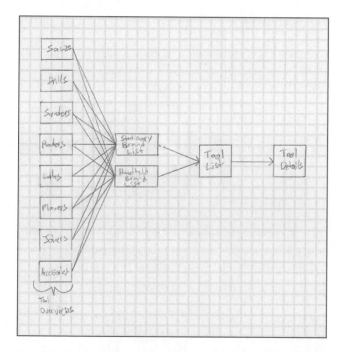

Figure 5.1 A hand-drawn flowchart for the woodworker tools app

This seems very reasonable, so you walk some users through the flowchart and you learn there is a big problem with your flow. Experienced woodworkers can have very strong opinions about brands, but a lot of new woodworkers have no idea which brands are good. Their choice ends up being arbitrary, making this step unnecessary. You also find that some users are specifically looking for battery-powered tools, and this flow doesn't offer any easy way to do that. One more issue they ran into was looking for clamps. It seems that clamps are vital to woodworking and, although you reasonably consider them an accessory, they're sought after enough to make them worth promoting to the top level. In addition, some of the other tools such as planers and joiners weren't looked at by any of the novice woodworkers.

Wow, that's a lot of feedback saying that the flowchart is wrong. Does that mean you screwed up? No! Your flowchart was a first stab at organizing the app and it generated all this valuable feedback! Not bad for some crude pencil work and a little time with some users. This is where the iteration comes in. Now that you have this great feedback, you can create an updated flowchart that addresses the concerns found in the first one and test it with users. Repeat this process as much as you need to get a solid flowchart. Once it is ready, you should create a digital version (if you haven't already) and detail it with all the other states you are going to need to worry about. These states are things like loading and failure. By getting these in your flowcharts, you'll have a much better idea of how much effort will be required for the app and you can ensure that people are thinking about them from the beginning. Figure 5.2 shows an example of an updated flowchart.

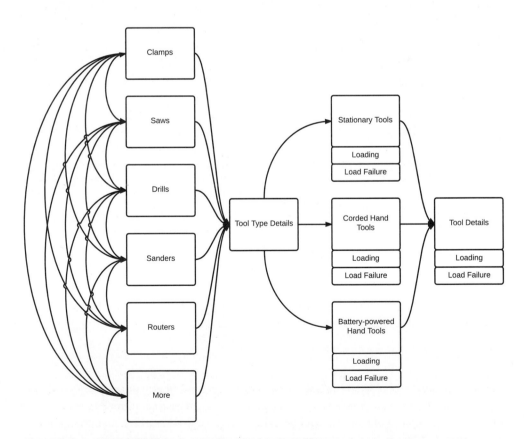

Figure 5.2 A refined digital flowchart for the woodworker tools app

Wireframes

Wireframes represent the skeleton of your app. They attempt to explain the layout without any visual treatment to focus on functionality and usability. Wireframes ensure that data is grouped logically, touch targets are reasonably placed, the information hierarchy makes sense, and the data to be displayed on a given screen makes sense.

There are many different tools for wireframing. Starting out with a simple sheet of paper and a writing utensil is a great way to quickly try out a few different ideas. You can use a pen to force yourself to keep moving and trying new things without tweaking what's there or a pencil for a more detailed draft. You don't need to be an artist to create good wireframes. Look at the difference between the three wireframes in Figure 5.3; they all illustrate the same screen but with different levels of fidelity. They all let you quickly see if something seems to work or not.

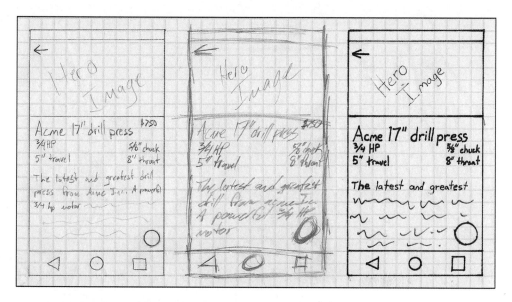

Figure 5.3 Regardless of whether your style is pretty average, excessively sketchy, or precise and bold, wireframing is an excellent way to try out different layouts with minimal effort

There are a few techniques you can apply to make your wireframes look better. First, stencils are a great way to make sure you are consistent, so consider picking up some such as the Android UI Stencil Kit (http://www.uistencils.com/products/android-stencil-kit). Next, break your sketching into small pieces. Many shapes are just a bunch of straight lines, so it's worth spending some time practicing drawing straight lines. Sure, it's not the most exciting thing to do, but it makes a major difference in how sharp your wireframes look. When you're first getting better at drawing lines, put a dot at your starting point and at your finishing point. Concentrate on moving your arm (not your wrist!). Watch where you want the line to go rather than where you're currently drawing. It won't take long before you can draw straight lines without giving it any thought.

One more thing that comes in handy is knowing how to draw a circle or arc. Just like with drawing a line, you don't want to rely on your wrist. Instead, find a pivot point and move the paper. For large circles and arcs, the tiny bone opposite of your thumb near your wrist provides the pivot point. Put it down on the paper and then hold the pen or pencil like you normally would. If you need a full circle, rotate the paper while keeping your drawing hand stationary. If you just need an arc, you can move your elbow while keeping your wrist straight. Need a medium-sized circle or arc? You can use one of the knuckles of your pinky finger as the pivot point (usually the middle knuckle works best, but it depends how you hold the pen or pencil). If you need a small circle or arc, you can hold the pen or pencil between your index and middle fingers and put your middle finger against the paper as the pivot point (see Figure 5.4). If nothing else, you can always try to find something that's round and the approximate size you need (such as a pen cap) to trace around.

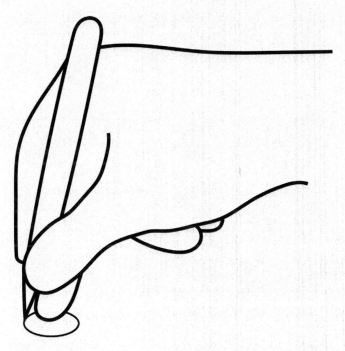

Figure 5.4 By using your middle finger as a pivot point and rotating the paper, you can create small but precise circles

When you're ready to work with software to create more polished wireframes, a lot of different tools are available to you. Many designers are already familiar with vector-based programs such as Adobe Illustrator (http://www.adobe.com/products/illustrator.html) and Inkscape (https://inkscape.org) and prefer to stick with those. Some tools that are good for flowcharts are also good for wireframes such as the previously mentioned Omnigraffle. Another popular tool that's available on Macs is Sketch (http://bohemiancoding.com/sketch/), which has features that extend beyond just wireframes. If you're looking for a tool that's available as a desktop app and a web app, give Balsamiq a try (https://balsamiq.com/); it uses a "sketch-like" style to keep the focus on what you really want to test with wireframes. Wireframe Sketcher (http://wireframes-ketcher.com/) is another cross-platform tool you might consider. Really, there are a lot of tools out there and there isn't a single tool that works best for everyone. Give a few different tools a try and do a quick Google search for more if none of these work for you.

It is important to remember that the purpose of wireframing is not graphical design. Your wireframes should generally not use custom colors unless they are for defining content groups, showing interaction (e.g., a touch or swipe), or showing alignment. In fact, many wireframing tools use sketch-like graphics to help keep the focus on the content and its positioning, rather than its appearance. It is fine to use native components (such as Material Design buttons), but avoid adding in your own custom controls with any more detail than necessary. You can show a custom chart, but you should not add gradients or other visual treatments. Ultimately, the purpose is to put the emphasis on the content positioning and its hierarchy and not on the visual design. This is your opportunity to determine positioning and sizing of elements on the screen relative to the other elements.

Starting with Navigation

The beginning of any project can be intimidating, as you stare at a blank paper waiting for inspiration. Some people are able to just dive right in; others need to be more methodical. If you fall into the latter group, sometimes it helps to start with the pieces. After having created a flowchart, determining navigation should be relatively easy.

The simplest form of navigation uses fixed tabs (see Figure 5.5 for an example). It ensures that the major sections of your app are visible, it creates a clear hierarchy, and interaction is obvious. The downsides are that tabs work best when you have only a few major sections, and they also

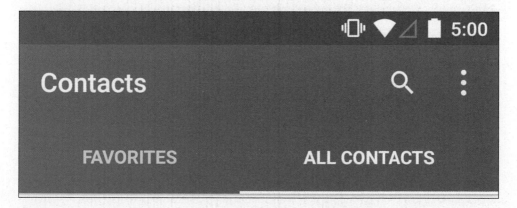

Figure 5.5 Even with just two sections, tabs are a great form of navigation when those sections are equally important

take up some screen space. The content represented by tabs should be swipeable, so that you can change tabs by swiping almost anywhere on the screen. Tabs should also only appear at the top of the section they're appropriate for. For instance, if you were building an app for podcasts, you might have a tab for discovering new podcasts, a tab for podcasts in your library that you haven't listened to, and a tab for podcasts that you have listened to. If the user is on the tab for discovering new podcasts and taps on a suggestion to go to the detail page for a podcast, the tabs should not appear on that detail page. In general, if your app has two to four sections, you should strongly consider tabs.

A variation on tabs is scrollable tabs (see Figure 5.6 for an example). This is where you have tabs at the top again, but they are in a horizontally scrollable view, allowing you to fit more than you can when they're fixed. This allows you to use tabs for apps that might have five or six sections while still giving you the benefit of being obvious to users. Users might not realize the view can scroll, so selecting a tab should move it to the center of the view if it isn't at the edge. This allows you to show the other tabs that are available and teaches users that these tabs aren't static.

Figure 5.6 Notice that as the selected tab changes, it scrolls the view. This scrolling and the cut off tabs on the edges both tell the user that more content is available than what is shown on the screen

An increasingly common form of navigation is the navigation drawer or nav drawer (see Figure 5.7 for an example). It shows a hamburger icon (the icon with three horizontal lines) that can be tapped to slide the drawer in from the left. A user can also swipe from the left edge of the screen to display the drawer. The advantage of the navigation drawer is that it allows you to have a large number of top sections without using screen space when the drawer is hidden. It does have the major problem of discoverability because it is effectively invisible and it can cause confusion with navigation with the back button. Tapping a section swaps out the content on the screen rather than drilling in, which means the back button should not go back to that section (you aren't adding to the backstack); however, the transitions often occur as the drawer is sliding back out of the way, preventing users from seeing the visual cues that transitions provide.

Another navigation scheme is to have a central page that provides links out to other sections, if needed. This works well when you have some core information that the user wants to see and either no secondary actions or just a few uncommon ones. For instance, an app that is primarily designed to just show elevations on a map should jump directly to that map view. A search feature can be in the app bar, but you don't really need any tabs or other navigation.

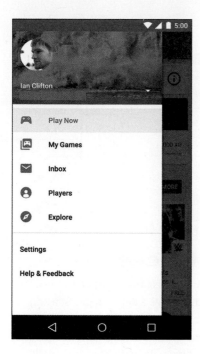

Figure 5.7 The navigation drawer is an increasingly common form of navigation

It is often very helpful to see how other apps handle problems similar to yours. It's very valuable to see how the native apps that were designed by Google work because they tend to best reflect the current state of Android design and UX. You should also look at popular third-party apps to see how they handle some of the challenges your app faces. You can learn both what apps do well and what they do poorly by spending some time exploring them.

Considering the woodworking tools app, what navigational strategy would you use? There are probably seven sections: clamps, saws, drills, sanders, routers, lathes, and more. You might be able to put lathes into the more section, but you're really at the limit of how many items you want as scrollable tabs. Perhaps a navigation drawer is a good start? Looking at your updated flowchart, you can also see that choosing a tool type pushes the user toward another decision: stationary, handheld with a power cord, or handheld with a battery. You might want to go to a page about the tool type, explaining the general purpose of the tool with three buttons to dig into one of those categories. You might instead want to go straight to one of those categories, so that you can immediately show content. Another option is to combine those two and go to a page about the tool type with four tabs: About, stationary, handheld, and battery (see Figure 5.8 for an example flowchart with this organization). This is the situation where wireframing is particularly helpful. It would take a lot of work to build out all three of these possibilities, and you'd end up throwing away two-thirds of that. Instead, you can relatively quickly test out what these options look like and try them with users.

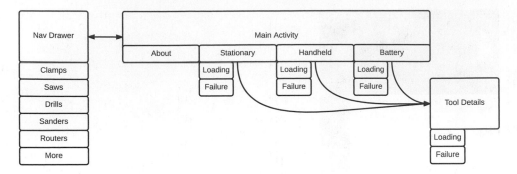

Figure 5.8 The revised flowchart for the woodworking tools app

Continuing with Content Pieces

Now that you have thought about and wireframed navigation, it is time to get on to the content. Each of the tools needs to appear in a list and it needs to have a details page. Starting with the presentation in the list can sometimes be easier because you have to focus on what is most important and eliminate everything else. Once you have a decent list presentation, you can build the detail page from there, ensuring that common elements are consistently presented.

When creating a list of content, you need to think about what is most important and what is different between items. Weight might be very important for some tools, but it isn't as important to put in the list view if all tools in that list weigh roughly the same. That means a little bit of research can be helpful. Similarly, knowing real examples can make a big difference in how you organize the info, how big or small you make fonts, and so on. For instance, if you're making a list of news stories, you want to know what the normal length of headlines is so that you don't end up with ellipses in every item after two words.

There are a lot of techniques for learning what is most important. The simplest is to just ask real users. This will generally get you pretty close, but there are often important things users don't think about or don't realize are important, so a helpful technique is to actually watch users and ask questions. For example, you could watch users navigating a woodworking tool site and after seeing them drill in and back out of tools a few times, ask what they're looking for or what is causing them to back out. Also consider what a photo can get you. It's a nice visual, but it can often convey information more effectively than words and a photo is especially helpful for users who might be unfamiliar with what they're looking for.

After working with some real users yet again (hopefully you're seeing the value of users by now), you might discover that the name, price, power, and photo of tools is most important. Alignment is imperative when starting to lay out content, so it's a good idea to start with the most vital element (say, the photo in this case), and lay the other elements around it with consideration about how they align in a list. Photos in a list will generally be in one of three places: the left (start), the right (end), or the background. If you have photos for only some of the items, you generally don't want to put them at the left edge because you will end up with a zigzag effect (see Figure 5.9) unless you include generic thumbnails that don't add user value. Photos in the background are best when the content area is large, ensuring the text that over-lays them does not completely obscure them. These list items are likely to be pretty small, so either the right side or the left side will be best. Given that this list will be hand-curated, photos should be available for all items, so the left side seems good.

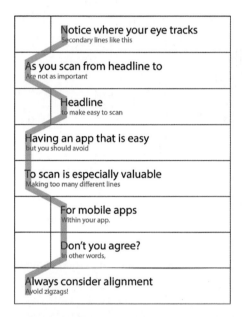

Figure 5.9 The pink highlight indicates the path of your eye when looking from item heading to item heading; the empty squares represent photos

The name is the next most important element. Given the variation in length, making sure it has as much room as possible is a good idea, so the top left seems like a good choice. Price is a very comparable element, so putting it on the right side to make it easy to scan might work. Finally, the power can go directly below the name. Figure 5.10 demonstrates what this could look like.

Wireframing a Detail Page

The detail page should have some, if not all, of the same elements that the list items have. Here, you have more room for a large photo, so the photo is once again a good starting point. Putting it at the top allows you to give the detail page a large, hero image that can help the transition from list to detail. The other content that was on the list item should go near the top of the

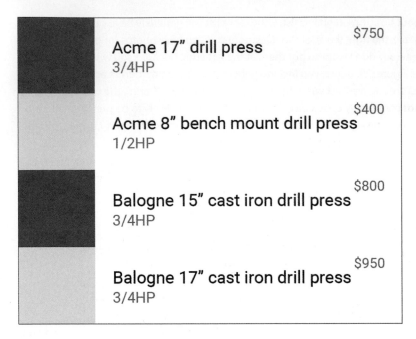

Figure 5.10 Possible layout of list items; it's important to look at multiple stacked versions to see potential issues with alignment

page. It could ultimately go just below the photo or even over the bottom of the photo. Next, figure out what other features are worth including that might not have been important enough for the list (maybe the weight is appropriate here?). These glanceable features go up near the top so that they can quickly be taken in and the user can back out if the tool doesn't match his or her needs. You'll probably include a description of the tool as well. You'll also want a button for buying the tool.

When you need to test out text alignment and you don't actually have real text content available, you can use what's called "lorem ipsum" text. It's essentially filler text meant to allow you to focus on typography, alignment, and other aspects of the page without worrying about the text content itself. The text is inspired by Latin, but altered to be improper and nonsensical. A quick web search for "lorem ipsum generator" will lead you to plenty of pages that can supply text for you to copy and paste. There are also variations such as "bacon ipsum," "hipster ipsum," and others that you can find by searching for "lorem ipsum alternative."

The app bar often contains secondary actions on detail pages, but there isn't any immediate need for any in this app. That means the bar can just contain the up navigation and might not even need a title. See Figure 5.11 for what the detail page wireframe looks like.

Figure 5.11 One possible layout for the tool detail page; notice that the lack of color helps you focus on size and alignment

> **note**
>
> **THE UP INDICATOR** Many people are initially confused by the up indicator in Android. It shows as a left-facing arrow now (it used to be a chevron) on the left of your app bar. In many cases, it has the same behavior as the back button, but there is a subtle—though important—difference. The back button should go back to the screen you were just viewing, but the up indicator should go up a level in the hierarchy.
>
> To make this clearer, imagine that the woodworking app has a "related tools" section on the detail page (page A) and tapping a tool there jumps to its detail page (page B). You could continue to tap on other related tools (page C, D, etc.) and see their info. The back button would take you to the detail page that lead you to the one you're currently on (going from page D to C to B to A); the up navigation would send you back to the list of tools (skipping pages C, B, and A).

Supporting Multiple Devices

Early on in design considerations is the best time to start thinking about supporting different devices. A common mistake that designers make is to design with entirely one device in mind. It is a lot easier to balance the content on a screen when you design that content for one screen size only, but that is a bad practice to fall into. Besides, users can change font sizes, and that means views are going to be pushed around as needed.

Sometimes it can be helpful to do wireframing without any device borders to contain it. What does that UI look like in its natural form? How wide should a text view be before you make the content wrap to the second line? Is the button connected to the bottom right of the content or the bottom right of the screen?

Playing around with the content positioning early on can make it clear how you can better support not only different devices but also landscape and portrait orientations specifically. Although many apps do not support landscape orientation on phones, there is little reason not to. The amount of work involved is not significant if you are already following best practices and planning to support a variety of device sizes.

Tablets generally fit two fragments side-by-side in what is referred to as the "master/detail" flow (where "master" refers to your list of content and "detail" refers to the detailed information about the item selected from that list). Of course, there's nothing preventing you from doing something totally different. Many of the best tablet apps have completely custom tablet layouts that take much better use of the available space than simply moving fragments around can give you. Others are able to provide a very simple interface where the user doesn't have to change screens because it can all fit on the tablet screen. See Figure 5.12 for an example of what the woodworking tools app might look like on a tablet with minimal work by reusing what will already be built for the phone version.

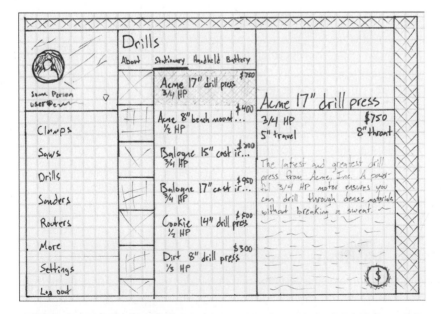

Figure 5.12 A simple wireframe illustrating a tablet layout where the navigation, tool list, and tool details are all visible; it would also be worth trying with the navigation hidden as a drawer to see if the extra breathing room for the other content helps with usability

Naming Conventions

Following clear naming conventions will undoubtedly keep your resources easier to organize and track. Chances are, many of your assets will go through revisions, so you should consider that when naming. For instance, a name such as `background_red.png` is unclear. Where will it be used? What happens when the design changes and the background has to be blue? Instead, name assets based on function. Your `background_red.png` might be used on just one page and be named appropriately (e.g., if it is only used on the settings screen, it might be called `background_settings.png`); if it's used for a group of pages, it should reflect that group (e.g., an image used for all secondary pages might be called `background_secondary.png`).

Android also has conventions for specific assets (see http://developer.android.com/design/style/iconography.html#DesignTips). Icons, for instance, start with "`ic_`" and then the icon type. For example, `ic_dialog_warning.png` would be the icon used in a warning dialog. Typically, filenames have a suffix that indicates the state. For example, `button_primary_pressed.9.png` would be the primary button in its pressed state; chances are you'd also have a `button_primary_focused.9.png` and others. Usually, the `StateDrawable` (see Chapter 4 "Adding App Graphics and Resources") is named either with no state (e.g., `button_primary.xml`) or with a suffix to indicate that it's stateful (e.g., `button_primary_stateful.xml` or `button_primary_touchable.xml`). This book will use the former, but remember that these are all just conventions, not requirements. Use what makes sense to you; just be consistent. See Table 5.1 for more examples.

Table 5.1 Asset Naming Conventions

Asset Type	Prefix	Examples
Buttons	`button`	`button_primary.9.png` `button_subdued.9.png`
Dialog icons	`ic_dialog`	`ic_dialog_confirm.png` `ic_dialog_warning.png`
Dividers	`divider`	`divider_light.9.png` `divider_list.9.png`
Launcher icons	`ic_launcher`	`ic_launcher_main.png` `ic_launcher_map.png`
Map icons	`ic_map`	`ic_map_destination.png` `ic_map_pin.png`
Status bar/notification icons	`ic_stat_notify`	`ic_stat_notify_error.pn` `ic_stat_notify_playing.png`
Tab icons	`ic_tab`	`ic_tab_list.png` `ic_tab_map.png`
Traditional menu icons	`ic_menu`	`ic_menu_help.png` `ic_menu_settings.png`

Crude Resources

Android is very adaptable to changes in assets, which means you can quickly throw a 50×50 image into a list view, find out it feels too small, and try a 100×100 image. At this stage, resources are expected to be incomplete, but do not underestimate the value of creating some simple resources to start getting a feel for the grouping of content. Eventually, you'll have a nicely designed default thumbnail for images, but for now you can throw a box in there to help visualize how that space will be taken up.

If you follow naming conventions, such as those in Table 5.1, it will be much easier to swap out assets and see how something different looks. In most cases, it's enough to start by supplying just high-resolution assets such as all XXHDPI or XXXHDPI assets. Later in the process, when the assets are closer to finalized, you can create files for each of the other densities.

Summary

You cannot overestimate the value of planning when it comes to app development. In this chapter you learned the importance of working with real users, and how to define both goals for the users and goals for the business/product. You learned about creating high-level flow-charts based on the goals and then jumped head-first into wireframes. If you have not done any wireframing before reading this chapter, you might still be feeling a little overwhelmed or confused about which program you should use for your wireframes. Give a few of them a try. You can recreate some of the wireframes shown in this chapter or build your own to get a feel for which program works best for you—and don't be afraid to break out your pen or pencil.

After reading this chapter, you should find navigation to be much clearer. It is particularly important that you understand the difference between the back button and "up" navigation, as discussed in this chapter. If you're still unsure, see how the native Android apps handle this. In the next chapter, you will see how to develop prototype apps using the wireframes from this chapter, and you will learn to implement navigation so that you can see which really will work best for this woodworking tools app.

CHAPTER 6

PROTOTYPING AND DEVELOPING THE APP FOUNDATION

After having done the initial design work in the previous chapter, it is now time to start developing. This is often one of the most exciting parts of developing an app; you can go from no code to a working prototype very quickly. This chapter focuses on the process of implementing wireframes and testing the prototype with real users. The key here is that you are not creating final code, but testing the theory of the initial design and adapting as you find what works and what doesn't.

Organizing into Activities and Fragments

The first part of developing an app is breaking the design down into manageable chunks. What are the activities and fragments? In an ideal world, you have been presented with (or created yourself) wireframes and flowcharts for phones and tablets, allowing you to easily see what part of the UI is reused and how. In the real world, you might be starting on the app before even the phone wireframes are done.

To maintain flexibility, you can break every screen into a fragment first and then create each activity that is needed to hold them together. If you have a flowchart to look at, usually each block can be a fragment. Looking at Figure 6.1, which was one of the flowcharts from the previous chapter, you can see that you essentially have two parts: the overall tool section with tabs and the tool details. You can create a single activity that manages all of the screens, but it's probably easier to split the app into two activities. One activity handles the navigation drawer and tabs; the other activity handles the tool details.

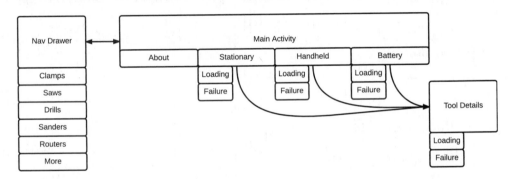

Figure 6.1 The wireframe of the tool app

The navigation drawer can be done as a fragment or as a layout that the activity manages, depending on your preference. The About tab is probably a fragment that has parameters to say what tool type to display info for. Each of the other tabs is a fragment, but you don't necessarily have to create a unique `Fragment` class for each. It's quite likely that the Stationary, Handheld, and Battery tabs are very similar, so you might have a fragment that displays a tool list based on parameters. Finally, you have the tool details fragment. Where appropriate, you can choose to just implement an activity without a fragment to save time for the prototype.

Keep in mind, your goal at this point is not necessarily the exact architecture of the final app. Instead, you want something that can reasonably represent the flowchart and wireframes, so that you can test what works and what doesn't work with this initial organization. In most cases, you're going to find issues with the design that require changes. Sometimes the issues are minor and easily accommodated; other times they're major and require significant reworking of your app.

Creating the First Prototype

When creating the initial project, you don't need to worry about getting everything perfect. You can easily change the name of your app later. In fact, the Android tools now are significantly better than they were in years past, so even changing the package (which is used as the app ID) is very easy.

One consideration that comes up early on is the minimum SDK level. For a prototype, just target the newest version of Android and set the `minSdkVersion` to whatever you need just for your test device(s). When you're dealing with a prototype, you want to rapidly test out the organization of the content, not the implementation. If you end up finding out that the prototype has some core issues and needs to be redesigned, any time that you had spent on compatibility is wasted. In general, virtually everything you would do in a prototype with the latest version of Android can be done on older versions, perhaps with libraries or a bit of custom work, so worrying about compatibility before you even know if your design needs refinement is premature. Of course, there are always exceptions. If you are specifically supporting older versions of Android (maybe you're writing an app that will be preloaded on a low-end phone that runs an older version of Android or you're designing it to be used by a particular demographic that has devices with older versions of Android), it might be a good idea to support those in the prototype to make sure any possible compatibility issues stand out, letting you better estimate how much time development will take. For more information on the `minSdkVersion` attribute, see http://developer.android.com/guide/topics/manifest/uses-sdk-element.html.

As you get started with your prototype, it can be helpful to take advantage of the code templates Android Studio has built-in. This means that you can quickly create activities for the shell of an app, often without worrying about a lot of the details like declaring activities in the manifest or importing the support library because the details are often handled for you. Unfortunately, at time of writing, many of the templates have not been updated to match the Material Design guidelines. In some cases, that may interfere with the testing of your prototype, but in other cases the differences might be insignificant, so you just have to decide if the templates get you something that will be useful to test. You should also be aware of the various sample projects that are available from Google directly through Android Studio. See http://developer .android.com/samples/index.html for more information.

For instance, if you create an activity that uses the navigation drawer pattern using the current templates, you'll end up with something similar to Figure 6.2. Unlike this older implementation, any new navigation drawer should always go over the app bar because that app bar is associated with the content currently on the screen and the navigation drawer is not. If you believe this difference between the older style app bar and the newer style will impact the prototype, then you can implement this is with the `Toolbar` class as an app bar rather than the built in action bar methods. If you're getting confused about all these types of bars, remember that these are all "toolbars." An app bar is the toolbar that's at the top. The original term for app bar was "action bar," so a lot of documentation and methods use that term still. When you see

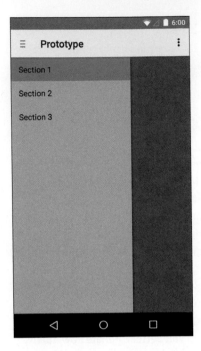

Figure 6.2 The outdated style of navigation drawer

`Toolbar` in monospace, that means the specific class provided in Android 5.0 or in the support library as `android.support.v7.widgets.Toolbar`.

Tabs

Confusing semantics out of the way, it's time to create an app. In this case, a blank activity is fine because we'll go through the full process of creating a navigation drawer and then adding tabs. First, we need to make sure that we have the Design library included in the dependencies section of our `build.gradle` file. Because the Design library is dependent on the AppCompat library (which is dependent on Support-V4), it's the only dependency we need to add. Remember too that the full code for this example prototype is included in the source code for this book in the `Prototype` folder for this chapter.

Now we can get that pesky toolbar out of the way. We want to ensure that the app's theme does not add a toolbar at the top already, so open your `styles.xml` file and update the parent to `Theme.AppCompat.Light.NoActionBar`. Depending on how you created the project, Android Studio may have created multiple copies of `styles.xml` for different versions of Android. This isn't necessary for the prototype, so you can delete all but the main one in `res/values`.

Now we can add a toolbar to the main layout. Because we'll be adding it to multiple layouts, it's a good idea to specify the toolbar in its own XML file so that it can be included elsewhere. Listing 6.1 shows an example saved as `toolbar.xml`.

Listing 6.1   Example of a Simple Toolbar Layout

```xml
<?xml version="1.0" encoding="utf-8"?>
<android.support.v7.widget.Toolbar
    xmlns:android="http://schemas.android.com/apk/res/android"
    android:id="@+id/toolbar"
    android:layout_width="match_parent"
    android:layout_height="?attr/actionBarSize"
    android:elevation="4dp"
    android:background="?attr/colorPrimary"/>
```

With the toolbar layout created, we can update the layout for the main activity. The whole thing will be wrapped with a DrawerLayout, inside of which there are two views. The first is the main content, which will be a LinearLayout containing the Toolbar, a TabLayout, and a ViewPager. The second is the NavigationView from the Design library. Listing 6.2 shows what this should look like. The `Toolbar` and `TabLayout` have the same background color and elevation, which will make them appear like one cohesive piece without complicating the view hierarchy. This might be a fragment at a future point, but keeping it this way is easy and effective right now. We'll create the navigation drawer's header layout and menu shortly.

Listing 6.2   Layout for the Main Activity

```xml
<?xml version="1.0" encoding="utf-8"?>
<android.support.v4.widget.DrawerLayout
    xmlns:android="http://schemas.android.com/apk/res/android"
    xmlns:app="http://schemas.android.com/apk/res-auto"
    android:id="@+id/drawer_layout"
    android:layout_width="match_parent"
    android:layout_height="match_parent"
    android:fitsSystemWindows="true">

    <!-- The main content -->
    <LinearLayout
        android:layout_width="match_parent"
        android:layout_height="match_parent"
        android:orientation="vertical">

        <include layout="@layout/toolbar" />

        <android.support.design.widget.TabLayout
            android:id="@+id/tabs"
            android:layout_width="match_parent"
            android:layout_height="wrap_content"
            android:background="?attr/colorPrimary"
            android:elevation="4dp"
            app:tabMode="scrollable" />

        <android.support.v4.view.ViewPager
            android:id="@+id/viewpager"
```

```
                    android:layout_width="match_parent"
                    android:layout_height="match_parent" />
        </LinearLayout>

        <!-- The nav drawer -->
        <android.support.design.widget.NavigationView
                android:id="@+id/navigation_view"
                android:layout_width="wrap_content"
                android:layout_height="match_parent"
                android:layout_gravity="start"
                app:headerLayout="@layout/nav_drawer_header"
                app:menu="@menu/nav_drawer" />

    </android.support.v4.widget.DrawerLayout>
```

Before we start populating the tabs, we're going to need some other pieces of the app ready.

Navigation Drawer

The navigation drawer is the other big piece of navigation, but before making the drawer, we need to define the types of tools that the drawer is organized into. This is a great case for an enum because Java enums are full classes, which means they can have methods and constructors. This lets you create a `ToolType` enum that can tell you the string resource ID for its name and description. Be sure to define the name and description for each type in `strings.xml` just like any other UI strings. Listing 6.3 shows what this could look like.

Listing 6.3   The Enum for Populating the Drawer

```java
public enum ToolType {
    CLAMPS(R.string.clamps, R.string.clamps_description),
    SAWS(R.string.saws, R.string.saws_description),
    DRILLS(R.string.drills, R.string.drills_description),
    SANDERS(R.string.sanders, R.string.sanders_description),
    ROUTERS(R.string.routers, R.string.routers_description),
    MORE(R.string.more, R.string.more_description),
    ;

    private final int mToolNameResourceId;
    private final int mToolDescriptionResourceId;

    private ToolType(@StringRes int toolName, @StringRes int
➥toolDescription) {
        mToolNameResourceId = toolName;
        mToolDescriptionResourceId = toolDescription;
    }

    @StringRes
    public int getToolDescriptionResourceId() {
```

```
            return mToolDescriptionResourceId;
    }

    @StringRes
    public int getToolNameResourceId() {
        return mToolNameResourceId;
    }
}
```

Now we can create the navigation drawer menu. Like all menus, it goes in the `res/menu` folder. We can call it `nav_drawer.xml` to make the purpose obvious. The menu needs to contain a group (though it can have more than one) and the group needs to have `checkableBehavior` set to `single`. This ensures that an item can be "checked" (i.e., selected as the current item) and that checking another item will uncheck the previous one. Within the group there are the size individual items. Listing 6.4 shows what this menu can look like.

Listing 6.4   The `nav_drawer.xml` Menu

```xml
<?xml version="1.0" encoding="utf-8"?>
<menu xmlns:android="http://schemas.android.com/apk/res/android">
    <group android:checkableBehavior="single">
        <item
            android:id="@+id/nav_clamps"
            android:title="@string/clamps"
            android:checked="true"
            />
        <item
            android:id="@+id/nav_saws"
            android:title="@string/saws"
            />
        <item
            android:id="@+id/nav_drills"
            android:title="@string/drills"
            />
        <item
            android:id="@+id/nav_sanders"
            android:title="@string/sanders"
            />
        <item
            android:id="@+id/nav_routers"
            android:title="@string/routers"
            />
        <item
            android:id="@+id/nav_more"
            android:title="@string/more"
            />
    </group>
</menu>
```

With that ready, we need to make the navigation drawer header. This is the layout that is used at the top of the navigation drawer. In a real app, we'd worry about the background and interactivity, but we're just focused on making a prototype, so this can be pretty simple. We create a new layout called `nav_drawer_header.xml` that contains a vertical `LinearLayout` with an `ImageView` and two `TextViews`. The values can all be hardcoded for now; we just need to make sure it looks close enough to get the point across when we evaluate the prototype with users. Listing 6.5 shows this simple layout.

Listing 6.5   The `nav_drawer_header.xml` Layout

```xml
<?xml version="1.0" encoding="utf-8"?>
<LinearLayout
    xmlns:android="http://schemas.android.com/apk/res/android"
    android:orientation="vertical"
    android:layout_width="match_parent"
    android:layout_height="150dp"
    android:background="#FF777777"
    android:paddingBottom="8dp"
    android:paddingLeft="16dp"
    android:paddingRight="16dp"
    android:paddingTop="24dp"
    android:gravity="bottom">

    <ImageView
        android:layout_width="64dp"
        android:layout_height="64dp"
        android:id="@+id/imageView"
        android:src="@drawable/profile"
        />

    <TextView
        android:fontFamily="sans-serif-medium"
        android:layout_width="wrap_content"
        android:layout_height="wrap_content"
        android:layout_marginTop="8dp"
        android:text="Pat Woodworker"
        android:textColor="#FFFFFF"
        android:id="@+id/textView"/>

    <TextView
        android:layout_width="wrap_content"
        android:layout_height="wrap_content"
        android:text="pdubs@patthewoodworker.com"
        android:textColor="#FFFFFF"
        android:id="@+id/textView2"/>
</LinearLayout>
```

Tool Representation

If you have real JSON that represents your data, you can take advantage of libraries such as GSON (https://code.google.com/p/google-gson/) or Jackson (https://github.com/FasterXML/jackson) that can take JSON and convert it to a simple Java object (commonly called a POJO or plain old Java object) and vice versa with very little effort. If your web API already exists, you might even be able to use it in the prototype without much effort by taking advantage of great libraries such as Retrofit (http://square.github.io/retrofit/).

Of course, most of the time you won't have anything ready at this stage, so we're going to assume nothing else is available yet and handle manually creating the data we want to display and the class that represents it. First, we can create the `Tool` class. The tool detail page requires the tool name, price, description, and a few pieces of metadata that are different for each type of tool (e.g., the drill press had horsepower, travel distance, and throat measurement). In a real app, it would make sense to have a subclass for each tool type because the metadata can vary so much, but we can do this somewhat generically now with just a string array to speed up the prototyping process.

Because we're going to need to be able to pass this class around in the app between activities and fragments, we should make it implement `Parcelable`. This interface provides a way of breaking a class down into primitive values stored in a `Bundle` class and restoring it from primitives in a bundle. This is more efficient than `Serializable`, but it is far more tedious to implement. Fortunately, you don't have to do the heavy work. If you open Android Studio's settings and go to the Plugins section, there is a button at the bottom that says, "Browse Repositories." Click this button and search for "parcelable." You should see the plugin called "Android Parcelable code generator" in the list as shown in Figure 6.3, so install it. After you close out the dialog windows to get back to Android Studio, it will tell you that it has to restart to use the new plugin; go ahead and do that now. When you get back into Android Studio, you can use the code insertion feature by right clicking or using the shortcut keys (Alt + Insert for Windows and Linux; Command + N on Mac) and select "Parcelable" to automatically generate all the code for you. Listing 6.6 shows a basic implementation of this class, including the parcelable bits.

Listing 6.6 The `Tool` Class

```
public class Tool implements Parcelable {

    private static final int DETAILS_COUNT = 3;

    private final String mName;
    private final String mPrice;
    private final String[] mDetails;
    private final String mDescription;
```

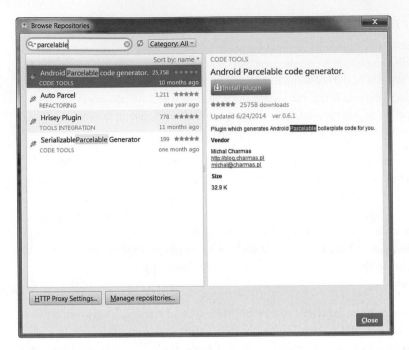

Figure 6.3 A search for the Android Parcelable code generator plugin in Android Studio

```java
public Tool(String name, String price, String[] details, String
➥ description) {
    mName = name;
    mPrice = price;
    mDetails = new String[DETAILS_COUNT];
    if (details != null) {
        for (int i = 0; i < details.length; i++) {
            mDetails[i] = details[i];
        }
    }
    mDescription = description;
}

public String getDescription() {
    return mDescription;
}

public String[] getDetails() {
    return mDetails;
}

public String getName() {
    return mName;
}
```

```java
    public String getPrice() {
        return mPrice;
    }

    @Override
    public int describeContents() {
        return 0;
    }

    @Override
    public void writeToParcel(Parcel dest, int flags) {
        dest.writeString(this.mName);
        dest.writeString(this.mPrice);
        dest.writeStringArray(this.mDetails);
        dest.writeString(this.mDescription);
    }

    private Tool(Parcel in) {
        this.mName = in.readString();
        this.mPrice = in.readString();
        this.mDetails = in.createStringArray();
        this.mDescription = in.readString();
    }

    public static final Parcelable.Creator<Tool> CREATOR = new
➥ Parcelable.Creator<Tool>() {
        public Tool createFromParcel(Parcel source) {
            return new Tool(source);
        }

        public Tool[] newArray(int size) {
            return new Tool[size];
        }
    };
}
```

Now that we have a way to represent each tool, we have to figure out how to get some data. One technique that is sometimes helpful is to have a class that generates instances for you using some predefined values. You can create arrays of acceptable values for each field and then choose from them by picking at random and you'll end up with something that should be reasonable enough for basic testing. Listing 6.7 demonstrates some arrays you might set up with acceptable values for a `ToolTestUtils` class.

Listing 6.7   Examples of Predefined Values as Arrays

```java
private static final String[] BRANDS = {
        "Ace", "Bosch", "DeWalt", "Irwin", "Jet", "Kreg",
        "Makita", "Porter Cable", "Skil", "Stanley", "Stihl",
};
```

```
private static final String[] DETAILS_HP = {
        "1/4 HP", "1/2 HP", "3/4 HP", "1 HP", "1 1/2 HP", "2 HP",
};

private static final String[] DETAILS_CLAMP_TYPE = {
        "Bar", "Spring", "Quick-Grip", "Pipe", "Parallel",
};

private static final String[] DETAILS_INCHES = {
        "2\"", "5\"", "12\"", "18\"", "24\"", "36\"", "48\"",
};

private static final String[] DETAILS_BATTERY = {
        "12V", "18V", "20V", "24V", "32V", "48V",
};

// ... You get the idea
```

Next, you need to add a constructor, so that you can create a `Random` class with a particular seed, and a method to generate a `Tool` using that `Random`. The reason for passing in a particular seed is that it enables you to get exactly the same results, so you can ensure that your list of stationary drills is always the same. It also means that you can use this class later on for automated tests because you can create a lot of useful values and repeat results. The method for generating each object isn't particularly interesting; it's mostly just grabbing a random option from an array. There are a few specific checks to see which tab has been selected and choose more realistic options, but it looks more complicated than it is. Listing 6.8 shows the rest of the class (note that the sanders, routers, and more sections don't have their details filled in; the first three sections should be enough to get a feel for the prototype).

Listing 6.8 The Code for Generating Test `Tool` Instances

```
private final Random mRandom;

public ToolTestUtils() {
    this(0);
}

public ToolTestUtils(long seed) {
    mRandom = new Random(seed);
}

public Tool getNewTool(ToolType toolType, ToolPagerAdapter.Tab tab) {
    final String brand = getRandom(BRANDS);
    String name = brand + " ";
    String price = null;
    final String[] details = new String[3];
    switch (toolType) {
```

```
    case CLAMPS:
        details[0] = getRandom(DETAILS_CLAMP_TYPE);
        details[1] = getRandom(DETAILS_INCHES);
        name += details[1] + " " + details[0] + " Clamp";
        details[1] += " opening";
        price = getRandom(PRICE_LOW);
        break;
    case SAWS:
        details[0] = getRandom(DETAILS_BLADE_SIZE);
        details[1] = getRandom(DETAILS_HP);
        if (tab == ToolPagerAdapter.Tab.BATTERY) {
            details[2] = getRandom(DETAILS_BATTERY);
        }
        if (tab == ToolPagerAdapter.Tab.STATIONARY) {
            name += getRandom(TYPES_SAWS_STATIONARY);
        } else {
            name += getRandom(TYPES_SAWS_NOT_STATIONARY);
        }
        break;
    case DRILLS:
        details[0] = getRandom(DETAILS_HP);
        if (tab == ToolPagerAdapter.Tab.BATTERY) {
            details[1] = getRandom(DETAILS_BATTERY);
        }
        if (tab == ToolPagerAdapter.Tab.STATIONARY) {
            details[2] = getRandom(DETAILS_INCHES) + " throat";
            name += getRandom(TYPES_DRILLS_STATIONARY);
        } else {
            name += "Drill";
        }
        break;
    case SANDERS:
        name += "Sander";
        break;
    case ROUTERS:
        name += "Router";
        break;
    case MORE:
        name += "Tool";
        break;
}

if (price == null) {
    if (tab == ToolPagerAdapter.Tab.STATIONARY) {
        price = getRandom(PRICE_HIGH);
    } else {
        price = getRandom(PRICE_MEDIUM);
    }
}
```

```java
        String description = "The latest and greatest from " + brand +
    " takes " + toolType.name().toLowerCase(Locale.getDefault()) + " to a
    whole new level. Tenderloin corned beef tail, tongue landjaeger boudin
    kevin ham pig pork loin short loin shoulder prosciutto ground round.
    Alcatra salami sausage short ribs t-bone, tongue spare ribs kevin
    meatball tenderloin. Prosciutto tail meatloaf, chuck pancetta kielbasa
    leberkas tenderloin drumstick meatball alcatra cow sausage corned beef
    pork belly. Shoulder swine hamburger tail ham hock bacon pork belly
    leberkas beef ribs jowl spare ribs.";

        return new Tool(name, price, details, description);
};

public ArrayList<Tool> getNewTools(ToolType toolType, ToolPagerAdapter.
Tab tab, int count) {
    final ArrayList<Tool> results = new ArrayList<>(count);
    for (int i = 0; i < count; i++) {
        results.add(getNewTool(toolType, tab));
    }
    return results;
};

private String getRandom(String[] strings) {
    return strings[mRandom.nextInt(strings.length)];
}
```

Tab Fragments

We need a fragment for the About tab and a list fragment for the other three tabs. For the About tab, we can create a simple fragment called `ToolAboutFragment` that takes a `ToolType` enum and displays the name and description. For the real app, we'll likely want something more detailed, perhaps with photos, but this should be enough for the prototype. Creating a new `Fragment` class in Android Studio via File -> New -> Fragment -> Fragment (Blank) will give you a fragment and layout to start with.

Listing 6.9 shows one way of organizing the fragment's layout. By making the root view a vertically oriented linear layout, we can just drop the two text views in. Setting the first one to have a text appearance of `?android:attr/textAppearanceLarge` allows us to take advantage of attributes that are built in to Android and create a visual hierarchy. Another attribute to notice in this file is `tools:text`. The `tools` namespace lets you specify values for attributes that are just used for working with Android Studio and not in the app. By specifying `tools:text` in this way, you override whatever (if anything) was put for `android:text`, allowing you to test text in the design view without it affecting your actual app. This is great for cases where the default is empty because you will programmatically assign a value. Although we're only using the `tools` namespace to set the text here, you can use it for other Android attributes too. Want a view to stand out while you tweak it in the design tab? You could set its background via `tools:background` to a right red.

Listing 6.9 The Layout for the About Fragment

```xml
<?xml version="1.0" encoding="utf-8"?>
<LinearLayout xmlns:android="http://schemas.android.com/apk/res/android"
              xmlns:tools="http://schemas.android.com/tools"
              android:layout_width="match_parent"
              android:layout_height="match_parent"
              android:orientation="vertical"
              android:paddingLeft="@dimen/activity_horizontal_margin"
              android:paddingRight="@dimen/activity_horizontal_margin"
              android:paddingTop="@dimen/activity_vertical_margin"
              android:paddingBottom="@dimen/activity_vertical_margin"

              tools:context="com.iangclifton.woodworkingtools.
➥ ToolAboutFragment">

    <TextView
        android:id="@+id/title"
        android:layout_width="match_parent"
        android:layout_height="wrap_content"
        android:textAppearance="?android:attr/textAppearanceLarge"
        tools:text="@string/clamps" />

    <TextView
        android:id="@+id/description"
        android:layout_width="match_parent"
        android:layout_height="wrap_content"
        android:textAppearance="?android:attr/textAppearanceMedium"
        tools:text="@string/clamps_description" />


</LinearLayout>
```

Now the fragment just needs to be updated to know the `ToolType` it is displaying and to set the appropriate text views. The convention used for passing values to a fragment that are required is to create a static `newInstance` method that takes those values, creates an instance of the fragment, sets those values as the fragment's arguments, and then returns the fragment. This ensures that the arguments are set before the fragment needs them and it also keeps you from creating a custom constructor that will remove the required default (empty) constructor. Because Android can recreate your fragments via the default constructor using reflection, not having one can cause a crash that's not obvious. Setting the arguments the way we are in this `newInstance` method means that Android can use the default constructor to recreate the fragment and the arguments will be restored for us. Listing 6.10 shows the fragment.

Listing 6.10   The About Fragment

```java
public class ToolAboutFragment extends Fragment {

    private static final String ARG_TOOL_TYPE = "toolType";

    private ToolType mToolType;

    public static ToolAboutFragment newInstance(ToolType toolType) {
        final ToolAboutFragment fragment = new ToolAboutFragment();
        final Bundle args = new Bundle();
        args.putString(ARG_TOOL_TYPE, toolType.name());
        fragment.setArguments(args);
        return fragment;
    }

    public ToolAboutFragment() {
        // Required empty public constructor
    }

    @Override
    public void onCreate(Bundle savedInstanceState) {
        super.onCreate(savedInstanceState);
        final Bundle args = getArguments();
        if (args == null) {
            throw new IllegalStateException("No arguments set; use
➥ newInstance when constructing!");
        }
        mToolType = ToolType.valueOf(args.getString(ARG_TOOL_TYPE));
    }

    @Override
    public View onCreateView(LayoutInflater inflater, ViewGroup
➥ container, Bundle savedInstanceState) {
        final View rootView = inflater.inflate(R.layout.fragment_tool_
➥ about, container, false);
        TextView textView = (TextView) rootView.findViewById(R.id.title);
        textView.setText(mToolType.getToolNameResourceId());
        textView = (TextView) rootView.findViewById(R.id.description);
        textView.setText(mToolType.getToolDescriptionResourceId());

        return rootView;
    }
}
```

The `ToolListFragment` that will be used for the other three tabs can be created in the same way, but you should change the super class from `Fragment` to `ListFragment`. The List-Fragment class handles displaying a loading state, an empty state, or a list at any given time.

We only need to worry about the list of content right now, and we need to pass two pieces of content to do that: the `ToolType` enum and the tab that was selected. Because we haven't defined the tabs yet, let's do that now. We can create a new class that extends `FragmentPagerAdapter` called `ToolPagerAdapter`. This class will be responsible for constructing the fragments that are displayed when the user taps a tab or swipes between tabs. Within it, we can define an enum called `Tab` with a class for each tab pointing to a string resource similar to what we did for `ToolType`. The adapter's constructor will need the `FragmentManager` (to pass to the super class constructor), the `Resources` (for loading the strings displayed on the tabs), and the `ToolType` (used when constructing the `ToolListFragment`). Rather than keeping the resources around, we can immediately use the resources to load the string titles into an array. We need to override `getItem` to return a new fragment of the appropriate type. In this case, we need the `ToolAboutFragment` to be instantiated if the first (0 position) tab is selected, our in-progress `ToolListFragment` to be instantiated if any of the next three tabs is selected, or an exception to be thrown for any other position (just in case we add more tabs later and forget to handle them). One extra bit we do is override `getItemId`, which returns a unique ID for each fragment so that the super class can reuse existing fragments. When you tap the Stationary tab, the super class will look to see if a fragment of that ID has already been created, reusing it if it has. Because we don't want the fragment for stationary drills to be used when tapping the tab for stationary saws, we represent the tool type with the tens digit and the tab position with the ones digit to create a simple unique ID. The complete `ToolPagerAdapter` class is in Listing 6.11.

Listing 6.11 The `ToolPagerAdapter` Class

```
public class ToolPagerAdapter extends FragmentPagerAdapter {

    public enum Tab {
        ABOUT(R.string.about),
        STATIONARY(R.string.stationary),
        HANDHELD(R.string.handheld),
        BATTERY(R.string.battery);

        private final int mStringResource;

        Tab(@StringRes int stringResource) {
            mStringResource = stringResource;
        }

        public int getStringResource() {
            return mStringResource;
        }
    }

    private final Tab[] mTabs = Tab.values();
    private final CharSequence[] mTitles = new CharSequence[mTabs.
➥length];
    private final ToolType mToolType;
```

```java
    private final ToolType[] mToolTypes = ToolType.values();

    public ToolPagerAdapter(FragmentManager fm, Resources res, ToolType
➥ toolType) {
        super(fm);
        mToolType = toolType;
        for (int i = 0; i < mTabs.length; i++) {
            mTitles[i] = res.getString(mTabs[i].getStringResource());
        }
    }

    @Override
    public Fragment getItem(int position) {
        switch (position) {
            case 0:
                return ToolAboutFragment.newInstance(mToolType);
            case 1:
            case 2:
            case 3:
                return ToolListFragment.newInstance(mToolType,
➥ mTabs[position]);

        }
        throw new IllegalArgumentException("Unhandled position: " +
➥ position);
    }

    @Override
    public int getCount() {
        return mTabs.length;
    }

    @Override
    public CharSequence getPageTitle(int position) {
        return mTitles[position];
    }

    @Override
    public long getItemId(int position) {
        for (int i = 0; i < mToolTypes.length; i++) {
            if (mToolTypes[i] == mToolType) {
                return (i * 10) + position;
            }
        }
        throw new IllegalArgumentException("Invalid position (" +
➥ position + ") or ToolType (" + mToolType + ")");
    }
}
```

With the adapter for our tabs ready, we need to update the main activity. The `onCreate` method has the typical `setContentView` call and the toolbar setup. Then it needs to set up the drawer. We have to set up the navigation icon in the toolbar and also the click listener that triggers the opening of the drawer. We also need to make the activity implement `OnNavigationItemSelectedListener` and call the setter for that listener on our `NavigationView`. If this is the first time the activity is launching (i.e., the `Bundle` passed into `onCreate` is null), then we should also set up all the tabs.

We'll create a `setupTabs` method that takes the position and sets up the `ViewPager` as needed. It needs to create a `ToolPagerAdapter` based on the position (using the appropriate `ToolType`). Then it can clear out all existing tabs, create tabs from the adapter, add the page listener, set the adapter, and set the tab listener. The `OnTabSelectedListener` simply needs to set the current item based on the position of the tab. In this example, we are simply finding the views each time, which isn't very efficient. It's good enough for a prototype, but it would be better to retain these references in a real app.

We can implement `onNavigationItemSelected` by using a switch on the ID of the `MenuItem` that was selected (this represents the item in the drawer that was created from the XML we wrote). The switch just needs to set the current position, but you might also do other handling here in future. Be sure to set the `MenuItem` as checked, call `setupTabs` with the new position, and close the drawer. Note that many apps would also set the title here, but our design displays the section under the tabs, so it might be redundant to show it in the app bar as well.

One more thing we need to do is handle the navigation drawer state. That means we should override `onSaveInstanceState` to store the current nav position (don't forget to call through to the super method). We should also override `onRestoreInstanceState`, calling through to the super method, and adding a few lines of code to set things back up. We retrieve the position from the `Bundle`, and then we get the `MenuItem` that represents that position to call `setChecked` on it. Finally, we trigger our `setupTabs` method.

Listing 6.12 shows what the activity looks like now and Figure 6.4 shows the state of the navigation in the UI at this point.

Listing 6.12   The Updated `MainActivity`

```
public class MainActivity extends AppCompatActivity implements
➥ NavigationView.OnNavigationItemSelectedListener {
    private static final String TAG = "MainActivity";

    private static final String SELECTED_POSITION = "selectedPosition";

    private int mCurrentNavPosition;
    private DrawerLayout mDrawerLayout;
    private NavigationView mNavigationView;
```

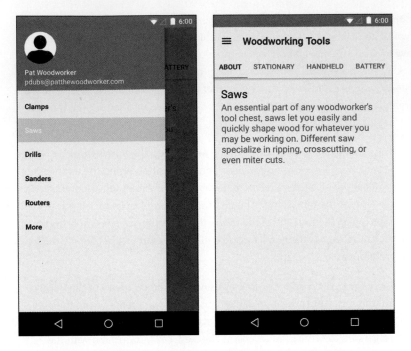

Figure 6.4 The navigation drawer on the left and the tabs on the right

```java
private Toolbar mToolbar;
private ToolType[] mToolTypes = ToolType.values();

@Override
protected void onCreate(Bundle savedInstanceState) {
    super.onCreate(savedInstanceState);
    setContentView(R.layout.activity_main);

    mToolbar = (Toolbar) findViewById(R.id.toolbar);
    setSupportActionBar(mToolbar);

    // Enable opening of drawer
    mDrawerLayout = (DrawerLayout) findViewById
➥(R.id.drawer_layout);
    mToolbar.setNavigationIcon(R.drawable.ic_menu_black_24dp);
    mToolbar.setNavigationOnClickListener(new View.
➥OnClickListener() {
        @Override
        public void onClick(View v) {
            mDrawerLayout.openDrawer(GravityCompat.START);
        }
    });

    // Add drawer listener
    mNavigationView = (NavigationView) findViewById
➥(R.id.navigation_view);
```

```java
        mNavigationView.setNavigationItemSelectedListener(this);

        // Set up tabs and title
        if (savedInstanceState == null) {
            setupTabs(0);
        }
    }

    @Override
    public boolean onNavigationItemSelected(MenuItem menuItem) {
        switch (menuItem.getItemId()) {
            case R.id.nav_clamps:
                mCurrentNavPosition = 0;
                break;
            case R.id.nav_saws:
                mCurrentNavPosition = 1;
                break;
            case R.id.nav_drills:
                mCurrentNavPosition = 2;
                break;
            case R.id.nav_sanders:
                mCurrentNavPosition = 3;
                break;
            case R.id.nav_routers:
                mCurrentNavPosition = 4;
                break;
            case R.id.nav_more:
                mCurrentNavPosition = 5;
                break;
            default:
                Log.w(TAG, "Unknown drawer item selected");
                break;
        }

        menuItem.setChecked(true);
        setupTabs(mCurrentNavPosition);
        mDrawerLayout.closeDrawer(GravityCompat.START);
        return true;
    }

    @Override
    protected void onRestoreInstanceState(Bundle savedInstanceState) {
        super.onRestoreInstanceState(savedInstanceState);
        mCurrentNavPosition = savedInstanceState.getInt(SELECTED_
➡ POSITION, 0);
        final Menu menu = mNavigationView.getMenu();
        final MenuItem menuItem = menu.getItem(mCurrentNavPosition);
        menuItem.setChecked(true);
        setupTabs(mCurrentNavPosition);
    }
```

```java
@Override
protected void onSaveInstanceState(Bundle outState) {
    super.onSaveInstanceState(outState);
    outState.putInt(SELECTED_POSITION, mCurrentNavPosition);
}

private void setupTabs(int position) {
    final ViewPager viewPager = (ViewPager) findViewById
➥(R.id.viewpager);
    final TabLayout tabLayout = (TabLayout) findViewById
➥(R.id.tabs);
    final ToolPagerAdapter toolPagerAdapter = new ToolPagerAdapter
➥(getSupportFragmentManager(), getResources(), mToolTypes[position]);
    tabLayout.removeAllTabs();
    tabLayout.setTabsFromPagerAdapter(toolPagerAdapter);
    viewPager.addOnPageChangeListener(new TabLayout.TabLayoutOnPage
➥ChangeListener(tabLayout));
    viewPager.setAdapter(toolPagerAdapter);
    tabLayout.setOnTabSelectedListener(new TabLayout.
➥OnTabSelectedListener() {
        @Override
        public void onTabSelected(TabLayout.Tab tab) {
            viewPager.setCurrentItem(tab.getPosition());
        }

        @Override
        public void onTabUnselected(TabLayout.Tab tab) {

        }

        @Override
        public void onTabReselected(TabLayout.Tab tab) {

        }
    });
}
}
```

Before we get back to the list fragment, we need to make an adapter that will be used to create the views, which means we also need a layout that will display the list items. We can either make this layout have a RelativeLayout as the root or a LinearLayout, the former has the advantage of a shallower view hierarchy and the latter has the advantage of being able to center the text vertically as a group even if the metadata is missing. We'll go with the LinearLayout approach in this case, but either is fine. Listing 6.13 shows this simple layout, which we save as list_item_tool.xml. Typically, layouts are named based on the root use and then the specific type (in our case we have a list item that represents a tool). A layout for a fragment that displays details about bacon might be called fragment_bacon_details.xml but you might call it activity_bacon_details.xml if you planned to use it in an activity. Because the files are organized alphabetically, this helps visually group the layouts based on their use. Of course, this is a convention, so you can use whatever naming scheme works best for you.

Listing 6.13   The `list_item_tool.xml` Layout

```xml
<LinearLayout xmlns:android="http://schemas.android.com/apk/res/android"
              xmlns:tools="http://schemas.android.com/tools"
              android:layout_width="match_parent"
              android:layout_height="wrap_content"
              android:orientation="horizontal">

    <ImageView
        android:layout_width="@dimen/thumbnail_size"
        android:layout_height="@dimen/thumbnail_size"
        android:id="@+id/thumbnail"
        android:contentDescription="@null"
        android:layout_marginBottom="@dimen/default_padding"
        android:layout_marginStart="@dimen/default_padding"
        android:layout_marginTop="@dimen/default_padding"
        tools:src="#FFBBBBBB" />

    <LinearLayout
        android:layout_width="match_parent"
        android:layout_height="wrap_content"
        android:padding="@dimen/default_padding"
        android:gravity="center_vertical"
        android:orientation="vertical">

        <TextView
            android:id="@+id/price"
            android:layout_width="match_parent"
            android:layout_height="wrap_content"
            android:gravity="end"
            android:textAppearance="?android:attr/textAppearanceMedium"
            android:lines="1"
            tools:text="$200"/>

        <TextView
            android:id="@+id/name"
            android:layout_width="match_parent"
            android:layout_height="wrap_content"
            android:textAppearance="?android:attr/textAppearanceLarge"
            android:textSize="18sp"
            tools:text="Acme 17" Bench Mount Drill Press"/>

        <TextView
            android:id="@+id/meta"
            android:layout_width="match_parent"
            android:layout_height="wrap_content"
            android:textAppearance="?android:attr/textAppearanceMedium"
```

```
                  android:textSize="16sp"
                  tools:text="1/2 HP"/>

         </LinearLayout>

   </LinearLayout>
```

The adapter we make that uses the `list_item_tool.xml` layout can extend from `Array-Adapter`, cutting down on the amount of code we need to write. Our `ToolArrayAdapter` can pass a `List` of `Tool` instances to the super's constructor. The constructor normally takes an ID for a text view, which it then uses to set the text displayed for each item using the `get-String` method of the object, but we can pass `-1` here because we'll implement the `get-View` method ourselves. Remember that `getView` receives a `convertView`, which is a view previously returned by `getView` for an item that is now off the screen. It can be null if there are no previous views being recycled, so we just need to inflate the layout we made in that case. In a real app, you should never use `findViewById` every time `getView` is called. You can use the common "View Holder" pattern (basically you have a separate object that keeps all the view references for you), which is covered in Chapter 8 "Applying the Design," or you can use a custom view, which is covered in Chapter 12 "Combining Views for Custom Components." For a prototype, calling `findViewById` more than necessary is okay.

One extra thing we want to do is to vary the thumbnails with different shades of gray to help simulate different images. We'll make a simple method that takes an `int` and returns a color. We'll define three colors, so we can switch over the absolute value (to get rid of any negatives) modulus three. If you're not familiar with the modulus operator, it returns what the remainder would be when dividing numbers (e.g., 10 divided by 3 will give you 3 and the remainder is dropped off because we're dealing with integers but 10 modulus 3 gives you 1). By using three, we guarantee that the number returned will be zero, one, or two, so we just have to return a color for each of those. In this case we can hardcode the colors because they're just here for the prototype. These will be different shades of gray such as `0xff777777`. Using `0x` says that the value is in hexadecimal format just like how you specify a color in XML. The rest of the values are in pairs (where `00` is the lowest value and `ff` is the highest) `ff` is for the alpha value, so `ff` is fully opaque. The red, blue, and green pairs can be anything you want. By making the three pairs the same, you create a gray. The last bit we need to do is get an `int` that we can use to key off of. You could pass in the position of the view, which would give you a very regular pattern of your grays, but that pattern is very noticeable and can cause people to try to understand why the pattern is there when that isn't at all the focus of the prototype. Instead, we want something somewhat random, but we can "cheat" by just using the hash code of the tool's name. A hash code is intended to be used for data structures such as a hash map, which means the range of possible values should be well distributed across instances of the object. In other words, the hash code for one tool's name is unlikely to be the same as for another tool, but the hash code for a given tool's name will always be the same. This is perfect for our needs. You can see how everything comes together for the `ToolArrayAdapter` in Listing 6.14.

Listing 6.14   The `ToolArrayAdapter`

```java
public class ToolArrayAdapter extends ArrayAdapter<Tool> {

    private final LayoutInflater mLayoutInflater;

    public ToolArrayAdapter(Context context, List<Tool> objects) {
        super(context, -1, objects);
        mLayoutInflater = LayoutInflater.from(context);
    }

    @Override
    public View getView(int position, View convertView, ViewGroup
 parent) {
        if (convertView == null) {
            convertView = mLayoutInflater.inflate(R.layout.list_item_
 tool, parent, false);
        }
        final Tool tool = getItem(position);

        // Set TextViews
        TextView textView = (TextView) convertView.findViewById
 (R.id.price);
        textView.setText(tool.getPrice());
        textView = (TextView) convertView.findViewById(R.id.name);
        textView.setText(tool.getName());
        textView = (TextView) convertView.findViewById(R.id.meta);
        textView.setText(tool.getDetails()[0]);

        // Set color for thumbnail
        convertView.findViewById(R.id.thumbnail).setBackgroundColor
 (getThumbnailColor(tool.getName().hashCode()));

        return convertView;
    }

    private int getThumbnailColor(int key) {
        switch (Math.abs(key) % 3) {
            case 0:
                return 0xff777777;
            case 1:
                return 0xff999999;
            case 2:
                return 0xffbbbbbb;
        }

        return 0;
    }
}
```

Figure 6.5 The tool list populated with test data

We can finally get back to our `ToolListFragment`. Its `newInstance` method will take both a `ToolType` enum and a `ToolPagerAdapter.Tab` enum, and we need to update the fragment to make use of the adapter we just made. Using the `ToolTestUtils` we created earlier, we can populate the adapter with 20 tools to give the basic feel we expect the app to have once there is real data. The fragment also needs to handle clicks, so we can update it to implement `AdapterView.OnItemClickListener`. In the `onItemClick` method, we get the `Tool` object from our adapter and then start the `ToolDetailActivity`, which we need to make next. The full fragment is in Listing 6.15, and an example of the UI is in Figure 6.5. You may find that the entire app is extremely bland (and excessively gray) at this point. That's okay! The less final an app looks, the more comfortable most people feel in critiquing it. Remember, you're not worried about color choice at this point.

Listing 6.15 The `ToolListFragment`

```
public class ToolListFragment extends ListFragment implements
➥ AdapterView.OnItemClickListener {

    private static final String ARG_TOOL_TYPE = "toolType";
    private static final String ARG_TAB = "tab";

    private ToolType mToolType;
    private ToolPagerAdapter.Tab mTab;
    private ToolArrayAdapter mToolArrayAdapter;
```

```
    public static ToolListFragment newInstance(ToolType toolType,
➥ ToolPagerAdapter.Tab tab) {
        final ToolListFragment fragment = new ToolListFragment();
        final Bundle args = new Bundle();
        args.putString(ARG_TOOL_TYPE, toolType.name());
        args.putString(ARG_TAB, tab.name());
        fragment.setArguments(args);
        return fragment;
    }

    public ToolListFragment() {
        // Required empty public constructor
    }

    @Override
    public void onCreate(Bundle savedInstanceState) {
        super.onCreate(savedInstanceState);
        final Bundle args = getArguments();
        if (args == null) {
            throw new IllegalStateException("No arguments set; use
➥ newInstance when constructing!");
        }
        mToolType = ToolType.valueOf(args.getString(ARG_TOOL_TYPE));
        mTab = ToolPagerAdapter.Tab.valueOf(args.getString(ARG_TAB));
        final ArrayList<Tool> tools = new ToolTestUtils
➥ (mTab.hashCode()).getNewTools(mToolType, mTab, 20);
        mToolArrayAdapter = new ToolArrayAdapter(getActivity(), tools);
        setListAdapter(mToolArrayAdapter);
    }

    @Override
    public void onActivityCreated(Bundle savedInstanceState) {
        super.onActivityCreated(savedInstanceState);
        getListView().setOnItemClickListener(this);
    }

    @Override
    public void onItemClick(AdapterView<?> adapterView, View view, int
➥ position, long id) {
        final Tool tool = mToolArrayAdapter.getItem(position);
        ToolDetailActivity.startActivity(getActivity(), tool);
    }
}
```

Tool Details

To save a tiny bit of time, we're going to implement the detail activity without using a fragment. That means we need to create a blank activity with Android Studio and then get started on the

Figure 6.6 The tool detail page

layout. Figure 6.6 shows what we're going to build. The root of this layout will be a `Relative-Layout`. Our toolbar will go on the top, followed by a `ScrollView` that contains just about everything else, and then a floating action button (FAB) will be added to the bottom-right corner. The `FloatingActionButton` view comes from the Design library. Inside the `ScrollView`, we'll have another `RelativeLayout` that positions everything how we want it. All the content is just text and a single image, so this layout is fairly simple. The complete layout is in Listing 6.16.

Listing 6.16 The `activity_tool_detail.xml` Layout

```
<RelativeLayout xmlns:android="http://schemas.android.com/apk/res/android"
                xmlns:app="http://schemas.android.com/apk/res-auto"
                xmlns:tools="http://schemas.android.com/tools"
                android:layout_width="match_parent"
                android:layout_height="match_parent"
                android:orientation="vertical"

tools:context="com.iangclifton.woodworkingtools.
➥ ToolDetailsActivityFragment">

    <include layout="@layout/toolbar" />

    <ScrollView
        android:layout_width="match_parent"
        android:layout_height="wrap_content"
```

```
android:layout_below="@id/toolbar"
android:fillViewport="true">

<RelativeLayout
    android:layout_width="match_parent"
    android:layout_height="wrap_content"
    android:paddingBottom="80dp">

    <ImageView
        android:id="@+id/image"
        android:layout_width="match_parent"
        android:layout_height="220dp"
        android:layout_alignParentStart="true"
        android:layout_alignParentTop="true"
        android:layout_marginBottom="8dp"
        android:contentDescription="@null"
        android:src="#FFBBBBBB"/>

    <TextView
        android:id="@+id/name"
        android:layout_width="wrap_content"
        android:layout_height="wrap_content"
        android:layout_alignBottom="@+id/image"
        android:layout_alignStart="@+id/image"
        android:paddingBottom="8dp"
        android:paddingLeft="@dimen/activity_horizontal_margin"
        android:paddingRight="@dimen/activity_horizontal_margin"
        android:textAppearance="?android:attr/textAppearanceLarge"
        android:textSize="26sp"
        tools:text="Acme 17&quot; drill press"/>

    <TextView
        android:id="@+id/detail_0"
        android:layout_width="wrap_content"
        android:layout_height="wrap_content"
        android:layout_above="@+id/detail_2"
        android:layout_alignStart="@+id/image"
        android:paddingLeft="@dimen/activity_horizontal_margin"
        android:paddingRight="@dimen/activity_horizontal_margin"
        android:textColor="@color/black_87"
        android:textSize="20sp"
        tools:text="3/4 HP"/>

    <TextView
        android:id="@+id/detail_1"
        android:layout_width="wrap_content"
        android:layout_height="wrap_content"
        android:layout_alignStart="@id/detail_0"
        android:layout_below="@id/detail_0"
        android:paddingLeft="@dimen/activity_horizontal_margin"
```

```xml
        android:paddingRight="@dimen/activity_horizontal_margin"
        android:textColor="@color/black_87"
        android:textSize="20sp"
        tools:text="5" travel"/>

    <TextView
        android:id="@+id/detail_2"
        android:layout_width="wrap_content"
        android:layout_height="wrap_content"
        android:layout_alignEnd="@+id/price"
        android:layout_below="@+id/price"
        android:paddingLeft="@dimen/activity_horizontal_margin"
        android:paddingRight="@dimen/activity_horizontal_margin"
        android:textColor="@color/black_87"
        android:textSize="20sp"
        tools:text="8" throat"/>

    <TextView
        android:id="@+id/description"
        android:layout_width="wrap_content"
        android:layout_height="wrap_content"
        android:layout_alignParentStart="true"
        android:layout_below="@id/detail_1"
        android:layout_marginTop="16dp"
        android:paddingLeft="@dimen/activity_horizontal_margin"
        android:paddingRight="@dimen/activity_horizontal_margin"
        android:textAppearance="?android:attr/
➥ textAppearanceMedium"
        tools:text="The latest and greatest drill press from
Acme Inc. A powerful 3/4 HP motor ensures you can drill through dense
materials without breaking a sweat. Tail pork belly pancetta shank.
Salami ham biltong ball tip pig corned beef jerky turkey meatloaf
shank hamburger flank filet mignon porchetta rump. Beef ribs kevin
drumstick landjaeger pastrami tail jowl ground round porchetta chuck
swine sausage doner jerky. Doner landjaeger bresaola spare ribs short
loin tenderloin pancetta fatback kielbasa capicola prosciutto. Beef
tenderloin tail sirloin rump tongue short ribs picanha pork chop,
landjaeger porchetta. Filet mignon shank shoulder bacon sausage
frankfurter."/>

    <TextView
        android:id="@+id/price"
        android:layout_width="wrap_content"
        android:layout_height="wrap_content"
        android:layout_alignEnd="@+id/image"
        android:layout_below="@+id/image"
        android:paddingLeft="@dimen/activity_horizontal_margin"
        android:paddingRight="@dimen/activity_horizontal_margin"
        android:textColor="@color/black_87"
```

```
                    android:textSize="20sp"
                    tools:text="$750"/>

        </RelativeLayout>

    </ScrollView>

    <android.support.design.widget.FloatingActionButton
        android:id="@+id/fab"
        android:layout_width="wrap_content"
        android:layout_height="wrap_content"
        android:layout_alignParentBottom="true"
        android:layout_alignParentEnd="true"
        android:layout_margin="@dimen/default_padding"
        android:src="@drawable/ic_buy"/>

</RelativeLayout>
```

Back in the `ToolDetailActivity` class, we need to make sure the `Tool` is an extra in the
`Bundle` that is added to the `Intent` that launches the activity, so we create a helper method
called `startActivity` to do all the work. This is a handy pattern because it keeps code
outside of the activity from having to know which extras are required and which keys to use.
The `onCreate` method just pulls out the `Tool` and sets each of the text views in the layout.
Because we're repeating the process of finding a view, casting it to a `TextView`, and setting
the text, we can create a simple helper method for that. Listing 6.17 shows this simple activity
completed.

Listing 6.17   The `ToolDetailActivity`

```
public class ToolDetailActivity extends AppCompatActivity {

    private static final String EXTRA_TOOL = "com.iangclifton.
➥ woodworkingtools.TOOL";

    public static void startActivity(Context context, Tool tool) {
        final Intent intent = new Intent(context,
➥ ToolDetailActivity.class);
        intent.putExtra(EXTRA_TOOL, tool);
        context.startActivity(intent);
    }

    @Override
    protected void onCreate(Bundle savedInstanceState) {
        super.onCreate(savedInstanceState);
        setContentView(R.layout.activity_tool_detail);

        final Toolbar toolbar = (Toolbar) findViewById(R.id.toolbar);
```

```java
        setSupportActionBar(toolbar);
        getSupportActionBar().setDisplayHomeAsUpEnabled(true);

        final Tool tool = getIntent().getParcelableExtra(EXTRA_TOOL);
        if (tool == null) {
            throw new IllegalStateException("Tool not available as
➥ extra; use startActivity when creating an activity instance");
        }

        findAndSetTextView(R.id.name, tool.getName());
        findAndSetTextView(R.id.price, tool.getPrice());
        findAndSetTextView(R.id.detail_0, tool.getDetails()[0]);
        findAndSetTextView(R.id.detail_1, tool.getDetails()[1]);
        findAndSetTextView(R.id.detail_2, tool.getDetails()[2]);
        findAndSetTextView(R.id.description, tool.getDescription());
    }

    private void findAndSetTextView(int id, String text) {
        final TextView textView = (TextView) findViewById(id);
        textView.setText(text);
    }
}
```

With all of this done, we now have a reasonable prototype that we can test with users. To keep this chapter from going on too long, we didn't implement the actual purchase screen (what happens when you press the FAB), but we can explain to users that the purchase feature isn't complete. It's actually fairly common that some pieces will be missing in your prototype (maybe your privacy policy hasn't made it through the gauntlet of lawyers or a particular screen depends on a third-party SDK), so don't let that discourage you from showing what you have so far to users.

Evaluating the First Prototype

Now that you have a working prototype, you can begin testing. First, give it a try yourself. If you coded everything, you've likely interacted with all of the core pieces, but that's often with a focus on just making them function. You're definitely going to have a biased perspective, but you can still catch some of the possible issues either to immediately fix or to keep an eye on when real users interact with the prototype. Does the organization seem logical and simple? Is the positioning and spacing of elements enough to make them appear grouped where they should? Can you easily tell one list item from the next? Some of these can easily be addressed when graphical design is applied to the app such as the distinction between list items, but more significant issues like the organization can require you to step back and make changes to the flow, wireframes, and prototype.

Once you have either fixed the sharp edges or made notes of what to keep an eye on, it's time to get the app in the hands of real users.

Working with Users

The first time you ever show users a working prototype of your app can be exciting and a bit scary. You're not sure what to expect, and you may have a tendency to be defensive. Remember, the users aren't criticizing you; they're critiquing your design theory. You want to be receptive to all feedback at this point and, after working with enough users, you can decide which feedback to act on. You should also keep in mind that people tend to point out things that feel wrong or look out of place far more than they point out what feels right. If you create a painting masterpiece but put a random streak of a bright, out-of-place color across it, how many people do you think will comment about all the details that make the painting great before pointing out that strange streak?

One more thing to consider is that, while some people are eager to critique, others feel like they are being rude by pointing out any issues. It's important to be encouraging ("Wow, that's really good feedback!") rather than discouraging ("Really, that actually matters to you?"). You can also provide encouragement by saying things such as "We feel something just doesn't work on this page, but we haven't figured out what," which makes people feel like they're helping by pointing out all the issues rather than just being negative. A very valuable technique is to get users to think aloud. This is where you have your users talk through what they're thinking as they interact with the app. The dialog might be something like this:

"This looks like an app that has a lot of different drills. I'm not really sure what the difference is between handheld and battery. Let's see what the handheld tab has. Oh maybe these are corded tools. If I tap one of those, it looks like this page has all the detail info. I'm not sure why there's a floating dollar sign."

It's a bit tricky to do well, but it can be exceedingly useful even when it's not done perfectly. You can also get different feedbacks depending on how you direct the users to interact with the app.

Open-Ended

One of the ways you can have users interact with the app is with open-ended exploration. This means you are handing the prototype to a user and letting them just explore it, talking through what they're finding. This type of feedback can be good at revealing what users don't find or interact with, such as if users never try to touch an item in a list.

Specific Goal

Another way to have users interact with the app is to give a specific goal. This goal will depend on the app and should be realistic. For example, in a music streaming app, you might have a user listen to a specific song, which gives you insight into whether users tend to search (and do they search song names, artists, albums, lyrics, etc.) or browse, and you'll see snags along the way. For the tool app, you can give users the task of buying a particular tool that may have requirements such as buying a table saw for under $600.

It can even be helpful to have the users perform a task that can't be completed. It might seem a bit weird, but this lets you see other behavior that isn't exhibited when the users find exactly what they're looking for. Generally, people are encouraged to keep trying as long as they feel like they're making progress. For example, you might be searching for something on a website, drilling into categories that are more and more specific to what you're looking for. Suddenly, you get to a page that doesn't go any deeper and doesn't have what you're looking for. What do you do? Your behavior at this point is very telling of the design.

Dynamic Goal

Having multiple users attempt to accomplish the same goal can help you determine if that goal is easy to accomplish and if a given user is an outlier (if you test with just one person and that person gives up, does that mean your organization was bad overall or was it just bad for this one particular user); however, users will have goals that you don't anticipate or don't think to test. If you describe goals that are slightly less specific or that are more dependent on the users' experience, you may discover something new.

For instance, you can ask the user "What kind of projects do you like to work on?" Once the user has responded, you can follow up with "Pretend you have to create a new woodworking shop from scratch and have to buy all new power tools. Use the app to buy the most important tools for that project." This type of scenario is going to result in a different experience for each user, but you might find out something valuable in addition to just how users navigate the app. You may learn that half of users tend to think about saws before anything else or most users think of price first. These insights can help you revise the app to better meet the needs of your users.

Real User Feedback

Enough of the theory, what does real user feedback actually look like and what do you do with it? Some of the feedback will be spoken by users. For example, putting this prototype in front of users, here is a very small subset of user feedback:

1. I don't understand how the clamps are organized. What the heck is a battery-powered parallel clamp?
2. It feels like there is a missing line in the list.
3. Do you really have a jigsaw with a 12-inch blade? I'd love to see that!
4. I don't know what a router is.
5. What is a quick-grip clamp? It seems like it's easy to grip any kind of clamp.

The first item here is a shortcoming of the prototype. Because we didn't specifically handle clamps, the generated text didn't necessarily make sense for them, but it does reveal a good point: The way we organize the clamps is probably going to be different from how we organize power tools.

Figure 6.7 The list of sanders with no metadata

The second item was in response to the list of sanders (shown in Figure 6.7), which didn't have any metadata to display below the name of each tool in our list. We should make sure each item has metadata or consider if our layout needs to change for cases when metadata isn't available.

The third item is another shortcoming of the prototype. It is pretty common to have a fair bit of feedback related to the prototype not handling all cases. Just consider whether the feedback might be hinting at a problem with the design so far (like the first item) or if it's just an issue with the prototype (like this item).

The fourth item is interesting. Because the users are beginning users, many of them may be unfamiliar with certain tools. This particular user didn't even try tapping the router section to see the about page, so it's worth considering how to encourage users to explore tools more.

The fifth item is similar to the previous one but it's a little more specific. The user knows what clamps are but not what a particular type is. Our design didn't consider individual types, just overall tools.

The other kind of feedback that you'll receive, whether you realize it or not, is behavioral. What did your users actually do when they interacted with the app and what does it mean? Here are some examples:

1. Several users didn't interact with the navigation drawer even when they needed to in order to complete a goal.

2. Some users who did interact with the navigation drawer selected an item, changed tabs, and then immediately reopened the navigation drawer.

3. Some users tried to scroll down past the list of twenty items when given the task "Find a table saw for under $300."

The first item is very troubling. It's likely that many users did not realize that the navigation drawer was available. Given that the only indication of it is the hamburger menu that isn't necessarily immediately obvious to all users, it might be valuable to have the drawer start opened, slightly open and then close, or even closed with a different main screen explaining that the drawer is available.

The second item is more difficult to interpret. Why would users reopen the navigation drawer immediately after selecting a tab? Don't be afraid to ask the users why they do certain things. In this case two users said they weren't sure whether they were still on the right tool section after changing tabs. Another said, "I was seeing if this menu on the side changed after I moved to the other tab." This suggests that it's not obvious whether the top level navigation is the drawer with tabs being subnavigation or if it's the other way around. We might have hoped that the fact that the navigation drawer covers the tabs would help convey its importance, but users don't always pick up clues we think we're leaving nor do they always behave how we'd expect, which shows the importance of testing with real users. Given that both the first item and the second item affected many of our users and both are related to the navigation drawer, it is worth creating a prototype with an alternative.

The third item shows that users are looking for more content. We specifically gave them a task that couldn't be accomplished, and they tried to scroll past the list we provided. Asked why, users said they were trying to load more tools to find one that was the right price. Great! This means users are familiar with the pattern of autoloading more items in a list and that they were confident that the stationary saw section was the right place to find the table saw (which is correct).

Next Steps

It can be difficult to decide how to approach all the user feedback you receive while testing your prototype. Sometimes it's helpful to start with the biggest problem (either the one affected the most users or the one that most significantly impacts the organization of the prototype) and see what other issues might be related. For instance, our biggest problem was the navigation drawer. It was nonobvious and caused confusion even for those who found it. Related to that, we had a user that very specifically didn't tap on an item in the drawer because it was unfamiliar. Perhaps we can address all of these by putting the tools directly on a main screen, letting users drill into them from there so that the main screen doesn't have any tabs? With them on the main screen, we have the opportunity to test having images or text to help explain what the tools are.

We also need to consider how to organize the clamps section and the more section, which don't make sense when they're organized the same way as the others. Perhaps the tabs can be based on the currently selected tool type. Because they're going to be on another screen, it isn't as strange to have different tabs as it would be with our current navigation.

Once you have considered the user feedback and how you can address it, it's time to update your wireframes and your prototype. Then you test with users again. It might seem like you've solved all the issues, so why bother testing again? Have you ever written some code, tried it out only to find there's a bug, fixed that bug, and tried it again (perhaps to find a new bug)? This iterative User-Centered Design process is exactly the same. The real difference is that computers will do what you tell them to (even when it's not what you really meant), but you never know what users will do.

Summary

In this chapter, you learned how to quickly create prototype apps based on wireframes. You should now feel confident creating layouts that can demonstrate wireframes on a real device, although you will get more practice in future chapters. The important thing to take away from this chapter is that the wireframe is a theory, and you create a prototype to test that theory. To actually test that theory, you work with real users and understand their interactions with your app. Sometimes you find that you have to completely throw out all the wireframes, but that's okay. Proving that something does not work is an important part of iterating on the app, and it's far better to throw it out now than to develop the whole thing and release it only to find out you have a core issue that you didn't know about.

The next chapter shows how design can be applied to wireframes. The design retains the information hierarchy of the wireframes but can give the app a completely different feel.

CHAPTER 7

DESIGNING THE VISUALS

Now that you have completed wireframes and prototypes, you should have a good foundational knowledge upon which to build your designs. Good graphical design is a combination of art and science, understanding how to make something both beautiful and functional. Even if you're a developer reading this book who will have a designer handle creating comps, slices, and assets, it is very beneficial to understand the basics of what goes into a good design.

Wireframes and Graphical Design

Although wireframes were primarily covered in Chapter 5, "Starting a New App," you should come back to them after trying to create prototypes and improve them. The cycle is iterative, like any development process, and having a solid set of wireframes will lead to a much better graphical design.

At this point, it may seem like the graphical design is just coloring between the lines created by the wireframes, but it is never that easy, nor should it be that limited. The wireframes serve as a logical grouping of content, an expectation of user interaction and user experience. They are intended to make the user expectations blatant. You would likely draw a box around related form elements in a wireframe, but the actual visual design might have just a background difference or even a common treatment to the form elements letting their visual proximity create the same grouping that the obvious box did in the wireframes.

Graphical design serves the two sides of the app: what the stakeholders want and what the users need. On one side, you have brand requirements. On the other, you have user expectations. The graphical design has to marry those together and, ideally, do it in a visually pleasing way. The produced designs that show exactly how the app should look are called "comps." Sometimes the design will include comps for all the main screens and states plus directions for other scenarios to be supported (such as empty pages, loading states, and long titles).

Chances are you know what the brand requirements are. There is a certain logo to use, a specific color palette to work with, and other constraining factors. Knowing the user side of the equation is a little harder. Some of this comes out in the wireframes, where you can define the user interface (UI) based on what makes sense to the target audience. An interactive book aimed at young children should have large touch areas and large fonts, but a painting app for artists is going to have precise touch controls and an interface based largely on iconography that borrows from what the artists have learned from other creative apps.

Tools

Just like with wireframing, there are countless tools out there for graphical design. The most known is Adobe's ubiquitous Photoshop (http://www.adobe.com/products/photoshop.html). It is exceedingly powerful and offers pixel-level precision. You can use filters, layer blending, and custom masks to create impressive visuals. But, as Uncle Ben said, with great power comes a steep learning curve (or something like that). If you're inexperienced with Photoshop, you can quickly become frustrated with simple tasks like creating arrows. The closest open source program is Gimp (http://www.gimp.org/). It isn't as full-featured or as polished as Photoshop, but it does work on Linux and is free. If you're on a Mac and looking for something a bit more polished than Gimp, consider Pixelmator (http://www.pixelmator.com/mac/).

Another Adobe product that can be used for graphic design is Illustrator (http://www.adobe.com/products/illustrator.html). Since Illustrator is vector-based, it can make it easier to create some assets. Remember that vector graphics describe lines and shapes relative to each other, which means they can scale infinitely. With design trends moving away from textures and heavy blending, Illustrator is well suited for graphic design of modern apps. The closest open source equivalent is Inkscape (https://inkscape.org/en/). It has most of the core features from Illustrator, but there are a lot of important features that are lacking in comparison. Of course, free is an appealing price for those on a budget.

There are also some newer tools such as Sketch (http://bohemiancoding.com/sketch/) for OS X. You should take some time searching for whichever tool works for you. You may even find that you use different tools for different design tasks.

Styles

Looking across art throughout history, you can see there are many different styles, and graphical design of apps is the same. There is no need for you to learn all the different styles at this point, but understanding a few of the big ones that have had particular impact in mobile apps can help as you determine how to approach graphically designing your own apps. An app doesn't necessarily fit into one category perfectly; it can mix and match as desired.

Skeuomorphism

Skeuomorphism is probably the design style that is most polarizing; people either love it or hate it. In simple terms, skeuomorphism is designing an object to mimic another, particularly elements that were required in the original. For instance, a software button might have a texture that makes it look metallic and pressing it causes the graphics to change, giving it the appearance of being depressed; the physical button that this software mimics required that movement to complete or break an electrical circuit. You'll also see detailed imitations of microphones and even tape recorders with a spinning supply reel.

The benefit of skeuomorphism is that it allows people to grasp onto a concept because it can be familiar such as the idea of pushing a button despite that they're really just touching a piece of glass that doesn't move in response. It also gives graphic designers the opportunity to create extremely life-like designs. The disadvantage is that it limits your design based on constraints of the object that's being emulated even when that might not make sense.

Design trends have been moving away from skeuomorphism for many years, and every designer is likely to give you a different reason for that. Skeuomorphism isn't inherently bad, but one of the big challenges of this design style is the tendency to put more emphasis on visual appearance than the actual user experience. Consider how many calculator apps mimic pocket calculators. Even when Apple released the first iPhone with an impressive touchscreen and a powerful processor, the calculator app drew heavy design influence from the Braun ET44 pocket calculator. With all this technology, shouldn't there be a better design than mimicking limited calculators of decades past?

Minimalism

Minimalism is a design language that relies on as little visual design as possible. That doesn't mean that no effort goes into it (in fact, good minimalist designs are very challenging to create); it means the effort goes into determining exactly what elements are required and eliminating any superfluous. For example, many designs include dividers between sections such as in lists, but a minimalist design might visually cluster those sections so that the divider is implied. Boxes around elements and colored sections are often eliminated by using proximity.

Flat Design

Flat design eliminates texture and the shadows that are used to create a sense of depth, giving it a minimalist quality. Gradients and other embellishments are also avoided. Although not strictly required for flat design, bright colors are frequently used as a means of grouping content or creating emphasis. Microsoft's design language (known widely as "Metro") relies on a lot of the elements of flat design, but it puts particular emphasis on typography in an effort to move away from the heavy reliance on icons that many designs have.

With iOS 7, Apple ditched their skeuomorphic design language, moving toward a flatter (but not purely flat) design. Although Apple still uses a few shadows here and there, they have largely eliminated shadows as an indicator of depth. Panels slide in and out, obscuring other content to appear in front. Sometimes Apple uses a translucent blurring effect (similar to the "Aero" style first used in Windows Vista) that further reinforces that the panel is in front of other content.

As you can probably already tell, design tends to shift and evolve borrowing elements from other places and changing them to match differing needs.

Material Design

And what about Material Design? It is a bit of all three. It uses the concept of "paper" meant to mimic real life paper but with fewer constraints (such as the ability to grow, shrink, or join multiple pieces together). This paper might be considered skeuomorphic, indeed it even casts shadows at higher elevations, but it doesn't have texturing like real paper. The surface itself is flat. The ink applied to Material Design's paper is often bright and vivid, which is more common with flat designs. Material Design is also focused on the content and takes a more minimalistic approach to embellishments. Anything added to a Material Design layout is intended to be purposeful and add to the experience.

The designs discussed in this book focus primarily on Material Design. That isn't meant to say that any other style is "wrong," but Material Design has two major benefits: it is a current trend (which means your apps will look modern and fit in) and it is a comprehensive design language that has been well thought out.

Lighting

For years, most app designs have had lighting that comes from either the top left or the top center of the screen. This causes raised shapes to be slightly brighter at the top where the light reflects more directly (sometimes referred to as a "hot spot") and slightly darker at the bottom where the shape is in shadow. Depressed shapes are the opposite with shadows at the top and brighter spots at the bottom. Figure 7.1 illustrates this better than words can.

Figure 7.1 The left image looks elevated while the right image looks depressed

Material Design has a key light (definition) at the top center of the screen, casting light directly down, but it also has an ambient light. If you take a photo of someone outside on an overcast day, the light will be very even as it filters through the clouds. To make that person stand out more, you can use a light shining on that person from the front, often from an angle. This light gives that person more shape and draws attention; it's a key light. Despite that you are shining a light on the front of the person the shadow behind your subject isn't black. Light comes down from the sun, bouncing around through the clouds, and off of the trees and the rest of the environment to give some lighting to nearly all surfaces. This light that seems to be everywhere is called ambient light. It creates soft shadows (hold your hand a few inches above a surface and you can see the shadows below it), and these soft shadows are a key part of Material Design. They show when a surface is elevated and by how much. They also create a soft aesthetic that is visually pleasing.

Generally speaking, you want shadows to be subtle, adding dimensionality to your layout without taking the focus away from the content. Shadows are a visual cue that something is elevated, helping to create depth and separate different UI layers. Combined with purposeful color choices, shadows can draw attention to particular parts of your design (such as a floating action button).

Colors

Books have been written on color theory. The way our eyes and visual cortex process wavelengths to see color is complex and fascinating. The way our brains create associations and meanings based on those colors is no simpler. That means there isn't an easy answer to color choice, but there are certainly a few tips that can help steer you in the right direction.

The Science

Before diving into specific colors, it's a good idea to know a few of the ways of thinking about colors. You already know the idea of making colors from red, green, and blue channels. This is an additive process where more color brings you brighter and whiter colors. In print, CMYK is often used. This subtractive process combines cyan, magenta, yellow, and black to create all other colors. The more color you add, the closer you get to black. These are both ways to think of colors based on how individual channels can be combined, but another way to think about colors is hue, saturation, and brightness (or HSB).

Hue is basically color. If you take a color wheel (shown in Figure 7.2), the hue correlates to a particular degree. It doesn't have a sense of how bright/dark or vibrant/subdued the color is; hue is simply the color somewhere along the spectrum.

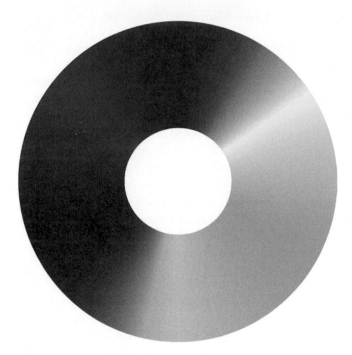

Figure 7.2 A typical color wheel

Saturation is how pure the hue is. A saturation of zero would be a medium gray without any of the hue applied; a saturation of 100% would be entirely the color chosen without gray. All values in between are a mixture of gray and the hue. Figure 7.3 shows how a single hue can range from 0% saturation to 100%. That means that a color with a higher saturation will appear more vibrant than a color with lower saturation, which can look dull or muddied. Figure 7.4 shows a range of colors in columns. The hue is exactly the same for each rectangle in the column, but the rows show saturations of 25%, 50%, 75%, and 100%. You can see that the colors at the

Figure 7.3 A range of saturation from 0% on the left to 100% on the right

Figure 7.4 Columns of different hues with each row at a different saturation

bottom with full saturation are significantly more vivid than the colors higher up, which have a gray, muddied appearance.

Brightness is how much black is mixed in. With a value of 0% for brightness, you've have pure black. A value of 100% means that you aren't adding any black, so you have the brightest value for the hue that you've chosen. Figure 7.5 shows a brightness range for cyan. Sometimes this is referred to as "value" (making the abbreviation HSV) because our perception of brightness is slightly different based on hue; a yellow will seem to be brighter than blue even when the saturation and brightness are the same.

Figure 7.5 Cyan from 0% brightness on the left to 100% on the right

Why bother thinking about colors in terms of HSB instead of RGB? After all, RGB is pretty simple, right? One advantage of HSB is that it lets you quickly compare the saturation of colors and the brightness of colors. Another is that it is easier to choose related colors. Consider the colors Google recommends for Material Design (available at http://www.google.com/design/spec/

style/color.html). For each color, they provide several variants labeled with numbers from 50 to 900 along with the RGB hex values. Taking purple as an example, the colors range from #F3E5F5 to #4A148C. If you're human, you probably don't get much meaning out of those hex values. In comparison, the HSB values for the lightest color are 292, 7%, and 96%, respectively; the HSB values for the darkest color are 267, 86%, and 55%. You can see that the hue shifts some, but the significant changes are with saturation and brightness. Figure 7.6 plots these out in a chart to visualize how these values change from the 50 color to the 900 color. Because hue is a degree value, the chart shows its value divided by 360 to plot it on the same axis as the saturation and brightness.

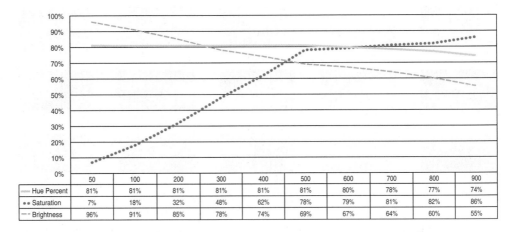

	50	100	200	300	400	500	600	700	800	900
Hue Percent	81%	81%	81%	81%	81%	81%	80%	78%	77%	74%
Saturation	7%	18%	32%	48%	62%	78%	79%	81%	82%	86%
Brightness	96%	91%	85%	78%	74%	69%	67%	64%	60%	55%

Figure 7.6 Chart plotting the hue, saturation, and brightness of the suggested purple

You can see that the saturation change is almost completely linear until the 500 color and then it's very flat. The brightness has a relatively consistent drop off. The hue is interesting because it is almost unchanged from the 50 color to the 500 and then shifts to lower values, pushing it toward blue. Although the exact values of each of Google's suggest colors are different, the trends are very similar. Saturation increases as the brightness decreases. Purple had a pretty significant hue shift in the darker colors, but most of Google's other color suggestions only vary the hue by a few degrees.

Choosing Colors

Armed with a better understanding of colors, you might still be wondering how to pick them. The Material Design guidelines recommend picking a color from the 500 level as your primary, a color from the 700 or 800 level as your darker primary, and a separate accent color. You can certainly create any kind of color scheme you want, but starting with this simple pattern can work well. So how do you choose your primary color?

This part isn't so scientific. Color choice has an incalculable number of factors from cultural meanings to color harmony and even visual impairment considerations. Some colors are viewed as warmer (reds, oranges, and yellows), which feel more energetic; others are cooler (greens, blues, and purples), which are more calming. Cultural meanings can be difficult, especially if your product will be available worldwide or in a region you're unfamiliar with, but you can even think of the ones you know. For instance, red is often a color associating with stopping or with warnings. It's a bold color choice that Google made work for the Gmail app and Google+. Given the popularity of those apps, you may wish to opt for another color.

Orange is sometimes associated with warnings as well, but it also conveys excitement and warmth. I developed an app called Permission Informant to let users easily see which apps on their devices were using which permissions. I chose orange for that app because it had both conveyed some sense of caution around permissions and gives a strong and bold vibrancy to the app that otherwise has few visual elements. Figure 7.7 shows the main screen of the Permission Informant app.

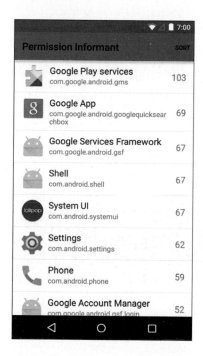

Figure 7.7 The Permission Informant app, which uses a vivid orange primary color

Yellow is a cheerful color, but it is perceived as extremely bright. It can be a difficult color to use as your primary color due to that brightness, but it can work well for apps that want to create a playful excitement. It can be a good choice for apps targeted at kids or any audience where being upbeat can be beneficial.

Green is strongly associated with nature and sometimes with finances as well. It can be a good choice for most apps because it doesn't clash with many other colors (though you may have to tone down reds) and you can even create a visually interesting app with multiple shades of green.

Blue is one of the most frequently chosen colors. It works well with most colors other than yellow. It's the color of the sky and the ocean, so we're naturally used to seeing large sections of blue. It's viewed as a safe choice used by some of the biggest brands out there, so its popularity may be something to consider. If you're choosing blue, your design will probably be fine, but it might not stand out against Facebook, Twitter, and many others that have chosen blue as well.

Violet is a very rich color full of vibrancy. Being a mix of red and blue, you can add more red to give it a warmer feel or more blue for a cooler feel. It's sometimes associated with royalty, but it doesn't have strong meanings in most cultures.

If your app is focused almost entirely on displaying photos, you might opt to not have a strong primary color. Traditionally, these types of apps have been white, gray, or black because those colors won't interfere with the colors in photos. You can also experiment with colors that have a very low saturation, such as Google's blue-gray, which has just 31% saturation at the 500 level.

If your app has a particular brand color already, you might use that. For instance, maybe your brand color is #268056, a green with some cyan mixed in. It could be used as your primary color, but you need to come up with a darker version. The HSB values of this green are 152, 70%, and 50%, respectively. From the previous section, you know that a darker version will have an increased saturation and a decreased brightness. The exact amount depends on the desired effect, but you always want to make design choices appear purposeful. In other words, you don't want two colors that are almost identical because the difference will look like a mistake. By increasing the saturation to 80% and decreasing the brightness to 35%, the color looks sufficiently darker with the same hue.

The accent color you choose should be sufficiently different from your primary color to stand out. It keeps your application looking vibrant while drawing attention to specific elements such as a floating action button or interactive controls. There are no hard rules about choosing an accent color, but one of the easy ways is to look near the opposite side of the color wheel from your primary color. It doesn't need to be exactly opposite, but you generally want it to be a warm color if your primary color is cool and vice versa. Figure 7.8 shows the green from the previous paragraph near the bottom right of the color wheel with the colors closest to it faded out somewhat. Any of the colors that are vibrant (opposite of that green) are potentially good candidates for accent colors. You can choose one of the accent colors that lines up with one of Google's suggestions (any of the "A" colors below the primary colors) or you can create your own by selecting a hue that is somewhere roughly opposite of the primary color and then adjusting the saturation and brightness. Most accent colors will have high values for the saturation and brightness, though you can experiment to see what works. Figure 7.9 is an example of the two greens and a purple accent.

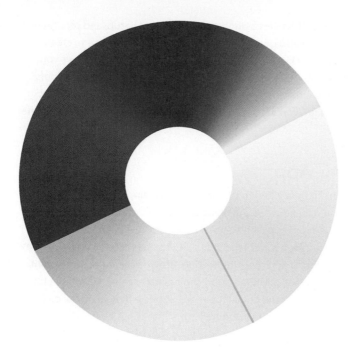

Figure 7.8 Color wheel showing the primary color at the bottom right and potential accent colors at the top left

Figure 7.9 An example color scheme with a primary color on the left, primary dark color in the middle, and accent color on the right

Still need help deciding? There are plenty of tools for determining full color schemes that can help you decide. For instance, Adobe's Color (previously called Kuler) is a nice tool that's easy to use (https://color.adobe.com/create/color-wheel/), but there are many others out there, so don't be afraid to take a look at others.

Color vision deficiencies (colloquially referred to as "color blindness") are another consideration when choosing colors. The most common forms affect the ability to differentiate red and green hues from one another, but there are also color vision deficiencies that affect the ability to differentiate yellow and blue and even to differentiate color altogether (although quite rare). If you're using a recent version of Photoshop, you can preview your designs to get a feel for how they look to those with color vision deficiencies by going to View, Proof Setup, and picking one of the Color Blindness options. You can also go to Window, Arrange, New Window to create another view of the same document. Picking Window, Arrange, Tile All Vertically allows you to see both of these views side by side. You can then apply one of the color blindness proofs to easily compare full-color vision to either common color vision deficiency. One quick check you can do to help ensure your design works is to convert it to grayscale and ensure that all the essential elements are still obvious.

The Woodworking App

With all this knowledge, how could it be applied to the woodworking app from the previous chapters? What primary color would make sense? An obvious choice might be brown. It's the color of wood, so it may work well for the app. The Material Design brown has a lower saturation that makes the color feel mellow, even a bit bland. By taking that color and increasing the saturation, the brown looks more vibrant and more interesting. Brown is near the same point as orange on the color wheel, making blue and cyan good choices for accents. Given that blue is so common, cyan might make the app stand out a little more. Just like that, an initial color scheme is available to start working with as seen in Figure 7.10.

Figure 7.10 The color scheme for the woodworking app

Text Considerations

You will primarily communicate with your users through visuals and through text. Getting the text right is as important as getting your visuals right, so be sure to give text the proper level of consideration. Both the appearance of your text and its content influence how effectively a user can read and interpret what you're communicating.

When creating comps, use real text. It's easy to fall into the habit of using "lorem ipsum" filler text, but that can create a disconnect from the real content. How long are the titles? Is the text full of long, scientific terms or short capitalized acronyms? By using real text in your designs, you are forced to consider whether text should wrap and how full or empty the design will really be. This is one of the times when it is very useful for designers to work with the development team (including any server-side developers, when applicable) to get examples of real content. If a designer just creates a screen that shows a list of country names for the user to pick from, "U.S.A." might fit the design perfectly, but how does it look when the server actually returns "United States of America" instead?

In cases where you are designing for an app that does not yet have any real text defined, it's a little harder to make sure the comps are representative of the final product. Sometimes you can look at similar apps to get a feel for what kinds of text they handle. Other times you just have to take a stab at it and potentially revise once the real text is determined.

Text Contrast

To be easily read, your app's text must have enough contrast with its background. According to the WCAG (Web Content Accessibility Guidelines), your text should have a *minimum* 4.5-to-1 contrast ratio. There are a variety of online tools for determining contrast ratios such as the one at snook.ca (http://www.snook.ca/technical/colour_contrast/colour.html) and the one by Lea Verou (http://leaverou.github.com/contrast-ratio). There are also simple desktop programs that can make calculating contrast easy as well. Contrast Analyser for Windows and Mac is available at http://www.paciellogroup.com/resources/contrast-analyser.html and allows you to quickly check contrasts by using eyedropper tools for picking colors from anywhere on your screen.

Why should you care about maintaining this contrast ratio for text? After all, isn't this intended for people with visual impairments who actually represent a fairly small percentage of users? Although it's easy to dismiss the need for high contrast because it does not always let you create the visual design that you want, it's important to remember that this affects far more people than you might realize. Yes, there are the obvious users who benefit the most from higher contrast, such as those with color vision deficiencies and older users with presbyopia, but high-contrast text makes the app easier to use for everyone, even those with excellent vision. Consider also that your app may run on a variety of devices, each of a different size with a different screen technology. Add in that many devices are woefully reflective and users may be outside in the sun, and suddenly it seems everything is working against designs that don't ensure a high contrast in the text.

Hopefully, you are doing your designing on a high-quality monitor that has been calibrated, but you still have to keep in mind that the app will be running on devices with AMOLEDs, which usually have high-contrast ratios and can have oversaturated colors. It will also run on low-quality TFT LCDs, which often display only a fraction of the full color gamut. Throw some glare on top of a screen with lowered brightness because the user is trying to squeeze the last bit of battery life out of the device, and high contrast becomes vital.

One more consideration with text contrast is the pattern of the background. Whenever possible, the background should be a solid color or a simple gradient. A background with lines, zigzags, and other shapes will interfere with the user's ability to see the text. If it is okay to make the text difficult to read, then the text must not be very important. If the text is not important, why is it in your app?

Text Sizes, Styles, and Capitalization

Text sizes should be established very early on in the design process. It's too easy to decide on sizes for each individual screen and end up with a dozen different sizes in the app. By limiting the number of sizes, you allow the user to quickly learn what they mean. A good starting point is 24sp for headlines and titles, 16sp for subheadings, 14sp for body text, and 12sp for captions and fine print.

You can always adjust the font sizes as needed, but sticking to a small set of sizes will keep your design consistent. These sizes will be reasonably consistent across devices (e.g., text that is 24dp will appear to be about the same size on multiple devices), with the caveat that the user can increase font sizes. In general, you do not need to design for each possible font size that the user could change to, but you should keep in mind that the sizes can be changed. For instance, try to avoid designing something that requires the text to be an exact height and breaks otherwise.

Android supports the typical range of styling for text such as bold, italic, and underline. As with any design, use these sparingly. If everything is bold, nothing is. If an entire paragraph is in italics, it is simply harder for the user to read. If every other word is underlined, there is a lot of visual clutter for the user to make sense of.

Using all capitals should be limited to brief labels or actions (such as "DELETE" on a button). A large amount of capitalized text is difficult to read, so avoid ever using capitals for body text or any significant portion of text, which can include items in a list.

Text Spacing

Unfortunately, Android is extremely limited when it comes to spacing in text. Line spacing, also called "leading" (and pronounced 'ledding'), can be adjusted by a multiplier (e.g., use 1 or 1.5) and an extra amount that's added or subtracted. For example, you can use a line spacing of 1.5 and add 2sp to each line, but you cannot do much more than that. One important thing to know is that if you are decreasing the line spacing, you may end up clipping descenders (the portion of a letter that goes below the baseline, such as the bottom of a *g*), so you may have to compensate with extra padding.

Android does not natively support adjusting kerning or tracking. Implementing custom kerning is a nontrivial effort, so it's best to pick a font that already has a default kerning that works for your design. The hours that would be spent developing a custom view to display a font with a slightly different kerning can be better spent on other aspects of the app.

Text Shadows

Text shadows can be used to give a little extra to some text, but they're largely unused in apps following Material Design. This is because letters are created with ink and ink is two dimensional. It dyes the paper; it doesn't float above the paper.

Android has one particular quirk about the way it handles text shadows. Essentially the shadow is drawn and then the text is drawn on top of it. This sounds obvious and generally works, but having partially transparent text means that the shadow shows through the text. In some cases, this can be what you want, but it often just works to muddy the text. You end up with your text color where the shadow isn't, a mix of your text color and the shadow where they overlap, and just the shadow outside of that.

Custom Fonts

Traditionally, Android used the Droid family of fonts. The Droid fonts worked but they were not as clean as some more popular fonts such as Helvetica. Fortunately, the font Roboto was specifically designed for Android and added in Ice Cream Sandwich (Android 4.0). For most designs, this font should be considered first because it has been specifically built for mobile devices of varying densities and tends to render better across screen types, including those that don't use traditional RGB striping. Google continues to improve Roboto, morphing it into a better font with every iteration, so you might consider including the latest version in your app if you support older versions of Android that don't have the latest version.

You can divide and group typefaces in a variety of ways, but this book will simply break them into serif, sans serif, monospace, and script as shown in Figure 7.11.

Serif fonts were considered the standard for a long time. They get their name from serifs, which are lines at the ends of strokes. Figure 7.12 shows these lines highlighted to make them more obvious. Serif fonts are commonly used in print, particularly in novels or books with dense text.

Figure 7.11 Four categories of fonts

Serif

Figure 7.12 A serif font with the serifs in red

Sans serif fonts are fonts that don't have serifs ("sans" is French for "without"). Roboto, the primary font of Android, is a sans serif font. As serif fonts had been the norm for a long time, the appearance of fonts without serifs around 200 years ago earned them the name "grotesque." Other terms evolved such as gothic, which was used commonly in America after a sans serif font of that name was created. Eventually, the name sans serif became the standard, but you'll still run into many others if you read much about typography.

Sans serif fonts are generally considered more modern and (debatably) easier to read on digital displays. They work well on high-density displays, which are common on mobile devices now, and have largely become the standard typeface for digital content.

If you've done any development, you've undoubtedly used monospace fonts. As the name implies, these fonts have the same spacing for every character. This was out of necessity in early typewriters, but it's still desirable in cases where aligning characters is important (such as programming). Many non-monospace typefaces keep all numeric characters the same size because aligning numbers is somewhat common.

Script typefaces are those that imitate cursive form. If you aren't a skilled designer, you should just stay away from these. They're difficult to read, so the number of use cases in which they make sense is very small and largely reserved for things that need to appear more traditional or formal (such as wedding invitations).

What does all this mean to you? Well, if you did not follow any of that, then you should use Roboto. If you are dead set on using another font, be sure to test it on multiple screens (consider densities as well as subpixel layouts). Many thin/light fonts will not look good on low-density displays, especially those that use a PenTile matrix.

Accessible Vocabulary

Text is not all about appearance. One of the important things to consider with text is how understandable it is to the end user. If you're targeting a general audience, that means you have to consider a variety of educational levels. Whenever possible, use plain, obvious language. For instance, don't say "reauthenticate" when you can say "log in again." Avoid technical jargon, use words consistently, and be succinct.

Other Considerations

It is easy to design for the ideal case, but you also have to consider each of the other states of the app. What does it look like when content is loading? What about when it fails to load? What if the content is longer or shorter than expected?

Varying Text Lengths

Although it was mentioned earlier, it's worth mentioning again: Use real content for your comps. Forcing yourself to use real content means your comps are much more likely to encounter the same scenarios that the developer will have to handle. If you design all your comps for ideal text sizes ("Hey, I've got enough room for a four-letter username, so 'Jake' would be perfect!"), you end up with great comps that don't help the development of the app as much as they should. The developer ends up trying to make reasonable guesses as to how to handle the real content and the developer probably has neither a background in design nor the time to really consider how the UI will be affected. Of course, that doesn't mean every case needs to be designed. Oftentimes, it is enough to design for the 80-percent case (in other words, pick text that is representative of 80% of use cases) and include details about how to handle others (e.g., "limit text to one line and ellipsize").

Image Availability and Size

Include placeholder images for any images that will be loaded dynamically. The user experience becomes very jarring when images suddenly appear and text jumps around on the page to accommodate those images. Be sure to consider the aspect ratio of images. If you're connecting to a service that you have no control over for the images, you are going to need to take a representative sample and see how they look cropped in different ways. Do they need to fill the space or be fully displayed? Should they be enlarged if they're too small?

Transparency and the 3× Rule

Transparency has many uses in design. It is a simple way of lowering contrast and blending parts of a UI together. Transparency can also be used for visual effects such as crossfading between two images. However, there is an important performance consideration with transparency. Many devices are fill-rate limited. That means they can only push so many pixels (typically due to a limited graphics pipeline). You might think that a device only needs to push as many pixels as are displayed on the screen, but that's not always the case. If you have several layers, you may have to draw pixels on top of pixels. In the case of software rendering, pixels are typically drawn using the painter's algorithm. The farthest/deepest layer is drawn first, then the next layer on top of that, and the next one, and so forth. Because of this drawing method, the device may be drawing pixels that are covered up entirely, thus wasting bandwidth. Hardware rendering can often be smarter, which can optimize opaque layers, but it still has to calculate for mixing partially transparent pixels.

The problem with transparency is that regardless of the rendering method, the pixels must be blended. That means having a black background and a white foreground with 50% transparency will draw all the black pixels and then the white pixels. If that is drawing 60 times per second, you have less than 17 milliseconds per frame to draw every pixel on the screen twice. Add more transparent pixels and suddenly you're drawing three times as many pixels as the screen displays in 17 milliseconds. It doesn't take long before the result is a choppy UI, particularly during animation and scrolling.

The general rule of thumb is to avoid drawing more than three times the total pixels on the screen. This isn't a hard limit and some devices can handle more than this, but sticking to this limit means that your UI will appear smooth on a variety of devices.

Standard Icons

The Android design site has a section specifically on iconography that is well worth reading (http://developer.android.com/design/style/iconography.html). It covers the different types of icons and their technical requirements, but it also links out to the Material Design guidelines where appropriate. Be sure to read these thoroughly before creating any icons for your app, whether they're launcher icons, notification bar icons, action bar icons, or something else entirely.

Android's launcher icons can be any shape you desire, so consider using shape to help users locate your app. For example, if your app is a world exploration app, your icon might be an image of the world, effectively a circle. Do not just create a rounded rectangle because it's common or can be used on iOS as well. Shape is one of the key visual indicators that people use to identify something, so use this flexibility of Android to your advantage. For details on creating app icons, see Appendix A, "Google Play Assets."

Navigation and Transitions

Considering navigation and transitions between UI early and often will help ensure that you create a better overall user experience. What does the UI look like while it is being interacted with? What about when swiping between lists? How does the next screen animate in? Just like the rest of the design, these considerations aren't just aesthetic. For example, the way in which the next view animates in affects whether the user perceives it as a new page and thus whether he or she thinks the back button will reverse the transition. Animations are covered more in Chapter 9, "Polishing with Animations."

Error Cases

Do not forget your error cases. Do not forget your error cases. No, repeating that was not a mistake. Gracefully handling errors is a significant user experience consideration that should be well designed. This covers everything from the user entering an invalid email address to the device running out of storage space. It is very common to not design for these cases and to end up with a thrown together result such as an ugly pop-up that just says, "No space available." That is neither good looking nor useful for the user. In fact, these non-designed errors can feel rather jarring, which makes them much more troubling to the user. Instead of thinking, "Oh, I forgot the 'at' symbol in my email address," the user might think, "What did I break?"

If an app is well designed, even the error states are designed and feel like they belong. Error messages should simply acknowledge a problem and give the user enough information to act on the problem, without being judgmental. Sometimes you can use simple animations to draw the user's attention to an error (such as a minor shake of an `EditText` field). Other times it is enough to use color to indicate where a problem lies.

Designing Step-by-Step

In the previous chapter, user studies revealed that the initial wireframes weren't quite ready. The navigation drawer wasn't ideal and combining it with tabs on the main screen caused issues, so a new wireframe was created. Figure 7.13 shows the new wireframe for the main screen. Notice that each tool type is given a large image as well as the name. Through user testing, it became clear that including an image significantly helped users understand each section.

By simply adding the color scheme created earlier in the chapter, the main screen looks like Figure 7.14. This little splash of a vivid brown is beginning to bring some life to the app.

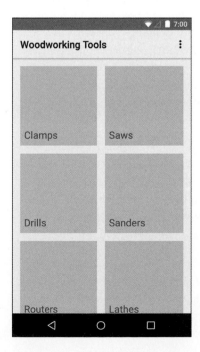

Figure 7.13 Updated wireframe for the woodworking app's main screen

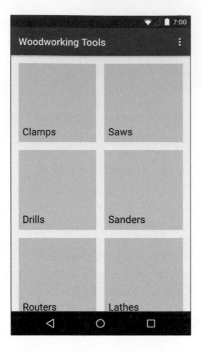

Figure 7.14 Beginning the design with the color scheme

It might seem like there isn't much to design here; however, even deciding how to display the combined text plus image can take a fair bit of effort and experimentation. Any time you place text over an image, you have to be careful to ensure readability. Generally, you want the text fairly large to help it stand out from the background. You also want to ensure enough contrast with the image, which is the bigger challenge. Images could have any color of background, so just plunking some text on top and hoping for the best means you're likely to have some of the text very readable when the background image just happens to work and some text that is virtually impossible to read.

There are three main ways to handle this: (1) change the brightness of some or all of the photo, (2) add a background to the text, and (3) blur the background behind the text. The part that you're adding to help the readability is called a scrim (the term comes from a piece of equipment in photography called a scrim, which is generally fabric that will reduce the intensity of light). You can also combine these for the effect you want. You should generally use either white or black text because they will have more contrast than anything in between.

Assuming white text is desirable, the simplest change is darkening the image. By adding 50% black to an image, white text on it is guaranteed to have at least a decent level of contrast. This solution might be easy, but it tends to be a poor choice for larger images because the image becomes more difficult to see, which partly defeats the purpose of having it in the first place. You could instead just darken the portion of the image behind the text. This gives you a crisp

Figure 7.15 The original image at the left, the full-image scrim in the center, and the text area scrim on the right

edge to the scrim that may or may not be the effect you're looking for. Figure 7.15 shows the original image with white text, the full image scrim, and the text area scrim.

If you want to darken the background of just the text, but you don't want a harsh edge, you can use a gradient that darkens the bottom portion of the most and fades out higher up. You can also use text shadows with the blur value high enough to ensure that the shadow isn't immediately obvious. Figure 7.16 shows both these techniques.

Figure 7.16 A gradient scrim on the left and a scrim using a blurred text shadow on the right

Another technique is using a blur. By blurring the portion of the image immediately behind the text, you ensure that there aren't harsh lines that might interfere with the text, but you don't necessarily ensure enough contrast. You can both blur the background behind the text and darken it slightly to improve the contrast. Figure 7.17 shows the background blur with and without the darkened portion.

Figure 7.17 A blurred background on the left and a blurred background that's also darkened on the right

With all these options, which one do you choose? Sometimes it helps to see all of them together at a smaller size so you can better tell how readable the text is (see Figure 7.18). All of these techniques can work, but some work better than others. For the design of the woodworking app, the scrim will be a combination of a background blur and the crisp text area scrim, using the primary dark color. This gives a sharp look that helps attract attention to the text and also keeps the image feeling warmer than a black or gray scrim would. See Figure 7.19 to see how the screen looks with this applied.

Figure 7.18 All of the scrim examples side-by-side can help make it easier to decide which works best for your use

When you have a solid set of wireframes ready that have been tested with real users, the design process goes much faster. Using that solid foundation, you can add in a color scheme and begin painting the broad areas like the status bar and the app bar. After that, filling in images and determining how the text around them will look can significantly help shape the design.

Figure 7.19 The updated main screen with scrims applied

Summary

Designing an effective UI is a lot of work. You have to consider what stakeholders want and what users need, somehow finding the balance between using existing patterns and visuals and creating a new, recognizable design. You also have to consider what is technically feasible, which brings up the importance of having the designer(s) and developer(s) communicate early and often. That communication is extremely valuable because it also forces the designer to talk through why the design is the way it is (what is it trying to accomplish), ensuring that the developer understands the decisions and knows which aspects are most important when the design might not be able to be perfectly met in code. Establish your patterns early (fonts, text sizes, color palette, touch states, and so on) and ensure that they are consistent. Use color as a secondary indicator and follow conventions where applicable.

In the next chapter, you will see how to begin implementing an actual design.

CHAPTER 8

APPLYING THE DESIGN

Once you have a design ready to implement, you have to start breaking it apart into the various Android views needed to re-create the design as faithfully as possible. The first step to this is to really understand the design, and this means that the designer and developer need to communicate early and often. Once the developer knows what the designer intends, the developer can communicate what assets are needed and begin implementing the design. This chapter focuses on both the communication between the developer and the designer and the techniques a developer can use to create the design in the app.

Working with the Designer

One of the challenges when applying design to an Android app is that developers and designers tend to speak different languages. Developers use Android Studio and Gradle; designers use Photoshop and Illustrator. Developers speak in density-independent pixels and scale-independent pixels; designers speak in pixels and points. Developers typically focus on function and designers focus on form; the best designers and developers consider both form and function.

One other thing to consider in the differences between developers and designers is that there are specialties. Developers often don't realize that there are many types of design specialties such as graphic design (a focus on the visual elements of a design) and interactive design (a focus on how the user interacts with the visual elements of a design). Most designers, especially in the mobile environment, have experience with several of the design specialties, but they often have more expertise in one specialty. The same is true of developers. Many designers don't realize there are different specialties for developers. A developer can have extensive user interface (UI) implementation experience, creating incredibly smooth UIs and yet balk at implementing the A-star algorithm. Similarly, a developer can implement low-level data transmission protocols with his or her eyes closed and yet have no idea how to use OpenGL.

The sooner you can get past the "designers make it pretty; developers make it work" mentality and acknowledge the subtleties of others' expertise, the sooner you can start working as a team. Learn the key parts of each other's vocabulary where your work directly interacts. For example, a developer should understand what the designer means by terms such as comps (comprehensive layouts are essentially the final design that most represent what the product should look like on device) and slices (the individual graphics assets that make up the design, such as the image for a button). Designers should understand the basic idea of a view and an app bar, for instance. A designer who really understands what a fragment is can design in a way that is easier for a developer to work with.

Once you have started to work with each other, ask questions. A designer should not be afraid to ask questions such as "Can this interaction be made smoother?" or "Do we have control over the alignment of this text?" A developer should not be afraid to ask, "What does this look like when scrolling between items?" or "What's the goal of this font style?" Speaking of goals, it's a great idea to have the designer explain to the developer the overarching theme and reasoning behind choices. There are going to be times when the developer has to do some interpretation of the design, such as when handling an obscure edge case, and knowing the intent of the designer can help ensure a cohesive visual experience for the user.

Stay in constant communication. If you want a broken app, a great way to develop it is to have the designer create something in a dark corner and then hand it off to the developer to implement in a different dark corner. Designers often like to push the limits of what can be done to create an exciting user experience, so having developer feedback early can help. The designer also won't know the level of effort behind most development. Without communication, you can end up in a situation like this: The developer spends 2 weeks with his or her head down in RenderScript creating a fabulous scrolling carousel and neglecting the other features. Then the designer sees it and wonders why everything else looks terrible. The developer explains how much effort the carousel was and how the other parts didn't seem as significant, and then the designer says, "Oh, well that's not really an important part of the design. I just thought it'd be cool if the items curved slightly as they went off the screen."

Slicing the Graphics Assets

One of the important parts of going from gorgeous comps to an amazing UI is "slicing," which refers to cutting the pieces of the comps into specific assets that the app needs. Sometimes this process is easy, such as saving out the background for a page. Other times it involves some work, such as when a given asset actually spans several layers in Photoshop (or whatever graphical tool is used). Designers frequently use layers to achieve various visual effects, from multiplying colors to adding gloss, so it is not always just the case of cropping a portion of the screen and saving to a new file. Additionally, many assets will work best as nine-patch images. To best slice the assets, the designer needs to explain the effect that is desired and the developer has to explain how to cut up the pieces to get that effect, keeping in mind the device constraints.

The Easy Slices

Some slices are just plain easy to create. Assets such as the background can often just be used as is or with some minimal resizing. Assets that should be tiled just need to be sliced into pieces that can be tiled either by repeating the tile or by mirroring it. See Figure 8.1

Figure 8.1 An example of using a repeating tile background

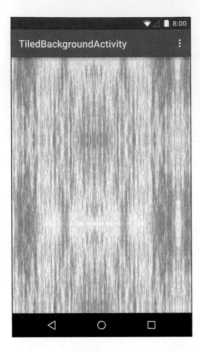

Figure 8.2 An example of using a mirrored tile background

for an example of a background that has been tiled by simply repeating the same image (red lines added to show where the edges of the tiles are). Figure 8.2 demonstrates tiling by mirroring (i.e., it flips the image to align the edges). Tiled assets and simple gradients work well for backgrounds because they can support a variety of screen sizes without appearing distorted, but it's far more common to use flat colors for a modern design. See Listing 8.1 for an example of an XML drawable that tiles an image via mirroring (change "mirror" to "repeat" for standard tiling.)

Listing 8.1   An XML Drawable That Tiles an Image

```
<?xml version="1.0" encoding="utf-8"?>
<bitmap xmlns:android="http://schemas.android.com/apk/res/android"
        android:src="@drawable/bg_tile"
        android:tileMode="mirror" />
```

Other easy slices are placeholder images, logos, and images that can basically be used as is, such as existing icons. You can download a large array of Android app bar and other icons via the Google design site (http://www.google.com/design/spec/resources/sticker-sheets-icons .html), which saves you work and ensures you are using the standard icons your users will already understand. If you still need something else, consider using the Android Asset Studio to generate your icons (http://romannurik.github.io/AndroidAssetStudio/).

Nine-Patch Images

Containers are commonly able to be sliced into nine-patch images because they are intended to fit variably sized content while giving some sense of edges or grouping. A nine-patch image is simply an image that has some extra pixels specifying what portion of the image can stretch and where content can go within the image. For example, buttons are usually containers that have text or an icon in them. The middle portion of a button needs to be big enough to fit whatever the text is in it (keeping in mind that the amount of space required to explain the button's action will vary for different languages and for different font sizes). The defining feature of a button is usually the edge, which lets it stand out as something touchable by casting a shadow or catching the light. The corners are sometimes rounded, so you want to preserve that radius but extend the flat sides to fit the content. Figure 8.3 shows a single nine-patch image that has been automatically resized for different content sizes.

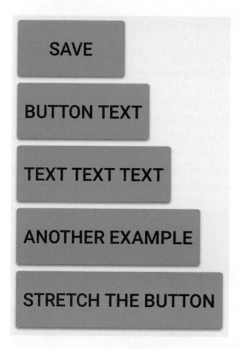

Figure 8.3 A nine-patch image that is resized depending on the content inside

The two main ways that designers create nine-patch images are the `draw9patch` tool that comes with the Android SDK and the program they already use for creating images (e.g., Photoshop). The `draw9patch` tool has the advantage of giving previews of the image being resized horizontally, vertically, and in both directions. Despite the fact that a specialized tool exists for creating nine-patch images, they are actually extremely easy to create in Photoshop, GIMP, or any other image manipulation software, which is sometimes preferable because creating nine-patches this way more easily fits into a typical design workflow.

Figure 8.4 This is a typical button image that's been sliced from a design

If you have an existing asset that you want to make into a nine-patch image, open it in a separate file. For example, you might have a button such as the one in Figure 8.4. Although all you need to do to make an image into a nine-patch is to add pixels to the outside, it's best to first eliminate some of the redundancy in the image. For example, this image is essentially four rounded corners with everything in between filled in. Figure 8.5 shows the filler pixels in red to make it easier to see which parts of the image are repeated (red) and which aren't (the corners).

Figure 8.5 All of the filler pixels have been colored red; these can be deleted from the image

By deleting the red section and bringing the ends together, you can save a lot of wasted space and you also make sure that the button will work well in a variety of situations (such as when the string on it might be short, such as "okay"). You also want to crop it tightly so there are no wasted pixels. Then, expand the canvas by two pixels vertically and horizontally, ensuring that your content is centered. Create fully opaque black pixels on the left where the image can stretch vertically and black pixels on the top where it can stretch horizontally.

Use black pixels on the right and bottom to indicate where content can be placed (such as the "okay" text). Frequently, the pixels indicating content location will be directly across from the pixels that indicate where the image can stretch, but that's not always the case. In the end, you should have something like Figure 8.6.

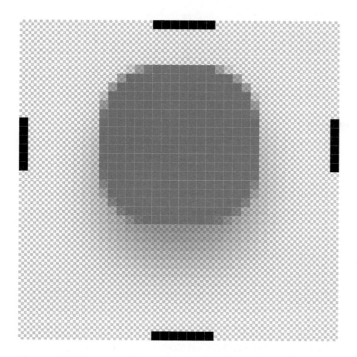

Figure 8.6 The image after cutting out the filler pixels and drawing the nine-patch bounds

Android 4.3 added the concept of optical bounds to nine-patch images. The optical bounds are indicated with red pixels on the right and bottom rather than black. The idea of the optical bounds is that the full size of the image isn't necessarily the way it should visually line up with another view. For example, you might have a button that should have its bottom edge line up with a photo next to it. The button casts a shadow when raised, so you want to align the bottom of the button (not the shadow) with the bottom of the photo. Optical bounds allow you to say what part of the image is a shadow or other element that shouldn't contribute to the visual size of it. The concept is very useful, but optical bounds are largely unused in practice because prior versions of Android still

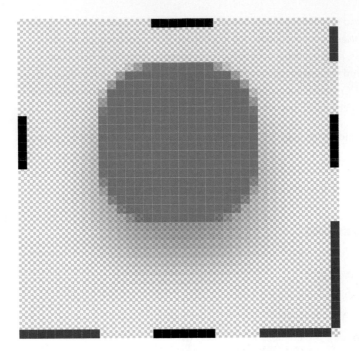

Figure 8.7 A nine-patch with optical bounds indicated with red

have to be handled in other ways and Android 5.0 added support for shadows. Figure 8.7 shows how the previous button nine-patch would be updated for optical bounds.

Generating Alternate Sizes

Although Android will scale images for you, you'll want to test the appearance of the images on a few devices of different densities and determine when you need to make scaled assets yourself. Generally, it is enough to support two density buckets (such as XXXHDPI and XXHDPI) and let Android scale for the rest, but you should keep in mind that devices with lower densities are typically less powerful, so providing lower density assets is always a consideration. It is generally worth trying out the app on a few lower density devices to help make the decision.

Assets should be created at a resolution much higher than what most devices will display. They can then be resized for each of the densities you need. At the very least, your assets should be created with XXXHDPI in mind, though many assets now can be easily designed as vectors and exported to PNGs because modern app design is less heavy (fewer gradients, textures, blending effects, etc.).

Unfortunately, there are times when you'll find that a certain asset is not resized well by one of the automated tools and you need to resize it by hand. There is no simple step-by-step guide for resizing images because it depends on the content of the image and how much you're shrinking it, but there are a few tips to consider. If the image is based on a vector asset, work with the vector asset again instead of shrinking the image that's already rasterized. Try different scaling algorithms. For shrinking images, Photoshop's "Bicubic Sharper" works the best in most cases, but not all. In cases where you are dealing with shrinking an image to exactly half the size in each dimension (such as when going from XHDPI to MDPI), bilinear can give good results. Keep in mind that other software has other algorithms (e.g., GIMP has Lanczos3 but Photoshop does not), so you may need to try other tools if you're not satisfied with what your usual software is giving you.

Themes and Styles

Once you've received a design, work with the designer to understand the visual patterns. In some cases, the patterns will have already been established by the wireframes, so you just need to update the colors or font treatment and everything will look good; however, most of the time the design is different enough from the wireframes (or the wireframes were never actually created) that you need to do quite a bit of work.

For apps that follow Material Design, your overall app theme should extend one of the AppCompat themes that is closest to what you want. In most cases, you will probably base your theme on `Theme.AppCompat.Light.NoActionBar`. The "Light" portion of the name means that this theme overall has a light appearance, so it will have lightly colored backgrounds and darkly colored text. The "NoActionBar" portion means that the app bar will not be added automatically, so you can add your own `Toolbar` instance. In most cases, the use of the support libraries means that you no longer have to create version-specific `styles.xml` files.

First, you should add your colors to `colors.xml` in the `res/values` directory (creating the file, if needed) and then add the references to `styles.xml`. As long as you're extending from `AppCompatActivity` for each of your activities, the library will handle coloring the status bar your dark primary color, the app bar your primary color, and various interactive views your accent color.

Next, you can create any broad styles that repeat throughout your design. Try to use the function of the style for the name (such as "Header") rather than the appearance of it (such as "BigRedText"). What if you really do have two headers, one with big red text and one with big blue text? Ask the designer why. Is it because one is a top-level header and one is a subheader? Is one used for the main page and another for the detail page? If nothing else, try to break them up without exact color. For example, you might have a header that is dark text and one that is light. Something like "Header.Light" is a much better name than "Header.Red" because it's more likely to be true even after design updates. The red color might have shifted to orange or even green as the design evolves, but it's probably still going to be dark text if the background is light or light text if the background is dark.

Ideally, the designer creates a style guide that explains all the styles, but the rapid environment of mobile applications means that is commonly not the case. Sometimes styles are called out in the "redlines" (typically a document containing multiple comps that have been marked up to specify spacing, assets, and so on) for specific screens instead of in a full guide. And other times the developer has to interpret the comps to figure out what is intended.

Breaking Comps into Views

In Chapter 6, "Prototyping and Developing the App Foundation," you learned how to break wireframes into views. Wireframes are often very easy to split into views because each piece of information being presented tends to map to a specific view. Breaking comps into views can be a little more challenging, especially if you did not have the advantage of seeing any wireframes.

Take a look at Figure 8.8, which shows the design created in the previous chapter. How would you break this up? The base of the layout is two parts: a `Toolbar` and a `GridView`. This can easily be done with a vertical `LinearLayout`. The `GridView` consists of individual items that could be broken up in a few ways. There's an image, which either means an `ImageView` or a background for another view, and there's text best displayed with a `TextView`. Using an `ImageView` gives you more control over an image's appearance than simply using the background of another view, so that's generally the way to go when you want better control over the image such as how it is scaled. Each grid item can be a `FrameLayout` because that's the simplest implementation of `ViewGroup`, and it supports gravity for positioning the `TextView` at the bottom. Figure 8.9 shows how these individual views come together to create the design.

Figure 8.8 The main screen's design from the previous chapter

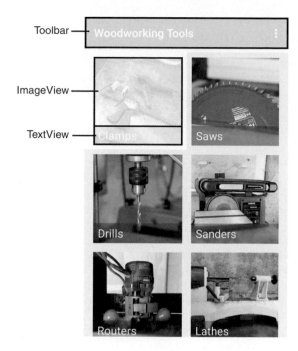

Toolbar ——

ImageView ——

TextView ——

Figure 8.9 Breaking up the design into individual views

Developing the Woodworking App

Knowing how to break the design into views is just the first step. The actual implementation of a design can be straightforward or it can be exceedingly challenging.

The Main Screen

We'll start this one with a fresh project because it is sufficiently different from the prototype. The app needs an activity (we'll call it `ToolGridActivity`) and a fragment for that activity (called `ToolGridFragment`). The activity is going to be extremely simple. All it needs do to is to set up the toolbar. The layout will contain the fragment, so it doesn't need to be instantiated by the activity. Listing 8.2 shows what the activity's layout (called `activity_tool_grid.xml`) should look like (it uses a reference to a toolbar layout just like the prototype did) and Listing 8.3 shows the `onCreate` method of the activity.

Listing 8.2   The Layout for the Main Activity

```
<?xml version="1.0" encoding="utf-8"?>
<LinearLayout xmlns:android="http://schemas.android.com/apk/res/android"
              xmlns:tools="http://schemas.android.com/tools"
              android:layout_width="match_parent"
              android:layout_height="match_parent"
              android:orientation="vertical"
    >
```

```
<include layout="@layout/toolbar"/>

<fragment
    android:id="@+id/fragment"
    android:name="com.auidbook.woodworkingtools.ToolGridFragment"
    android:layout_width="match_parent"
    android:layout_height="match_parent"
    tools:layout="@layout/fragment_tool_grid"/>

</LinearLayout>
```

Listing 8.3   The onCreate Method of the Activity

```
@Override
protected void onCreate(Bundle savedInstanceState) {
    super.onCreate(savedInstanceState);
    setContentView(R.layout.activity_tool_grid);

    final Toolbar toolbar = (Toolbar) findViewById(R.id.toolbar);
    setSupportActionBar(toolbar);
}
```

The fragment is pretty simple as well. It just inflates the layout, which is simply a GridView, and then it sets up and assigns the adapter that we'll make shortly. The one interesting thing to note about the layout is the property clipToPadding. When true, any content in the view that is covered by the padding is not drawn. This causes the scrolled grid items to appear to appear and disappear arbitrarily, so setting it to false causes them to appear to come from the bottom of the screen and scroll under the app bar at the top. Listing 8.4 shows this layout and Listing 8.5 shows the onCreateView method of the fragment.

Listing 8.4   The Layout for the ToolGridFragment

```
<?xml version="1.0" encoding="utf-8"?>
<GridView xmlns:android="http://schemas.android.com/apk/res/android"
        android:id="@+id/gridview"
        android:layout_width="match_parent"
        android:layout_height="match_parent"
        android:numColumns="2"
        android:verticalSpacing="16dp"
        android:horizontalSpacing="16dp"
        android:paddingBottom="@dimen/activity_vertical_margin"
        android:paddingLeft="@dimen/activity_horizontal_margin"
        android:paddingRight="@dimen/activity_horizontal_margin"
        android:paddingTop="@dimen/activity_vertical_margin"
        android:clipToPadding="false"
    />
```

Listing 8.5 The `onCreateView` Method of the Fragment

```
@Override
public View onCreateView(LayoutInflater inflater, ViewGroup container,
                         Bundle savedInstanceState) {
    final View rootView = inflater.inflate(R.layout.fragment_tool_grid,
➥ container, false);
    final GridView gridView = (GridView) rootView.findViewById
➥ (R.id.gridview);
    mToolGridAdapter = new ToolGridAdapter(getActivity());
    gridView.setAdapter(mToolGridAdapter);
    gridView.setOnItemClickListener(this);
    return rootView;
}
```

The app is going to need to know what types of tools there are just like the prototype, so we can copy the `ToolType` enum over, but we need to make a change. This design displays images for each type, so the constructor needs to be updated to take an image resource. Listing 8.6 shows the enum with the updated image information.

Listing 8.6 The Updated `ToolType` Enum

```
public enum ToolType {
    CLAMPS(R.string.clamps, R.string.clamps_description, R.drawable.
➥ hero_image_clamps),
    SAWS(R.string.saws, R.string.saws_description, R.drawable.
➥ hero_image_saw),
    DRILLS(R.string.drills, R.string.drills_description, R.drawable.
➥ hero_image_drill),
    SANDERS(R.string.sanders, R.string.sanders_description, R.drawable.
➥ hero_image_sander),
    ROUTERS(R.string.routers, R.string.routers_description, R.drawable.
➥ hero_image_router),
    LATHES(R.string.lathes, R.string.lathes_description, R.drawable.
➥ hero_image_lathe),
    MORE(R.string.more, R.string.more_description, R.drawable.
➥ hero_image_more),
    ;
    private final int mToolNameResourceId;
    private final int mToolDescriptionResourceId;
    private final int mToolImageResourceId;

    private ToolType(@StringRes int toolName, @StringRes int
➥ toolDescription, @DrawableRes int toolImage) {
        mToolNameResourceId = toolName;
        mToolDescriptionResourceId = toolDescription;
        mToolImageResourceId = toolImage;
    }
```

```
    @StringRes
    public int getToolDescriptionResourceId() {
        return mToolDescriptionResourceId;
    }

    @StringRes
    public int getToolNameResourceId() {
        return mToolNameResourceId;
    }

    @DrawableRes
    public int getToolImageResourceId() {
        return mToolImageResourceId;
    }
}
```

Before we jump into the adapter, there are two things to figure out. The first is keeping the images square. Although we can easily scale or crop the images themselves to be square, a real app might be getting these from a server, which can't guarantee the aspect ratio. Therefore, we can create a very simple subclass of ImageView that ensures that it is always square. Creating SquareImageView and having it extend ImageView, the only thing we have to do here is update the onMeasure method, which has to call setMeasuredDimension with the correct dimensions to use. Because we want the image to be square, we can pass the width for both dimensions. Listing 8.7 shows this basic class.

Listing 8.7   The SquareImageView Class

```
public class SquareImageView extends ImageView {

    public SquareImageView(Context context) {
        super(context);
    }

    public SquareImageView(Context context, AttributeSet attrs) {
        super(context, attrs);
    }

    public SquareImageView(Context context, AttributeSet attrs, int
➥ defStyleAttr) {
        super(context, attrs, defStyleAttr);
    }

    public SquareImageView(Context context, AttributeSet attrs, int
➥ defStyleAttr, int defStyleRes) {
        super(context, attrs, defStyleAttr, defStyleRes);
    }
    @Override
    protected void onMeasure(int widthMeasureSpec, int heightMeasureSpec) {
```

```
        super.onMeasure(widthMeasureSpec, heightMeasureSpec);
        setMeasuredDimension(getMeasuredWidth(), getMeasuredWidth());
    }
}
```

We can't quite get to the adapter yet though; we need to figure out how we're going to handle this background blurring in the design. This type of scrim, discussed in the previous chapter, is only a few seconds of work in an image editing program, but it's a bit more work to implement in code. To contain all the logic, we'll create another custom view called CaptionedImageView that extends FrameLayout. Whenever creating a custom view that contains children, it can be handy to create an XML layout that defines all those children instead of trying to programmatically create them. Listing 8.8 shows captioned_image_view.xml, which will be inflated by this custom view. Notice that the root tag is merge. XML requires a root tag, but we don't actually want a FrameLayout defined here. If we did, our custom view would inflate this layout and add the FrameLayout to itself, which would effectively be wasted because it is already a FrameLayout. You could inflate the layout and then programmatically pass the children from the inflated FrameLayout to the custom view, but that still creates a layout that isn't actually used. By employing the merge tag, we avoid that waste and can directly add multiple children to our custom view.

Listing 8.8   The Layout Used by the Custom CaptionedImageView Class

```
<?xml version="1.0" encoding="utf-8"?>
<merge xmlns:android="http://schemas.android.com/apk/res/android"
       xmlns:tools="http://schemas.android.com/tools"
       >
    <com.auidbook.woodworkingtools.SquareImageView
        android:id="@+id/image"
        android:layout_width="match_parent"
        android:layout_height="match_parent"
        android:scaleType="centerCrop"
        tools:src="@drawable/hero_image_clamps"/>

    <TextView
        style="@style/GridItemTitle"
        android:id="@+id/text"
        android:layout_width="match_parent"
        android:layout_height="wrap_content"
        tools:text="@string/clamps"
        android:layout_gravity="bottom"/>
</merge>
```

Our CaptionedImageView needs to do three things: inflate the layout, listen to layout changes, and create the blur. The first part we do by creating a simple init method that is called from each of the constructors. The second part is needed so we know when the ImageView and `TextView` have been sized, and we can grab the correct portion of the image to blur. The final part is the bulk of the work and that's the actual blurring of the image.

After we inflate the layout, we store the view references, store the color to draw on the scrim (this is just the same as our primary dark color, but with the alpha lowered), and add an `OnLayoutChangeListener` to the `TextView`, which will be called any time the size of the `TextView` changes. We can implement that interface with our custom view to keep the code simple. The only method of that interface is `onLayoutChange` which is given the view that changed sizes, the old positions, and the new positions. All we need to do here is verify that the view is visible and it has a size, triggering our `updateBlur` method if both are true.

The `updateBlur` method first makes sure the drawable used in the ImageView is a `BitmapDrawable` because we know how to blur bitmaps but not necessarily other types. We calculate the ratio of the height of the `TextView` to the height of the `ImageView`, which will tell us how much of the bitmap to use for the blur. We get the actual `Bitmap` object from the drawable and determine the height of the bitmap to use for the blur (we just want the portion that is behind the text).

Now we can create a new `Bitmap` object that represents the portion of the image that we are going to blur and a new `Bitmap` that will be the original image with the blurred portion overlaid on the bottom.

The actual blur happens in the next few lines by using RenderScript. RenderScript allows you to define calculations that can be executed on the GPU when possible (falling back to the CPU if the GPU isn't capable). The Android team has created some "intrinsic" scripts, which are extremely efficient functions for common operations (like blurring or convolutions). Not only are they efficient, but they keep you from having to bother with C code. This process is a few steps, but it's extremely powerful.

1. Create the `ScriptIntrinsicBlur`.
2. Create the `Allocation` instances, which represent a portion of memory that will be used for passing data to or from the script.
3. Set the blur radius in pixels.
4. Set the input `Allocation` (the `Bitmap` the script will operate on).
5. Call `forEach` with the output `Allocation`.

The `forEach` method is a special RenderScript method that executes on a single element in the `Allocation` (in our case, an element is a pixel). This method can be executed on dozens or even hundreds of GPU cores at the same time, which is what makes it very fast. After we have the output `Allocation` ready, we need to copy it into our output `Bitmap` instance. This bitmap now contains all the blurred pixels. One more thing we want to do is darken all the pixels of the blurred portion to help ensure we have enough contrast with the text using the `drawColor` method of `Canvas` (the `Canvas` class is covered in detail in Chapter 11, "Working with the Canvas and Advanced Drawing," but you can simply think of it as a method of drawing pixels on a bitmap for now).

With all the hard work done, we make a copy of the original bitmap and draw the blurred pixels on top of the bottom portion of it. Just tell the `ImageView` to display this new `Bitmap` instance and we're done.

Because there isn't an easy way of being notified when the `ImageView` has its image changed, we can add a `setImageResource` to our class that will update the `ImageView` and trigger the blurring.

The `CaptionedImageView` class is shown in Listing 8.9. You may need to go through it carefully to understand what is happening, but having any experience at all with RenderScript will put you ahead of a lot of Android developers.

Listing 8.9 The `CaptionedImageView` Class

```
public class CaptionedImageView extends FrameLayout implements View.
➥ OnLayoutChangeListener {

    private Drawable mDrawable;
    private TextView mTextView;
    private SquareImageView mImageView;
    private int mScrimColor;

    public CaptionedImageView(Context context) {
        super(context);
        init(context);
    }

    public CaptionedImageView(Context context, AttributeSet attrs) {
        super(context, attrs);
        init(context);
    }

    public CaptionedImageView(Context context, AttributeSet attrs, int
➥ defStyleAttr) {
        super(context, attrs, defStyleAttr);
        init(context);
    }

    public CaptionedImageView(Context context, AttributeSet attrs, int
➥ defStyleAttr, int defStyleRes) {
```

```
        super(context, attrs, defStyleAttr, defStyleRes);
        init(context);
    }

    public SquareImageView getImageView() {
        return mImageView;
    }

    public TextView getTextView() {
        return mTextView;
    }
    @Override
    public void onLayoutChange(View v, int left, int top, int right,
➡ int bottom, int oldLeft, int oldTop, int oldRight, int oldBottom) {
        if (v.getVisibility() != VISIBLE) {
            return;
        }
        final int height = bottom - top;
        final int width = right - left;
        if (height == 0 || width == 0) {
            return;
        }
        updateBlur();
    }

    public void setImageResource(@DrawableRes int drawableResourceId) {
        mDrawable = getResources().getDrawable(drawableResourceId);
        mImageView.setImageResource(drawableResourceId);
        updateBlur();
    }

    private void updateBlur() {
        if (!(mDrawable instanceof BitmapDrawable)) {
            return;
        }
        final int textViewHeight = mTextView.getHeight();
        if (textViewHeight == 0) {
            return;
        }

        // Determine the size of the TextView compared to the height of
➡ the ImageView
        final float ratio = (float) textViewHeight / mImageView.
➡ getHeight();

        // Get the Bitmap
        final BitmapDrawable bitmapDrawable = (BitmapDrawable)
➡ mDrawable;
        final Bitmap originalBitmap = bitmapDrawable.getBitmap();
```

```java
        // Calculate the height as a ratio of the Bitmap
        int height = (int) (ratio * originalBitmap.getHeight());

        // The y position is the number of pixels height represents
➥ from the bottom of the Bitmap
        final int y = originalBitmap.getHeight() - height;

        final Bitmap portionToBlur = Bitmap.createBitmap(originalBit
➥ map, 0, y, originalBitmap.getWidth(), height);
        final Bitmap blurredBitmap = portionToBlur.copy(Bitmap.
➥ Config.ARGB_8888, true);

        // Use RenderScript to blur the pixels
        RenderScript rs = RenderScript.create(getContext());
        ScriptIntrinsicBlur theIntrinsic = ScriptIntrinsicBlur.create
➥ (rs, Element.U8_4(rs));
        Allocation tmpIn = Allocation.createFromBitmap(rs, portionToBlur);
        Allocation tmpOut = Allocation.createFromBitmap(rs, blurredBitmap);
        theIntrinsic.setRadius(25f);
        theIntrinsic.setInput(tmpIn);
        theIntrinsic.forEach(tmpOut);
        tmpOut.copyTo(blurredBitmap);
        new Canvas(blurredBitmap).drawColor(mScrimColor);

        // Create the new bitmap using the old plus the blurred portion
➥ and display it
        final Bitmap newBitmap = originalBitmap.copy(Bitmap.
➥ Config.ARGB_8888, true);
        final Canvas canvas = new Canvas(newBitmap);
        canvas.drawBitmap(blurredBitmap, 0, y, new Paint());
        mImageView.setImageBitmap(newBitmap);
    }

    private void init(Context context) {
        inflate(context, R.layout.captioned_square_image_view, this);
        mTextView = (TextView) findViewById(R.id.text);
        mImageView = (SquareImageView) findViewById(R.id.image);
        mScrimColor = getResources().getColor(R.color.grid_item_scrim);
        mTextView.addOnLayoutChangeListener(this);
    }
}
```

With all the difficult work done, we can now create the `ToolGridAdapter`. It will extend `BaseAdapter`, operating on an array of our `ToolType` values. The `getView` method creates a new `CaptionedSquareImageView` if the `convertView` is null, then it simply sets the image resource and text to display. All the hard work is already done for us in the custom view class. The adapter is shown in Listing 8.10.

Listing 8.10   The `ToolGridAdapter` Class

```java
public class ToolGridAdapter extends BaseAdapter {

    private final ToolType[] mToolTypes = ToolType.values();
    private final Context mContext;

    public ToolGridAdapter(Context context) {
        mContext = context;
    }

    @Override
    public int getCount() {
        return mToolTypes.length;
    }

    @Override
    public ToolType getItem(int position) {
        return mToolTypes[position];
    }

    @Override
    public long getItemId(int position) {
        return position;
    }

    @Override
    public View getView(int position, View convertView, ViewGroup
➥ parent) {
        final CaptionedImageView captionedImageView;
        if (convertView == null) {
            captionedImageView = new CaptionedImageView(mContext);
        } else {
            captionedImageView = (CaptionedImageView) convertView;
        }

        final ToolType toolType = mToolTypes[position];
        captionedImageView.setImageResource(toolType.
➥ getToolImageResourceId());
        captionedImageView.getTextView().setText(toolType.
➥ getToolNameResourceId());
        return captionedImageView;
    }
}
```

With all this work done, we can run the app on a device and see how it looks. Chances are, you'll notice that it looks good but there's "jank" when scrolling. Jank is the opposite of smoothness; it's any hiccup in the UI. Your app should run at 60 frames per second, but that gives you only

16 milliseconds per frame, so it doesn't take much to miss a frame. Whenever a frame is dropped, the resulting jank is the jerky movement that can ruin an otherwise polished app.

Chapter 10, "Using Advanced Techniques," will explain how to find what is causing jank and, more importantly, how to fix it. For now, your focus should be on function. Once everything is working how it should, you can move on to improving the efficiency.

The Tool List

After the user selects the tool type, we need to show the next screen, which has been revamped to show an About tab, explaining what the tool is, and other tabs dependent on the type. Figure 8.10 shows the design for this page.

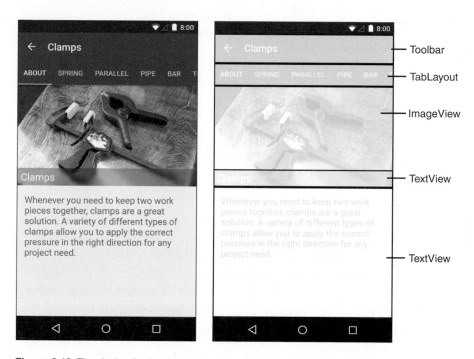

Figure 8.10 The design for the About tab on the left with applicable views on the right

The tool list includes tabs, so we need to make sure the design support library is added as a dependency in our `build.gradle` file. We can either open the file directly to add `compile 'com.android.support:design:22.2.1'` to the dependencies section or go to File -> Project Structure, select the module on the left and the Dependencies tab on the right to add it. With the design support library added, we can create a new activity (called `ToolListActivity`). The layout is going to be a LinearLayout with our Toolbar from before, a `TabLayout`, and a `ViewPager`. Listing 8.11 shows the full layout.

Listing 8.11   The Layout Used by `ToolListActivity`

```xml
<?xml version="1.0" encoding="utf-8"?>
<LinearLayout xmlns:android="http://schemas.android.com/apk/res/android"
              xmlns:tools="http://schemas.android.com/tools"
              xmlns:app="http://schemas.android.com/apk/res-auto"
              android:layout_width="match_parent"
              android:layout_height="match_parent"
              android:orientation="vertical"
    >
    <include layout="@layout/toolbar"/>

    <android.support.design.widget.TabLayout
        android:id="@+id/tabs"
        android:layout_width="match_parent"
        android:layout_height="wrap_content"
        android:background="?attr/colorPrimary"
        android:elevation="4dp"
        app:tabMode="scrollable"
        app:theme="@style/ThemeOverlay.AppCompat.Dark.ActionBar"/>

    <android.support.v4.view.ViewPager
        android:id="@+id/viewpager"
        android:layout_width="match_parent"
        android:layout_height="match_parent"/>

</LinearLayout>
```

One particular thing we need to do is to modify the `AndroidManifest.xml` file. The default behavior when the user presses the up navigation (the arrow at the top left in the app bar) is to create a new `Intent` to launch the parent activity. We don't want that process to create the activity from scratch, so we can update the manifest to add `android:launchMode="singleTop"` to both of our activities. Activities that have this set behave exactly the same as regular activities (which default to `standard` launch mode) with one special exception: When the activity is on the top of the task stack, an `Intent` that would ordinarily create the activity will instead be delivered to the `onNewIntent()` method of the existing activity. In this particular app, the effect that has is that tapping the up navigation will not create a new instance of the activity, so everything that has already been loaded will still be there.

We need to create a `ToolAboutFragment` that will be the default tab that's shown when a user has tapped a particular tool type from the main screen. It uses a photo of the tool type with the name overlaid just like the main screen, creating a visual continuity. Below that is a blurb of text about the type of tool. The layout is shown in Listing 8.12. The one important part to realize is that the image isn't square. This means that we'll need to update our code to handle non-square images.

Listing 8.12   The Layout Used by the `ToolAboutFragment`

```xml
<?xml version="1.0" encoding="utf-8"?>
<LinearLayout xmlns:android="http://schemas.android.com/apk/res/android"
              xmlns:tools="http://schemas.android.com/tools"
              android:layout_width="match_parent"
              android:layout_height="match_parent"
              android:orientation="vertical"
              tools:context="com.auidbook.woodworkingtools.
➥ ToolAboutFragment">

    <com.auidbook.woodworkingtools.CaptionedImageView
        android:id="@+id/hero_image"
        android:layout_width="match_parent"
        android:layout_height="wrap_content"/>

    <TextView
        android:id="@+id/description"
        android:layout_width="match_parent"
        android:layout_height="wrap_content"
        android:textAppearance="?android:attr/textAppearanceMedium"
        android:paddingLeft="@dimen/activity_horizontal_margin"
        android:paddingRight="@dimen/activity_horizontal_margin"
        android:paddingTop="@dimen/activity_vertical_margin"
        android:paddingBottom="@dimen/activity_vertical_margin"
        tools:text="@string/clamps_description" />

</LinearLayout>
```

We can update our `SquareImageView` to add a `setSquare` method. This method sets a boolean field that is checked in `onMeasure`. If it is true, then we force the layout to be square, otherwise we do nothing (the super method calls `setMeasuredDimension`). Listing 8.13 shows the updated class.

Listing 8.13   The Updated `SquareImageView` Class

```java
public class SquareImageView extends ImageView {

    private boolean mSquare = true;

    public SquareImageView(Context context) {
        super(context);
    }

    public SquareImageView(Context context, AttributeSet attrs) {
        super(context, attrs);
    }
```

```
    public SquareImageView(Context context, AttributeSet attrs, int
➥ defStyleAttr) {
        super(context, attrs, defStyleAttr);
    }

    public SquareImageView(Context context, AttributeSet attrs, int
➥ defStyleAttr, int defStyleRes) {
        super(context, attrs, defStyleAttr, defStyleRes);
    }

    /**
     * Enable or disable displaying as a square image
     *
     * @param square boolean true to make the image square
     */
    public void setSquare(boolean square) {
        if (square != mSquare) {
            mSquare = square;
            requestLayout();
        }
    }

    @Override
    protected void onMeasure(int widthMeasureSpec, int
➥ heightMeasureSpec) {
        super.onMeasure(widthMeasureSpec, heightMeasureSpec);
        if (mSquare) {
            setMeasuredDimension(getMeasuredWidth(), getMeasuredWidth());
        }
    }
}
```

The `ToolAboutFragment` is pretty simple. It needs to take the tool type just like we've
done before, then it updates the layout. We get the `CaptionedImageView` and get its
`SquareImageView` reference to tell it to not be square. Then we set the text, the image, and
the description. Listing 8.14 shows the fragment.

Listing 8.14   The `ToolAboutFragment` Class

```
public class ToolAboutFragment extends Fragment {

    private static final String ARG_TOOL_TYPE = "toolType";

    private ToolType mToolType;

    public static ToolAboutFragment newInstance(ToolType toolType) {
        final ToolAboutFragment fragment = new ToolAboutFragment();
        final Bundle args = new Bundle();
```

```java
        args.putSerializable(ARG_TOOL_TYPE, toolType);
        fragment.setArguments(args);
        return fragment;
    }

    public ToolAboutFragment() {
        // Required empty public constructor
    }

    @Override
    public void onCreate(Bundle savedInstanceState) {
        super.onCreate(savedInstanceState);
        final Bundle args = getArguments();
        if (args == null) {
            throw new IllegalStateException("No arguments set; use
 newInstance when constructing!");
        }
        mToolType = (ToolType) args.getSerializable(ARG_TOOL_TYPE));
    }

    @Override
    public View onCreateView(LayoutInflater inflater, ViewGroup
 container, Bundle savedInstanceState) {
        final View rootView = inflater.inflate(R.layout.fragment_tool_
 about, container, false);

        final CaptionedImageView captionedImageView =
 (CaptionedImageView) rootView.findViewById(R.id.hero_image);
        captionedImageView.getImageView().setSquare(false);
        captionedImageView.getTextView().setText(mToolType.
 getToolNameResourceId());
        captionedImageView.setImageResource(mToolType.
 getToolImageResourceId());
        final TextView textView = (TextView) rootView.findViewById
 (R.id.description);
        textView.setText(mToolType.getToolDescriptionResourceId());

        return rootView;
    }
}
```

Now we can create the `ToolListFragment`. It is very similar to the class we created for our prototype and the design is shown in Figure 8.11. The biggest difference is that we get the list of tools from a new class (using an updated `ToolTab`). That new class is monotonous, containing just a bunch calls to construct a new `Tool` object over and over depending on the type of tool that was passed. It contains a few hundred hardcoded values, so it's not listed here (the full source code is available with the rest of the source code for this book at https://github.com/ IanGClifton/auid2). Think of it as our `ToolTestUtils` version 2.0. A real app would be getting this data from a server somewhere, so we just have a simple class to give us data to work with.

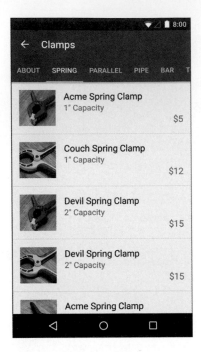

Figure 8.11 The design for the tool lists

One important thing we have to do is update the `Tool` class so that it can take an int image resource ID for the main photo and for the thumbnail. This means that the methods for converting the `Tool` into a `Parcel` and vice versa need to be updated as well, plus we need to add accessors for the image resource IDs. The updated class is in Listing 8.15.

Listing 8.15   The Updated `Tool` Class

```
public class Tool implements Parcelable {

    private static final int DETAILS_COUNT = 3;

    private final String mName;
    private final String mPrice;
    private final String[] mDetails;
    private final String mDescription;
    private final int mImageResourceId;
    private final int mThumbnailResourceId;

    public Tool(String name, String price, String[] details, String
➥ description, @DrawableRes int imageResourceId, @DrawableRes int
➥ thumbnailResourceId) {
        mName = name;
        mPrice = price;
```

```java
        mDetails = new String[DETAILS_COUNT];
        if (details != null) {
            System.arraycopy(details, 0, mDetails, 0, details.length);
        }
        mDescription = description;
        mImageResourceId = imageResourceId;
        mThumbnailResourceId = thumbnailResourceId;
    }

    public String getDescription() {
        return mDescription;
    }

    public String[] getDetails() {
        return mDetails;
    }

    public String getName() {
        return mName;
    }
    public String getPrice() {
        return mPrice;
    }

    public int getImageResourceId() {
        return mImageResourceId;
    }

    public int getThumbnailResourceId() {
        return mThumbnailResourceId;
    }

    @Override
    public int describeContents() {
        return 0;
    }

    @Override
    public void writeToParcel(Parcel dest, int flags) {
        dest.writeString(mName);
        dest.writeString(mPrice);
        dest.writeStringArray(mDetails);
        dest.writeString(mDescription);
        dest.writeInt(mImageResourceId);
        dest.writeInt(mThumbnailResourceId);
    }

    private Tool(Parcel in) {
        mName = in.readString();
        mPrice = in.readString();
```

```
        mDetails = in.createStringArray();
        mDescription = in.readString();
        mImageResourceId = in.readInt();
        mThumbnailResourceId = in.readInt();
    }

    public static final Parcelable.Creator<Tool> CREATOR = new
➥ Parcelable.Creator<Tool>() {
        public Tool createFromParcel(Parcel source) {
            return new Tool(source);
        }

        public Tool[] newArray(int size) {
            return new Tool[size];
        }
    };
}
```

The list items have a minor change from the prototype: The price for each item is now at the bottom. You can copy the layout in from the prototype and then just cut the price `TextView` and paste it below the other two. That's simple enough, right? The `ToolArrayAdapter` is also copied from the prototype with a minor change. Instead of setting the background of the image view to a shade of gray, we just set the image resource to the `Tool` object's thumbnail. Listing 8.16 shows the updated class.

Listing 8.16   The `ToolArrayAdapter` Class

```
public class ToolArrayAdapter extends ArrayAdapter<Tool> {

    private final LayoutInflater mLayoutInflater;

    public ToolArrayAdapter(Context context, List<Tool> objects) {
        super(context, -1, objects);
        mLayoutInflater = LayoutInflater.from(context);
    }

    @Override
    public View getView(int position, View convertView, ViewGroup
➥ parent) {
        if (convertView == null) {
            convertView = mLayoutInflater.inflate(R.layout.list_item_
➥ tool, parent, false);
        }
        final Tool tool = getItem(position);

        // Set TextViews
        TextView textView = (TextView) convertView.findViewById
➥ (R.id.price);
```

```
    textView.setText(tool.getPrice());
    textView = (TextView) convertView.findViewById(R.id.name);
    textView.setText(tool.getName());
    textView = (TextView) convertView.findViewById(R.id.meta);
    textView.setText(tool.getDetails()[0]);

    // Set thumbnail
    final ImageView imageView = (ImageView) convertView.
➡ findViewById(R.id.thumbnail);
    imageView.setImageResource(tool.getThumbnailResourceId());

    return convertView;
    }
}
```

With everything ready for the about screen and the tool list, we just need to add the tabs. First, we make the `ToolTab` class that is referenced in `ToolListFragment`. This class will represent the tab, so it needs to know the text to display for the tab name, it needs to know the tool type that's being displayed, and it needs an ID of some sort. The class also has an accessor for each of those and implements `Parcelable` so that it can be stored in the arguments `Bundle` of a fragment. The class is shown in Listing 8.17.

Listing 8.17 The `ToolTab` Class

```
public class ToolTab implements Parcelable {

    private final int mStringResourceId;
    private final int mTabId;
    private final ToolType mToolType;

    public ToolTab(int tabId, @NonNull ToolType toolType, @StringRes
➡ int stringResourceId) {
        mTabId = tabId;
        mToolType = toolType;
        mStringResourceId = stringResourceId;
    }

    public int getStringResourceId() {
        return mStringResourceId;
    }

    public int getTabId() {
        return mTabId;
    }

    public ToolType getToolType() {
        return mToolType;
    }
```

```
    @Override
    public int describeContents() {
        return 0;
    }

    @Override
    public void writeToParcel(Parcel dest, int flags) {
        dest.writeInt(mStringResourceId);
        dest.writeInt(mTabId);
        dest.writeSerializable(mToolType);
    }

    private ToolTab(Parcel in) {
        mStringResourceId = in.readInt();
        mTabId = in.readInt();
        mToolType = (ToolType) in.readSerializable();
    }

    public static final Parcelable.Creator<ToolTab> CREATOR = new
➥ Parcelable.Creator<ToolTab>() {
        public ToolTab createFromParcel(Parcel source) {
            return new ToolTab(source);
        }

        public ToolTab[] newArray(int size) {
            return new ToolTab[size];
        }
    };
}
```

Now we can finally make the `ToolPagerAdapter`, which extends from
`FragmentPagerAdapter`. This class will create the fragments that are needed for each tab.
It is similar to the class of the same name from our prototype, but the tabs are represented by
our new `ToolTab` class (because we have different tabs for different tools). There is a simple
method that creates a List of `ToolTab` objects depending on which `ToolType` the adapter
is for. This is another case where a real app might get this data from somewhere else (it could
be a local configuration or even a dynamically loaded JSON configuration from a server
somewhere), but this gives us a simple solution that works well. Listing 8.18 shows the adapter.

Listing 8.18 The `ToolPagerAdapter` Class

```
public class ToolPagerAdapter extends FragmentPagerAdapter {

    private final CharSequence[] mTitles;
    private final List<ToolTab> mToolTabs;
    private final ToolType mToolType;
    private final ToolType[] mToolTypes = ToolType.values();
```

```java
    public ToolPagerAdapter(FragmentManager fm, Resources res, ToolType
➥ toolType) {
        super(fm);
        mToolType = toolType;
        mToolTabs = getToolTabs(toolType);
        mTitles = new CharSequence[mToolTabs.size()];
        for (int i = 0; i < mTitles.length; i++) {
            mTitles[i] = res.getString(mToolTabs.get(i).
➥ getStringResourceId());
        }
    }

    @Override
    public Fragment getItem(int position) {
        if (position == 0) {
            return ToolAboutFragment.newInstance(mToolType);
        }
        return ToolListFragment.newInstance(mToolTabs.get(position));
    }
    @Override
    public int getCount() {
        return mToolTabs.size();
    }

    @Override
    public long getItemId(int position) {
        for (int i = 0; i < mToolTypes.length; i++) {
            if (mToolTypes[i] == mToolType) {
                return (i * 10) + position;
            }
        }
        throw new IllegalArgumentException("Invalid position
➥ (" + position + ") or ToolType (" + mToolType + ")");
    }

    @Override
    public CharSequence getPageTitle(int position) {
        return mTitles[position];
    }

    private List<ToolTab> getToolTabs(ToolType toolType) {
        int i = 0;
        final List<ToolTab> toolTabs = new ArrayList<>();
        toolTabs.add(new ToolTab(i++, toolType, R.string.about));
        switch (toolType) {
            case CLAMPS:
                toolTabs.add(new ToolTab(i++, toolType,
➥ R.string.spring_clamps));
                toolTabs.add(new ToolTab(i++, toolType,
➥ R.string.parallel_clamps));
```

```
                            toolTabs.add(new ToolTab(i++, toolType,
➥ R.string.pipe_clamps));
                            toolTabs.add(new ToolTab(i++, toolType,
➥ R.string.bar_clamps));
                            toolTabs.add(new ToolTab(i++, toolType,
➥ R.string.toggle_clamps));
                        break;
                    case SAWS:
                            toolTabs.add(new ToolTab(i++, toolType,
➥ R.string.table_saws));
                            toolTabs.add(new ToolTab(i++, toolType,
➥ R.string.band_saws));
                            toolTabs.add(new ToolTab(i++, toolType,
➥ R.string.circular_saws));
                            toolTabs.add(new ToolTab(i++, toolType,
➥ R.string.jig_saws));
                        break;
                    case DRILLS:
                            toolTabs.add(new ToolTab(i++, toolType,
➥ R.string.drill_presses));
                            toolTabs.add(new ToolTab(i++, toolType,
➥ R.string.handheld));
                        break;
                    case SANDERS:
                            toolTabs.add(new ToolTab(i++, toolType,
➥ R.string.stationary));
                            toolTabs.add(new ToolTab(i++, toolType,
➥ R.string.handheld));
                        break;
                    case ROUTERS:
                            toolTabs.add(new ToolTab(i++, toolType,
➥ R.string.routers));
                        break;
                    case LATHES:
                            toolTabs.add(new ToolTab(i++, toolType,
➥ R.string.lathes));
                        break;
                    case MORE:
//                          toolTabs.add(new ToolTab(i++, toolType, R.string.more));
                        break;
            }
            return toolTabs;
        }
    }
```

Now we have an adapter to give us the tabs we need, two different fragments to handle the tab selection, and an adapter to create the list of tools to display. It's time to put everything together by updating the `ToolListActivity`. By now, these patterns should be looking familiar. We have a static method to simplify starting the activity with the necessary intent extra. We set the content view and set up the toolbar (note that we enable the up navigation by calling `setDisplayHomeAsUpEnabled(true)` here). We get the extra from the intent, using it to set the title. Finally, we set up the tabs.

When you have an enum, there are a few different ways you can store it in a `Bundle` (the class that handles intent extras and fragment arguments), but the easiest is to take advantage of Java's built in serialization. For a normal class (i.e., not an enum), this method of serialization is not efficient because reflection is used to get the name, field names, and values to store as bytes, and then the deserialization process converts those bytes into an instance of the class and sets all the fields. For an enum, the runtime will only store the name and the deserialization process will just call `valueOf(name)` to create the appropriate enum. Many developers are under the mistaken impression that enums are serialized the same way as regular classes, so they go through the hassle of getting the enum's name to store and calling `valueOf(name)` themselves. This works, it is essentially the same as what happens when you just take advantage of serialization here.

Listing 8.19 shows the activity. With that done, we just need to create the detail activity and we'll have an app!

Listing 8.19 The `ToolListActivity` Class

```
public class ToolListActivity extends AppCompatActivity implements
➥ TabLayout.OnTabSelectedListener {

    private static final String EXTRA_TOOL_TYPE = "com.auidbook.
➥ woodworkingtools.TOOL_TYPE";

    private ToolType mToolType;
    private ViewPager mViewPager;

    public static void startActivity(Context context, ToolType toolType) {
        final Intent intent = new Intent(context, ToolListActivity.class);
        intent.putExtra(EXTRA_TOOL_TYPE, toolType);
        context.startActivity(intent);
    }

    @Override
    protected void onCreate(Bundle savedInstanceState) {
        super.onCreate(savedInstanceState);
        setContentView(R.layout.activity_tool_list);

        final Toolbar toolbar = (Toolbar) findViewById
➥ (R.id.toolbar);
        setSupportActionBar(toolbar);
        getSupportActionBar().setDisplayHomeAsUpEnabled(true);
```

```
        mToolType = (ToolType) getIntent().
➡ getSerializableExtra(EXTRA_TOOL_TYPE);
        if (mToolType == null) {
            throw new IllegalStateException("ToolType not available as
➡ extra; use startActivity");
        }
        setTitle(mToolType.getToolNameResourceId());

        // Set up tabs
        mViewPager = (ViewPager) findViewById(R.id.viewpager);
        final TabLayout tabLayout = (TabLayout) findViewById
➡ (R.id.tabs);
        final ToolPagerAdapter toolPagerAdapter = new ToolPagerAdapter
➡ (getSupportFragmentManager(), getResources(), mToolType);
        tabLayout.setTabsFromPagerAdapter(toolPagerAdapter);
        mViewPager.addOnPageChangeListener(new TabLayout.TabLayoutOnPag
➡ eChangeListener(tabLayout));
        mViewPager.setAdapter(toolPagerAdapter);
        tabLayout.setOnTabSelectedListener(this);
    }
    @Override
    public void onTabSelected(TabLayout.Tab tab) {
        mViewPager.setCurrentItem(tab.getPosition());
    }

    @Override
    public void onTabUnselected(TabLayout.Tab tab) {}

    @Override
    public void onTabReselected(TabLayout.Tab tab) {}
}
```

The Tool Details

The tool details activity and layout are very similar to the prototype versions. Figure 8.12 shows the design. Notice that the app bar at the top displays only the up nav arrow (no title) and it is on top of the image. To hide the title, we simply get a reference to the support action bar and call `setDisplayShowTitleEnabled(false)` on it.

To get the up nav arrow in front of the image, we need to update the layout slightly. It will now be a `FrameLayout` as the base which contains the `ScrollView` from the prototype (with the image and name removed in favor of our `CaptionedImageView` class), the `Toolbar`, and the `FloatingActionbutton`. The `Toolbar` specifically has its background set to transparent. Listing 8.20 shows the layout.

Figure 8.12 The design for the tool details

Listing 8.20   The Layout for the Details Screen

```xml
<?xml version="1.0" encoding="utf-8"?>
<FrameLayout xmlns:android="http://schemas.android.com/apk/res/android"
             xmlns:app="http://schemas.android.com/apk/res-auto"
             xmlns:tools="http://schemas.android.com/tools"
             android:layout_width="match_parent"
             android:layout_height="match_parent"
    >

    <ScrollView
        android:layout_width="match_parent"
        android:layout_height="wrap_content"
        android:fillViewport="true">

        <RelativeLayout
            android:layout_width="match_parent"
            android:layout_height="wrap_content"
            android:paddingBottom="80dp">

            <com.auidbook.woodworkingtools.CaptionedImageView
                android:id="@+id/hero_image"
                android:layout_width="match_parent"
                android:layout_height="wrap_content"/>
```

```xml
        <TextView
            android:id="@+id/detail_0"
            android:layout_width="wrap_content"
            android:layout_height="wrap_content"
            android:layout_above="@+id/detail_2"
            android:layout_alignStart="@+id/hero_image"
            android:paddingLeft="@dimen/activity_horizontal_margin"
            android:paddingRight="@dimen/activity_horizontal_margin"
            android:textSize="20sp"
            tools:text="3/4 HP"/>

        <TextView
            android:id="@+id/detail_1"
            android:layout_width="wrap_content"
            android:layout_height="wrap_content"
            android:layout_alignStart="@id/detail_0"
            android:layout_below="@id/detail_0"
            android:paddingLeft="@dimen/activity_horizontal_margin"
            android:paddingRight="@dimen/activity_horizontal_margin"
            android:textSize="20sp"
            tools:text="5" travel"/>

        <TextView
            android:id="@+id/detail_2"
            android:layout_width="wrap_content"
            android:layout_height="wrap_content"
            android:layout_alignEnd="@+id/price"
            android:layout_below="@+id/price"
            android:paddingLeft="@dimen/activity_horizontal_margin"
            android:paddingRight="@dimen/activity_horizontal_margin"
            android:textSize="20sp"
            tools:text="8" throat"/>

        <TextView
            android:id="@+id/description"
            android:layout_width="wrap_content"
            android:layout_height="wrap_content"
            android:layout_alignParentStart="true"
            android:layout_below="@id/detail_1"
            android:layout_marginTop="16dp"
            android:paddingLeft="@dimen/activity_horizontal_margin"
            android:paddingRight="@dimen/activity_horizontal_margin"
            android:textAppearance="?android:attr/
➥ textAppearanceMedium"/>

        <TextView
            android:id="@+id/price"
            android:layout_width="wrap_content"
            android:layout_height="wrap_content"
```

```
            android:layout_alignEnd="@+id/hero_image"
            android:layout_below="@+id/hero_image"
            android:paddingLeft="@dimen/activity_horizontal_margin"
            android:paddingRight="@dimen/activity_horizontal_margin"
            android:textSize="20sp"
            tools:text="$750"/>

    </RelativeLayout>

</ScrollView>

<android.support.v7.widget.Toolbar
        android:id="@+id/toolbar"
        android:layout_width="match_parent"
        android:layout_height="?attr/actionBarSize"
        android:elevation="0dp"
        android:background="@android:color/transparent"
        app:theme="@style/ThemeOverlay.AppCompat.Dark.ActionBar" />

<android.support.design.widget.FloatingActionButton
        android:id="@+id/fab"
        android:layout_width="wrap_content"
        android:layout_height="wrap_content"
        android:src="@drawable/ic_buy"
        app:borderWidth="0dp"
        android:layout_gravity="bottom|end"
        android:layout_margin="@dimen/default_padding" />

</FrameLayout>
```

Now we just need to update the activity to set the values on the `CaptionedImageView` class and we're set. Don't forget to call `setSquare(false)` to make sure that we get the right aspect ratio. Listing 8.21 shows the activity.

Listing 8.21   The `ToolDetailActivity` Class

```
public class ToolDetailActivity extends AppCompatActivity {

    private static final String EXTRA_TOOL = "com.auidbook.
➥ woodworkingtools.TOOL";

    public static void startActivity(Context context, Tool tool) {
        final Intent intent = new Intent(context,
➥ ToolDetailActivity.class);
        intent.putExtra(EXTRA_TOOL, tool);
        context.startActivity(intent);
    }
```

```java
@Override
protected void onCreate(Bundle savedInstanceState) {
    super.onCreate(savedInstanceState);
    setContentView(R.layout.activity_tool_detail);

    final Toolbar toolbar = (Toolbar) findViewById(R.id.toolbar);
    setSupportActionBar(toolbar);
    getSupportActionBar().setDisplayShowTitleEnabled(false);
    getSupportActionBar().setDisplayHomeAsUpEnabled(true);

    final Tool tool = getIntent().getParcelableExtra(EXTRA_TOOL);
    if (tool == null) {
        throw new IllegalStateException("Tool not available as
    extra; use startActivity when creating an activity instance");
    }

    final CaptionedImageView captionedImageView =
    (CaptionedImageView) findViewById(R.id.hero_image);
    captionedImageView.getImageView().setSquare(false);
    captionedImageView.getTextView().setText(tool.getName());
    captionedImageView.setImageResource(tool.getImageResourceId());

    findAndSetTextView(R.id.price, tool.getPrice());
    findAndSetTextView(R.id.detail_0, tool.getDetails()[0]);
    findAndSetTextView(R.id.detail_1, tool.getDetails()[1]);
    findAndSetTextView(R.id.detail_2, tool.getDetails()[2]);
    findAndSetTextView(R.id.description, tool.getDescription());
}

private void findAndSetTextView(int id, String text) {
    final TextView textView = (TextView) findViewById(id);
    textView.setText(text);
}
}
```

Basic Testing Across Device Types

There are countless variations of Android devices out there, so it's nearly impossible to really test your app against them all. Fortunately, it is relatively easy to test against groups of devices that you intend to support, especially if you are not doing anything complex with the GPU (in other words, not using any manufacturer- or chip-specific features). Typically, only graphically intense games have to consider what GPU is on a given device, and a regular app can more or less never interact with the GPU directly. This means that you can focus on device sizes and device densities. For "normal"-sized devices (i.e., phone-sized), recent flagship devices have been XXHDPI, but you should consider that many users get their devices on contract, so they could be using a device that's a few years old. Further, many developing countries are releasing new devices that XHDPI or even HDPI, so you can't discount the lower resolutions if your app will be widely available. In general, it's good to test against both a high-end device and a device that's near the end of its lifespan but still supports the version of Android that you've set as your minimum.

You should also consider testing against a Nexus 7 as the de facto large device; although it has been discontinued, it represents a fair share of the market and you can pick up a used version relatively cheaply. There are two versions of the Nexus 7, but testing against either one will be helpful because the screen is the same physical size (the newer version, the "Nexus 7 (2013)" has a higher resolution). These devices present a bit of a challenge. In portrait mode, they are very similar to phones. The screens are larger, but they do not quite feel tablet sized. This means that many apps will work pretty well with little to no modification. Switch your Nexus 7 to landscape though, and you suddenly have a device that feels much more like a tablet. It's wide enough to have two panes of content, so you have to consider what that means for your design.

Finally, you should test against "xlarge" or 9–12 inch tablets such as the Nexus 9 and 10. These tablets do not represent a substantial portion of the Android market right now, but their sales are growing. Most apps are not optimized for these tablets, so this means that optimizing your app lets you stand out. People tend to like using one app across their devices, so if your app is the only one of its kind that works well across all devices, you just earned yourself some additional installs and users who are likely to be loyal. Just remember than these tablets almost always require changes to the layouts to make efficient use of their extra space, whereas the Nexus 7 can frequently work fine with apps designed for phones.

Summary

This chapter focused on the communication between designers and developers and how to go from comps to designed apps. In particular, you have learned the considerations necessary for slicing assets, how to create styles that reflect the comps, and how to break the comps into Android layouts. You also got a taste of RenderScript for some efficient blurring.

In the next chapter, you will add more polish to your apps. Instead of focusing on static layouts, you will learn how to make your apps more fluid. By animating transitions in your app, not only does it look nicer, but you help the user understand how things are changing and, more importantly, why.

CHAPTER 9

POLISHING WITH ANIMATIONS

Animations have slowly become more and more important in apps. Not long ago, it was common for all actions to have sudden and nonobvious consequences, but animations have become an expectation now. Material Design has placed particular emphasis on the fluidity of design, making it more important than ever to include animations in your app.

Purpose of Animations

Many people mistakenly assume animations are just there for show or that they are just "eye candy" of some sort, but animations are a major part of user experience. They can certainly make an app feel more fun, but the real purpose is to explain changes to users. The past few chapters have been about overall hierarchy answering questions of how the app is organized and how screens are organized, but that doesn't answer the question of how you transition from one screen to the next or how you change from one state to the next.

If the user submits a form and there's an error, having the message suddenly somewhere on the screen means the user has to hunt for what changed. Although errors are a particularly good case for animation (they're unexpected, so the extra guidance is even more useful), animations can be beneficial even with normal interactions. Tapping a list item should push the unrelated items off the screen, animate any changes to the content that is staying (such as the thumbnail and title of the item that was tapped), and then bring in the new content. Animating the content in this way creates a sense of continuity that you don't get when you just drop all the new content in with one single motion.

Now might be a good time to play with a few of your favorite apps and pay attention to the animations. When you tap an email in Gmail's list, the app bar updates based on what's applicable to the detail page, the other emails go away, and the subject of the email you tapped animates to the top. When you tap an app in Google Play, the icon animates up into place and the top background uses a circular reveal. As you explore apps paying particular attention to animations, you'll likely also notice that there are still quite a few quirks like a toolbar flickering or font sizes changing suddenly. With many developers and designers paying more attention to animations than before and various libraries changing to better support animations, some of these growing pains can stand out.

View Animations

View animations were the primary animation method in Android originally and they're supported by all versions of Android. They basically work as tween animations, which means you specify a start and an end state and the states in between are calculated. For instance, you might specify that a view starts fully transparent and ends as a fully opaque view. With a linear animation, your view would be about halfway transparent at the midpoint. These tween animations support changes in transparency (alpha), size (scale), position (translate), and rotation (rotate).

With view animations, you can also supply an interpolator, which adjusts how far along an animation is at a given time. Interpolators work by taking a float as an input that is between 0 (the start of the animation) and 1.0 (the end of the animation) and returning a float that is the modified position. The returned float can return values outside of the start and end positions, which can allow the animation to undershoot and overshoot the start and end points. For example, you might have a view that's supposed to move 100dp to the right. An interpolator might cause the view to go to 120dp and then come back to the left 20dp.

> **note**
>
> View animations affect the drawing of the view, not the actual positioning. This means that if you animate a button from the left side of the screen to the right side, the click listening will still be happening on the left side despite the fact that the button appears to be on the right side. To avoid that problem, either use property animations or adjust the layout positioning within the parent after the animation has completed.
>
> View animations are also limited to the bounds of the parent view. This means that if you are animating an image that exists inside a `ViewGroup` that takes up the upper half of the screen, the image cannot animate to the bottom half of the screen (the view will be clipped if it exceeds the bounds of the parent).

Many views take advantage of view animations, such as the `ViewAnimator` class and its subclasses. These classes make it easy to crossfade between a loading indicator and the content view, for example, but they cannot do things such as animate the background of a view between two colors or affect objects that aren't views. Generally speaking, you don't need to use view animations anymore if the minimum version of Android that you're supporting is 3.0 or newer. Property animations came to Android at that point and have significant advantages, including that they can actually affect the position of the view and not just where it is drawn.

Property Animations

In Android 3.0 (Honeycomb), the property animation system was introduced. The idea is that you can animate any property (a field or class variable) of any object, so they can do the same things as view animations and a whole lot more. At time of writing, devices running a version of Android older than 3.0 account for about 4% of all devices accessing Google Play.

> **note**
>
> The property animation system was introduced in API level 11, so this means that you need to avoid using any of these classes on previous versions of Android. If your app supports older versions of Android, consider using the NineOldAndroids library by Jake Wharton (available at http://nineoldandroids.com/), which makes these objects available for Android 1.0 apps and up.

The first class to know for property animation is the `ValueAnimator`. This class handles all the timing and the value computations. It also keeps track of whether the animation repeats, what listeners should be notified of the new values, and more. This class does not directly modify any properties; it just supplies the mechanism for doing so, which means is helpful for a variety of use cases.

The next class to know about will make your life a lot easier. The `ObjectAnimator` is a subclass of `ValueAnimator` that allows you to specify an object that has properties to animate. This object needs a setter method for that property (so if you want to animate "alpha," the object needs a `setAlpha` method) that can be called for each update. If you do not specify a starting value, it also needs a getter method (e.g., `getAlpha()`) to determine the starting point and the range of animation.

Taking a look at a simple example will help clarify how to use an `ObjectAnimator`. If you wanted to animate a view from fully opaque to fully transparent and back again over the course of 5 seconds, how much code would be required? See Listing 9.1 for the answer.

Listing 9.1   A Simple `ObjectAnimator` Example

```
final ObjectAnimator anim = ObjectAnimator.offFloat(myView, "alpha",
➡ 1f, 0f, 1f);
anim.setDuration(5000);
anim.start();
```

As you can see, the code required is quite minimal. You create an `ObjectAnimator` by using the static `offloat` method. The first value passed is the object to animate. The second value is the name of the property to animate. The rest of the values are the floats to animate among. You can specify just one float, in which case the value is assumed to be the end animation value and the begin value will be looked up by calling `getAlpha` in this case. The `setDuration` method takes the number of milliseconds to animate for.

You can also combine multiple animations. For instance, you might want to animate a view to the right 200 pixels and down 50 pixels at the same time. In this case, you create the two `ObjectAnimator` instances and combine them with an `AnimatorSet` by calling the `playTogether` method with both animations (alternatively, you could call `playSequentially` to play one and then the other). The code looks like Listing 9.2.

Listing 9.2   Combining Animations with `AnimationSet`

```
ObjectAnimator animX = ObjectAnimator.offFloat(myView, "x", 200f);
ObjectAnimator animY = ObjectAnimator.offFloat(myView, "y", 50f);
AnimatorSet animationSet = new AnimatorSet();
animationSet.setDuration(5000);
animationSet.playTogether(animX, animY);
animationSet.start();
```

You can actually make this a bit more efficient by using `PropertyValueHolder` objects, but there is an even better way called `ViewPropertyAnimator`, which is covered a little later in the chapter.

Property Animation Control

Property animations are very powerful and quite flexible. You can trigger events that occur at specific times within the animation such as when it first starts or when it begins to repeat. You can use custom type evaluators to animate any kind of property instead of just floats and integers. Interpolators allow you to specify custom curves or changes to the animation speeds and values. You can even use key frames to define an exact state for a given moment within a greater animation.

Listeners

You will commonly use listeners to trigger events related to animations. For instance, you might animate the alpha (transparency) of a view until it is gone and use a listener to actually remove that view from the view hierarchy at the end of the animation.

`AnimatorListener` allows you to receive the high level events for the animation including when it starts, stops, ends, and repeats. `Animator` (such as `ValueAnimator` or `ObjectAnimator`) has an `addListener` method that lets you add any number of `AnimatorListener` instances. In many cases you only need to implement one or two of these methods, so it can be handy to know about `AnimatorListenerAdapter`. That class implements all of the interface's methods with stubs, so you can just override whichever ones you need.

If you use `ValueAnimator` directly, you will use `AnimatorUpdateListener` to receive an update for every frame of an animation. Your implementation of `onAnimationUpdate` will be called so that you can call `getAnimatedValue` to the most recent animation value and apply that to whatever you need for your animation.

Type Evaluators

Android supports animating ints, floats, and colors. These are supported with the `IntEvaluator`, `FloatEvaluator`, and `ArgbEvaluator` respectively. If you're animating from 0 to 100, the `IntEvaluator` tells Android what value to use at a given point; at 50%, the animation will give a value of 50. What about 50% of an arbitrary object though? You can create your own custom `TypeEvaluator` to handle these situations. There is a single method to implement called `evaluate` that takes the percent through the animation as a float between 0 and 1 (so 50% would be 0.5f), the start value, and the end value. A simple example might animate between an empty string and the string "Animation!" The evaluator could return the portion of the string represented by the percent (50% would return "Anima"), allowing you to actually animate the characters in a `TextView`, for instance, using the same mechanism you use for animating the position or alpha of that view.

Let's make a simple `TypeEvaluator` subclass that handles `CharSequence` instances called `CharSequenceEvaluator`, which would let us animate more representations of text, including strings. The evaluator needs to handle empty text or a null value as well as if one of the `CharSquence` instances is longer than the other. The overall goal is to animate from one bit of text to the other by taking the initial value (say, the word "Bacon") and replacing characters as it works toward the final value (e.g., "Power"). At 40% into the animation, it should be taking the first 40% of the final value's characters ("Po" in our example) and the rest from the initial value (the "con" from "Bacon"), creating a mix of the characters ("Pocon") until it eventually transitions fully to the final value.

First, we need to handle some edge cases. A developer using the code might accidentally animate from an empty text value or null to an empty text value or null. We should immediately check the lengths of the `CharSequence` start and end values and just return if they're both empty. In our `evaluate` method, we may be given a float that's less than 0 or greater than 1. This might seem strange (How can you be less than 0% or more than 100% of the way through an animation?), but this allows supporting what's called anticipating (values under 0%) and overshooting (values over 100%) with interpolators, which are covered more shortly. If you were animating a box from the left side of the screen to the right side, you might want it to actually go a little past the right side (overshoot) and then come back to where it is supposed to end up. This can be used for different effects, such as making the object appear to move so fast that it can't slowdown in time, but this doesn't make much sense for our `CharSequenceEvaluator`. What do you show if you're beyond the final `CharSequence`? Instead of figuring that out, we'll just return the full starting `CharSequence` if we receive a float of less than 0 and the full ending `CharSequence` if we receive a float of more than 1.

The bulk of the `evaluate` method just figures out how many characters have changed by multiplying the length of the longer `CharSequence` by the float that's passed in and then uses that many characters from the final value and the remainder from the initial value (remember, because the animation is starting at the first character of the text and working toward the end, the end portion will come from the initial value; you could just as easily make a type evaluator that animates from the last character to the first if that's what you wanted). In cases where the final value isn't as long as the initial value (such as if you were animating from "Suitcase" to "Food"), once the animation has gone far enough to display all of the final value, it displays fewer and fewer of the initial value's characters almost as if someone were pressing the delete key (so you'd see "Foodcase" and then "Foodase" and so forth). Listing 9.3 shows the source code for the `CharSequenceEvaluator`.

Listing 9.3 The `CharSequenceEvaluator`

```
public class CharSequenceEvaluator implements
➥ TypeEvaluator<CharSequence> {

    @Override
    public CharSequence evaluate(float fraction, CharSequence
➥ startValue, CharSequence endValue) {
```

```java
        final int initialTextLength = startValue == null ? 0 :
startValue.length();
        final int finalTextLength = endValue == null ? 0 : endValue.
length();

        // Handle two empty strings because someone's probably going to
do this for some reason
        if (initialTextLength == 0 && finalTextLength == 0) {
            return endValue;
        }

        // Handle anticipation
        if (fraction <= 0) {
            return startValue;
        }
        // Handle overshooting
        if (fraction >= 1f) {
            return endValue;
        }

        // Fraction is based on the longer CharSequence
        final float maxLength = Math.max(initialTextLength,
finalTextLength);
        final int charactersChanged = (int) (maxLength * fraction);
        if (charactersChanged == 0) {
            // Handle anything that rounds to 0
            return startValue;
        }

        if (finalTextLength < charactersChanged) {
            // More characters have changed than the length of the
final string

            if (finalTextLength == 0) {
                // Moving toward no string, so just substring the
initial values
                return startValue.subSequence(charactersChanged,
initialTextLength);
            }

            if (initialTextLength <= charactersChanged) {
                // Use the endValue because the startValue has been
passed
                return endValue.subSequence(0, charactersChanged);
            }
            // Both CharSequences have characters to use
        return endValue + startValue.subSequence(charactersChanged,
initialTextLength).toString();
        }
```

```
        // endValue is longer than the number of characters that have
➥ changed
        if (initialTextLength <= charactersChanged) {
            // Already animated away start, use fraction of end
            return endValue.subSequence(0, charactersChanged).
➥ toString();
        }

        return endValue.subSequence(0, charactersChanged).toString() +
➥ startValue.subSequence(charactersChanged, initialTextLength);
    }
}
```

One thing to keep in mind when creating an evaluator is that you want things to be as efficient as possible. Each call of the `evaluate` method is milliseconds after the previous one, so you don't want to create and throw away objects if you can help it.

Time Interpolators

Animations use a concrete implementation of the `TimeInterpolator` interface. An interpolator has a very simple purpose defined by a single method, `getInterpolation`, and that is to take in a float and return a float. This allows you to have animations that aren't linear. The animator will tell the interpolator how much of the animation is finished (again as a float between 0 and 1) and the interpolator will give a different float that is used by the type evaluator to determine how far along the animation is.

An example will make this clearer. For instance, if you create an interpolator that just takes the input value, multiplies it by itself, and returns the result, consider how that affects the numbers coming out. When the animation is 10% done, the animator will ask the interpolator for its interpolation of 0.1f. The interpolator will multiply that by itself, which returns 0.01f. That value is passed to your type evaluator to get a new value. This means that if you were animating a box 100px, at 10% it would go just 1px. When it's 20% done, the interpolator is going to multiply 0.2f by itself and get 0.04f, so the box will be 4px from the starting point. At 30% done, the interpolator will return 0.09f (0.3f times 0.3f) and 0.16f at 40%. You can start to see that each step of the way the amount that the box moves will be more and more significant. At 80% it will have moved 64px and at 90% it will have moved 81px. By simply returning the value multiplied by itself, you create a basic accelerating interpolator.

Android offers several interpolators, so you rarely have to make one yourself. Table 9.1 shows the interpolators that are available, but don't be afraid to make your own. The source code for this book has an AnimationExamples project in the `chapter09` folder. You can run it to easily test any of these interpolators with different durations.

Table 9.1 `TimeInterpolator` Implementations in Android

Class Name	Description
`AccelerateDecelerateInterpolator`	Starts slowly, goes very quickly in the middle, and ends slowly; this is useful for animations that start and end on the screen.
`AccelerateInterpolator`	Starts slowly and gets faster as it goes; this is useful for animations that start on the screen and end off the screen.
`AnticipateInterpolator`	Like `AccelerateInterpolator` but it has a "tension" that causes it to start with negative values, so an animation that moves a box to the right will start with it moving left some and then shooting to the right almost as if it were put into a slingshot.
`AnticipateOvershootInterpolator`	Behaves like an `AnticipateInterpolator` for the first half but it will go beyond the end value before returning, so box that was moving right would go beyond the end point and then move back to the left to settle down almost as if it were caught by a slingshot.
`BounceInterpolator`	Animates like a bouncing ball. You can imagine dropping a rubber ball from above the ground. When the ball hits the ground, it will go back up before gravity takes over to bring it back down. It repeats this process a few times, each bounce not going as high as the one before, until it ends.
`CycleInterpolator`	Imagine a sine wave where the Y coordinate represents the float that is returned by the interpolator and X represents time, you'll have a basic understanding of this interpolator. It takes an int to determine how many cycles the wave has, creating an oscillation where the top of the wave represents the final value for your animation and the center line represents the starting point. This means a box in the center of your screen that you animate to the right side will animate from the center to the right edge, from the right edge to the left edge, and from the left edge to the right edge. This is repeated based on how many cycles you set in the constructor.
`DecelerateInterpolator`	Starts at the maximum speed and then slows at the end; this is useful for animations that start from off screen and finish on screen.
`FastOutLinearInInterpolator`	In the support library, this interpolator uses a lookup table to describe the motion. In simple terms, it starts out like an `AccelerateInterpolator` and ends like a `LinearInterpolator`.

Class Name	Description
FastOutSlowInInterpolator	In the support library, this interpolator uses a lookup table to describe the motion. In simple terms, it starts out like an AccelerateInterpolator and ends like a DecelerateInterpolator.
LinearInterpolator	Animates at a constant speed with no speed changes.
LinearOutSlowInInterpolator	In the support library, this interpolator uses a lookup table to describe the motion. In simple terms, it starts out like a LinearInterpolator and ends like a DecelerateInterpolator.
OvershootInterpolator	Like AccelerateInterpolator but it has a "tension" that causes it to go beyond the end of the animate before settling, so an animation that moves a box to the right will move it beyond the end position and then spring back to the end as if caught by a slingshot.
PathInterpolator	Added in Android 5.0 (API level 21), this interpolator animates based on a path that you give it. The X position represents time and the Y position represents the float that will be returned. All kinds of interesting paths can be supported provided that you ensure you have only one Y value for any given X value and there are no gaps (a given X value from 0 to 1 has a corresponding Y value).

Key Frames

In the animation world outside of Android, key frames are the important frames of an animation. They mark the beginning and end of a single smooth motion (such as a car traveling from the left side of the screen to the right side). Android mirrors this concept with the Keyframe class, which contains the values an animation should have at a particular time. In most cases, you won't need to directly interact with this class. Behind the scenes, an IntKeyframe, FloatKeyframe, or ObjectKeyframe (all are static inner classes of the abstract Keyframe class) will be created for you as necessary. If you want to precisely control your animations, you can use the static methods of Keyframe to pass in a time (expressed as a float where 0 is the start of the animation and 1 is the end) and a value and get back a Keyframe instance to use in your animation. Listing 9.4 demonstrates how you can use key frames to animate the rotation of a view from 0 degrees to 90 degrees, hesitate briefly, and then animate back from 90 degrees to 0 degrees. The full source for this demo is in the KeyframeDemo project within the chapter09 source code.

Listing 9.4   A Simple Demonstration of the `Keyframe` Class

```
public class MainActivity extends AppCompatActivity implements View.
➥ OnClickListener {

    @Override
    protected void onCreate(Bundle savedInstanceState) {
        super.onCreate(savedInstanceState);
        setContentView(R.layout.activity_main);

        final Toolbar toolbar = (Toolbar) findViewById(R.id.toolbar);
        setSupportActionBar(toolbar);

        findViewById(R.id.button).setOnClickListener(this);
    }

    @Override
    public void onClick(final View button) {
        button.setEnabled(false);
        View icon = findViewById(R.id.icon);

        Keyframe keyframe1 = Keyframe.ofFloat(0f, 0f);
        Keyframe keyframe2 = Keyframe.ofFloat(.4f, 90f);
        Keyframe keyframe3 = Keyframe.ofFloat(.6f, 90f);
        Keyframe keyframe4 = Keyframe.ofFloat(1f, 0f);
        PropertyValuesHolder propertyValuesHolder = PropertyValuesHolder.
➥ ofKeyframe("rotation", keyframe1, keyframe2, keyframe3, keyframe4);
        ObjectAnimator rotationAnim = ObjectAnimator.ofPropertyValuesH
➥ older(icon, propertyValuesHolder);
        rotationAnim.setDuration(5000);
        rotationAnim.addListener(new AnimatorListenerAdapter() {
            @Override
            public void onAnimationEnd(Animator animation) {
                button.setEnabled(true);
            }
        });
        rotationAnim.setInterpolator(new
➥ AccelerateDecelerateInterpolator());
        rotationAnim.start();
    }
}
```

ViewPropertyAnimator

In Android 3.1, the Android team introduced the `ViewPropertyAnimator`. By calling `animate()` on any `View` object, you get a `ViewPropertyAnimator` that has simple methods for changing alpha, rotation, scale, translation, and so on. Each of these methods returns the

`ViewPropertyAnimator`, so you can easily chain several methods together. Take a look at Listing 9.5 to see how simple the code can become.

Listing 9.5 Using `ViewPropertyAnimator`

```
myView.animate().setDuration(5000).x(200f).y(50f).start();
```

The animation that was already impressive at just six lines can now be just one (shown on multiple lines here for readability). What's even more impressive is that, behind the scenes, this superconcise code is even more efficient than the previous example!

In many cases, `ViewPropertyAnimator` will give you everything you want. You can animate all the typical properties as well as set the interpolator, update listener, end or start actions, and more.

Animating Form Errors

Form errors are a common element to apps that need animation, especially because they usually represent a minor change to an existing page. You generally have two considerations with a form error: (1) Ensure the error catches the user's eye and (2) Ensure the error is visible on the screen. For the first consideration, you should make your errors red (#DD2C00) unless that clashes with your background. You should also animate them in when possible. In most cases, a simple alpha animation from 0f to 1f will be sufficient. For the second consideration, you need to see if the form error is on the screen. If not, scroll it onto the screen. Smoothly scrolling to the first (top-most) error is generally preferable. It allows the user to understand the spatial change and potentially see other errors during the scroll. For instance, in a `ScrollView`, you can simply call `smoothScrollTo` with the x and y coordinates (generally, this will be 0 for x, and simply the y position of the view with an error).

The Android design library makes it easy to handle errors and use a UI pattern called "float label," shown in Figure 9.1. The float label pattern is when you have an area to input text (generally an `EditText` in the case of Android) and there is no label. Instead, the area where you input text has a hint that suggests what you should type. Depending on the implementation, either selecting that view or typing in it causes the hint to animate away and become the label itself. The advantage of this pattern is that it allows you to significantly compact forms. The disadvantage is that the labels and hints have to be the same, which is often less useful (e.g., a traditional form field might have a label of "email address" but the hint would have "example@domain.com"). If you find that the float label pattern works for your needs, the `TextInputLayout` from the design library makes this easy. Listing 9.6 shows a simple layout that implements two `TextInputLayout` instances surrounding `EditText` views. Remember that you need to include the design library in your `build.gradle` file (`compile 'com.android.support:design:22.2.1'`). Given how rapidly all the support

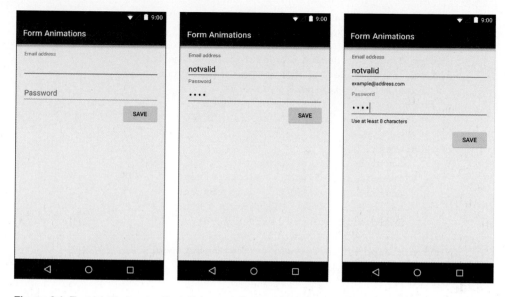

Figure 9.1 Float labels showing the initial state (left), the completed state (center), and the error state (right)

libraries have been developing, there is likely to be a newer version out by the time you read this. In general, you should use the newest version available but older versions remain available in case code depended on something that later changed.

Listing 9.6   A Layout Containing a Simple Form

```
<LinearLayout xmlns:android="http://schemas.android.com/apk/res/android"
              xmlns:tools="http://schemas.android.com/tools"
              android:layout_width="match_parent"
              android:layout_height="match_parent"
              android:paddingLeft="@dimen/activity_horizontal_margin"
              android:paddingRight="@dimen/activity_horizontal_margin"
              android:paddingTop="@dimen/activity_vertical_margin"
              android:paddingBottom="@dimen/activity_vertical_margin"
              android:orientation="vertical"
              tools:context=".MainActivity">

    <android.support.design.widget.TextInputLayout
        android:id="@+id/input_email"
        android:layout_width="match_parent"
        android:layout_height="wrap_content">

        <EditText
            android:id="@+id/email"
            android:layout_width="match_parent"
            android:layout_height="wrap_content"
```

```
                    android:hint="@string/email_hint"
                    android:inputType="textEmailAddress"/>

    </android.support.design.widget.TextInputLayout>
    <android.support.design.widget.TextInputLayout
            android:id="@+id/input_password"
            android:layout_width="match_parent"
            android:layout_height="wrap_content">

        <EditText
                android:id="@+id/password"
                android:layout_width="match_parent"
                android:layout_height="wrap_content"
                android:hint="@string/password_hint"
                android:inputType="textPassword"/>

    </android.support.design.widget.TextInputLayout>

    <Button
            android:id="@+id/button_save"
            android:layout_width="wrap_content"
            android:layout_height="wrap_content"
            android:text="@string/save"
            android:layout_gravity="end"/>

    <TextView
            android:id="@+id/success"
            android:layout_width="wrap_content"
            android:layout_height="wrap_content"
            android:textAppearance="?android:attr/textAppearanceLarge"
            android:text="@string/success"
            android:visibility="gone"/>

</LinearLayout>
```

With just some simple logic to tie everything together in the activity, you can display error messages as needed. The `TextInputLayout` handles the animations with two simple methods. First, `setError` allows you to set the text to be displayed as an error. The `setErrorEnabled` method allows you to disable (or enable) the current error. With just a little code, it's easy to check a field to make sure it's an email address and another to check for a minimum length. Remember, `getText` on a `TextView` (which `EditText` extends) never returns null, so you can safely check the length without first checking for null. Listing 9.7 shows the activity code.

Listing 9.7   Activity Code for Handling Form Errors

```
public class MainActivity extends AppCompatActivity implements View.
➥ OnClickListener {

    private static final int MIN_PASSWORD_LENGTH = 8;
```

```java
    private TextView mTextViewEmail;
    private TextInputLayout mTextInputLayoutEmail;
    private TextView mTextViewPassword;
    private TextInputLayout mTextInputLayoutPassword;
    private View mViewSuccess;

    @Override
    protected void onCreate(Bundle savedInstanceState) {
        super.onCreate(savedInstanceState);
        setContentView(R.layout.activity_main);

        findViewById(R.id.button_save).setOnClickListener(this);
        mTextInputLayoutEmail = (TextInputLayout) findViewById
(R.id.input_email);
        mTextViewEmail = (TextView) mTextInputLayoutEmail.
findViewById(R.id.email);
        mTextInputLayoutPassword = (TextInputLayout) findViewById
(R.id.input_password);
        mTextViewPassword = (TextView) mTextInputLayoutPassword.
findViewById(R.id.password);
        mViewSuccess = findViewById(R.id.success);
    }

    @Override
    public void onClick(View v) {
        boolean hasError = false;

        // Validate email address
        if (Patterns.EMAIL_ADDRESS.matcher(mTextViewEmail.getText()).
matches()) {
            mTextInputLayoutEmail.setErrorEnabled(false);
        } else {
            mTextInputLayoutEmail.setError(getString
(R.string.email_error));
            hasError = true;
        }

        // Validate password
        if (mTextViewPassword.getText().length() >= MIN_PASSWORD_
LENGTH) {
            mTextInputLayoutPassword.setErrorEnabled(false);
        } else {
            mTextInputLayoutPassword.setError(getString
(R.string.password_error));
            hasError = true;
        }

        if (hasError) {
            mViewSuccess.setVisibility(View.GONE);
        } else {
```

```
                    mViewSuccess.setVisibility(View.VISIBLE);
            }
        }
    }
```

Animating Icons

Chapter 4, "Adding App Graphics and Resources," briefly covered using an
`AnimatedVectorDrawable` to animate the path of a less-than symbol to a greater-than
symbol. That's worth exploring in a bit more detail. Many of your app icons are going to
come from the giant collection of Material Design icons available (https://github.com/google/
material-design-icons), so how do you animate between two arbitrary icons in this collection?

Animating Vector Icons

Just like Chapter 4, "Adding App Graphics and Resources," showed, you need three files for a
vector animation. You need the initial `VectorDrawable` (which uses the `vector` XML tag),
the `AnimatedVectorDrawable` (which uses the `animated-vector` XML tag), and the
`ObjectAnimator` (which uses the `objectAnimator` XML tag). Let's look at this process a
little closer. What are the steps to animate from the icon for left-aligned text to justified text?

First, create a new XML drawable with a `vector` root node called `ic_align_left`. Remember
that the height and width are the size you want it to render to and the viewport height and
width are the size of the SVG space. If you aren't sure what the SVG space was, you can open the
SVG file and look for the width and height attributes in the root `svg` node.

Create a single child `path` node. It needs a name (this is what the animation uses to target this
node), so something simple like "lines" works. It needs the stroke and fill colors defined (black
is fine for now). Finally, it needs the path data. Within the Material Design icons is a folder called
"editor" (as in, icons typically used for a text editor). Depending on which version you check out,
there may be a folder in there to open called "production." Then you should see the "svg" folder.
This is where the SVG versions of all editor icons reside. The icon for left-aligned text is called
`ic_format_align_left_48px.svg`. The name of that means it is an icon ("ic") for formatting
("format") and the specific formatting it applies is align left. The 48px at the end means it is
on a canvas of 48 units by 48 units (that's the viewport width and height in your drawable). If
you open this in a text editor, you should see something like Listing 9.8. Note that the icons are
occasionally refreshed, which means that the exact contents might be different for you but the
specific version seen here is included in the `chapter09` folder of the source code for this book.

Listing 9.8   The SVG Contents of the Left-Aligned Icon

```
<svg xmlns="http://www.w3.org/2000/svg" width="48" height="48"
➡ viewBox="0 0 48 48">
```

```
    <path d="M30 30h-24v4h24v-4zm0-16h-24v4h24v-4zm-24 12h36v-4h-
➥ 36v4zm0 16h36v-4h-36v4zm0-36v4h36v-4h-36z"/>
    <path d="M0 0h48v48h-48z" fill="none"/>
</svg>
```

The first `path` node has a `d` attribute that contains the path data for drawing the icon. Don't worry about understanding it yet; just copy the contents from the SVG file to the `pathData` attribute in your vector drawable or into the strings file and reference it like any other string. Your `ic_align_left` file should look like Listing 9.9.

Listing 9.9   The `ic_align_left` Drawable

```
<?xml version="1.0" encoding="utf-8"?>
<vector xmlns:android="http://schemas.android.com/apk/res/android"
        android:height="@dimen/icon_size"
        android:width="@dimen/icon_size"
        android:viewportHeight="48"
        android:viewportWidth="48">

    <path
        android:name="lines"
        android:strokeColor="#000000"
        android:fillColor="#000000"
        android:pathData="@string/svg_align_left" />

</vector>
```

You can use this drawable just like any other drawable, but there's a bit more to do for animating it. Next create an `AnimatedVectorDrawable` XML file (it has the animated-vector root node) called `ic_anim_align_left_justified.xml`. This is a very small file that basically ties the previous drawable to an animation. It looks like Listing 9.10.

Listing 9.10   The `ic_anim_align_left_justified` Drawable

```
<?xml version="1.0" encoding="utf-8"?>
<animated-vector xmlns:android="http://schemas.android.com/apk/res/android"
                 android:drawable="@drawable/ic_align_left">

    <target
        android:animation="@animator/align_left_justified"
        android:name="lines" />
</animated-vector>
```

Now comes the `align_left_justified.xml` animator, which goes in the "animator" folder. It is an object animator that gives the duration of the animation and the values to animate from the align-left icon to the justified icon. The data for the `valueTo` node (which is the SVG data to animate to) comes from the `ic_format_align_justify_48px.svg` file. You should have something like Listing 9.11 for your animator.

Listing 9.11 The `align_left_justified` Animator

```
<?xml version="1.0" encoding="utf-8"?>
<objectAnimator xmlns:android="http://schemas.android.com/apk/res/android"
                android:duration="300"
                android:propertyName="pathData"
                android:valueFrom="@string/svg_align_left"
                android:valueTo="@string/svg_align_justify"
                android:valueType="pathType">

</objectAnimator>
```

Next up, you need a layout to display this animation. An easy option is to make the `AnimatedVectorDrawable` the source of an `ImageView`. Then all you need is a trigger to start the animation. For demonstration purposes, you can simply add an `OnClickListener` to the `ImageView` and trigger the animation from there. Be sure to cast the drawable to an `AnimatedVectorDrawable` and then call the `start` method. Listing 9.12 demonstrates this.

Listing 9.12 Casting to an `AnimatedVectorDrawable` and Animating

```
public void onClick(View v) {
    final ImageView imageView = (ImageView) v;
    final AnimatedVectorDrawable avd = (AnimatedVectorDrawable)
➥ imageView.getDrawable();
    avd.start();
}
```

Now, it's time to tap that `ImageView` and enjoy the beautiful animation you put together. Wait. That animation isn't what we want! Instead of the shorter lines growing to make the justified icon, lines are moving around in a confusing animation. Figure 9.2 shows a few frames of this.

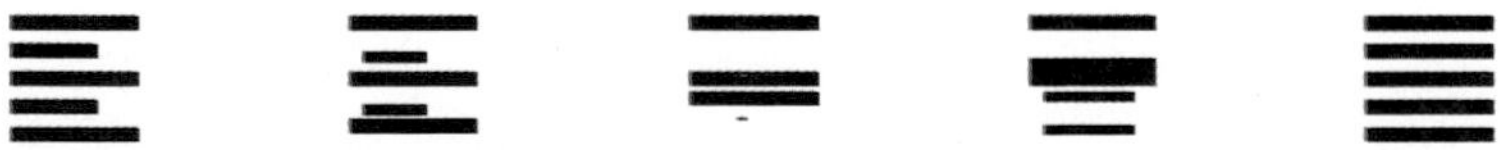

Figure 9.2 The bad SVG animation

What's going on? Unfortunately, the order in which the lines are drawn in the two SVG files is not consistent. If you assumed that they were each drawn from top to bottom, you were mistaken. This presents a bit of a challenge. The whole point of using these existing SVG icons is so that you don't have to draw them yourself. Fortunately, that bizarre SVG data can be changed directly.

Table 9.2 Basic SVG Path Commands

Command Letter	Meaning
M	Move to (without drawing)
L	Line from the current position to the specified position
H, V	Horizontal or Vertical line from the current position to the specified position
Z	Close the current path
A, C, Q, S, T	Curves of various types

SVG data isn't really meant to be read by humans, but knowing just a few of the letters used can help a lot in understanding how you should modify the SVG to suit your needs. Letters symbolize commands. They're followed by numbers that represent the coordinates. Capital letters are followed by absolute coordinates and lowercase letters are followed by relative coordinates. Table 9.2 shows the basic SVG path commands that you'll commonly see. With the exception of the curve commands, these aren't too farfetched.

Looking at the start of the path data for the left alignment SVG through the "z" command (which closes the path, you should see "M30 30h-24v4h24v-4z." The first part of this ("**M30 30**h-24v4h24v-4z") is a command to move 30 units to the right and 30 down. Next is the command to draw a horizontal line left 24 units ("M30 30**h-24**v4h24v-4z"). The "v" command comes after that, moving 4 units down ("M30 30h-24**v4**h24v-4z"). Another "h" command moves back to the right 24 units ("M30 30h-24v4**h24**v-4z"). A final "v" command moves up 4 units ("M30 30h-24v4h24**v-4**z"). The last command, "z," marks this path as closed ("M30 30h-24v4h24v-4**z**"). It's pretty obvious that reading SVG manually is a big hassle, but you should see that it's not too complex if you take it one step at a time. Looking a little more at this SVG data, you can probably tell that the commands aren't drawing the lines from top to bottom. Unlike raster-based image formats, SVG data can be in any order. Many drawing programs will put it in the order that you draw or create shapes, but some will change the order or make adjustments automatically.

Armed with a basic understanding of SVG commands, you can pretty easily (though extremely tediously) create your own graphics by hand. Fortunately, you usually don't need to. Instead of using the SVG data for the icon that symbolized justified text, you can easily modify the SVG commands from the left alignment path that way all the lines will be drawn in a consistent order and you only have to adjust the size of the lines. You know that the shorter lines are 24 units across and the longer ones are 36 (24 + 12) based on the "h" commands. Starting off with the initial move command, you should increase the movement to 42 (30 + 12). Now just change every instance of 24 to 36 and the SVG data suddenly looks just like the icon for justified alignment. Now you can run the app and see the animation work correctly. The shorter lines simply grow until they are as long as the other lines. Listing 9.13 shows the paths excerpted from the strings file, so you can see how the left-align path is changed to make the justified path. This might be a bit confusing, so it can be helpful to open the SVG file in a browser and a text editor. Make changes to the text and then refresh the browser to see how that affects the rendered icon.

Listing 9.13   The Two Strings That Represent the Icons

```
<string name="svg_align_left">M30 30h-24v4h24v-4zm0-16h-24v4h24v-4zm-24
➥ 12h36v-4h-36v4zm0 16h36v-4h-36v4zm0-36v4h36v-4h-36z</string>
<string name="svg_align_justify">M42 30h-36v4h36v-4zm0-16h-36v4h36v-
➥ 4zm-36 12h36v-4h-36v4zm0 16h36v-4h-36v4zm0-36v4h36v-4h-36z</string>
```

With that custom SVG data created, you should now be able to see the proper animation. Figure 9.3 shows some of the frames.

Figure 9.3 The good SVG animation

Animating Raster Icons

Most apps are going to have to support versions of Android prior to 5.0 for a while, so this means that you will have to decide how you want to handle supporting versions of Android that didn't have `AnimatedVectorDrawable`. If you're just rotating a vector, you can easily rotate a raster image instead, but what about when you're morphing from one path to another? A good option is to create a frame-by-frame animation that mimics the experience. This works on all versions of Android, so it's up to you whether you want to use frame-by-frame animation for all versions of Android or for all versions below 5.0 and use vector animation for 5.0 and newer.

The easiest way to do frame-by-frame animation is by using an `AnimationDrawable` that is specified in XML within an `animation-list` node. The child nodes will all be `item` nodes that typically have a drawable and a duration (in milliseconds) specified. Listing 9.14 shows an example.

Listing 9.14   The `AnimationDrawable` XML File

```
<?xml version="1.0" encoding="utf-8"?>
<animation-list xmlns:android="http://schemas.android.com/apk/res/android"
    android:oneshot="true">

    <item android:drawable="@drawable/ic_format_align_left_black_48dp"
        android:duration="17" />

    <item android:drawable="@drawable/ic_format_align_left_black_48dp_01"
        android:duration="17" />

    <item android:drawable="@drawable/ic_format_align_left_black_48dp_02"
        android:duration="17" />
```

```
<item android:drawable="@drawable/ic_format_align_left_black_48dp_03"
      android:duration="17" />

<item android:drawable="@drawable/ic_format_align_left_black_48dp_04"
      android:duration="17" />

<item android:drawable="@drawable/ic_format_align_left_black_48dp_05"
      android:duration="17" />

<item android:drawable="@drawable/ic_format_align_left_black_48dp_06"
      android:duration="17" />

<item android:drawable="@drawable/ic_format_align_left_black_48dp_07"
      android:duration="17" />

<item android:drawable="@drawable/ic_format_align_left_black_48dp_08"
      android:duration="17" />

<item android:drawable="@drawable/ic_format_align_left_black_48dp_09"
      android:duration="17" />

<item android:drawable="@drawable/ic_format_align_left_black_48dp_10"
      android:duration="17" />

<item android:drawable="@drawable/ic_format_align_left_black_48dp_11"
      android:duration="17" />

<item android:drawable="@drawable/ic_format_align_justify_black_48dp"
      android:duration="17" />

</animation-list>
```

Just like any drawable, you can use this as the background for a view or as the image that an
`ImageView` displays. To trigger the animation, you simple get a reference to the drawable, cast
it to an `AnimationDrawable` and call the `start` method (almost exactly the same process as
with vectors). Listing 9.15 shows how to do this. The full source code for this example is in the
RasterIconAnimations project of `chapter09` folder.

Listing 9.15   Triggering the Frame-by-Frame Animation

```
public void onClick(View v) {
    ImageView imageView = (ImageView) v;
    AnimationDrawable animationDrawable = (AnimationDrawable)
➥ imageView.getDrawable();
    animationDrawable.start();
}
```

Simple Transitions

In addition to animating individual views and images, Android supports animations to transition entire layouts. The simplest form is the `LayoutTransition` class, which was added in Android 3.0 when property animations first appeared. The general idea is that views animate in response to views appearing or views disappearing (this could be views being added and removed from the hierarchy or views transitioning from `VISIBLE` to `GONE` and vice versa). This means you can have up to four different animations: (1) the view appearing, (2) the view disappearing, (3) the view moving in response to a view appearing, and (4) the view moving in response to a view disappearing.

Like many things in Android, you can use layout transitions from XML or Java. By simply adding `android:animateLayoutChanges="true"` to your layout in XML, the `LayoutTransition` class will be used with all the default animations. If you want more control, you can create a `LayoutTransition` class in Java, configure it however you'd like, and then pass it into `ViewGroup`'s `setLayoutTransition` method.

As convenient as this method of animating layout transitions is, sometimes you're animating between complete view hierarchies such as changing activities or fragments. Other times you need significantly more control or you want to swap out significant portions of the view hierarchy. Fortunately, Android also has mechanisms for handling all of those cases.

Scene Transitions

If you want to do something more complicated than a basic layout transition, Android's `Scene` class will come in handy. It was introduced in Android 4.4 with the idea of making transitions much more powerful while still very easy (if you're supporting previous versions of Android, third party libraries that add backward compatibility are available such as the Transitions Everywhere library https://github.com/andkulikov/transitions-everywhere). The idea is that a scene represents a portion of the view hierarchy at a particular point in time. You have another scene that represents a portion of the view hierarchy that generally has some elements in common (though it doesn't have to). You can easily tell Android, "Animate from this first scene to the second scene," and everything is handled for you. Android will compare which views are in both scenes (and if properties change on them) and which are in one scene and not the other. This allows Android to fade out a view that is not in the second scene but keep a view in place that doesn't change regardless of how else the view hierarchy may have changed. You can also override transitions and add actions that are triggered when scenes enter or leave.

For a simple example, let's create two layouts. The first, `scene1.xml`, is a `RelativeLayout` with a `TextView` (set at the bottom left of the parent) and an `ImageView` that's a 48dp square at the top left. Listing 9.16 shows this simple layout.

Listing 9.16   Layout for the First Scene

```xml
<?xml version="1.0" encoding="utf-8"?>
<RelativeLayout xmlns:android="http://schemas.android.com/apk/res/android"
                android:layout_width="match_parent"
                android:layout_height="match_parent">

    <TextView
        android:layout_width="wrap_content"
        android:layout_height="wrap_content"
        android:textAppearance="?android:attr/textAppearanceMedium"
        android:text="@string/some_text"
        android:id="@+id/textView"
        android:layout_alignParentBottom="true"
        android:layout_alignParentStart="true"/>

    <ImageView
        android:layout_width="48dp"
        android:layout_height="48dp"
        android:id="@+id/imageView"
        android:src="@color/accent"
        android:layout_alignParentTop="true"
        android:layout_alignParentStart="true"
        android:contentDescription="@null"/>

</RelativeLayout>
```

Next, we create `scene2.xml`, which is a `LinearLayout`, horizontally oriented. It has the `TextView` and `ImageView` from the previous scene, but the `ImageView`'s weight is set to 1 and its width is set to 0. This means that after the `TextView`'s width is accounted for, the `ImageView` will use the rest of the width. Listing 9.17 shows this second scene.

Listing 9.17   Layout for the Second Scene

```xml
<?xml version="1.0" encoding="utf-8"?>
<LinearLayout xmlns:android="http://schemas.android.com/apk/res/android"
              android:orientation="horizontal"
              android:layout_width="match_parent"
              android:layout_height="match_parent">

    <TextView
        android:layout_width="wrap_content"
        android:layout_height="wrap_content"
        android:textAppearance="?android:attr/textAppearanceMedium"
        android:text="@string/some_text"
        android:id="@+id/textView"/>
```

```
<ImageView
    android:layout_width="0dp"
    android:layout_height="48dp"
    android:id="@+id/imageView"
    android:src="@color/accent"
    android:layout_weight="1"
    android:contentDescription="@null"/>


</LinearLayout>
```

The main layout just has a button, to trigger the animation, and a `FrameLayout` that the scenes can be added to. The activity needs to create the scenes that it will transition between. The `Scene` class has a static `getSceneForLayout` method. This method takes the `ViewGroup` that the scene should be added to, the layout to actually use for creating the scene, and a `Context` for inflating the layout. Scenes need a transition when you want to smoothly animate between them. The Transition abstract class is basically capturing the properties of the views to determine how to change them. For instance, the `ChangeBounds` class, which extends `Transition`, captures the physical positioning info (where is the view and how big is it). Just like you're used to, you can set the duration, interpolator, and more.

To display a scene without animating, you can use the `TransitionManager`'s static `go` method, passing the `Scene` object you wish to show. When you wish to animate between `Scene` objects, you use the same static `go` method, but you pass in the `Transition` class that you wish to use. Listing 9.18 shows the activity code and Figure 9.4 shows a few frames of the animation. The full source code is in the SceneTransitions project of the `chapter09` folder.

Listing 9.18 The Activity Code That Triggers the Scene Changes

```
public class MainActivity extends AppCompatActivity implements View.
➥ OnClickListener {

    private Scene mCurrentScene;
    private Scene mScene1;
    private Scene mScene2;
    private ViewGroup mSceneRoot;
    private Transition mTransition;

    @Override
    protected void onCreate(Bundle savedInstanceState) {
        super.onCreate(savedInstanceState);
        setContentView(R.layout.activity_main);

        final Toolbar toolbar = (Toolbar) findViewById(R.id.toolbar);
        setSupportActionBar(toolbar);

        mSceneRoot = (ViewGroup) findViewById(R.id.scene_root);
```

```
        mScene1 = Scene.getSceneForLayout(mSceneRoot, R.layout.scene1,
➥ this);

        mScene2 = Scene.getSceneForLayout(mSceneRoot, R.layout.scene2,
➥ this);

        mTransition = new ChangeBounds();
        mTransition.setDuration(DateUtils.SECOND_IN_MILLIS);
        mTransition.setInterpolator(new
➥ AccelerateDecelerateInterpolator());
        TransitionManager.go(mScene1);
        mCurrentScene = mScene1;

        findViewById(R.id.button).setOnClickListener(this);
    }

    @Override
    public void onClick(View v) {
        if (mCurrentScene == mScene1) {
            TransitionManager.go(mScene2, mTransition);
            mCurrentScene = mScene2;
        } else {
            TransitionManager.go(mScene1, mTransition);
            mCurrentScene = mScene1;
        }
    }
}
```

Figure 9.4 Frames from the scene transition

Activity Transitions

One of Android's weakest points in transitions has always been activities. There was a default animation with a very limited ability to change it. The best practice was generally leaving it in place as it served to explain to users that they had navigated deeper into the app and the back button could take them to the previous activity. A big part of Material Design is changing this flawed concept of moving from one static arrangement of views to the next. If you tap a thumbnail for a music album, the detail activity shouldn't just appear from the side. It should evolve from the content already on the screen. That thumbnail can grow to a larger image of the album. The album title can shift positions while the rest of the list is pushed out. Then the new content can slide into place. Not only does this look immeasurably better, it actually improves the user experience by helping the user to understand which parts of the screen were already there, which parts are new, and where to shift focus.

The same transitions framework that was introduced in KitKat and used for the previous scene transitions was expanded upon in Android 5.0, allowing it to work for fragments and activities. The overall concept is very similar to working with scenes. Instead of automatically animating between two scenes, Android automatically animates between two activities, though there's just a little more plumbing. This handles a lot of the behind-the-scenes headaches that you'd have to deal with if you wanted to do these kinds of animations manually.

The general idea behind using transitions between activities is that you match a particular view (such as a thumbnail on the current page) to a view on the next screen. Because the next view isn't instantiated yet, you refer to it by its `transitionName`, which is just a string that identifies it for transitions. That string can be anything you want, but many people put it in the `strings.xml` file with the rest of their strings and prefix the name with "transition" to make it more organized. The information is passed between the activities by way of a `Bundle` instance (just like with intent extras). Fortunately, most of this is easier than it sounds.

Let's open up the woodworking tools app from the previous chapter and add transitions to it. We're going to animate the image and tool name from the first screen to the second screen. First, we need to define a couple of strings for the text and the image that will animate (e.g., `transition_image_view`); the strings themselves don't matter as long as they are unique. Then, open up the `captioned_image_view.xml` layout and set the transition names.

Remember that the `ToolGridFragment` is where we handle clicks on one of the tools on the main screen. Within the `onClickItem` method, we know that the clicked view was a `CaptionedImageView`, so we cast to that specific class to get the `ImageView` and `TextView`. We use the static `makeSceneTransitionAnimation` method of the `ActivityOptionsCompat` class to create the data we need to pass to the activity (note that there is an `ActivityOptions` class, but it's generally a best practice to make a habit of using the compatibility version to avoid worrying about the version of Android that is on the device). That method needs an `Activity` instance, which we can get with `getActivity`, and then it needs the matches of views to transition names. If you are only animating one view, you can pass in that view and the string; otherwise, you can use the `Pair` object one or more times (which, as you can probably guess, is just a generic container that holds two object references). We need to create a pair for the image and a pair for the text. Now, when we call the static `startActivity` method, we need to pass in the `Bundle` that we get when we call `toBundle` on our `ActivityOptionsCompat` instance. Listing 9.19 shows the `onClickItem` method.

Listing 9.19   The Updated `onClickItem` Method

```
public void onItemClick(AdapterView<?> adapterView, View view, int
➥ position, long id) {
    final CaptionedImageView captionedImageView = (CaptionedImageView)
➥ view;
    ActivityOptionsCompat activityOptions = ActivityOptionsCompat.make
➥ SceneTransitionAnimation(
            getActivity(),
            new Pair<View, String>(captionedImageView.getImageView(),
➥ getString(R.string.transition_image_view)),
            new Pair<View, String>(captionedImageView.getTextView(),
➥ getString(R.string.transition_text_view))
    );
    ToolListActivity.startActivity(getActivity(), mToolGridAdapter.
➥ getItem(position), activityOptions.toBundle());
}
```

We need to update the `startActivity` method in `ToolListActivity` to accept the `Bundle` we are passing in. Instead of starting the activity from the `Context` we passed in, we want to update the method to take an `Activity` instead. This lets us use `ActivityCompat`'s `startActivity` static method instead, which allows us to pass in a `Bundle` without worrying about whether the app is running on a version of Android new enough to support that. Listing 9.20 shows the updated method.

Listing 9.20   The Updated `startActivity` Method

```
public static void startActivity(Activity activity, ToolType toolType,
➥ Bundle activityOptions) {
    final Intent intent = new Intent(activity, ToolListActivity.class);
    intent.putExtra(EXTRA_TOOL_TYPE, toolType);
    ActivityCompat.startActivity(activity, intent, activityOptions);
}
```

In normal cases, this is everything we need to do to get things to work. We've given the views the transition names they need. We've created a `Bundle` that has all the metadata needed to do the animation. We've started the activity with the `Bundle`. That's it right? Well, not quite. We have one challenge which is that our larger instance of the `CaptionedImageView` on the second screen is in `ToolAboutFragment` and that fragment is created (milliseconds) later by the `ViewPager` via our adapter. It doesn't seem like much time difference when interacting with the app, but when the new activity wants to run the animation, the fragment that contains the final views isn't ready yet. This means that it doesn't know how to animate them. The trick is that we need to postpone the animation until the views are ready. Fortunately, this is pretty easy. We call `postponeEnterTransition` in the `onCreate` method of the activity. Now we just have to call `startPostponedEnterTransition` when the views are ready. By using an

`OnPreDrawListener`, we can get a call that tells us just before the `ViewPager` draws the views. This listener is added to the `ViewTreeObserver` from the view we care about (the ViewPager). Adding a one-shot `OnPreDrawListener` that fires once and then removes itself is a fairly common practice in many advanced UI techniques. Figure 9.5 shows some frames from the completed animation.

Figure 9.5 Frames from the activity transition

With the animation to the new activity working correctly, we now have to consider the animation back. If you tap a tool, see the "About" page, and then tap back, you'll see everything animate how you'd expect. But what about if you tap a tool, see the "About" page, then change tabs before going back? In that case, the animation will be problematic. By default, a `ViewPager` keeps one page to each side available (to allow scrolling to be smooth). This means that changing from the "About" tab to the tab just to the right of it will cause the view to be sitting off to the left of the screen. Pressing back at this point animates the view back into place. It's a little strange, but not terrible. The strange part comes from moving more than one tab to the right. When the "About" page moves to the left once, it's just off screen. When it moves left again, the views are destroyed. Pressing back at that point means there is no view to animate, so you end up with a hole where the image should go and then suddenly the image pops back into place. It's a jarring experience.

Fixing issues like this is relatively easy and this same technique can be used for other dynamic changes to your view hierarchy. You call `setEnterSharedElementCallback` and provide a `SharedElementCallback`. This callback is triggered to handle customizing animations dynamically. All we need to do is provide an implementation of the `onMapSharedElements` method, which is meant to allow customizing the mapping of transition names to views (like what we passed in by creating the `Pair` objects). You can do some very clever things here, but we just need to check if we are displaying the "About" page and clear the mapping if we are not. In other words, if we aren't showing the big image at the top of the screen, then don't do any custom animation back to the previous activity. The additions to the `onCreate` method are shown in Listing 9.21. The full source code for the updated woodworking tools app is in the WoodworkingTools project within the `chapter09` folder.

Listing 9.21   The Additions to the `onCreate` Method

```java
// Handle animation from previous activity
postponeEnterTransition();
mViewPager.getViewTreeObserver().addOnPreDrawListener(new
ViewTreeObserver.OnPreDrawListener() {
    @Override
    public boolean onPreDraw() {
        mViewPager.getViewTreeObserver().removeOnPreDrawListener(this);
        startPostponedEnterTransition();
        return true;
    }
});


setEnterSharedElementCallback(new SharedElementCallback() {
    @Override
    public void onMapSharedElements(List<String> names, Map<String,
➥ View< sharedElements) {
        if (mViewPager.getCurrentItem() != 0) {
            // Not displaying the about page, which has the hero
➥ image
            names.clear();
            sharedElements.clear();
        }
    }
});
```

Circular Reveal Transitions

Another nice feature added in Android 5.0 is the circular reveal. Just as the name suggests, it's an animation that reveals views in a circular pattern (of course, you can also use it to hide views). With a single method call, you can get an `Animator` that will handle the visuals. You just need to tell it the view to clip the animation to, the x and y coordinates for the center of the circle (this could be where the user tapped or the center of the view to show/hide), and the starting and ending radius.

First, we need a fresh activity layout. This simply needs a button to trigger the reveal, a `FrameLayout` that is revealed, and a button within that layout that can hide everything again. Listing 9.22 shows the layout. Note that the `FrameLayout` is initially invisible.

Listing 9.22   The Activity Layout

```xml
<RelativeLayout xmlns:android="http://schemas.android.com/apk/res/android"
                xmlns:tools="http://schemas.android.com/tools"
                android:layout_width="match_parent"
                android:layout_height="match_parent"
                tools:context=".MainActivity">

    <android.support.v7.widget.Toolbar
        android:id="@+id/toolbar"
        android:layout_height="wrap_content"
        android:layout_width="match_parent"
        android:minHeight="?attr/actionBarSize"
        android:background="?attr/colorPrimary" />

    <Button
        android:layout_width="wrap_content"
        android:layout_height="wrap_content"
        android:text="@string/reveal"
        android:id="@+id/button_reveal"
        android:layout_below="@+id/toolbar"
        android:layout_centerHorizontal="true"/>

    <FrameLayout
        android:id="@+id/container"
        android:background="#F8BBD0"
        android:layout_width="match_parent"
        android:layout_height="match_parent"
        android:layout_below="@+id/button_reveal"
        android:layout_alignParentStart="true"
        android:visibility="invisible">

        <Button
            android:layout_width="wrap_content"
            android:layout_height="wrap_content"
            android:text="@string/hide"
            android:id="@+id/button_hide"
            android:layout_gravity="center"/>
    </FrameLayout>

</RelativeLayout>
```

Next, we just handle the button clicks. We first find the center of the circle, which will just be the center of the `FrameLayout`. Then we determine the radius to start and finish with. We know that one radius will be 0 (either it's starting from nothing and then revealing the full layout or it's starting from the full layout and shrinking to nothing). The other radius needs to be big enough to fill the rectangular view with a circle. This means that we need the distance from the center of the view to one of the corners. We know the distance from the center point to the right side (half the width) and from the center point to the top (half the height), so we can use the Pythagorean theorem to determine the hypotenuse. This means that we square the horizontal distance and the vertical distance, add those together, and then take their square root.

With all of the math out of the way, we use the static `createCircularReveal` method of `ViewAnimationUtils` to get our `Animator` object. If we are hiding the views, we need to listen to the animation and set the visibility back to invisible. Finally, we just start the animation. Listing 9.23 shows the full activity, and Figure 9.6 shows a few frames of the animation.

Listing 9.23 The Activity Code for a Circular Reveal

```java
public class MainActivity extends AppCompatActivity implements View.
➥ OnClickListener {

    View mContainer;

    @Override
    protected void onCreate(Bundle savedInstanceState) {
        super.onCreate(savedInstanceState);
        setContentView(R.layout.activity_main);

        final Toolbar toolbar = (Toolbar) findViewById(R.id.toolbar);
        setSupportActionBar(toolbar);

        mContainer = findViewById(R.id.container);
        findViewById(R.id.button_reveal).setOnClickListener(this);
        findViewById(R.id.button_hide).setOnClickListener(this);
    }

    @Override
    public void onClick(View v) {
        // Determine center
        final int x = (mContainer.getRight() - mContainer.getLeft()) / 2;
        final int y = (mContainer.getBottom() - mContainer.getTop()) / 2;

        // Determine radius sizes
        final int containerWidth = mContainer.getWidth() / 2;
        final int containerHeight = mContainer.getHeight() / 2;
        final int maxRadius = (int) Math.sqrt((containerWidth *
➥ containerWidth) + (containerHeight * containerHeight));
        final int startingRadius;
        final int finalRadius;
        if (v.getId() == R.id.button_reveal) {
            startingRadius = 0;
            finalRadius = maxRadius;
            mContainer.setVisibility(View.VISIBLE);
        } else {
            startingRadius = maxRadius;
```

```
                        finalRadius = 0;
                    }

                    // Animate
                    final Animator animator = ViewAnimationUtils.createCircularReveal
➡   (mContainer, x, y, startingRadius, finalRadius);
                    if (v.getId() == R.id.button_hide) {
                        animator.addListener(new AnimatorListenerAdapter() {
                            @Override
                            public void onAnimationEnd(Animator animation) {
                                mContainer.setVisibility(View.INVISIBLE);
                            }
                        });
                    }
                    animator.start();
                }
            }
```

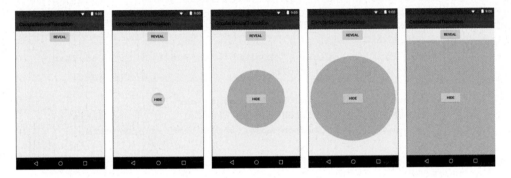

Figure 9.6 Frames from the circular reveal animation

Summary

In this chapter you learned the purpose of animations and how to apply them in a variety of ways. You learned about the older view animations as well as the more efficient and powerful property animations, plus the ways of applying animations to scenes and activity transitions. You also learned about using a circular reveal transition. In addition to all of these topics, you encountered advanced techniques such as using an OnPreDrawListener to run code immediately before a view is drawn.

This marks the end of the second part of this book. Next up, you'll focus on advanced topics to make your apps even better.

CHAPTER 10

USING ADVANCED TECHNIQUES

The second part of the book covered the full app development process starting with simple ideas and wireframes, turning those into designs, implementing the designs, and tying everything together with beautiful animations. Throughout the process, you relied on users to provide continuous feedback. With all the core work done, most developers consider the process done, but there are a lot of advanced techniques to learn and implement including analyzing and improving the efficiency of your layouts.

Identifying Jank

Unfortunately, development is never as easy as write it once and everything is perfect. In addition to typical bugs that cause the app to crash or misbehave, you're also going to have performance issues to figure out. When you scroll a view and it seems to stutter or hiccup, dropping frames, the experience is bad. These hiccups are sometimes called "jank," which is the opposite of smoothness. You want your app to be as fluid as possible, so eliminating jank can significantly improve the feel of your app.

In many cases, you will see jank but not know what is causing it. For instance, the implementation of the custom view which blurs a portion of an image in the woodworking tools app might be smooth on one device and not smooth on another, causing jank each time a new set of tool images comes into view. What's going on here? If you have difficulty seeing jank, an easy way to help visualize it is by going into the developer options of your phone and turning on Profile GPU rendering (the past few versions of Android have the "On screen as bars" choice so that you don't have to grab the output from `adb`). Go back to the app and scroll around for a bit. A graph of the rendering time will be displayed on top of the UI. The X-axis represents rendering over time and the Y-axis represents the amount of time taken for a frame. The horizontal green line is the limit (16 milliseconds); anything above that line means something is taking too long and causing jank. Figure 10.1 shows an example.

Figure 10.1 Profiling GPU rendering in real time

You should notice that there are multiple graphs on the screen; one for each "window." One represents the status bar, one represents the navigation bar, and one represents the visible application. Some devices will show the navigation bar and application graph on top of each other, like in Figure 10.1, but you can discern between them by interacting with the app and watching the graph draw itself. The bars are also made of three colors. The purple at the base is used to indicate the draw time; this is the process of converting your draw commands into what's called a display list. A display list is a group of OpenGL commands that have been compiled for execution. Once that's done, the renderer has to execute the display list by communicating with the GPU, represented by the red. At the top of each line is an orange cap. Typically, that cap is small because it represents the amount of time the CPU is waiting for the GPU to acknowledge the commands, which is nearly always fast if you're not doing any custom GPU work.

Using Systrace to Understand Jank

This is a good way to see when the problems happen and you might have some sense of what is going on as you scroll and see the spikes, but it doesn't help much with narrowing down exactly what's going on. That's where the Systrace tool comes in. Systrace logs a significant amount of data about what's going on while it is running and outputs the data as an interactive HTML file. Typically you run it for a brief time (say, 5 seconds), interacting with the app during that time to reproduce the jank, and then you analyze the created HTML file to understand what was taking so long that frames were dropped. Note that not all devices have Systrace available, so it's best used on Nexus devices.

You may recall that in Chapter 8, "Applying the Design," we called out the jank created during scrolling on the main screen of the app. Now it's time to come back to that issue, track down what exactly was causing it with Systrace, and fix it. First, we know that the jank seemed most noticeable when a new item was coming onto the screen. To make this easier to test, we're going to increase the `verticalSpacing` attribute in the `GridView` within `fragment_tool_grid.xml` from 16dp to 200dp. This will add enough spacing between items that only about two rows show up on a typical phone, which means two rows are off screen and can be scrolled on to create jank. One of the most important parts of fixing any bug, whether it's a crash or just a UI hiccup, is being able to easily reproduce it so that you can verify your changes fix it.

First, we can run Systrace without making any other changes. Open Android Device Monitor (under the Tools menu and the Android submenu). You should see your device in the Devices tab on the left. Select it and then pick the confusing Systrace icon above (called out in Figure 10.2). The next window, shown in Figure 10.3, allows you to configure Systrace. Be sure to pick a reasonable name and location. The default 5 seconds and buffer size are both typically fine. You must enable application traces from the app by clicking the dropdown and pick the package name of the app if you want to use any additional logging within your app (it's a good habit to select your app every time). If you don't see the app, be sure that you've selected the correct device and you've installed a debug version of the app (the default build type in Android Studio is a debug build).

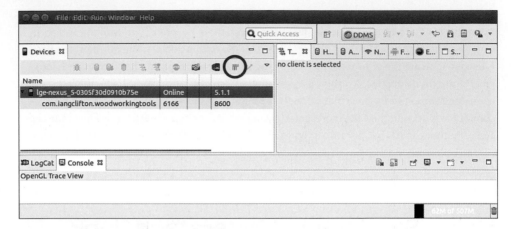

Figure 10.2 The Systrace icon in Android Device Monitor

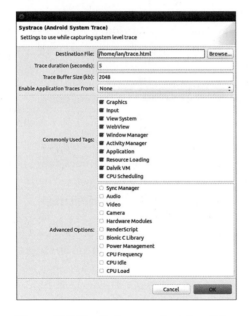

Figure 10.3 The Systrace configuration dialog

Systrace works by tracking the starting and stopping points of events. The events are identified by strings called tags. Android has several built in that are enabled by default as well as some advanced ones that are typically off. For now, leave the commonly used tags all enabled and turn on RenderScript in the advanced options below (remember, we used RenderScript to blur the portion of the image behind the text).

When you click OK, you'll see a dialog informing you that it is collecting trace information. Sometimes it can help to wait briefly (1–2 seconds) before interacting and then start interacting with the app to reproduce the jank. The wait lets you create a baseline for how long events take when there is no interaction, but it's up to you whether that's useful. Once the time is up, the data is pulled off the device and the HTML file is generated (Systrace currently doesn't tell you that everything is ready; the dialog just goes away and the file appears where you specified). Open it in your browser and prepare to be confused. You should see something like Figure 10.4 in your browser.

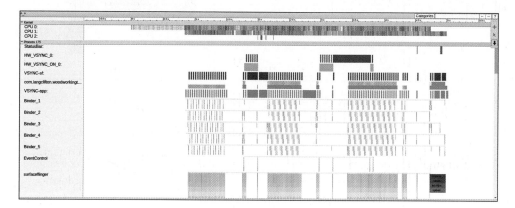

Figure 10.4 The Systrace output in a browser

The HTML will display as a bunch of colorful lines and boxes that make no sense at first. The display shows time along the X-axis and various events along the Y-axis. The wider a box is, the longer it took to perform that operation. At the top will be the CPU info, if you had that enabled. Then you'll have various info, much of which won't be useful to you right now. Further down, you will see "surfaceflinger." SurfaceFlinger takes buffers of pixel data, composites them, and then pushes them to the display. Big gaps in the SurfaceFlinger section when the UI should have been changing (such as while scrolling) are generally problems, but we can scroll down more to the app (the name should be on the left, though it is often cut off for longer names) for more detail.

The controls for the Systrace HTML page are not particularly user friendly. Pretend your Systrace output is as exciting as a first-person shooter and put your fingers on the W, A, S, and D keys. The W and S keys zoom in and out, respectively, while the A and D keys pan. You can also click and drag the mouse up or down to zoom. Double-clicking the mouse creates a guideline under the mouse that you can then position by clicking where you want it. Once you've placed more two guidelines or more, you can see the time between them at the top. At time of writing, the documentation for Systrace is outdated, so the best source for learning the bizarre controls is by clicking the question mark at the very top right when viewing a Systrace file.

Scroll down to the woodworking tools app (it should be the largest section) as shown in Figure 10.5. If you see several huge sections such as `obtainView` that report they never finished, then Systrace is lying to you. The way the tool works is very simple. Each time a developer wants to

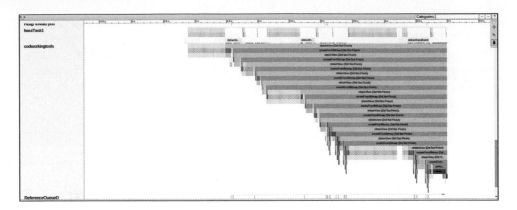

Figure 10.5 The Systrace output showing the app events

track something (including the events that are tracked inside of Android itself), the developer uses the `Trace` class (made available to application developers in Android 4.3; you can also use `TraceCompat` from the support library), calling `beginSection`. When you begin a new section, you give it a name, which shows up in the colored bars here. When that event you were tracking is done, you call `endSection`. Simple, right? The problem is that ending a section always ends the most recently started section. This means that if you forget to call `endSection` such as when you bail out of a method early due to an exception, your section will not end at the right time, if at all. There are a few places where this can happen in the Android system code, unfortunately, so you can receive Systrace output that tells you something like `obtainView` did not finish when you know it did (the view appeared on the screen).

Fortunately, you can "fix" the output of Systrace yourself by calling `endSection` where it was missing. If you see this bug, then after each call to the static `createFromBitmap` method of `Allocation`, call `TraceCompat`'s `endSection` method. This fixes the missing calls in `Allocation` (a bug fix has been accepted for this in the Android source code itself, but it hasn't yet made it into a major release) and now you can run Systrace again. Scrolling down to the woodworking tools app, you should now see only a few rows with most of the entries significantly smaller than they were. The areas where each tracked section is just a sliver are generally good (remember, the X-axis is time) and the larger ones are generally bad. If you use W on your keyboard (or click and drag up), you can zoom in on one of those bigger sections. Double-clicking with the mouse will begin the placement of a timing guideline that you can then position by moving the mouse and place by clicking. Creating two of these will tell you the time between them. Figure 10.6 shows that one of the `obtainView` sections took 155 milliseconds, which is more than eight frames! Keep in mind the power of the device you're testing on as well. In this case, the test was on a Nexus 5. A Nexus 6 might not drop as many frames (a quick test shows it closer to 90 milliseconds), but the Nexus 5 is still in the middle range of Android devices (especially when you look at markets across the world).

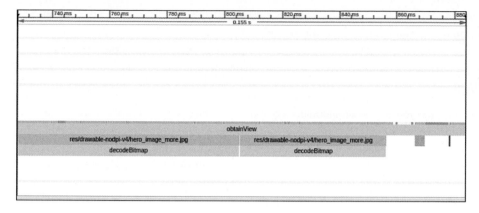

Figure 10.6 Analyzing the details of the Systrace output

The `obtainView` section we've been looking at comes from `AbsListView`'s package-private method of the same name. Because we can be reasonably sure that the Android system code around this is fast, the problem is within the `getView` method of our `ToolGridAdapter`. In the Systrace output, we can also see that the image for the view is being decoded and that alone is taking almost four frames; looking closer, you can see the image is being decoded twice! Just fixing this issue will cut the total `obtainView` time almost in half.

Within the `getView` method, we call the `setImageResource` method of our `CaptionedImageView`. That method simply sets the reference to our drawable and sets the drawable for the image view and then moves on to the blur code. But look a little closer. The drawable reference is being created by inflating the drawable via our resources. The `ImageView` is then having its image set via the resource ID, which causes it to be inflated again. By simply changing that line to instead call `setImageDrawable` and pass in `mDrawable`, we eliminate that second instance of `decodeBitmap`, which was taking around 60 milliseconds.

Maybe you caught this back in Chapter 8, "Applying the Design," but this is the type of mistake that's very easy to make and yet might not be caught. Having a code review process helps increase the chance that this will be caught, but there are still times when it will slip by or you might be working on your own without anyone to review your code. By making use of Android's performance tracking tools, you can catch issues like this, and you will eventually start to get used to keeping your eyes out for these types of problems.

You can run the app with the change and immediately feel the difference, but it's still not smooth, so let's make better use of Systrace. We are reasonably sure that the slowdown is in this area, so let's update the `setImageResource` method so that the first line beings a new trace section and that section is ended in the last line of the method. You can call the sections anything you want, but you can consider a prefix if you're adding a lot of related sections, so something like "BLUR — setImageResource" tells you that this section is part of the overall blurring process and is specifically the `setImageResource` call. Diving into the `updateBlur` method, there are a lot of different places that might be the cause of slowdown. This is a case where intuition and experience will help you decide, but you can't go wrong with extra logging.

Anywhere that you create or manipulate a bitmap is a good place to track. For instance, the two lines that create the `portionToBlur` and `blurredBitmap` objects can be wrapped with `TraceCompat` calls (that is, put a call to `beginSection` before those objects are created and a call to `endSection` after). Wrapping the full RenderScript section is also a good idea. You can even add some sections within the RenderScript portion of the code to better understand what is taking time there. Listing 10.1 shows an example of the `setImageResource` and `updateBlur` methods.

Listing 10.1   An Example of Methods with Systrace Logging Added

```
public void setImageResource(@DrawableRes int drawableResourceId) {
    TraceCompat.beginSection("BLUR — setImageResource");
    mDrawable = getResources().getDrawable(drawableResourceId);
    mImageView.setImageDrawable(mDrawable);
    updateBlur();
    TraceCompat.endSection();
}

private void updateBlur() {
    if (!(mDrawable instanceof BitmapDrawable)) {
        return;
    }
    final int textViewHeight = mTextView.getHeight();
    if (textViewHeight == 0) {
        return;
    }

    // Determine the size of the TextView compared to the height of the
➥ ImageView
    final float ratio = (float) textViewHeight / mImageView.getHeight();

    // Get the Bitmap
    final BitmapDrawable bitmapDrawable = (BitmapDrawable) mDrawable;
    final Bitmap originalBitmap = bitmapDrawable.getBitmap();

    // Calculate the height as a ratio of the Bitmap
    int height = (int) (ratio * originalBitmap.getHeight());

    // The y position is the number of pixels height represents from
➥ the bottom of the Bitmap
    final int y = originalBitmap.getHeight() — height;
```

```
    TraceCompat.beginSection("BLUR — createBitmaps");
    final Bitmap portionToBlur = Bitmap.createBitmap(originalBitmap, 0,
➥ y, originalBitmap.getWidth(), height);
    final Bitmap blurredBitmap = portionToBlur.copy(Bitmap.
➥ Config.ARGB_8888, true);
    TraceCompat.endSection();

    // Use RenderScript to blur the pixels
    TraceCompat.beginSection("BLUR — RenderScript");
    RenderScript rs = RenderScript.create(getContext());
    ScriptIntrinsicBlur theIntrinsic = ScriptIntrinsicBlur.create(rs,
➥ Element.U8_4(rs));
    TraceCompat.beginSection("BLUR — RenderScript Allocation");
    Allocation tmpIn = Allocation.createFromBitmap(rs, portionToBlur);
    // Fix internal trace that isn't ended
    TraceCompat.endSection();
    Allocation tmpOut = Allocation.createFromBitmap(rs,
➥ blurredBitmap);
    // Fix internal trace that isn't ended
    TraceCompat.endSection();
    TraceCompat.endSection();
    theIntrinsic.setRadius(25f);
    theIntrinsic.setInput(tmpIn);
    TraceCompat.beginSection("BLUR — RenderScript forEach");
    theIntrinsic.forEach(tmpOut);
    TraceCompat.endSection();
    TraceCompat.beginSection("BLUR — RenderScript copyTo");
    tmpOut.copyTo(blurredBitmap);
    TraceCompat.endSection();
    new Canvas(blurredBitmap).drawColor(mScrimColor);
    TraceCompat.endSection();

    // Create the new bitmap using the old plus the blurred portion and
➥ display it
    TraceCompat.beginSection("BLUR — Finalize image");
    final Bitmap newBitmap = originalBitmap.copy(Bitmap.
➥ Config.ARGB_8888, true);
    final Canvas canvas = new Canvas(newBitmap);
    canvas.drawBitmap(blurredBitmap, 0, y, new Paint());
    mImageView.setImageBitmap(newBitmap);
    TraceCompat.endSection();
}
```

Running the app and using Systrace again, we can see that a particular instance of the obtainView call is now taking 90 milliseconds with the decodeBitmap portion roughly two-thirds of that. The RenderScript portion of our code is the majority of the rest of the time with almost half of the RenderScript time coming from the copyTo call. Let's start with the image loading portion, because that's the larger part.

Optimizing Images

There are a few big things you can do to speed up your use of images. First, you can shrink the image file sizes by stripping out metadata and adjusting the compression. Second, you can size them correctly (loading an image that's bigger than it is displayed is obviously slower than loading one that's exactly the size that will be displayed). Finally, you can keep them in memory to avoid loading them again.

Shrinking Images

Many people aren't aware that images can contain a lot more data than they need. For instance, JPEGs can be "progressive," which means they actually store multiple versions of the image at progressively higher levels of detail. This was particularly helpful for old webpages on dialup, when you wanted some sense of what the image was before all of it could be downloaded on the slow connection, but it causes the images to be much larger and Android doesn't use this extra data because the full image is already on the local disk. JPEGs can also store metadata in EXIF or XMP formats. These are two different formats for storing information about the photo such as when it was taken, what camera was used, and even how long the photo was exposed. That data is great for photographers but it adds bulk to the image that isn't helpful for our app, so it can be stripped out. Another common inclusion in JPEGs is actually a thumbnail of the image. This is intended to help file browsers and cameras themselves to display a thumbnail without having to read in massive images and scale them; it can be stripped out as well.

You can also adjust the compression of the image. Although a more compressed image will still take up the same amount of memory once it is decompressed and decoded, it can significantly decrease the loading time because the amount of data read from disk can be substantially decreased. JPEG is a lossy format, which means you lose image detail by compressing it, but you can decrease file sizes substantially with only minor changes in compression. Typically, the compression level is described in terms of quality where 100 is highest quality and least compression. Although you might want to keep quality closer to 100 for your own personal photos, that isn't necessary for most app images like what are in the woodworking tools app. The amount of compression you can use while maintaining quality will vary depending on what is in the image (e.g., details like thin letters will look poor faster than something like a tree in the background), but you can generally start at a quality level of 90 and see how it looks.

By stripping out all this extra data and changing the quality level to 90, we decrease the hero image sizes in the woodworking tools app substantially. For instance, the image of the clamps was 493KB and it is now 272KB. The smallest image (in terms of file size) was the drill at 165KB and even it shrank down to 64KB. Testing the app again shows that the time to decode the images has gone from about 60 milliseconds to about half that (with a fair bit of variation). Photoshop makes this pretty easy by picking "Save for Web" and ensuring that the quality is set how you want, it is not progressive, and no metadata is enabled. The process in GIMP is slightly different, starting with the "Export As" command that will give you an "Export Image as JPEG" dialog when saving as a JPEG; the dialog has "Advanced Options" where you want to make sure the image is not progressive, does not contain EXIF or XMP data, and does not have an embedded thumbnail.

Although these images are JPEGs, the same idea of shrinking down the file size applies to PNGs. PNGs are lossless, so you should always use the maximum compression. PNGs can be 8-bit (256 colors), 24-bit (red, green, and blue channels of 256 values each), or 32-bit (adding the alpha channel with 256 values). You can also save them with custom palettes, which can significantly shrink down the overall size. Many graphics programs support shrinking PNGs quite a bit themselves, so look for those options (such as a "save for web" feature). There are also third-party tools like "pngcrush," which will try many different ways of compressing and shrinking the image to give you a smaller file size.

Using the Right Sizes

Our "hero" images are being used as thumbnails, so they're actually significantly larger than what is displayed. The screen has a 16sp space on the left, center, and right of the thumbnail grid. In the case of the Nexus 5 (an XXHDPI device, which means the spaces are 48px), the spaces use a total of 144px. With a screen width of 1080px, we can subtract the 144px of space and divide the remainder by 2 (because there are two thumbnails in each row) to determine the thumbnails will be 468px in each dimension. That means we're loading a 1080 $\times$ 607 image (roughly 650,000px) when we really just need a 468 $\times$ 468 image (about 220,000px). If we run the same numbers for a Nexus 4, which is an XHDPI device with a screen width of 768px, we need an image that's 336px (about 110,000px). That means a Nexus 5 is loading almost three times as many pixels as needed and a Nexus 4 is loading almost six times as many pixels as needed! Not only is using larger images than necessary slower to load, it's slower to blur and takes up more memory.

There is a simple method we can use to handle this. First, we will create a few sizes to handle the most typical device configurations. Then we'll store all of these in the `drawables-nodpi` folder with a filename that indicates the size (for instance, `hero_image_clamps_468.png`) because we don't want Android to scale these images. It's a good idea to make sure the original images have updated names (e.g., `hero_image_clamps_1080.png`) to be consistent, and don't forget to make sure the images you save out have any extra data stripped (they should not be progressive JPEGs, they shouldn't have EXIF data, XMP data, or thumbnails embedded). Removing the extra data helps keep your APK smaller and also slightly decreases the loading time for the images. After that we just need some simple code to pick the best size.

Listing 10.2 demonstrates a simple `BitmapUtils` class that picks the best sized image. You might be wondering if there's a way to construct the drawable resource ID from a string. For instance, you could store the string "hero_image_clamps_" and then concatenate the appropriate size, then get the resource that references. Indeed, that is possible. With a reference to your resources like you get from `getResources()`, you can use the `getIdentifier` method, but that method actually uses reflection to figure out which resource you're referencing, so it is slow (defeating the purpose of optimizing this code in the first place). You should typically avoid using that method.

Listing 10.2   A `BitmapUtils` Class

```
public class BitmapUtils {

    private static final int THUMBNAIL_SIZE_336 = 336;
    private static final int THUMBNAIL_SIZE_468 = 468;

    public static int getScreenWidth(@NonNull Context context) {
        WindowManager windowManager = (WindowManager) context.
➥ getSystemService(Context.WINDOW_SERVICE);
        Display display = windowManager.getDefaultDisplay();
        Point point = new Point();
        display.getSize(point);
        return point.x;
    }

    /**
     * Returns a resource ID to a smaller version of the drawable, when
➥ possible.
     *
     * This is intended just for the hero images. If a smaller size of
➥ the resource ID cannot
     * be found, the original resource ID is returned.
     *
     * @param resourceId int drawable resource ID to look for
     * @param desiredSize int desired size in pixels of the drawable
     * @return int drawable resource ID to use
     */
    @DrawableRes
    public static int getPresizedImage(@DrawableRes int resourceId, int
➥ desiredSize) {
        switch (resourceId) {
            case R.drawable.hero_image_clamps_1080:
                if (desiredSize <= THUMBNAIL_SIZE_336) {
                    return R.drawable.hero_image_clamps_336;
                } else if (desiredSize <= THUMBNAIL_SIZE_468) {
                    return R.drawable.hero_image_clamps_468;
                }
                break;
            case R.drawable.hero_image_saw_1080:
                if (desiredSize <= THUMBNAIL_SIZE_336) {
                    return R.drawable.hero_image_saw_336;
                } else if (desiredSize <= THUMBNAIL_SIZE_468) {
                    return R.drawable.hero_image_saw_468;
                }
                break;
```

```
            case R.drawable.hero_image_drill_1080:
                if (desiredSize <= THUMBNAIL_SIZE_336) {
                    return R.drawable.hero_image_drill_336;
                } else if (desiredSize <= THUMBNAIL_SIZE_468) {
                    return R.drawable.hero_image_drill_468;
                }
                break;
            case R.drawable.hero_image_sander_1080:
                if (desiredSize <= THUMBNAIL_SIZE_336) {
                    return R.drawable.hero_image_sander_336;
                } else if (desiredSize <= THUMBNAIL_SIZE_468) {
                    return R.drawable.hero_image_sander_468;
                }
                break;
            case R.drawable.hero_image_router_1080:
                if (desiredSize <= THUMBNAIL_SIZE_336) {
                    return R.drawable.hero_image_router_336;
                } else if (desiredSize <= THUMBNAIL_SIZE_468) {
                    return R.drawable.hero_image_router_468;
                }
                break;
            case R.drawable.hero_image_lathe_1080:
                if (desiredSize <= THUMBNAIL_SIZE_336) {
                    return R.drawable.hero_image_lathe_336;
                } else if (desiredSize <= THUMBNAIL_SIZE_468) {
                    return R.drawable.hero_image_lathe_468;
                }
                break;
            case R.drawable.hero_image_more_1080:
                if (desiredSize <= THUMBNAIL_SIZE_336) {
                    return R.drawable.hero_image_more_336;
                } else if (desiredSize <= THUMBNAIL_SIZE_468) {
                    return R.drawable.hero_image_more_468;
                }
                break;
        }

        return resourceId;
    }
}
```

Testing out loading images that are the correct size for a Nexus 5 shows that we drop from the 30 milliseconds we saw after shrinking the file sizes in the previous section to just 7 milliseconds! This has also made our blurring code significantly faster (down from 30 milliseconds to about 15 milliseconds) because it's operating on fewer pixels. Overall, it is still taking about 22 milliseconds to get the view, so it's still slow, but the improvements so far have been substantial.

Before we move on, it's worth noting that you can also tackle this by loading the images at a smaller size using the `BitmapFactory` class, which supports subsampling. By subsampling, you can read a fraction of the number of pixels. For instance, if you have an image that was 1000px wide but you only need it at 500px wide, you can read every other pixel. This isn't as efficient as providing correctly sized images, but it is more universal.

The general idea is that you read in just the metadata about the image (which includes the dimensions) by making use of the `Options` class. Create a new instance of the `Options` class and set `inJustDecodeBounds` to true. Now when you decode the image with `decodeResources`, you use the `Options` object to tell it that you only want the bounds (the size of the image). The `Options` object will now have its `outWidth`, `outHeight`, and `outMimeType` set to the values of the actual image (and `BitmapFactory` will return null).

Once you know how big the image is, you figure out how to subsample the image. The `BitmapFactory` class works in powers of 2, so you can subsample every second pixel, every fourth pixel, every eighth pixel, and so forth. Using a simple while loop, we can double the sample size until the resulting image will be just larger than the desired width. Listing 10.3 shows a simple implementation of this method.

Listing 10.3   The `getSizedBitmap` Method

```
public static Bitmap getSizedBitmap(@NonNull Resources res,
➥ @DrawableRes int resId, int desiredWidth) {
    // Load just the size of the image
    BitmapFactory.Options options = new BitmapFactory.Options();
    options.inJustDecodeBounds = true;
    BitmapFactory.decodeResource(res, resId, options);

    // Options now has the bounds; prepare it for getting the actual
➥ image
    options.inSampleSize = 1;
    options.inJustDecodeBounds = false;

    if (options.outWidth > desiredWidth) {
        final int halfWidth = options.outWidth / 2;

        while (halfWidth / options.inSampleSize > desiredWidth) {
            options.inSampleSize *= 2;
        }
    }

    return BitmapFactory.decodeResource(res, resId, options);
}
```

This is a simple way of making your image loading more efficient and this technique can be used throughout your app; however, it isn't as efficient as having your images exactly the correct size.

Testing image loading with this method, the average speed is around 15 milliseconds (with a fair bit of variation), compared to the 30 milliseconds without this method or the 7 milliseconds with properly sized images.

Using an Image Cache

Every time you load an image from disk, it has to be decoded again. As we've seen, this process is often very slow. Worse, we can be loading the same image multiple times because the view that was displaying it goes off the screen and garbage collection is triggered and later it comes back on screen. An image cache allows you to specify a certain amount of memory to use for images, and the typical pattern is an LRU (least-recently-used) cache. As you put images in and ask for images out, the cache keeps track of that usage. When you put in a new image and there isn't enough room for it, the cache will evict the images that haven't been used for the longest amount of time, so that images you just used (and are most likely to still be relevant) stay in memory. When you load images, they go through the image cache, which will keep them in memory as long as the cache has room. That means the view going off screen and coming back on might not cause the image to have to be read from disk, which can save several milliseconds.

You can use the `LruCache` class that is in the support library to work with any version of Android. It has two generics, one for the keys and one for the values (the objects you cache). For images, you'll typically have a string key (such as a URL and filename), but you can use whatever makes sense for your needs. Because the `LruCache` class is designed to work in many situations, the concept of "size" can be defined by you. By default, the size of the cache is determined by the number of objects, but that doesn't make sense for our use. A single large image will take up a lot more memory than several smaller ones, so we can make the size measured in kilobytes. We need to override the `sizeOf` method to return the number of kilobytes a given entry is. We also need to decide on the maximum size of the cache. This will depend heavily on the type of app you're developing, but we can make this a portion of the overall memory available to our app. Let's start with an eighth of the total memory. We can also place an upper limit on the size of 16mb so that our app is well behaved on devices that give each VM much more memory that we necessarily need. Listing 10.4 shows this simple class.

Listing 10.4 The `BitmapCache` Class

```
public class BitmapCache extends LruCache<String, Bitmap> {
    public static final String TAG = "BitmapCache";

    private static final int MAXIMUM_SIZE_IN_KB = 1024 * 16;

    public BitmapCache() {
        super(getCacheSize());
    }

    @Override
    protected int sizeOf(String key, Bitmap bitmap) {
        return bitmap.getByteCount() / 1024;
    }
```

```
/**
 * Returns the size of the cache in kilobytes
 *
 * @return int total kilobytes to make the cache
 */
private static int getCacheSize() {
    // Maximum KB available to the VM
    final int maxMemory = (int) (Runtime.getRuntime().maxMemory()
➥ / 1024);
    // The smaller of an eighth of the total memory or 16MB
    final int cacheSize = Math.min(maxMemory / 8, MAXIMUM_SIZE_IN_KB);
    Log.v(TAG, "BitmapCache size: " + cacheSize + "kb");
    return cacheSize;
}
}
```

We can create the `BitmapCache` in our `BitmapUtils` class and then add some simple methods for interacting with it. In the case of our grid of images, we actually care more about the versions of the images that have been blurred along the bottom already, so we can directly cache those. Listing 10.5 shows the `BitmapUtils` methods we've added and Listing 10.6 shows the updated methods in `CaptionedImageView`.

Listing 10.5   The `BitmapUtils` Class Updated to Use the Cache

```
publicclass BitmapUtils {

    private static final int THUMBNAIL_SIZE_336 = 336;
    private static final int THUMBNAIL_SIZE_468 = 468;

    private static final BitmapCache BITMAP_CACHE = new BitmapCache();

    public synchronized static void cacheBitmap(@NonNull String key,
➥ @NonNull Bitmap bitmap) {
        BITMAP_CACHE.put(key, bitmap);
    }

    public synchronized static Bitmap getBitmap(@NonNull String key) {
        return BITMAP_CACHE.get(key);
    }

    public synchronized static Bitmap getBitmap(@NonNull Resources res,
➥ @DrawableRes int resId) {
        String key = String.valueOf(resId);
        Bitmap bitmap = BITMAP_CACHE.get(key);
        if (bitmap == null) {
            bitmap = BitmapFactory.decodeResource(res, resId);
            BITMAP_CACHE.put(key, bitmap);
```

```
        }
        return bitmap;
    }


    public static int getScreenWidth(@NonNull Context context) {
        WindowManager windowManager = (WindowManager) context.
getSystemService(Context.WINDOW_SERVICE);
        Display display = windowManager.getDefaultDisplay();
        Point point = new Point();
        display.getSize(point);
        return point.x;
    }


    /**
     * Returns a resource ID to a smaller version of the drawable, when
possible.
     *
     * This is intended just for the hero images. If a smaller size of
the resource ID cannot
     * be found, the original resource ID is returned.
     *
     * @param resourceId int drawable resource ID to look for
     * @param desiredSize int desired size in pixels of the drawable
     * @return int drawable resource ID to use
     */
    @DrawableRes
    public static int getPresizedImage(@DrawableRes int resourceId, int
desiredSize) {
        switch (resourceId) {
            case R.drawable.hero_image_clamps_1080:
                if (desiredSize <= THUMBNAIL_SIZE_336) {
                    return R.drawable.hero_image_clamps_336;
                } else if (desiredSize <= THUMBNAIL_SIZE_468) {
                    return R.drawable.hero_image_clamps_468;
                }
                break;
            case R.drawable.hero_image_saw_1080:
                if (desiredSize <= THUMBNAIL_SIZE_336) {
                    return R.drawable.hero_image_saw_336;
                } else if (desiredSize <= THUMBNAIL_SIZE_468) {
                    return R.drawable.hero_image_saw_468;
                }
                break;
            case R.drawable.hero_image_drill_1080:
                if (desiredSize <= THUMBNAIL_SIZE_336) {
                    return R.drawable.hero_image_drill_336;
                } else if (desiredSize <= THUMBNAIL_SIZE_468) {
                    return R.drawable.hero_image_drill_468;
                }
```

```
                          break;
                  case R.drawable.hero_image_sander_1080:
                      if (desiredSize <= THUMBNAIL_SIZE_336) {
                          return R.drawable.hero_image_sander_336;
                      } else if (desiredSize <= THUMBNAIL_SIZE_468) {
                          return R.drawable.hero_image_sander_468;
                      }
                      break;
                  case R.drawable.hero_image_router_1080:
                      if (desiredSize <= THUMBNAIL_SIZE_336) {
                          return R.drawable.hero_image_router_336;
                      } else if (desiredSize <= THUMBNAIL_SIZE_468) {
                          return R.drawable.hero_image_router_468;
                      }
                      break;
                  case R.drawable.hero_image_lathe_1080:
                      if (desiredSize <= THUMBNAIL_SIZE_336) {
                          return R.drawable.hero_image_lathe_336;
                      } else if (desiredSize <= THUMBNAIL_SIZE_468) {
                          return R.drawable.hero_image_lathe_468;
                      }
                      break;
                  case R.drawable.hero_image_more_1080:
                      if (desiredSize <= THUMBNAIL_SIZE_336) {
                          return R.drawable.hero_image_more_336;
                      } else if (desiredSize <= THUMBNAIL_SIZE_468) {
                          return R.drawable.hero_image_more_468;
                      }
                      break;
              }

          return resourceId;
      }

      public static Bitmap getSizedBitmap(@NonNull Resources res,
    ➥ @DrawableRes int resId, int desiredWidth) {
          // Load just the size of the image
          BitmapFactory.Options options = new BitmapFactory.Options();
          options.inJustDecodeBounds = true;
          BitmapFactory.decodeResource(res, resId, options);

          // Options now has the bounds; prepare it for getting the
    ➥ actual image
          options.inSampleSize = 1;
          options.inJustDecodeBounds = false;

          if (options.outWidth > desiredWidth) {
              final int halfWidth = options.outWidth / 2;

              while (halfWidth / options.inSampleSize > desiredWidth) {
```

```
            options.inSampleSize *= 2;
        }
    }

    return BitmapFactory.decodeResource(res, resId, options);
    }
}
```

Listing 10.6 The Updated `CaptionedImageView` Methods

```java
public void setImageResource(@DrawableRes int drawableResourceId) {
    TraceCompat.beginSection("BLUR — setImageResource");
    mDrawableResourceId = drawableResourceId;
    Bitmap bitmap = BitmapUtils.getBitmap(getResources(),
➥ mDrawableResourceId);
    mDrawable = new BitmapDrawable(getResources(), bitmap);
    mImageView.setImageDrawable(mDrawable);
    updateBlur();
    TraceCompat.endSection();
}

private void updateBlur() {
    if (!(mDrawable instanceof BitmapDrawable)) {
        return;
    }
    final int textViewHeight = mTextView.getHeight();
    final int imageViewHeight = mImageView.getHeight();
    if (textViewHeight == 0 || imageViewHeight == 0) {
        return;
    }

    // Get the Bitmap
    final BitmapDrawable bitmapDrawable = (BitmapDrawable) mDrawable;
    final Bitmap originalBitmap = bitmapDrawable.getBitmap();

    // Determine the size of the TextView compared to the height of the
➥ ImageView
    final float ratio = (float) textViewHeight / imageViewHeight;

    // Calculate the height as a ratio of the Bitmap
    final int height = (int) (ratio * originalBitmap.getHeight());
    final int width = originalBitmap.getWidth();
    final String blurKey = getBlurKey(width);
    Bitmap newBitmap = BitmapUtils.getBitmap(blurKey);
    if (newBitmap != null) {
        mImageView.setImageBitmap(newBitmap);
        return;
    }
```

```java
    // The y position is the number of pixels height represents from
➡ the bottom of the Bitmap
    final int y = originalBitmap.getHeight() - height;

    TraceCompat.beginSection("BLUR - createBitmaps");
    final Bitmap portionToBlur = Bitmap.createBitmap(originalBitmap,
➡ 0, y, originalBitmap.getWidth(), height);
    final Bitmap blurredBitmap = Bitmap.createBitmap(portionToBlur.
getWidth(), height, Bitmap.Config.ARGB_8888);
    TraceCompat.endSection();

    // Use RenderScript to blur the pixels
    TraceCompat.beginSection("BLUR - RenderScript");
    RenderScript rs = RenderScript.create(getContext());
    ScriptIntrinsicBlur theIntrinsic = ScriptIntrinsicBlur.create(rs,
➡ Element.U8_4(rs));
    TraceCompat.beginSection("BLUR - RenderScript Allocation");
    Allocation tmpIn = Allocation.createFromBitmap(rs, portionToBlur);
    // Fix internal trace that isn't ended
    TraceCompat.endSection();
    Allocation tmpOut = Allocation.createFromBitmap(rs,
➡ blurredBitmap);
    // Fix internal trace that isn't ended
    TraceCompat.endSection();
    TraceCompat.endSection();
    theIntrinsic.setRadius(25f);
    theIntrinsic.setInput(tmpIn);
    TraceCompat.beginSection("BLUR - RenderScript forEach");
    theIntrinsic.forEach(tmpOut);
    TraceCompat.endSection();
    TraceCompat.beginSection("BLUR - RenderScript copyTo");
    tmpOut.copyTo(blurredBitmap);
    TraceCompat.endSection();
    new Canvas(blurredBitmap).drawColor(mScrimColor);
    TraceCompat.endSection();

    // Create the new bitmap using the old plus the blurred portion and
➡ display it
    TraceCompat.beginSection("BLUR - Finalize image");
    newBitmap = originalBitmap.copy(Bitmap.Config.ARGB_8888, true);
    final Canvas canvas = new Canvas(newBitmap);
    canvas.drawBitmap(blurredBitmap, 0, y, new Paint());
    BitmapUtils.cacheBitmap(blurKey, newBitmap);
    mTextView.setBackground(null);
    mImageView.setImageBitmap(newBitmap);
    TraceCompat.endSection();
}
```

Given that on a typical device six of the seven images in the woodworking tools app are available on the first screen (once the spacing is back to normal); you might consider pre-caching the seventh image. By precaching them all, you will slightly increase the loading time of the app, but you will ensure that the scrolling is smooth. If you had even more images to handle, you might even move the image loading and blurring to a background thread. Although RenderScript is extremely fast, it still takes time pass the data to the GPU, process it, and pass that data back, so it's not a bad idea to push that work to a background thread if you're going to be doing it often.

Additional Performance Improvements

There are many causes of performance issues, but they are nearly always related to doing too much work on the UI thread. Sometimes you can affect these issues directly (like moving the loading of images to a background thread) and other times you have to be less direct (like maintaining a reference to an object you don't need to avoid garbage collection during an animation). Whether you have to be direct or not, knowing additional techniques to improve performance is always beneficial.

Controlling Garbage Collection

Garbage collection is one of those things that you can simultaneously love and hate. It's great because it lets you focus on the fun part of developing an app rather than worrying about tedious tasks like reference counting. It's horrible because it slows down your app when it happens. Although Android has had concurrent garbage collection for years now and its introduction helped a huge amount, garbage collection can still cause jank. Remember, you have just 16 milliseconds for each frame, so the garbage collector taking just 4 milliseconds is effectively taking 25% of your time for that frame.

Although you can't do much to control the garbage collector directly other than just triggering a collection, you can adjust the way you code your app to decrease the work it does or even simply change the timing. In particular, you should be conscious of where you are allocating memory and where you are releasing it. Every time you allocate memory, such as declaring an object or array, you are asking the system for a consecutive chunk of free memory. The fact that it's consecutive is important because that means even if you have 10mb free, you could ask for 500kb and still incur the cost of the VM reorganizing the memory if there isn't enough consecutive free memory available. Even if the virtual machine doesn't have to clear out memory, just moving chunks of memory around to make a large, consecutive section takes time. On the other side of that, every time you get rid of a reference to an object or an array and that was the last reference to that object or array, there is a chance the garbage collector will run. Halfway done with that animation and now you don't need those giant bitmaps? Removing your reference could cause the animation to pause or skip frames.

In general, you don't want to allocate or release memory in any method that is already potentially slow or gets called many times in succession. For instance, be careful in the onDraw and onLayout methods of View (both are covered in Chapter 13, "Developing Fully Custom Views"), getView of Adapter implementations, and any methods you trigger during animations. If you have to allocate objects, consider whether it's possible to keep them around or reuse them (such as in an object pool).

View Holder Pattern

ListView and other AbsListView implementations are excellent ways to effectively display a subset of a larger data set. They effectively reuse views to limit garbage collection and keep everything smooth, but it's still easy to run into problems. One of the most common methods to use within a getView call of an adapter is findViewById. For example, look at Listing 10.7 that shows a simple getView implementation.

Listing 10.7   An Example getView Method

```
public View getView(int position, View convertView, ViewGroup parent) {
    if (convertView == null) {
        convertView = mLayoutInflater.inflate(R.layout.list_item,
➥ parent, false);
    }

    ListItem listItem = getItem(position);
    ImageView imageView = (ImageView) convertView.findViewById
➥ (R.id.imageView);
    Drawable drawable = mContext.getDrawable(R.drawable.person);
    drawable.setTintMode(PorterDuff.Mode.SRC_ATOP);
    drawable.setTint(listItem.getColor());
    imageView.setImageDrawable(drawable);

    TextView textView = (TextView) convertView.findViewById
➥ (R.id.count);

    textView.setText(listItem.getCount());
    textView = (TextView) convertView.findViewById(R.id.title);
    textView.setText(listItem.getTitle());
    textView = (TextView) convertView.findViewById(R.id.subtitle);
    textView.setText(listItem.getSubtitle());

    return convertView;
}
```

Each getView call traverses the view to find the views that need to be updated. In this case, there are four separate findViewById calls. Each call will first check the convertView ID, then the children one at a time until a match is found. If this example has just the convertView plus the four views that are searched for, the first call will check two views to get the match, the next three, and so on. This leads to 14 view lookups in this simple case! The more complex the view, the longer it takes to traverse the hierarchy and find the views you are looking for.

The ideal solution would be to only have to find the views one time and then just retain the references, and that's what the view holder pattern does. Because you are reusing views (via the convert view), you have to traverse a finite number of views before you have found every view you care about in the list. By creating a class called ViewHolder that has references to each of the views you care about, you can instantiate that class once per view in the ListView and then reuse that class as much as needed. This class is implemented as a static inner class, so it is really just acting as a container for view references. See Listing 10.8 for a simple example of a class that takes the view and sets all the necessary references.

Listing 10.8   An Example of a ViewHolder Class

```
private static class ViewHolder {
    /*package*/final ImageView imageView;
    /*package*/final TextView count;
    /*package*/final TextView title;
    /*package*/final TextView subtitle;

    /*package*/ ViewHolder(View v) {
        imageView = (ImageView) v.findViewById(R.id.imageView);
        count = (TextView) v.findViewById(R.id.count);
        title = (TextView) v.findViewById(R.id.title);
        subtitle = (TextView) v.findViewById(R.id.subtitle);
    }
}
```

Looking back at the getView method, a few minor changes can significantly improve the efficiency. If convertView is null, inflate a new view as we already have and then create a new ViewHolder instance, passing in the view we just created. To keep the ViewHolder with this view, we call the setTag method, which allows us to associate an arbitrary object with any view. If convertView is not null, we simply call getTag and cast the result to the ViewHolder.

Now that we have the ViewHolder, we can just reference the views directly, so the rest of the getView code is not only much simpler than before but also better performing and easier to read. See Listing 10.9 for the updated getView call. Any time you use an adapter and you use the child views in the getView method, you should use this view holder pattern. For example, the ToolArrayAdapter in the woodworking tools app should be updated to use the view holder pattern; give it a try.

Listing 10.9   The `getView` Method Using a `ViewHolder`

```
public View getView(int position, View convertView, ViewGroup parent) {
    ViewHolder viewHolder;
    if (convertView == null) {
        convertView = mLayoutInflater.inflate(R.layout.list_item,
➡ parent, false);
        viewHolder = new ViewHolder(convertView);
        convertView.setTag(viewHolder);
    } else {
        viewHolder = (ViewHolder) convertView.getTag();
    }

    ListItem listItem = getItem(position);
    Drawable drawable = mContext.getDrawable(R.drawable.person);
    drawable.setTintMode(PorterDuff.Mode.SRC_ATOP);
    drawable.setTint(listItem.getColor());
    viewHolder.imageView.setImageDrawable(drawable);

    viewHolder.count.setText(listItem.getCount());
    viewHolder.title.setText(listItem.getTitle());
    viewHolder.subtitle.setText(listItem.getSubtitle());

    return convertView;
}
```

Eliminating Overdraw

Overdraw is when your app causes pixels to be drawn on top of each other. For example, imagine a typical app with a background, whether plain or an image. Now you put an opaque button on it. First, the device draws the background; then it draws the button. The background under the button was drawn but is never seen, so that processing and data transfer are wasted.

You might wonder how you can actually eliminate overdraw then, and the answer is that you do not need to. You only need to eliminate excessive overdraw. What "excessive" means is different for each device, but the general rule of thumb is that you should not be drawing more than three times the number of pixels on the screen (as detailed in Chapter 7, "Designing the Visuals"). When you go above three times the number of pixels, performance often suffers.

It's worth noting that some devices are better than others at efficiently avoiding drawing pixels when opaque pixels would be drawn right on top of them. GPUs that use deferred rendering are able to eliminate overdraw in cases where fully opaque pixels are drawn on fully opaque pixels, but not all Android devices have GPUs that use deferred rendering. Further, if pixels have any amount of transparency, that overdraw cannot be eliminated because the pixels have to be combined. That is why designs that contain a significant amount of transparency are inherently more difficult to make smooth and efficient than designs that do not.

Overdraw is easiest to eliminate when you can see it. Android 4.2 and newer offer a developer option to show GPU overdraw by coloring the screen differently based on how many times a pixel has been drawn and redrawn. To enable it, go to the device settings and then Developer options and scroll to the "drawing" section to enable the Show GPU Overdraw option (see Figure 10.7). When this option is checked, apps will be colored to show the amount of overdraw. Current versions of Android don't require restarting the app, but older versions do.

Figure 10.7 The Show GPU Overdraw option in Android's developer options

First, you should understand what the color tints mean. If there is no tint, there is no overdraw, and this is the ideal situation. A blue tint indicates a single overdraw (meaning the pixel was drawn once and then drawn again), and you can think of it as being "cold" because your device can easily handle a single level of overdraw (so the processor is not overheating). When something is tinted green, it has been overdrawn twice. Light red indicates an overdraw of three times, and dark red indicates an overdraw of four (or more) times (red, hot, bad!).

Large sections of blue are acceptable as long as the whole app is not blue (if it were, that'd suggest you're drawing the full screen and immediately redrawing it, which is very wasteful). Medium-sized sections of green are okay, but you should avoid having more than half of the screen green. Light red is much worse, but it's still okay for small areas such as text or a tiny icon. Dark red should make you cry. Well, maybe not cry, but you should definitely fix any dark red. These areas are drawn five times (or more), so just imagine your single device powering five full screens and you should realize how bad this is.

Figure 10.8 Simple app that shouldn't require much work by the device

Figure 10.8 shows a very simple design that is just a list of text. Judging by the simple appearance, it looks like the device has to do minimal work to get these pixels on the display; however, we can turn on the overdraw visualization and see how bad things actually are. Figure 10.9 shows the design tinted by the Show GPU Overdraw option. The full source code for this example is in the OverdrawExample project in the `chapter10` folder.

Figure 10.9 The same app with overdraw being displayed

First, you should know that the theme your app uses should have a window background. This can be a drawable and it is usually a simple color. Android uses this when your app is first being displayed to immediately show some visual indication of what your app should look like even before the views have been inflated. This makes the device feel more responsive because it can respond to the tap even before you've initiated the activity and inflated its views. This window background stays on the screen and everything else is painted on top. That means if you have an activity with a layout that also draws a background, you can very easily draw all pixels on the screen twice and then more times when the views are put on top.

Another common source of overdraw is with items in a `ListView`. The example is not only drawing a white background with the activity's base view right on top of the window background, it is drawing a white background for each list item over that, which is entirely unnecessary. By simply eliminating the extra backgrounds, the overdraw visualization (shown in Figure 10.10) is immediately improved.

Figure 10.10 Overdraw visualization after eliminating extra backgrounds

Remember that you don't need to eliminate all overdraw, but you should generally minimize it. You should be conscious of what views are drawing in front of and check the overdraw visualization now and then.

Hierarchy Viewer

Hierarchy Viewer is the unsung hero of layout optimization. It hasn't seen a whole lot of change since the early versions, but it still remains a great go-to tool for figuring out what is happening with your layouts. It can be used for simply figuring out why a view doesn't display or to figure out why a hierarchy is slow to load. It can even output your views as a PSD, allowing you to inspect positioning and colors with precision that is hard to match from simple screenshots.

If your device is running Android 4.0 (or lower) and is unlocked, everything should just work. If it's running 4.0 (or lower) and it is locked, you can use the ViewServer class from Romain Guy (https://github.com/romainguy/ViewServer) in your app (be sure to add the internet permission). If your device is running Android 4.1 or newer, you need to set an environment variable called `ANDROID_HVPROTO` with a value of `ddm`. In Windows, you can open My Computer, Property, Advanced, Environment Variables, and click New to create it. For Mac you'll open `.bash_profile` in your home directory (note that the file starts with a dot, which means it is hidden by default). Add a line that contains `export ANDROID_HVPROTO=ddm` and save the file. Now type source `~/.bash_profile` from the command line (this causes the file to be re-read so that the variable is immediately set). For Linux, you can follow the same steps as for Mac but the file is `.bashrc` in your home directory.

Open Android Device Monitor (under the Tools menu and the Android submenu). The Hierarchy Viewer is a different perspective, so open the Window menu and click the Open Perspective option. Select Hierarchy View and click OK. If you haven't already connected your device and opened the screen you want to inspect, do so now.

On the left side, you should see your device(s) listed. Select it and click the "Load view hierarchy" button (that's the icon next to the refresh button; you can also click the downward-facing triangle and select the option there). If the icon is grayed out, that typically means there is an issue communicating with the device and more details should be available in the console (usually on the bottom right). If you've already followed the directions from two paragraphs ago and it's still gray, you can also try closing out Android Studio (and anything else that might be communicating with the device) and then run Android Device Monitor directly (run `monitor` from the Android SDK tools directory).

Once the view hierarchy has loaded, the left window will show view properties, the center of the screen will be the detailed view hierarchy, the top right will be an overview, and the bottom right is the layout view that lets you see what portion of the screen the selected view is responsible for (the bottom right may be showing the console tab, so just click the Layout View tab). Your screen should look like Figure 10.11.

Each gray box in the tree view (the center window) represents a view. The boxes can have the class type (e.g., `LinearLayout`), the memory address, the ID (e.g., `id/content`), performance indicators, and a view index. The view index shows you the view's position within the parent, where the first child is position 0. The performance indicators are simply colored circles that indicate the time it took to measure the view, the time it took for the layout pass, and the time it took to draw the view. Newer versions of Hierarchy Viewer require you to click the icon with the three circles to obtain the layout times. These indicators on the gray boxes are broken into three groups. If a view is within the fastest 50% of views for the given indicator (e.g., draw time),

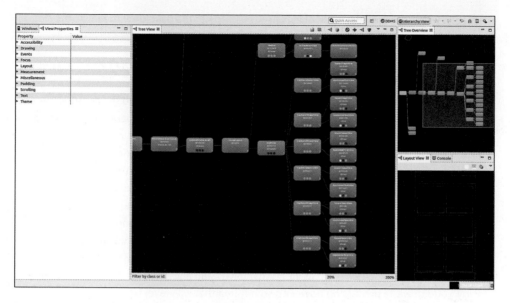

Figure 10.11 After the view hierarchy has been loaded, this is what you should see

that view will be green for that circle. If it's in the 50% of slow views, it will be yellow. If it is the slowest of all the views, it is red. It's important to realize these are relative indicators, so a view hierarchy that is extremely fast and efficient will still have a view with a red indicator for each circle just as an extremely slow hierarchy will.

By clicking a gray box, you can see an image of the view, a count of how many views this view represents (a 1 indicates the view itself; a 2 indicates the view plus a child view), and the exact times for measuring, laying out, and drawing the view. In the view properties (the left window), you can see virtually everything you could want to know about a view. This is extremely helpful when troubleshooting.

Finding Missing Views

One particularly handy use of Hierarchy Viewer is to figure out why a given view isn't showing up. There are many different reasons a view might not appear on the screen, so being able to see all the view's properties in one place plus a visual representation of the views in your hierarchy is incredibly useful. You can quickly see that a view's alpha is 0 or its visibility is set to invisible. You can tell if the view was sized incorrectly or positioned incorrectly. Before Android was blessed with Lint checks, pretty much every developer at one point (or many points) would have a `LinearLayout` and some child views with their widths set to `match_parent`, run the app, and then wonder why only the first child showed up. Simple things like forgetting the default orientation is horizontal can leave you with unexpected results, but Hierarchy Viewer can easily show you where a view is positioned and seeing it on the right edge of the screen instead of below the previous view is usually enough to get the developer to realize the simple mistake.

Eliminating Unnecessary Views

The biggest benefit Hierarchy Viewer can bring is helping you understand the complexity of your view hierarchy and eliminate extra views. The more complex your hierarchy, the longer your UI thread has to lock up on measuring, laying out, and drawing your views. You should look for views that have only a single child because those are often extraneous views that are easy to remove. You should also look for several sibling `TextViews` because you can often consolidate them (details are later in this chapter). It's a good idea to look for invisible views too. Although they aren't drawn, views that have visibility set to `INVISIBLE` are still measured and even a view that is `GONE` will slow down your view lookups and take up memory. If you sometimes need some views on a given screen but not always, use a `ViewStub` instead of inflating the entire view hierarchy and not drawing it. It's also a good idea to look out for views entirely outside of the screen (such as views that have been animated off the screen); it doesn't do any good to waste processing power on something that will never be seen.

Exporting to PSD

One of the extremely powerful but often overlooked features of Hierarchy Viewer is the ability to export a layout hierarchy as a Photoshop Document (a PSD file). This can be hugely valuable to designers, so make sure they are aware of this functionality. There is a rather forgettable-looking button above the tree view that appears to be three overlapping squares. That's the Capture Layers button. If you do not see it, you can also click the downward-facing triangle to get the list of options and select it from there. The resulting PSD can take a while to be generated, so be patient. If it fails, you will see an error in the console and can try again (occasionally it helps to reconnect the hardware device or restart the emulator).

Because this PSD is not using any advanced features such as layer masks, you can actually open it in GIMP and other tools as well. Along with the techniques discussed earlier in the chapter, this is an excellent method of detecting overdraw.

Exporting to a PSD is a great way for a developer and a designer to speak the same language. The designer can inspect in detail exactly what is going on with a layout by tweaking the layers and then tell the developer which layer has an issue (the layers are named after the view IDs when present, making it extra easy to associate a layer with a view). This also gives the designer the opportunity to make changes to further optimize the design. Perhaps initially a view seemed best at 50-percent opacity, but now the designer can tweak how opaque a view is just like any layer in Photoshop and determine that 40% is actually better.

One thing to note is that the layers are all rasterized. In simplistic terms, the pixels that each view creates are what are actually exported as layers. `TextViews` do not create actual Photoshop text layers, for instance. That also means that if you have a complex view that's drawing shapes, text, and images, only the resulting pixels are exported, so you can't see what each "layer" of that view looks like.

Custom Fonts

There are times when using a custom font can improve your app. Some apps designed for reading provide additional font choices for users; other apps might use fonts specific to their brand. When deciding on whether to use an additional font, consider how it helps the user experience. Don't include a font just because it's popular or makes the app look different from others; include a font because a usability study has shown that your app is easier to read with the font or because your brand requires it and you want to avoid using images for custom text.

The Roboto font family was built specifically for Android and is the default font for Android 4.0 (Ice Cream Sandwich) and above. Whenever possible, it is the font you should use. You can download the font from the Google design site (http://www.google.com/design/spec/resources/roboto-noto-fonts.html), and it includes multiple variations. In addition to Roboto regular, there is a thin version, light version, medium version, black version, and condensed version (as well as bold and italic versions where applicable).

Because this font was built for Android specifically, it displays very well on a variety of densities and screen types. Many of the most commonly used fonts today were designed for print, which is a very different medium than an electronic display, so some of the fonts that look great on paper do not reproduce as well onscreen. In particular, if you are considering light or thin fonts, be sure to test them on medium- and high-density displays and test them against low-end devices with AMOLEDs (most modern AMOLEDs are reasonably comparable to LCDs, even besting them in some measures, but older and lower quality AMOLEDs like the ones used for the Nexus S have a different subpixel arrangement than a traditional LCD and on top of that have a low enough resolution that the subpixel arrangement can cause display issues for very thin items).

If you do decide to use an alternate font, you need to put it in a directory called `assets` within the root directory of your project. The easiest way to use a custom font in your app is to extend `TextView` to create your own class. Listing 10.10 shows an example.

Listing 10.10   A Custom `TextView` for Displaying a Font

```
public class TextViewRobotoThin extends TextView {

    /**
     * This is the name of the font file within the assets folder
     */
    private static final String FONT_LOCATION = "roboto_thin.ttf";

    private static Typeface sTypeface;

    public TextViewRobotoThin(Context context) {
        super(context);
```

```
        setTypeface(getTypeface(context));
    }

    public TextViewRobotoThin(Context context, AttributeSet attrs) {
        super(context, attrs);
        setTypeface(getTypeface(context));
    }

    public TextViewRobotoThin(Context context, AttributeSet attrs, int
➥ defStyleAttr) {
        super(context, attrs, defStyleAttr);
        setTypeface(getTypeface(context));
    }

    @TargetApi(Build.VERSION_CODES.LOLLIPOP)
    public TextViewRobotoThin(Context context, AttributeSet attrs, int
➥ defStyleAttr, int defStyleRes) {
        super(context, attrs, defStyleAttr, defStyleRes);
        setTypeface(getTypeface(context));
    }

    /**
     * Returns the Typeface for Roboto Thin
     *
     * @param context Context to access the app's assets
     * @return Typeface for Roboto Thin
     */
    public static Typeface getTypeface(Context context) {
        if (sTypeface == null) {
            sTypeface = Typeface.createFromAsset(context.getAssets(),
FONT_LOCATION);
        }
        return sTypeface;
    }
}
```

At the top of the class is a static string specifying the name of the font file. Each of the normal constructors calls `setTypeface`. A public static method called `getTypeface()` will create the `Typeface` from the font file in the assets directory, if it hasn't already been created, and then return the `Typeface`. This is useful for times when you might access the `Typeface` for other uses (perhaps you do some custom drawing using this `Typeface` elsewhere). By having this public static method, anywhere in your code that needs this custom `Typeface` has one place to go, and you can just change the `FONT_LOCATION` if you need to change the font everywhere in the app.

You can now use this class anywhere you would use an ordinary `TextView`. For instance, you can replace the default "hello world" `TextView` with this in a new project. Figure 10.12 shows how this custom `TextView` looks on an actual device.

Figure 10.12 The custom `TextView` being displayed on a device

Complex TextViews

`TextView` is an extremely powerful view in Android. Obviously, they're able to display text, but they can also display several styles of text, different fonts or colors, and even inline images, all within a single `TextView`. You can have specific portions of text respond to click events and really associate any object you want with any portion of text. These ranges of text are generically referred to as "spans," as in a span (range) of bold text or a span of subscript.

Existing Spans

Android has a large number of prebuilt spans you can take advantage of. Because you can assign any object as a span, there isn't an actual span class. That's great in that it gives you a huge amount of flexibility, but it also means you have to dig a little to figure out what is supported.

First, you should know about the two main types of spans defined by the interfaces `CharacterStyle` and `ParagraphStyle`. As you can probably guess, these interfaces refer to spans that affect one or more characters and spans that affect entire paragraphs, respectively. Most spans will implement one of these two interfaces (although many implement more than just these). See the following list of built-in spans to get an idea about what is already supported:

- `AbsoluteSizeSpan`—A span that allows you to specify an exact size in pixels or density independent pixels.
- `AlignmentSpan.Standard`—A span that attaches an alignment (from `Layout.Alignment`).

- `BackgroundColorSpan`—A span that specifies a background color (the color behind the text, such as for highlighting).
- `ClickableSpan`—A span that has an `onClick` method that is triggered. (This class is abstract, so you can extend it with a class that specifies the `onClick` behavior.)
- `DrawableMarginSpan`—A span that draws a `Drawable` plus the specified amount of spacing.
- `DynamicDrawableSpan`—A span that you can extend to provide a `Drawable` that may change (but the size must remain the same).
- `EasyEditSpan`—A span that just marks some text so that the `TextView` can easily delete it.
- `ForegroundColorSpan`—A span that changes the color of the text (basically just called `setColor(int)` on the `TextPaint` object).
- `IconMarginSpan`—A span that draws a `Bitmap` plus the specified amount of spacing.
- `ImageSpan`—A span that draws an image specified as a `Bitmap`, `Drawable`, `URI`, or resource ID.
- `LeadingMarginSpan.Standard`—A span that adjusts the margin.
- `LocaleSpan`—A span that changes the locale of text (available in API level 17 and above).
- `MaskFilterSpan`—A span that sets the `MaskFilter` of the `TextPaint` (such as for blurring or embossing).
- `MetricAffectingSpan`—A span that affects the height and/or width of characters (this is an abstract class).
- `QuoteSpan`—A span that puts a vertical line to the left of the selected text to indicate it is a quote; by default the line is blue.
- `RasterizerSpan`—A span that sets the `Rasterizer` of the `TextPaint` (generally not useful to you).
- `RelativeSizeSpan`—A span that changes the text size relative to the supplied float (for instance, setting a 0.5 float will cause the text to render at half size).
- `ReplacementSpan`—A span that can be extended when something custom is drawn in place of the spanned text (e.g., `ImageSpan` extends this).
- `ScaleXSpan`—A span that provides a multiplier to use when calling the `TextPaint`'s `setTextScaleX(float)` method. (In other words, setting this to 0.5 will cause the text to be scaled to half size along the X-axis, thus appearing squished.)
- `StrikethroughSpan`—A span that simply passes `true` to the `TextPaint`'s `setStrikeThruText(boolean)` method, causing the text to have a line through it (useful for showing deleted text, such as in a draft of a document).
- `StyleSpan`—A span that adds bold and/or italic to the text.
- `SubscriptSpan`—A span that makes the text subscript (below the baseline).

- **SuggestionSpan**—A span that holds possible replacement suggestions, such as for a incorrectly spelled word (available in API level 14 and above).

- **SuperscriptSpan**—A span that makes the text superscript (above the baseline).

- **TabStopSpan.Standard**—A span that allows you to specify an offset from the leading margin of a line.

- **TextAppearanceSpan**—A span that allows you to pass in a TextAppearance for styling.

- **TypefaceSpan**—A span that uses a specific typeface family (monospace, serif, or sans-serif only).

- **UnderlineSpan**—A span that underlines the text.

- **URLSpan**—A ClickableSpan that attempts to view the specified URL when clicked.

Using Spans for Complex Text

One of the simplest ways to use spans is with the HTML class. If you have some HTML in a string, you can simply call HTML.fromHtml(String) to get an object that implements the spanned interface that will have the applicable spans applied. You can even supply an ImageGetter and a TagHandler, if you'd like. The styles included in the HTML will be converted to spans so, for example, "b" (bold) tags are converted to StyleSpans and "u" (underline) tags are converted to UnderlineSpans. See Listing 10.11 for a brief example of how to set the text of a TextView from an HTML string and enable navigating through and clicking the links.

Listing 10.11   Using HTML in a TextView

```
textView.setText(Html.fromHtml(htmlString));
textView.setMovementMethod(LinkMovementMethod.getInstance());
textView.setLinksClickable(true);
```

Another easy method for implementing spans is to use the Linkify class. The Linkify class allows you to easily create links within text for web pages, phone numbers, email addresses, physical addresses, and so on. You can even use it for custom regular expressions, if you're so inclined.

Finally, you can also manually set spans on anything that implements the Spannable interface. If you have an existing String or CharSequence that you'd like to make Spannable, use the SpannableString class. If you are building up some text, you can use the SpannableStringBuilder, which works like a StringBuilder but can attach spans. To the untrained eye, the app in Figure 10.13 is using two TextViews and an ImageView, but it actually has just a single TextView. See Listing 10.12 to understand how you can do this with one TextView and a few spans.

Figure 10.13 An app that seemingly uses more views than it really does

Listing 10.12 Using Spans with a `SpannableStringBuilder`

```
final SpannableStringBuilder ssb = new SpannableStringBuilder();
final int flag = Spannable.SPAN_EXCLUSIVE_EXCLUSIVE;
int start;
int end;

// Regular text
ssb.append("This text is normal, but ");

// Bold text
start = ssb.length();
ssb.append("this text is bold");
end = ssb.length();
ssb.setSpan(new StyleSpan(Typeface.BOLD), start, end, flag);

// Inline image
ssb.append('\n');
start = end + 1;
ssb.append('\uFFFC'); // Unicode replacement character
end = ssb.length();
ssb.setSpan(new ImageSpan(this, R.mipmap.ic_launcher), start, end, flag);

// Stretched text
start = end;
ssb.append("This text is wide");
end = ssb.length();
```

```
ssb.setSpan(new ScaleXSpan(2f), start, end, flag);

// Assign to TextView
final TextView tv = (TextView) findViewById(R.id.textView);
tv.setText(ssb);
```

RecyclerView

If you've been doing Android development for some time, you've probably come across issues with ListView. For most uses ListView is great. It handles everything you need and it is efficient; however, there are times when ListView doesn't do everything you want. For instance, animating views within ListView has a lot of challenges and there isn't a good way to change how the items are laid out.

To solve these issues, RecyclerView was created. Its name is a reference to the process of view recycling that we've discussed previously where a view that goes off screen can then be reused for a new view coming onto the screen. RecyclerView works similarly to ListView but with a more modular architecture. For instance, instead of assuming that you want your items vertically stacked, you supply a layout manager that handles determine how to lay out the items. Given that RecyclerView can do everything that ListView can, you might be wondering when you should still use ListView. The simple answer is to use ListView unless you encounter one of its limitations. Contrary to some opinions, ListView isn't dead and you shouldn't change all your ListViews over to RecyclerViews without reason. If you find that ListView doesn't work for you, that's the time to switch over to RecyclerView.

If you want a good starting point for playing around with RecyclerView, check out the sample. From Android Studio, open the File menu and select Import Sample and then type "Recycler View" in the search box. This will let you quickly set up a project that uses RecyclerView so that you can see how it works and experiment with it.

Layout Manager

To tell RecyclerView how to arrange the views, you need a layout manager. It's responsible for measuring and positioning views as well as handling the view recycling policy. Fortunately, there are some built in ones for the typical use cases. You'll commonly use LinearLayoutManager, which can give you a ListView-like display but also supports horizontal arrangement. You may also use GridLayoutManager or StaggeredGridLayoutManager for times when you want grids of items rather than just rows or columns.

Adapter

Like ListView, RecyclerView uses an adapter to supply its views, but it works a little differently (also note that it's RecyclerView.Adapter rather than android.widget.

Adapter). You commonly have to use the view holder pattern with adapters for `ListView` as described earlier in the chapter to avoid repeated calls to `findViewById`, but that pattern is built in to `RecyclerView` with an actual `ViewHolder` class. Rather than the `getView` method, this adapter has two methods. First, `onCreateViewHolder` is expected to create any views that are necessary, but it returns a new `ViewHolder` instance that references those views. Second, `onBindViewHolder` is expected to set all the views up for a given position using the `ViewHolder` instance.

Note that a key difference between `AdapterView` and `RecyclerView` is how you listen to clicks. Rather than assigning a single `onItemClickListener`, `RecyclerView` just uses the regular `onClickListener` and related classes. Typically any necessary listeners are set in `onCreateViewHolder` and the position or object(s) they care about are updated in `onBindViewHolder`.

Item Animator

Whenever the state of the `RecyclerView` changes, it needs to know how to animate the change and that's where the `ItemAnimator` abstract class comes in. A concrete implementation allows you to control the animations that are used to visualize these changes, so that your users can easily understand what happened. By default, `RecyclerView` uses the aptly named `DefaultItemAnimator`, but you can provide a custom implementation to precisely control the behavior.

Item Decoration

`RecyclerView` has one more trick up its sleeve and that's the concept of item decoration, which is based on the `ItemDecoration` abstract class. The idea is simple: sometimes you need to draw more than just the views that are displaying your data. For instance, you might draw dividers between items or visually group a section of items. `ItemDecoration` has both `onDraw` and `onDrawOver` methods. The former draws before the views are drawn (such as for backgrounds) and the latter draws after (meaning it draws in front of them). You can add multiple `ItemDecoration` implementations to your `RecyclerView` to get the effect you want, but you don't have to use any.

One additional feature `ItemDecoration` has is the ability to modify the position of views. By overriding `getItemOffsets`, you can adjust positions as needed, which allows you to manipulate the display in powerful ways such as visually clustering content based on proximity or spacing.

Summary

In this chapter, you learned a wide variety of topics that help advanced developers make even better apps. Using Systrace will allow you to get performance details that help you make informed decisions on how you can improve your app and help you identify issues that are easily missed like decoding an image twice. You saw multiple techniques for improving the efficiency of working with images from pre-sizing to background loading. Additional tools and techniques for performance improvements followed before getting into advanced uses of existing views by way of spans and the flexible `RecyclerView`.

In the next chapter, you'll dive right into the world of drawing in Android. You'll learn how to draw images and text as well as how to apply filters and compositing.

CHAPTER 11

WORKING WITH THE CANVAS AND ADVANCED DRAWING

Before diving into building completely custom views, it's a good idea to understand how to draw to the screen in Android. Drawing includes images, text, custom shapes, and more. Once you understand the basics, it's time to use color filters, shaders, and other advanced techniques for drawing anything you want.

Creating Custom Drawables

Android's `Drawable` class is a great abstraction for anything that can be drawn to the screen. In some ways it is like a view, but it is much easier to understand and work with for a variety of uses. By extending `Drawable` to create custom effects, you can easily add those effects to almost any view by setting the drawable as the background. Plus, virtually everything you learn about creating a custom `Drawable` class is also applicable to custom views. This means that a drawable is a good place to start experimenting with how you draw to the screen or to an image.

Behind the scenes, Android is using Skia, an excellent 2D C++ graphics library. Most of the drawing-related code you use in Android directly mirrors code from Skia, but Android has a lot of helpers to simplify common tasks and save you from some of the headaches that you might otherwise have to work through.

General Concept

The `Drawable` class has a few basic concepts you should know about to better understand the purpose of the methods. It has an "intrinsic" size and an actual drawn size. The intrinsic size is the ideal or natural size. For instance, a drawable that just draws a bitmap would have an intrinsic size that's identical to the bitmap's size. Drawables defined in XML usually have a width and a height attribute (such as we used previously with `VectorDrawable`) to define the intrinsic size. The actual drawn size is determined by the `setBounds` method. For instance, when you use an `ImageView`'s `setImageDrawable` method and pass in a drawable, it will call `setBounds` with a `Rect` (a class that represents a simple rectangle). Those bounds define the actual drawn size, but a class such as `ImageView` will use the intrinsic size to inform the bounds when possible.

The `Drawable` class also has a few methods that affect the actual drawing of the content. For instance, it has `setAlpha`, which allows the transparency level to be adjusted. It is up to you to actually implement this (fortunately, this is generally very easy).

There are four methods you must implement when you create a custom `Drawable` class.

- `draw(Canvas)` —Handles drawing to the canvas, similar to how `onDraw(Canvas)` works for views.
- `getOpacity()` —Returns an `int` that defines whether this drawable is translucent, transparent, or opaque. Each `int` is defined in `PixelFormat`.
- `setAlpha(int)` —Sets the alpha value from 0 (transparent) to 255 (opaque).
- `setColorFilter(ColorFilter)` —Sets the `ColorFilter` for the drawable.

Additional Important Methods

In addition to the required methods, there are several methods that you're likely to implement or at least use.

- `getBounds()` —Returns the `Rect` within which the drawable will fit.
- `getIntrinsicHeight()` —Returns the ideal height of the drawable.

- `getIntrinsicWidth()` —Returns the ideal width for the drawable.
- `onBoundsChange(Rect)` —Notifies your drawable that its bounds changed. This is the ideal place to do any one-time dimension calculations.
- `onLevelChange(int)` —Notifies your drawable that the level has changed. For example, a level can be used for a drawable that shows the amount of battery left (where the value would be between 0 and 100, but the drawable itself might only have five different appearances).
- `onStateChange(int[])` —Notifies your drawable that its state (e.g., whether it is pressed or focused) has changed.

Paint

The `Paint` class holds information about how to draw, such as the color, styles for filling and ending lines, and more. Nearly all the drawing calls performed by a `Canvas` object require a `Paint` object. A `Canvas` object will do something like draw a rectangle, but the `Paint` object will determine if it is anti-aliased, filled in, and so on.

Remember that you should avoid allocating objects in your `draw(Canvas)` method, so you should generally allocate your `Paint` objects elsewhere. Another option is to allocate them the first time `draw(Canvas)` is called and then retain the reference for future calls.

Canvas

The `Canvas` object that is passed in the `draw` method can be thought of as the tool that handles drawing. It is backed by a mutable `Bitmap` object that actually holds all the pixels. To draw, you need a `Paint` instance and something to draw, such as another bitmap or a rectangle. The `Canvas` class has a large number of methods for drawing and simplifying drawing. `Canvas` supports clipping (a clip is a portion of the bitmap that can be drawn onto, similar to using a marquee in an image program), drawing bitmaps, drawing shapes (arcs, rectangles, circles, and so on), adjusting the canvas with matrixes (including helper methods to simplify translation, rotation, scaling, and skewing), saving and restoring state (used for saving and restoring the state of the clip and matrixes), and some other helper methods.

You can also instantiate your own `Canvas` object by supplying it with a mutable `Bitmap` object like we did for the woodworking tools app. This is very useful when you need to perform some kind of drawing only once and want to retain the results. We'll see this again near the end of this chapter.

Whenever we talk about drawing to the screen, we're really talking about drawing to a `Bitmap` instance via the `Canvas` object. Android handles the process of getting the data from that `Bitmap` object to the screen. That means, from our perspective, anytime we talk about techniques for "drawing to the screen," those techniques could also be used for general image creation (such as if you wanted to programmatically create an image that is then emailed or shared via an `Intent`).

Working with Text

If you ever have to implement low-level code for actually creating the individual pixels of text on a screen, you should probably go running. It's extremely difficult with a lot of factors to consider, including the characteristics of the surprisingly complex fonts we work with. Fortunately, Android's system code takes care of much of the difficulty, so you can easily tell the system to put a given string on the screen, including wrapping it at a specific distance, and you won't have any difficulty determining how much room text takes up (so that you can position something after the text).

A Simple Text Drawable

Let's create a `SimpleTextDrawable` that just takes a string in the constructor and draws it. One important thing we want to do is to ensure that our `Paint` is anti-aliased to avoid jaggy, hard edges. The simplest way to do so is to pass in the `Paint.ANTI_ALIAS_FLAG` constant to the `Paint` constructor (though there is a `setAntiAlias` method). In `SimpleTextDrawable`'s constructor, we want to store the string that's passed in, set the color of the text, and set a size for it. The color of the text is controlled by the paint, so we simply have to call `setColor` and pass in an int that represents the color. For this example, we can use a hardcoded value (but feel free to get a color from a `Resources` instance, if desired). Setting the size is very similar. There is a `setTextSize` method on `Paint`, and we can simply use a hardcoded value to make the text large (but, again, feel free to get a dimension from `Resources` instead).

For our drawable to have a meaningful size, we implement the `getIntrinsicHeight` and `getIntrinsicWidth` methods. Our intrinsic dimensions should be large enough to contain the text. For this drawable, let's keep things simple and have the text on one line. This means that the height is just going to be the text height, which we can get with the `getTextSize` method of `Paint`. The width is a little trickier. We need to measure the number of pixels that the text will take up when drawn. Fortunately, `Paint` has a simple `measureText` method that we can simply pass our string into.

The `setColorFilter` and `setAlpha` methods just pass through to our Paint, so they're easy enough. We also need to implement `getOpacity`. Because we're creating anti-aliased text, some of these pixels will be translucent (meaning they will be partly transparent), so we return `PixelFormat.Translucent`.

Now for the real work: We need to actually write the text. In the `onDraw` method, we'll use one of the `Canvas` class methods called `drawText`. We pass in the string to draw, the x offset (we'll use 0), the y offset, and the `Paint` instance. One problem is that the text is drawn as if the y position represents a horizontal line to draw on, so the text will be above that position. In other words, we want to pass in the text size for the y position to push down the starting point enough for our text to fit. That's it! The actual drawing of this text takes a single method call and all the hard parts are done for you behind the scenes. Listing 11.1 shows the full `SimpleTextDrawable` class.

Listing 11.1 The Full `SimpleTextDrawable` Class

```java
public class SimpleTextDrawable extends Drawable {

    private static final int TEXT_COLOR = 0xFF311B92;

    private final Paint mPaint = new Paint(Paint.ANTI_ALIAS_FLAG);
    private final String mText;

    public SimpleTextDrawable(String text) {
        mText = text;
        mPaint.setColor(TEXT_COLOR);
        mPaint.setTextSize(100);
    }

    @Override
    public int getIntrinsicHeight() {
        return (int) mPaint.getTextSize();
    }

    @Override
    public int getIntrinsicWidth() {
        return (int) mPaint.measureText(mText);
    }

    @Override
    public void draw(Canvas canvas) {
        canvas.drawText(mText, 0, mPaint.getTextSize(), mPaint);
    }

    @Override
    public void setAlpha(int alpha) {
        mPaint.setAlpha(alpha);
        invalidateSelf();
    }

    @Override
    public void setColorFilter(ColorFilter cf) {
        mPaint.setColorFilter(cf);
        invalidateSelf();
    }

    @Override
    public int getOpacity() {
        return PixelFormat.TRANSLUCENT;
    }

}
```

Figure 11.1 The SimpleTextDrawable in action

To test this drawable, you can simply set it as the background of a view. Figure 11.1 shows an example of how this might look without padding.

A Better Text Drawable

One of the problems we have in that previous drawable is that it doesn't handle multiple lines. Once the text gets to the edge of the screen, it just keeps going instead of wrapping. You might think that you need to measure word-by-word to figure out where to wrap your text, but Android has help in store in the form of the Layout class. The name of this class isn't great because it is easily confused with views and layouts of that nature, but it is not the same. For text that doesn't change (like our example), there is the StaticLayout class. If our text could change, we'd use the DynamicLayout class. These classes do all the size calculations for you, making complex text display pretty easy.

We can create a class called BetterTextDrawable by starting with a copy of our previous drawable. In the constructor, we need to create a StaticLayout using our text, Paint instance, and the width of the text. We also have to specify an alignment (we'll use ALIGN_NORMAL), a spacing multiplier (remember a value of 1 is single-spaced and 2 is double-spaced), additional spacing, and whether to using the padding specified in the FontMetrics of the font.

This initial StaticLayout is used to give us intrinsic dimensions, so we can override the getIntrinsicHeight and getIntrinsicWidth methods and return the StaticLayout's getHeight and getWidth results, respectively.

Because we may be displayed at a size other than what we calculated, we need to implement the onBoundsChange method, which is given a Rect that tells us the size to constrain our drawable to. At that point, we can simply create a new StaticLayout. Our draw method can simply call through to the draw method of our StaticLayout and it handles all the text spacing, new lines, and so on. Listing 11.2 shows the full class and Figure 11.2 shows what it can look like.

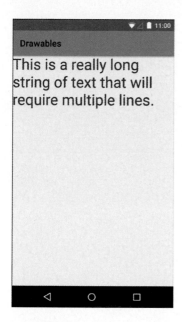

Figure 11.2 The BetterTextDrawable showing line wrapping

Listing 11.2 The Full BetterTextDrawable Class

```
public class BetterTextDrawable extends Drawable {

    private static final int TEXT_COLOR = 0xFF311B92;

    private final TextPaint mPaint = new TextPaint(new
➥ Paint(Paint.ANTI_ALIAS_FLAG));
    private final String mText;
    private StaticLayout mStaticLayout;

    public BetterTextDrawable(String text) {
        mText = text;
        mPaint.setColor(TEXT_COLOR);
        mPaint.setTextSize(100);
        mStaticLayout = new StaticLayout(mText, mPaint, (int) mPaint.
➥ measureText(mText), Layout.Alignment.ALIGN_NORMAL, 1, 0, false);
    }
```

```java
    @Override
    public int getIntrinsicHeight() {
        return mStaticLayout.getHeight();
    }

    @Override
    public int getIntrinsicWidth() {
        return mStaticLayout.getWidth();
    }

    @Override
    public void draw(Canvas canvas) {
        mStaticLayout.draw(canvas);
    }

    @Override
    public void setAlpha(int alpha) {
        mPaint.setAlpha(alpha);
        invalidateSelf();
    }

    @Override
    public void setColorFilter(ColorFilter cf) {
        mPaint.setColorFilter(cf);
        invalidateSelf();
    }

    @Override
    public int getOpacity() {
        return PixelFormat.TRANSLUCENT;
    }

    @Override
    protected void onBoundsChange(Rect bounds) {
        mStaticLayout = new StaticLayout(mText, mPaint, bounds.width(),
    ➥ Layout.Alignment.ALIGN_NORMAL, 1, 0, false);
    }
}
```

Depending on your use cases, you might also do some additional work to make this more efficient. For instance, if you're animating a view by shrinking or growing its height, you might have the onBoundsChange method compare the new width to the old width, to avoid creating a new StaticLayout when it hasn't changed.

Working with Images

Android has several methods to make working with images easier as well, so you don't have to worry about char arrays or other low-level representations of images. This means that common operations like copying one image into another (perhaps larger) image takes a line of code and you don't even have to worry about loops.

The typical path when working with images in a drawable is to get a `Bitmap` instance either via `BitmapFactory` or one of the static `Bitmap` methods and then draw it using one of the `Canvas drawBitmap` methods. Let's make a class called `SimpleBitmapDrawable` to take a closer look at this process.

First, the constructor should take a `Bitmap`, because we always want to have something to draw, but we can make a `setBitmap` method that handles receiving a new `Bitmap`. In the `setBitmap` method, we need to store a reference to the bitmap and call `invalidateSelf` (because we have something to draw).

Like with any drawable we make, we should override the `getIntrinsicHeight` and `getIntrinsicWidth` methods. Similar to the previous drawable, we can return the `getHeight` and `getWidth` results, respectively, from our `Bitmap` instance (instead of the `StaticLayout` instance).

Now we just need to override `draw`. There are several `drawBitmap` methods that `Canvas` offers us. In this case, let's use the method that takes the `Bitmap` instance, a source `Rect`, a destination `Rect`, and a `Paint`. The source `Rect` tells which portion of the bitmap to draw and the destination `Rect` tells where to draw it. Android will handle the scaling automatically. If we exclude the source `Rect` and use the bounds of the drawable as the destination `Rect`, we effectively stretch the image to fill the space allotted to the drawable. Figure 11.3 shows what this looks like when provided the small app icon. Listing 11.3 show the full source.

Figure 11.3 The `SimpleImageDrawable` showing the app icon

Listing 11.3 The Full `SimpleImageDrawable` Source

```java
public class SimpleImageDrawable extends Drawable {

    private Bitmap mBitmap;
    private final Paint mPaint = new Paint(Paint.ANTI_ALIAS_FLAG);

    public SimpleImageDrawable(Bitmap bitmap) {
        setBitmap(bitmap);
    }

    @Override
    public void draw(Canvas canvas) {
        canvas.drawBitmap(mBitmap, null, getBounds(), mPaint);
    }

    @Override
    public int getIntrinsicHeight() {
        return mBitmap.getHeight();
    }

    @Override
    public int getIntrinsicWidth() {
        return mBitmap.getWidth();
    }

    @Override
    public int getOpacity() {
        return PixelFormat.TRANSLUCENT;
    }

    @Override
    public void setAlpha(int alpha) {
        int oldAlpha = mPaint.getAlpha();
        if (alpha != oldAlpha) {
            mPaint.setAlpha(alpha);
            invalidateSelf();
        }
    }

    /**
     * Sets the {@link Bitmap} to draw and invalidates itself
     *
     * @param bitmap Bitmap to draw with rounded corners
     */
    public void setBitmap(@NonNull Bitmap bitmap) {
        mBitmap = bitmap;
        invalidateSelf();
    }

    @Override
    public void setColorFilter(ColorFilter cf) {
        mPaint.setColorFilter(cf);
```

```
        invalidateSelf();
    }
}
```

Color Filters

Android also has support for color filters. These filters provide ways of manipulating the pixels that are drawn in complex ways. You use these color filters by calling a `Paint` instance's `setColorFilter` method.

Lighting Color Filter

The `LightingColorFilter` class is a color filter that allows you to multiply and add to the RGB color channels. To use it, you simply construct a `LightingColorFilter`, passing in an int to multiply the color channels by and an int to add to each color channel, and then call `setColorFilter` on your `Paint` instance passing in the color filter. Each int you are passing in should be a full color. For instance, you can pass `0xFF00FF00` for the multiplier. The `0x` says that this is an int specified in hexadecimal. The first `FF` says don't change the alpha channel (effectively the same as multiplying a number by 1). The next `00` is to remove the red (multiplying the red by 0). The next `FF` keeps the green at its current level and the last `00` removes all blue. This alone would allow you to basically eliminate the red and blue pixels in an image, but you can also pass in a second int to the constructor that is added to the channels. For instance, if you pass in `0x000000BB` as the added int, you are saying not to add to any channel except blue. Given that we kept the green channel intact, this would make our icon a bit of a cyan color (green and blue mix). Figure 11.4 shows the effect of the color filter using these values.

Figure 11.4 The `LightingColorFilter` in use

Color Matrix

The `ColorMatrixColorFilter` is a lot like the `LightingColorFilter` but with more control. The color matrix is an array of ints to describe how to manipulate the channels. There are four sets of five values (one set for each channel in RGBA order). The first value in a set is the multiplier for the red channel. The second is the multiplier for green. The third is a multiplier for blue. The fourth is the multiplier for alpha, and the final one is the additional amount to add to the channel. This means that you can do interesting things like adjust the green channel of the image based on the values in the red channel. This lets you do some very powerful color manipulation.

At this point, many people are scared away from using the `ColorMatrixColorFilter`. Figuring out the exact values you need can be difficult and a lot of times you want some relatively simple effect. For instance, what if you wanted to make an image orange? If you control the images, then Photoshop makes this easy enough, but what about times when you're getting your images from a source outside of your control such as the web or from the OS itself? Older versions of Android didn't have the `setTint` method, but you can still use a `ColorMatrixColorFilter` to color images in a wide variety of ways programmatically.

First, create a new `ColorMatrix` and call `setSaturation`, passing in 0. This gives you a matrix which will convert an image to gray scale. Now you can create another `ColorMatrix` and use the `setScale` method to set the amount of color scaling (multiplying) for each channel. If we pass in `2f`, `0.68f`, `0.26f`, and `1f`, we'll end up with a bright orange (remember this is just how much to affect the red, green, blue, and alpha channels respectively). Next we need to combine the two matrices, so we call `postConcat` with our first matrix and pass in the second one. Now that we have a `ColorMatrix` that contains our manipulations, we can create a new `ColorMatrixColorFilter` and pass in our `ColorMatrix` and then call `setColorFilter` to apply it. Figure 11.5 shows our drawable with the `ColorMatrixColorFilter` applied and Listing 11.4 shows the lines of code to make it happen.

Listing 11.4   The `SimpleImageDrawable` Modified by a `ColorMatrixColorFilter`

```
final SimpleImageDrawable simpleImageDrawable = new
➥ SimpleImageDrawable(bitmap);
final ColorMatrix colorMatrix = new ColorMatrix();
colorMatrix.setSaturation(0);
final ColorMatrix colorScale = new ColorMatrix();
colorScale.setScale(2f, .68f, .26f, 1f); // Orange
colorMatrix.postConcat(colorScale);
simpleImageDrawable.setColorFilter(new
➥ ColorMatrixColorFilter(colorMatrix));
```

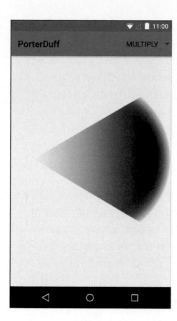

Figure 11.5 The `ColorMatrixColorFilter` in use

PorterDuff Image Compositing

Android supports PorterDuff image compositing. Thomas Porter and Tom Duff wrote a seven-page paper titled "Compositing Digital Images" back in 1984 that explained methods of combining two or more images that have become extremely common in applications for mobile and desktop.

Android identifies the specific compositing method by using an enum, which is really just telling the native code which method to call. Unfortunately, the Android documentation for `PorterDuff.Mode` enums is very limited. It gives you the name and a formula, and you're expected to understand the rest. At first, the formulas look a bit foreign, but most are not too bad once you understand what the letters mean and what the goal is.

For all the formulas, an *S* represents the source image and a *D* represents the destination image. An *a* represents the alpha channel and a *c* represents the color channels (a color being made of a red channel, a green channel, a blue channel, and an optional alpha channel). For all these composition modes, the color channels are treated individually and do not interact with other channels. If you are adding the source color to the destination color, you are adding the red channel of the source to the red channel of the destination, the green channel of the source to the green channel of the destination, and the blue channel of the source to the blue channel of the destination. Obviously, that's a bit wordy, so it can be expressed as "Sc + Dc" (source color plus destination color) instead.

Multiplication is not too much different, except you can better understand it by thinking of individual channels as `floats`. If 0 represents the minimum value of the channel and 1 represents the maximum value of the channel, you have infinite values (in reality it is limited by the precision of the data type, but that's an implementation detail). In fact, this is how OpenGL works. These values can be converted to a specific bit depth when needed (e.g., if you represent color with 256 values per channel, a value of `.25f` would be about 64). These channels can also be multiplied. For instance, you can take a green value of `.2f` and a green value of `.5f` and multiply them together you have a value of `.1f`, which equates to a color value of about 26.

Some of the modes to follow refer to the inverse of a channel. The inverse is what you get when you take the maximum value (`1f`) and subtract the current value. For instance, the inverse of `.25f` would be `.75f` because `1f - .25f` is `.75f`. This is not the opposite color (also called complementary color) because it is for a single channel. For example, if you had a fully green color (`0f` red, `1f` green, `0f` blue), the inverse would be magenta (`1f` red, `0f` green, `1f` blue).

Modes

Each of the PorterDuff methods is referred to as a `Mode` in Android. When using a `Paint` object, you can give it an `Xfermode` ("transfer mode") that is used when drawing. To give it a `PorterDuff.Mode`, you have to use the `PorterDuffXfermode` object, passing in the `Mode` enum that you want to use.

In some explanations of PorterDuff compositing, you might see the two images referred to as "A" and "B," but Android calls them the source ("SRC") image and the destination ("DST") image. In Android, the destination image is the one you are drawing the source into. Several of the methods have both a source image version and a destination image version, which can be helpful if the `Bitmap` backing your `Canvas` for one of your images is mutable but the other one is not. For example, `SRC_OVER` draws the source image over the top of the destination image. `DST_OVER` draws the destination image over the source image. To simplify the explanations, this book describes only the source versions in detail, but both types are included in the sample images.

As you look through these, you may realize many (if not all) are similar to the effects you have seen or used in graphics editing programs. Sometimes these are called "blend modes" or use other terminology but the concepts are exactly the same.

Clear
Formula: [0, 0]

"Clear" simply means that nothing will be drawn in the completed image. This is typically used to "erase" some portion of an image. See the example in Figure 11.6.

SRC **and** *DST*
Formula: [Sa, Sc]

Figure 11.6 The PorterDuff `Clear` mode shows neither the source nor the destination image

These two modes are fairly simple. If you use `SRC`, then only the source image is drawn. Similarly, if you use `DST`, only the destination image is drawn. You will probably rarely (if ever) use these because you can usually eliminate the need to create one of the two images earlier, if you are able to determine it is not needed. See the example of `SRC` and `DST` in Figure 11.7.

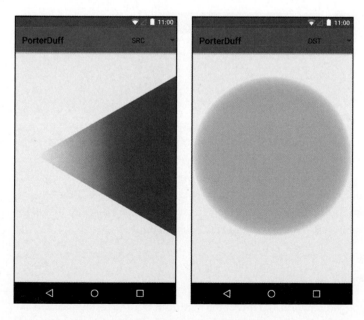

Figure 11.7 The PorterDuff `SRC` mode on the left and `DST` on the right

SRC_IN and DST_IN

Formula: [Sa × Da, Sc × Da]

"Source in" multiplies the source's alpha and color by the destination's alpha. This means that you're replacing the destination with the source where they overlap. Because both the color and alpha are multiplied, anywhere they don't overlap is cleared. In other words, the *source* is *in* place of the destination. See Figure 11.8 for an example.

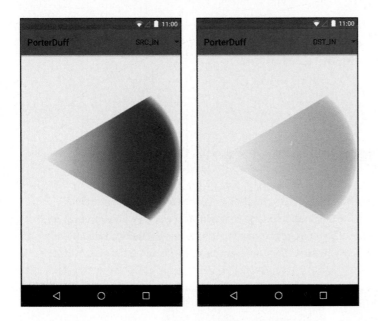

Figure 11.8 The PorterDuff SRC_IN mode on the left and DST_IN on the right

SRC_OUT and DST_OUT

Formula: [Sa × (1 − Da), Sc × (1 − Da)]

The "out" methods are basically the opposite of the "in" methods. When you're using SRC_OUT, only the part of the source image that does not overlap the destination image will be drawn. "Source out" multiplies the source's alpha and color by the inverse of the destination's alpha. Anywhere that the destination is fully transparent, the source will be fully opaque. If the destination is fully opaque somewhere, the source will not be visible. You are placing the *source* *out*side of the destination's alpha channel. See Figure 11.9 for an example.

SRC_OVER and DST_OVER

Formula: [Sa + (1 − Sa) × Da, Sc + (1 − Sa) × Dc]

"Source over" is a bit trickier to understand in terms of the math, but the end result is easy to understand. The *source* is placed *over* the top of the destination. The inverse of the source's

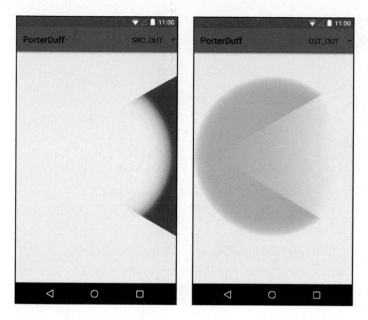

Figure 11.9 The PorterDuff SRC_OUT mode on the left and DST_OUT on the right

alpha channel is multiplied by the destination's alpha channel and then the source's alpha is added back to it. The color is also modified in a similar manner. The inverse of the source's alpha is multiplied by the destination's color and then the sources color is added. See Figure 11.10 for an example.

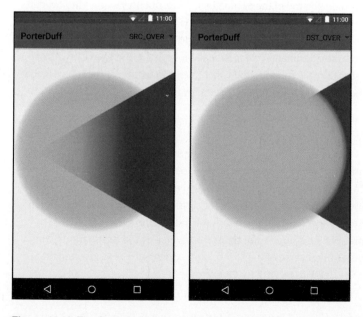

Figure 11.10 The PorterDuff SRC_OVER mode on the left and DST_OVER on the right

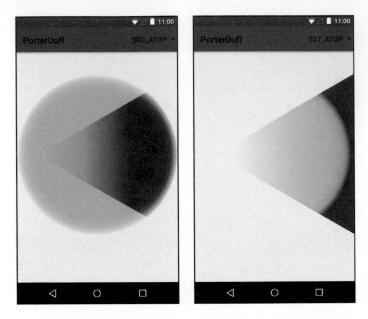

Figure 11.11 The PorterDuff `SRC_ATOP` mode on the left and `DST_ATOP` on the right

SRC_ATOP **and** *DST_ATOP*

Formula: [Da, Sc × Da + (1 − Sa) × Dc]

"Source atop" puts the source image on top of the destination image, but only where they overlap. It directly uses the destination's alpha channel for the resulting alpha values. The color is determined by taking the source color times the destination alpha and then adding back the result of the inverse of the source alpha multiplied by the destination color. Basically, it's putting the source on top of the destination using the destination's alpha value; then, for however transparent the source is, that amount of the destination shows through. See Figure 11.11 for an example.

Lighten

Formula: [Sa + Da − Sa × Da, Sc × (1 − Da) + Dc × (1 − Sa) + max(Sc, Dc)]

The "lighten" mode combines the two images and will only brighten the areas where they overlap. The areas that are fully opaque in one image and fully transparent in the other will take the opaque portions without modification. For the alpha channel, the source and destination alphas are added together and the product of the two is subtracted from that result. To determine the color, you multiply the source color times the inverse of the destination alpha, add the destination color times the inverse of the source, and add whichever is greater, the source or the destination color. See Figure 11.12 for an example.

Darken

Formula: [Sa + Da − Sa × Da, Sc × (1 − Da) + Dc × (1 − Sa) + min(Sc, Dc)]

Figure 11.12 The PorterDuff `Lighten` mode

The "darken" mode is extremely similar to the lighten mode. Anywhere that is opaque on one image and transparent in the other uses the opaque version without modification; however, anywhere that has some opacity in either image results in the color being darker because the final addition in the color calculation takes the darker of the two color values instead of the brighter. See Figure 11.13 for an example.

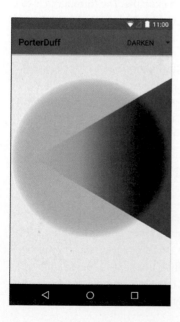

Figure 11.13 The PorterDuff `Darken` mode

Figure 11.14 The PorterDuff Add mode

Add
Formula: Saturate(S + D)

The "add" mode literally adds the source values to the destination values and then clamps them to the maximum value if they're too large. See Figure 11.14 for an example. The formula calls this clamping "saturate" because of the name of the Skia method, but it's just limiting the maximum value.

For instance, if the source has .7f for the red channel and the destination has .6f for the red channel, you get 1.3f. Because that's greater than the maximum value of 1f, the result is 1f. Addition always brightens colors (unless you're adding a black image, in which case it does not affect the other image). Note that this Mode was added in API level 11 despite the fact that the documentation does not say so.

Multiply
Formula: [Sa × Da, Sc × Dc]

The "multiply" mode is one of the easiest to understand from a math perspective, but it can take a few examples before you understand the visuals. The source alpha and destination alpha are multiplied to get the resulting alpha channel, so only pixels that are fully opaque in the source and destination images will be fully opaque in the resulting image. The source color and the destination color are multiplied to get the resulting color. The name "multiply" is obviously very fitting when you look at the math. Because you're multiplying values that are never bigger

Figure 11.15 The PorterDuff `Multiply` mode

than 1, you will never get a brighter color when multiplying. Multiplying pure white would just give you whatever the other color was because each channel is represented by a `1f`. This means that, except in the case of white, multiplying will always give you darker colors. Anywhere that is fully transparent on either image results in transparency. See Figure 11.15 for an example.

Screen
Formula: [Sa + Da − Sa × Da, Sc + Dc − Sc × Dc]

The "screen" mode results in images that are very similar to the "lighten" and "add" modes. In fact, the alpha channel is calculated the exact same way for lighten and screen; the difference is that the color for the screen mode is calculated the same way as the alpha (whereas the lighten mode handles it differently). See Figure 11.16 for an example. Note that this `Mode` was added in API level 11 despite the fact that the documentation does not say so.

Overlay
This is the one `Mode` where the formula is not included, and that's because it is variable. If double the destination color is less than or equal to the destination alpha, one formula is used; otherwise, another formula is used. The alpha is calculated the same way as screen, though. The key difference is the way that the colors are blended. See Figure 11.17 for an example. Note that this `Mode` was added in API level 11 despite the fact that the documentation does not say so.

XOR
Formula: [Sa + Da − 2 × Sa × Da, Sc × (1 − Da) + (1 − Sa) × Dc]

Figure 11.16 The PorterDuff `Screen` mode

Figure 11.17 The PorterDuff `Overlay` mode

"Exclusive or" is another that's easier to visually understand. Anywhere that the source and destination overlap is cleared. This is done by adding the source and destination alpha channels and subtracting double the product of the source and destination alpha channels. The color is determined by multiplying the source color by the inverse of the destination's alpha, multiplying the destination color by the inverse of the source's alpha, and combining the result. See Figure 11.18 for an example.

Figure 11.18 The PorterDuff XOR mode

Shaders

In a generalized sense, a shader provides the Paint object with pixels (colors) to draw. A simple example is a gradient such as a LinearGradient. When you use a Paint to draw a rectangle on the Canvas, for instance, the Paint gets the color for each pixel from the left to the right via the Shader instance. There are three types of shaders. The first is BitmapShader, which provides pixels from a bitmap. The second is a gradient shader, which allows you to draw a gradient that uses two or more colors. The concrete implementations are LinearGradient, RadialGradient, and SweepGradient. The last type of shader is called ComposeShader and it simply combines two shaders into one.

Round Images

To understand shaders better, it's a good idea to create a simple example. What if you wanted to create a round version of an image such as a profile picture? You would do this by drawing a circle with a BitmapShader. Although there is now a RoundedBitmapDrawable in the support library, understanding how you would implement something like this will make it more clear what's actually going on and how you might use a similar technique for a specific use case that you have down the road.

Making a copy of SimpleBitmapDrawable gives us a good starting point. We need to update the constructor to take an int that will be the radius to round the image with. The draw method will call drawRoundRect on the Canvas instance, passing in a RectF, our radius, and our

Figure 11.19 The `RoundBitmapDrawable` in action

`Paint` instance. We also need to update `setBitmap` so that after getting a reference to the new `Bitmap` instance, we create a new `BitmapShader` using that instance. When creating this type of shader, we have to specify the tiling mode, which is how the shader figures out which colors to use when you paint beyond the end of the bitmap. We're not going to be doing that, so the value we set doesn't really matter, but we can use `CLAMP`, which just means it repeats the very last column/row of pixels. Now we call the `Paint` instance's `setShader` method and pass in this `BitmapShader`. The last thing we need to do is override `onBoundsChange` and update our destination `RectF` that we use when drawing. Figure 11.19 shows an example of an image that has had the corners rounded using the drawable code in Listing 11.5.

Listing 11.5   The Full `RoundedBitmapDrawable` Source

```
public class RoundedImageDrawable extends Drawable {

    private Bitmap mBitmap;
    private int mRadius;
    private final Paint mPaint = new Paint(Paint.ANTI_ALIAS_FLAG);
    private final RectF mDestinationRectF = new RectF();

    public RoundedImageDrawable(Bitmap bitmap, int radius) {
        mRadius = radius;
        setBitmap(bitmap);
    }
```

```java
    @Override
    public void draw(Canvas canvas) {
        canvas.drawRoundRect(mDestinationRectF, mRadius, mRadius, mPaint);
    }

    @Override
    public int getIntrinsicHeight() {
        return mBitmap.getHeight();
    }

    @Override
    public int getIntrinsicWidth() {
        return mBitmap.getWidth();
    }

    @Override
    public int getOpacity() {
        return PixelFormat.TRANSLUCENT;
    }

    @Override
    public void setAlpha(int alpha) {
        int oldAlpha = mPaint.getAlpha();
        if (alpha != oldAlpha) {
            mPaint.setAlpha(alpha);
            invalidateSelf();
        }
    }

    /**
     * Sets the {@link Bitmap} to draw and invalidates itself
     *
     * @param bitmap Bitmap to draw with rounded corners
     */
    public void setBitmap(@NonNull Bitmap bitmap) {
        mBitmap = bitmap;
        final Shader shader = new BitmapShader(bitmap, Shader.
➥TileMode.CLAMP, Shader.TileMode.CLAMP);
        mPaint.setShader(shader);
        invalidateSelf();
    }

    @Override
    public void setColorFilter(ColorFilter cf) {
        mPaint.setColorFilter(cf);
        invalidateSelf();
    }
```

```
    @Override
    protected void onBoundsChange(Rect bounds) {
        mDestinationRectF.set(bounds);
    }

}
```

Gradient Fades

If you wanted to fade a portion of an image, you can simply combine two of the techniques from this chapter. First, you draw the gradient that you want, and then you draw the image over that gradient, using the `SRC_IN` mode.

We can start by copying `SimpleImageDrawable` and calling it `FadedImageDrawable`. We can create a `private final Xfermode` by creating a new `PortDuffXfermode` and passing in `SRC_IN`. Now we simply have to update the `setBitmap` method. We're going to create a new `Bitmap` with the static `createBitmap` method and then create a `Canvas` to draw into it with. Then we create a `LinearGradient`, which has a fairly lengthy constructor. The first pair of arguments specifies where the starting point is and the next two specify the ending point (as if you were drawing the line that the gradient follows). We're just going to fade from the top to the bottom, but you could make these whatever makes sense to you. Next, we pass the starting color and ending color. We only care about the alpha values, so we specify fully opaque and fully transparent, respectively. Finally, it requires a tiling mode, which we can use `CLAMP` for. With the shader ready, we can call `setShader` and pass in the `LinearGradient`.

With the local `Canvas` instance, we can simply draw a rectangle with `drawRect`. The shader makes that rectangle a gradient from fully opaque to fully transparent. After drawing the gradient, we pass null into `setShader` to avoid using it for the next part. We also call `setXfermode`, passing in the `Xfermode` we created earlier, and draw the bitmap. Because the `Xfermode` is using `SRC_IN`, the bitmap uses the alpha of the pixels already in the bitmap to determine the alpha of the pixels being drawn.

Lastly, we pass null into `setXfermode` to avoid using it when we actually draw the bitmap in the `draw` method. Triggering `invalidateSelf` ensures that `draw` will be called soon and this faded bitmap that we've created will be displayed. Figure 11.20 shows an example of an image using this drawable and the code is in Listing 11.6.

Listing 11.6 The Full `FadedImageDrawable` Source

```
public class FadedImageDrawable extends Drawable {

    private Bitmap mBitmap;
    private final Paint mPaint = new Paint(Paint.ANTI_ALIAS_FLAG);
    private final Xfermode mXfermode = new
➥ PorterDuffXfermode(PorterDuff.Mode.SRC_IN);
```

Figure 11.20 The FadedImageDrawable in action

```java
public FadedImageDrawable(Bitmap bitmap) {
    setBitmap(bitmap);
}

@Override
public void draw(Canvas canvas) {
    canvas.drawBitmap(mBitmap, null, getBounds(), mPaint);
}

@Override
public int getIntrinsicHeight() {
    return mBitmap.getHeight();
}

@Override
public int getIntrinsicWidth() {
    return mBitmap.getWidth();
}

@Override
public int getOpacity() {
    return PixelFormat.TRANSLUCENT;
}

@Override
public void setAlpha(int alpha) {
```

```
        int oldAlpha = mPaint.getAlpha();
        if (alpha != oldAlpha) {
            mPaint.setAlpha(alpha);
            invalidateSelf();
        }
    }

    /**
     * Sets the {@link Bitmap} to draw and invalidates itself
     *
     * @param bitmap Bitmap to draw with rounded corners
     */
    public void setBitmap(@NonNull Bitmap bitmap) {
        mBitmap = Bitmap.createBitmap(bitmap.getWidth(), bitmap.
getHeight(), Bitmap.Config.ARGB_8888);
        final Canvas canvas = new Canvas(mBitmap);
        final LinearGradient linearGradient = new LinearGradient(0, 0,
0, bitmap.getHeight(), 0xFF000000, 0x00000000, Shader.TileMode.CLAMP);
        mPaint.setShader(linearGradient);
        canvas.drawRect(0, 0, mBitmap.getWidth(), mBitmap.getHeight(),
mPaint);
        mPaint.setShader(null);
        mPaint.setXfermode(mXfermode);
        canvas.drawBitmap(bitmap, 0, 0, mPaint);
        mPaint.setXfermode(null);
        invalidateSelf();
    }

    @Override
    public void setColorFilter(ColorFilter cf) {
        mPaint.setColorFilter(cf);
        invalidateSelf();
    }

}
```

Summary

In this chapter, you learned about advanced image compositing techniques by using
PorterDuff.Modes. You should now understand how to create Bitmaps to draw into using
advanced painting techniques. You should know the basic concepts behind a Shader as well as
how to instantiate and apply them to Paint objects. You can bring all this knowledge together in
custom Drawables to make it easy to apply advanced drawing techniques to a variety of views.

In the next chapter, you'll begin to more deeply understand Android's views, including how
to apply the techniques from this chapter directly to a custom view without the need for a
separate drawable.

CHAPTER 12

DEVELOPING CUSTOM VIEWS

Android has a significant number of views already created for your use. Throughout this book, you've learned how to work with many of them, and in the previous chapter, "Working with the Canvas and Advanced Drawing," you learned how to create custom drawables that could display almost anything you could imagine. Now it is time to begin to combine the knowledge of drawing with an understanding of views to dive into creating your own.

General Concepts

Before you can start developing your own custom views, it's a good idea to understand the general concepts behind views. Views must know how to measure themselves, lay themselves out (and any children) out, draw themselves (although some views do not actually draw anything), and save/restore their own state. They also have to handle various input events such as clicks and swiping (interaction and scrolling are covered in Chapter 13, "Handling Input and Scrolling").

When you are first creating a view, you will find it very useful to look at the source code for views that are similar to what you want. Although you can check out the source code for Android to see how the views work (http://source.android.com/source/downloading.html), it is handy to use the Chrome extension "Android SDK Search." This extension adds a "view source" link to every class in the Android documentation (http://developer.android.com/reference), including the views. Note that many of the fields stored in views have package visibility, so you will see subclasses often accessing these fields directly, such as `mPaddingLeft`. In general, you should avoid doing the same to ensure that your code remains compatible with any changes to the Android classes outside of your control. You can nearly always store copies of the values in your own class when you need the performance benefit of avoiding a method call.

Measurement

The first part to understand about views is how measurement happens. Measurement is when a view says how big it would like to be given certain constraints. For instance, a view might be asked how tall it would like to be given a width of 300px.

The parent view will call each child view's `measure(int, int)` method, passing in two integers that represent the measurement specification for the width and height, respectively. This triggers the child's `onMeasure(int, int)` method with the same parameters, which is required to call `setMeasuredDimensions(int, int)` with the actual pixel values for the width and height of the view. Both `measure` and `setMeasuredDimensions` are final, so you will only ever override `onMeasure`. After that has happened, the view's `getMeasuredWidth()` and `getMeasuredHeight()` methods will return those dimensions.

The measurement specification is an integer packed with `MeasureSpec` (https://developer .android.com/reference/android/view/View.MeasureSpec.html) that has both a mode and a size. You will find that this and many other properties of views are stored as ints instead of objects to make all views more efficient. The mode can be one of `AT_MOST`, `EXACTLY`, and `UNSPECIFIED`. The `AT_MOST` mode means the child can specify any size for this dimension up to the size provided in the `MeasureSpec`. The `EXACTLY` mode says that the view must be the exact number of pixels passed in as the size (note that this is actual pixels and not density independent pixels, so you do not need to convert the value based on density). The `UNSPECIFIED` mode means that the parent has not provided any restrictions on the size of the child, so the child should determine its own ideal size.

The parent usually considers the `LayoutParams` of the child to determine what measurement specifications to pass down. For instance, a view's `LayoutParams` might specify `MATCH_PARENT` for the width, and the parent might then pass down a `MeasureSpec` that says the child will be exactly 768px (a possible exact width of the parent). However, regardless of what is requested by the `LayoutParams`, the `MeasureSpec` that is passed from the parent to the child is what must be obeyed.

Layout

The method `layout` is called on each view, triggering `onLayout` just as the `measure` method triggers `onMeasure`. In the `onLayout` method, each parent view can position its child views according to the sizes determined in the measurement phase. Once the positions for a given child are determined, its `layout` method is called. For instance, a vertically oriented `LinearLayout` might go through its children, positioning one, and using its height to position the next one (`LinearLayout` actually does significantly more than this, but this is the basic idea).

The four ints passed to the layout method are the left, top, right, and bottom pixel positions relative to the parent. The `onLayout` method receives a `boolean` that indicates if this is a new size and/or position along with those four ints.

There are times when a view determines that it needs to be laid out again because its size has changed. In this case, it calls the `requestLayout` method. For example, if you call `setImageDrawable` on an `ImageView` with a `Drawable` that is not the same size as the current `Drawable`, it will call `requestLayout` so that it can be given the right amount of space for the new `Drawable`.

Drawing

The drawing phase is when the view actually creates the pixels that it will display. This all happens in the `onDraw` method, which is the view equivalent of the `draw` method from the `Drawable` class. The view should avoid allocating any objects in this method (unless they are retained for future draws) and should be as efficient as possible to keep the user interface smooth.

If a view has determined that its drawing state has changed (such as when you give an `ImageView` a new `Drawable`), then it can call `invalidate` (just like a drawable calls `invalidateSelf`) to request that `onDraw` is called. The `invalidate` call is asynchronous; it merely flags the view as needing to be redrawn. This means that you can safely call it multiple times. For example, if you set the text of a `TextView`, `invalidate` will be called. If you then change the color of the text, `invalid` will be called again. None of the drawing will happen until the next drawing pass. When you need to invalidate a view from a background thread, you can use `postInvalidate`.

> **note**
>
> When views do not need to draw anything (such as `ViewGroups` that just lay out other views), they can call `setWillNotDraw`, passing in `true`. This allows Android to do some extra optimization. When extending existing views, be aware that some set this value to `true`, which means your `onDraw` method will never be called. For instance, a `LinearLayout` without dividers sets this to true. To check the current value, call `willNotDraw` on your view.

Saving and Restoring State

Views should be able to save and restore state themselves. For instance, a `ListView` might save the currently selected position, so that when the device is rotated and the views are recreated, it can select the new view that represents that position. There are two methods to handle here: `onSaveInstanceState` and `onRestoreInstanceState`. When saving state, a view should always call through to the super method to save its state and then create a new object that represents its own data to save (typically this is a custom class that extends `BaseSavedState`). When restoring state, a view will trigger the parent method and then restore anything it needs to.

Creating a Custom View

The previous chapter, "Working with the Canvas and Advanced Drawing," covered PorterDuff compositing and even used the `SRC_IN` mode to create a faded image. The PorterDuff modes can be very difficult to understand, so it is helpful to be able to easily try different modes and images and see what results. To that end, we'll create a new project and in it we'll create a class called `PorterDuffView` that extends the `View` class to easily combine two images with different modes.

To keep this view efficient, we should create class variables to store the `Paint` object called `mPaint`, the `Bitmap` (which will be the combination of the two images) called `mBitmap`, the default sizes of the images (`mDefaultBitmapWidth` and `mDefaultBitmapHeight`), and both the `Mode` as `mMode` and the `XferMode` called `mXferMode`. The `Paint` object can be immediately instantiated.

Each of the constructors should call out to `initDefaultBitmapDimens`. That method needs to simply read in the size of one of the images that will be used to set `mDefaultBitmapWidth` and `mDefaultBitmapHeight`. Since the images aren't needed at this time, just the dimensions are, we can use the `BitmapFactory.Options` trick of setting `inJustDecodeBounds`.

We need to add a method to allow you to set the `PorterDuff.Mode`, so we'll create a method called `setPorterDuffMode(PorterDuff.Mode)`. It should simply set the `mXferMode` to a new `PorterDuffXferMode` that takes the `Mode` that was passed in. It also needs to null out the reference to `mBitmap` because it will need to be re-created with the new `XferMode`. At this point, our `PorterDuffView` should look like Listing 12.1.

Listing 12.1   The Initial `PorterDuffView`

```
public class PorterDuffView extends View {

    /**
     * The width used for measuring when a bitmap has not been generated
     */
    private int mDefaultBitmapWidth;

    /**
     * The height used for measuring when a bitmap has not been generated
     */
    private int mDefaultBitmapHeight;

    /**
     * The Paint used to draw everything
     */
    private final Paint mPaint = new Paint(Paint.ANTI_ALIAS_FLAG);

    /**
     * The Bitmap containing the two images blended together
     */
    private Bitmap mBitmap;

    /**
     * PorterDuff Mode used to generate the Xfermode
     */
    private PorterDuff.Mode mPorterDuffMode = PorterDuff.Mode.CLEAR;

    /**
     * The Xfermode to combine the images with
     */
    private Xfermode mXfermode = new PorterDuffXfermode(mPorterDuffMode);

    public PorterDuffView(Context context) {
        super(context);
        initDefaultBitmapDimens();
    }

    public PorterDuffView(Context context, AttributeSet attrs) {
        super(context, attrs);
        initDefaultBitmapDimens();
    }

    public PorterDuffView(Context context, AttributeSet attrs, int
➡ defStyleAttr) {
        super(context, attrs, defStyleAttr);
```

```
        initDefaultBitmapDimens();
    }


    @TargetApi(Build.VERSION_CODES.LOLLIPOP)
    public PorterDuffView(Context context, AttributeSet attrs, int
➡ defStyleAttr, int defStyleRes) {
        super(context, attrs, defStyleAttr, defStyleRes);
        initDefaultBitmapDimens();
    }


    /**
     * Sets the new PorterDuff.Mode, removes the existing Bitmap and
➡ invalidates the view
     *
     * @param mode PorterDuff.Mode to use
     */
    public void setPorterDuffMode(PorterDuff.Mode mode) {
        if (mode == mPorterDuffMode) {
            // No change
            return;
        }
        mPorterDuffMode = mode;
        mXfermode = new PorterDuffXfermode(mode);
        mBitmap = null;
        invalidate();
    }


    private void initDefaultBitmapDimens() {
        BitmapFactory.Options options = new BitmapFactory.Options();
        options.inJustDecodeBounds = true;
        BitmapFactory.decodeResource(getResources(), R.drawable.shape1,
➡ options);

        mDefaultBitmapWidth = options.outWidth;
        mDefaultBitmapHeight = options.outHeight;
    }
}
```

Measuring

To determine how large the view will be, we need to override `onMeasure`. Remember that this method is automatically called for us and received an int for the width and an int for the height. Each of these ints is packed with a mode and a size, so we can make use of the `MeasureSpec` methods of `getMode` and `getSize` to do the bitmask work for us and get values we can easily work with. We first check if the mode is `EXACTLY`, because we can just directly use the size when that's the case (saving any calculations we would do otherwise). When it's not `EXACTLY`, we just add the padding on both sides and the desired content size (we'll use the mDefaultBitmapWidth). We need to also check if the mode is AT_MOST, ensuring that we don't pass a size bigger than desired if that's the mode. Listing 12.2 shows the full onMeasure method.

Listing 12.2   The onMeasure Method

```
@Override
protected void onMeasure(int widthMeasureSpec, int heightMeasureSpec) {

    // Calculate the width
    int width;
    int specMode = MeasureSpec.getMode(widthMeasureSpec);
    int specSize = MeasureSpec.getSize(widthMeasureSpec);

    if (specMode == MeasureSpec.EXACTLY) {
        width = specSize;
    } else {
        width = getPaddingLeft() + getPaddingRight() +
➥ mDefaultBitmapWidth;
        if (specMode == MeasureSpec.AT_MOST) {
            width = Math.min(width, specSize);
        }
    }

    // Calculate the height
    int height;
    specMode = MeasureSpec.getMode(heightMeasureSpec);
    specSize = MeasureSpec.getSize(heightMeasureSpec);

    if (specMode == MeasureSpec.EXACTLY) {
        height = specSize;
    } else {
        height = getPaddingTop() + getPaddingBottom() +
➥ mDefaultBitmapHeight;
        if (specMode == MeasureSpec.AT_MOST) {
            height = Math.min(height, specSize);
        }
    }

    // Set the calculated dimensions
    setMeasuredDimension(width, height);
}
```

Handling Layout

Once we've handled measuring, we need to handle layout. Our onLayout method will be triggered once the size and position of our view are determined. Because we don't have any children, we don't have to do anything, but this is actually a great place for us to check if the bitmap we may have created is the right size.

The general way that this view will work is that it will create a bitmap combining the two images when drawing and then it will retain and reuse that bitmap for future `onDraw` calls. This lazy initialization allows us to avoid creating a bitmap when the view isn't going to be displayed. This means that all we need to do here is set `mBitmap` to null if changed (a boolean we get when `onLayout` is called) is true.

Building the Bitmap

Next up, we'll make a method called `createBitmap` that will do the heart of the work. To support a range of image sizes, we will create a `Rect` that represents the image scaled to the size of the view. To keep the example simple, it will assume the images are square, so it just has to take the smaller of the width or height (called `minDimension`) and create a `Rect` based on that (thus, if the view is 500px by 800px, the resulting `Rect` is 500px by 500px).

We will use the static `createBitmap (int, int, Config)` method of `Bitmap` to create the actual `Bitmap` (`mBitmap`) we will draw into. The two `int`s represent the width and the height (in this case, both are the `minDimension`) and a `Config` that says how many bits are used to represent the colors in the `Bitmap`. We want to pass in `Config.ARGB_8888`, which means that the alpha, red, green, and blue channels each get 8 bits for 256 levels per channel. This is the highest quality configuration and is almost always the one you want to use. Using a lower quality configuration can result in visual artifacts and, depending on the images passed in, might make the compositing harder to understand.

Now we create a new `Canvas`, passing in the target `Bitmap` we just made. This `Canvas` will handle the calls to draw the images into the target `Bitmap`. To get a `Bitmap` instance of one of our images, we use the `BitmapFactory`'s static `decodeResource (Resources, int)` method, passing in a reference to `Resources`, which we can obtain with `getResources()`, and the identifier for our image (the example uses `R.drawable.shape1`). We use the `Canvas`'s `drawBitmap(Bitmap, Rect, Rect, Paint)` method to draw the newly loaded `Bitmap` into the target `Bitmap`. As mentioned in the previous chapter, there are several methods for drawing `Bitmaps`. This one takes the `Bitmap` to draw (the one we just loaded from `Resources`), a `Rect` that represents the portion of that `Bitmap` to use for drawing, a `Rect` that represents where to draw the `Bitmap`, and the `Paint`. We can leave the first `Rect` null, which means that the full image will be used. The second `Rect` will be the one we already created, and the `Paint` will be `mPaint`.

Next we use the `BitmapFactory` again to load our second image but, before drawing it, we call `setXfermode(mXfermode)` on our `Paint`. This sets it up to use the transfer mode when drawing (in this case, whichever `PorterDuff.Mode` has been set in the `PorterDuffXfermode` object). We draw this second `Bitmap` to the target `Bitmap` using the same `Canvas` method we used for the previous image. Finally, we remove the `Xfermode` from the `Paint` by calling `setXfermode(null)`.

When we're all done with the `createBitmap()` method, it should look like Listing 12.3.

Listing 12.3   The `createBitmap()` Method

```java
/**
 * Creates mBitmap using the set XferMode
 */
private void createBitmap() {

    // Prepare the Bitmap
    final int width = getWidth();
    final int height = getHeight();
    final Rect rect = new Rect();
    final int minDimen = Math.min(width, height);
    rect.right = minDimen;
    rect.bottom = minDimen;
    mBitmap = Bitmap.createBitmap(width, height, Bitmap.
➥ Config.ARGB_8888);
    final Canvas c = new Canvas(mBitmap);

    // Create the destination Bitmap and paint it
    Bitmap b = BitmapFactory.decodeResource(getResources(),
➥ R.drawable.shape1);
    c.drawBitmap(b, null, rect, mPaint);

    // Create the source Bitmap, set XferMode, and paint
    b = BitmapFactory.decodeResource(getResources(),
➥ R.drawable.shape2);
    mPaint.setXfermode(mXfermode);
    c.drawBitmap(b, null, rect, mPaint);

    // Remove the XferMode
    mPaint.setXfermode(null);
}
```

We are almost done with the custom view, but there is a little more to do. We need to override the `onDraw(Canvas)` method to actually draw our `mBitmap`. First, we check if `mBitmap` is null. If it is, call `createBitmap()`. Now it should make sense why we remove our `mBitmap` reference when setting a new `PorterDuff.Mode` in the `setPorterDuffMode` call (to create a new `Bitmap` using the new `Xfermode`). Although you should not allocate objects in the `onDraw(Canvas)` method, it is okay to do so when the object is then retained for future draw calls.

Outside of the `if` block, we simply call the passed-in `Canvas`'s `drawBitmap(Bitmap, float, float, Paint)` method. Notice that this one takes two floats instead of two `Rect`s. These floats specify the left and top positions in the canvas to draw the bitmap to. The bitmap will not be scaled. We are simply saying, "Start the top-left corner of the bitmap here and draw all that will fit." Because we already handled the scaling by using the `Rect` earlier, calling this method with the two floats is very efficient.

Saving and Restoring State

We want to save and restore the PorterDuff mode that is being used. To do this, we create a private static class called PorterDuffSaveState inside of our view that extends `BaseSavedState`. It needs a single member variable to store the `PorderDuff.Mode` value. There are two constructors, one that uses a `Parcel` and one that uses a `Parcelable`. That's a bit confusing, but the one that uses a `Parcel` is the one that's being restored and the one that's using a `Parcelable` is the one that's being saved. We need to override the `writeToParcel` method and simply call `writeSerializable` to save the mode. Similarly, we need to call `readSerializable` to get the mode in the constructor that takes a `Parcel`.

Now we can override `onRestoreInstanceState` and check if the `Parcelable` that was passed in is our custom type. If it is a different type, we can just call the super method and be done with it. If it is our type, we can cast it, call the super method, and then restore our mode.

Next up, we override `onSaveInstanceState`. We call through to the super method to get its `Parcelable`, then we construct our custom `PorterDuffSaveState`, passing in the `Parcelable`. We simply set the mode on our saved state and return the object.

Listing 12.4 shows the complete class, including the code required to handle saving and restoring state.

Listing 12.4 The Complete `PorterDuffView`

```
public class PorterDuffView extends View {

    /**
     * The width used for measuring when a bitmap has not been generated
     */
    private int mDefaultBitmapWidth;

    /**
     * The height used for measuring when a bitmap has not been generated
     */
    private int mDefaultBitmapHeight;

    /**
     * The Paint used to draw everything
     */
    private final Paint mPaint = new Paint(Paint.ANTI_ALIAS_FLAG);

    /**
     * The Bitmap containing the two images blended together
     */
    private Bitmap mBitmap;

    /**
     * PorterDuff Mode used to generate the Xfermode
```

```java
    */
    private PorterDuff.Mode mPorterDuffMode = PorterDuff.Mode.CLEAR;

    /**
     * The Xfermode to combine the images with
     */
    private Xfermode mXfermode = new PorterDuffXfermode(mPorterDuffMode);

    public PorterDuffView(Context context) {
        super(context);
        initDefaultBitmapDimens();
    }

    public PorterDuffView(Context context, AttributeSet attrs) {
        super(context, attrs);
        initDefaultBitmapDimens();
    }

    public PorterDuffView(Context context, AttributeSet attrs, int
➥ defStyleAttr) {
        super(context, attrs, defStyleAttr);
        initDefaultBitmapDimens();
    }

    @TargetApi(Build.VERSION_CODES.LOLLIPOP)
    public PorterDuffView(Context context, AttributeSet attrs, int
➥ defStyleAttr, int defStyleRes) {
        super(context, attrs, defStyleAttr, defStyleRes);
        initDefaultBitmapDimens();
    }

    /**
     * Sets the new PorterDuff.Mode, removes the existing Bitmap and
➥ invalidates the view
     *
     * @param mode PorterDuff.Mode to use
     */
    public void setPorterDuffMode(PorterDuff.Mode mode) {
        if (mode == mPorterDuffMode) {
            // No change
            return;
        }
        mPorterDuffMode = mode;
        mXfermode = new PorterDuffXfermode(mode);
        mBitmap = null;
        invalidate();
    }

    @Override
    public void onDraw(Canvas canvas) {
        if (mBitmap == null) {
```

```
            createBitmap();
        }
        canvas.drawBitmap(mBitmap, 0, 0, mPaint);
    }

    @Override
    protected void onLayout(boolean changed, int left, int top, int
➥ right, int bottom) {
        if (changed) {
            mBitmap = null;
        }
    }

    @Override
    protected void onMeasure(int widthMeasureSpec, int
➥ heightMeasureSpec) {

        // Calculate the width
        int width;
        int specMode = MeasureSpec.getMode(widthMeasureSpec);
        int specSize = MeasureSpec.getSize(widthMeasureSpec);

        if (specMode == MeasureSpec.EXACTLY) {
            width = specSize;
        } else {
            width = getPaddingLeft() + getPaddingRight() +
➥ mDefaultBitmapWidth;
            if (specMode == MeasureSpec.AT_MOST) {
                width = Math.min(width, specSize);
            }
        }

        // Calculate the height
        int height;
        specMode = MeasureSpec.getMode(heightMeasureSpec);
        specSize = MeasureSpec.getSize(heightMeasureSpec);

        if (specMode == MeasureSpec.EXACTLY) {
            height = specSize;
        } else {
            height = getPaddingTop() + getPaddingBottom() +
➥ mDefaultBitmapHeight;
            if (specMode == MeasureSpec.AT_MOST) {
                height = Math.min(height, specSize);
            }
        }

        // Set the calculated dimensions
        setMeasuredDimension(width, height);
    }
```

```
    /**
     * Creates mBitmap using the set XferMode
     */
    private void createBitmap() {

        // Prepare the Bitmap
        final int width = getWidth();
        final int height = getHeight();
        final Rect rect = new Rect();
        final int minDimen = Math.min(width, height);
        rect.right = minDimen;
        rect.bottom = minDimen;
        mBitmap = Bitmap.createBitmap(width, height, Bitmap.
➥ Config.ARGB_8888);
        final Canvas c = new Canvas(mBitmap);

        // Create the destination Bitmap and paint it
        Bitmap b = BitmapFactory.decodeResource(getResources(),
➥ R.drawable.shape1);
        c.drawBitmap(b, null, rect, mPaint);

        // Create the source Bitmap, set XferMode, and paint
        b = BitmapFactory.decodeResource(getResources(),
➥ R.drawable.shape2);
        mPaint.setXfermode(mXfermode);
        c.drawBitmap(b, null, rect, mPaint);

        // Remove the XferMode
        mPaint.setXfermode(null);
    }

    private void initDefaultBitmapDimens() {
        BitmapFactory.Options options = new BitmapFactory.Options();
        options.inJustDecodeBounds = true;
        BitmapFactory.decodeResource(getResources(), R.drawable.shape1,
➥ options);

        mDefaultBitmapWidth = options.outWidth;
        mDefaultBitmapHeight = options.outHeight;
    }

    @Override
    protected void onRestoreInstanceState(Parcelable state) {
        if (!(state instanceof PorterDuffSavedState)) {
            // Not our saved state
            super.onRestoreInstanceState(state);
            return;
        }

        final PorterDuffSavedState ourState = (PorterDuffSavedState) state;
```

```
        super.onRestoreInstanceState(ourState.getSuperState());
        setPorterDuffMode(ourState.mode);
    }

    @Override
    protected Parcelable onSaveInstanceState() {
        final Parcelable superState = super.onSaveInstanceState();
        final PorterDuffSavedState ourState = new PorterDuffSavedState
➥(superState);
        ourState.mode = mPorterDuffMode;
        return ourState;
    }

    private static class PorterDuffSavedState extends BaseSavedState {

        public PorterDuff.Mode mode;

        public PorterDuffSavedState(Parcel source) {
            super(source);
            mode = (PorterDuff.Mode) source.readSerializable();
        }

        public PorterDuffSavedState(Parcelable superState) {
            super(superState);
        }

        @Override
        public void writeToParcel(@NonNull Parcel dest, int flags) {
            super.writeToParcel(dest, flags);
            dest.writeSerializable(mode);
        }
    }
}
```

Now that we have a custom view, we need a layout to make use of the view. Edit `activity_main.xml` to simply be a vertically oriented `LinearLayout` with a `Toolbar`, `Spinner` and our custom view. The `Spinner` will be used to select the `PorterDuff.Mode` and our view will display it. The layout should look like Listing 12.5.

Listing 12.5 The Layout with the Custom View

```
<LinearLayout xmlns:android="http://schemas.android.com/apk/res/
➥android"
    xmlns:tools="http://schemas.android.com/tools"
    android:layout_width="match_parent"
    android:layout_height="match_parent"
    android:orientation="vertical"
```

```
    tools:context=".MainActivity">

    <android.support.v7.widget.Toolbar
        android:id="@+id/toolbar"
        android:layout_width="match_parent"
        android:layout_height="?attr/actionBarSize"
        android:elevation="4dp"
        android:background="?attr/colorPrimary" />

    <Spinner
        android:id="@+id/spinner"
        android:layout_width="wrap_content"
        android:layout_height="wrap_content"
        android:layout_marginBottom="@dimen/activity_vertical_margin"
        android:layout_marginLeft="@dimen/activity_horizontal_margin"
        android:layout_marginRight="@dimen/activity_horizontal_margin"
        android:layout_marginTop="@dimen/activity_vertical_margin" />

    <com.auidbook.porterduffview.PorterDuffView
        android:id="@+id/porter_duff_view"
        android:layout_width="match_parent"
        android:layout_height="match_parent"
        android:layout_marginBottom="@dimen/activity_vertical_margin"
        android:layout_marginLeft="@dimen/activity_horizontal_margin"
        android:layout_marginRight="@dimen/activity_horizontal_margin"
        android:layout_marginTop="@dimen/activity_vertical_margin" />
</LinearLayout>
```

Open the activity and add two variables to the class: `mAdapter`, which is an `ArrayAdapter` that holds `PorterDuff.Mode` enums, and `mPorterDuffView`, which is a reference to our custom view. In `onCreate(Bundle)`, we set the content view, set up the toolbar, and set the reference to `mPorterDuffView`. Then we get an array of all the available `PorterDuff.Mode`s by calling `PorterDuff.Mode.values()`. We create a new `ArrayAdapter`, passing in the `Context (this)`, `android.R.layout.simple_spinner_item` (for a basic layout), and our array of `PorterDuff.Mode`s. We need to also call `setDropDownViewResource(int)`, passing in `android.R.layout.simple_spinner_dropdown_item`.

We get a reference to the `Spinner` and set the `ArrayAdapter` on it. We also need to make the activity implement `OnItemSelectedListener` so that it will be notified of changes to the spinner, and call the `setOnItemSelectedListener` method, passing in the activity.

We don't need to do anything in the `onNothingSelected` method, but in the `onItemSelected` method, we need to update our custom view with the newly selected `PorterDuff.Mode` enum. To get the selected `Mode`, we call `getItem(int)` on our `ArrayAdapter`, passing in the position int. The complete activity is in Listing 12.6. Figure 12.1 shows this custom view in action.

Figure 12.1 The custom view in action

Listing 12.6   The Activity that Uses the Custom View

```
public class MainActivity extends AppCompatActivity implements
➥ AdapterView.OnItemSelectedListener {
    private ArrayAdapter<PorterDuff.Mode> mAdapter;
    private PorterDuffView mPorterDuffView;

    @Override
    protected void onCreate(Bundle savedInstanceState) {
        super.onCreate(savedInstanceState);
        setContentView(R.layout.activity_main);

        final Toolbar toolbar = (Toolbar) findViewById(R.id.toolbar);
        setSupportActionBar(toolbar);

        // Get reference to the PorterDuffView
        mPorterDuffView = (PorterDuffView) findViewById
➥ (R.id.porter_duff_view);

        // Create array of PorterDuff.Modes
        final PorterDuff.Mode[] porterDuffModes = PorterDuff.
➥ Mode.values();
        mAdapter = new ArrayAdapter<PorterDuff.Mode>(this,
➥ android.R.layout.simple_spinner_item, porterDuffModes);

        mAdapter.setDropDownViewResource(android.R.layout.
➥ simple_spinner_dropdown_item);
```

```
        final Spinner spinner = (Spinner) findViewById(R.id.spinner);
        spinner.setAdapter(mAdapter);
        spinner.setOnItemSelectedListener(this);
    }

    @Override
    public void onItemSelected(AdapterView<?> parent, View view, int
➡ position, long id) {
        mPorterDuffView.setPorterDuffMode(mAdapter.getItem(position));
    }

    @Override
    public void onNothingSelected(AdapterView<?> parent) {
        // Ignored
    }
}
```

Summary

In this chapter, you applied your knowledge gained working with drawables to custom views. You also learned about the measurement and layout processes for views as well as the methods used for saving and restoring state. With this knowledge, you can create most of the types of views you might need, but one big piece is missing and that's handling input. Handling input can be confusing, so the next chapter dives head-on into input, including handling any related scrolling.

CHAPTER 13

HANDLING INPUT AND SCROLLING

In the previous chapter, "Developing Custom Views," you worked through how to create a custom view that properly handles measurement, layout, drawing, and saving/restoring state. Now it's time to round out that knowledge with a deep look at handling input and scrolling.

Touch Input

Touch input is the primary means of interacting with views in Android. In most cases, you can use the standard listeners, such as `OnClickListener` and `OnLongClickListener`, to handle the interactions. In some cases, you need to handle custom, more complex touches. If a view already meets your needs but you just need to handle custom touches, then consider using the `OnTouchListener` to avoid having to subclass the view.

Touch events are reported with the `MotionEvent` object (which can also be used for other input types such as a trackball). `MotionEvents` track pointers (such as a user's fingers on the screen), and each pointer receives a unique ID; however, most interactions with pointers actually use the pointer index—that is, the position of the pointer within the array of pointers tracked by a given `MotionEvent`. A pointer index is not guaranteed to be the same, so you must get the index with `findPointerIndex(int)` (where the `int` argument is the unique pointer ID).

There are a lot of types of `MotionEvents` (you can see details at https://developer.android .com/reference/android/view/MotionEvent.html), but a few in particular you should know. `ACTION_DOWN` indicates that a new pointer is being tracked, such as when you first touch the screen. `ACTION_MOVE` indicates that the pointer has changed, usually location, such as when you drag your finger on the screen. `ACTION_UP` indicates that the pointer has finished, such as when you lift your finger from the screen. `ACTION_POINTER_DOWN` and `ACTION_POINTER_UP` indicate when a secondary pointer is starting to be tracked and is finishing, respectively, such as when you touch the screen with a second finger. `ACTION_CANCEL` indicates that the gesture has been aborted.

Android has several classes that simplify working with input. `GestureDetector` can be used to listen for common touch gestures. To use it, you simply pass the `MotionEvent` from your `onTouchEvent(MotionEvent)` method in the view to `onTouchEvent(MotionEvent)` on the `GestureDetector`. It specifies the `OnGestureListener` interface that defines various gesture-based methods such as `onFling` and `onLongPress`. You can use a `GestureDetector` to determine when any of these predefined gestures has taken place and then trigger your `OnGestureListener`. Because you often only need to handle a subset of the gestures available, there is a `SimpleOnGestureListener` that implements all the methods of `OnGestureListener` as empty methods or methods that simply return `false`. If you wanted to listen to just flings, you would override `onDown(MotionEvent)` to return `true` (returning `false` from this method will prevent the other methods from triggering because the touch event will be ignored) and override `onFling(MotionEvent, MotionEvent, float, float)` to handle the fling. Note that a compatibility version of `GestureDetector` appears in the support library called `GestureDetectorCompat`.

To simplify working with `MotionEvents`, there is a `MotionEventCompat` class in the support library. It provides static methods for working with `MotionEvents` so that you don't have to deal with masks manually. For instance, you can call `getActionMasked(MotionEvent)` to get just the action portion of the `int` (such as `ACTION_DOWN`) that is returned by a `MotionEvent`'s `getAction()` method.

Android also provides two classes for working with scrolling. The original is called `Scroller` and has been available since the beginning of Android's public release. The newer version is called `OverScroller` and was added in API level 9. Both of them allow you to do things such as animate a fling gesture. The main difference between the two is that `OverScroller` allows you to overshoot the bounds of the scrolling container. This is what happens when you fling a list quickly in Android, and then the list stops and the edge glows. The `OverScroller` determines how far beyond the list you have scrolled and converts that "energy" into the glow. You can also use `ScrollerCompat` if you need to support older versions of Android.

`EdgeEffect` was introduced in API level 14 (Ice Cream Sandwich) to standardize working with visual indicators of overscrolling. If you decide to create a custom view and want to have an `EdgeEffect` while still supporting older versions of Android, you can use the `EdgeEffectCompat` class from the support library. When running on pre-ICS versions of Android, it will simply have no effect.

Other Forms of Input

When Android was originally developed, it was designed to support a variety of form factors, and that meant it had to support multiple input types. Many of the original phones had touchscreens along with alternate input methods such as scroll wheels and directional pads. Although many Android devices today do not use these other input methods, it's still worth considering how users can interact with your views without touch input. In most cases, supporting other forms of input requires very little effort. Plus, supporting a directional pad, for instance, allows your app to run on Android TV or to be better used by devices with keyboards.

In general, you simply need to override `onKeyDown(int, KeyEvent)` to handle alternate forms of input. The first parameter is an int identifying which key was pressed (the `KeyEvent` object has constants for all the keys; for example, `KeyEvent.KEYCODE_ENTER` is the int representing the Enter key). The second parameter is the actual `KeyEvent` object that contains details such as whether another key is being pressed (to let you do things like check if Alt is being pressed while this key is being pressed) and what device this event originated from (e.g., an external keyboard).

Trackball events aren't common anymore but can be handled with your `onKeyDown(int, KeyEvent)` method, so you rarely need to consider them. For instance, if you do not specifically handle trackball events, a scroll to the right on a trackball will end up triggering `onKeyDown(int, KeyEvent)` with the "key" being `KEYCODE_DPAD_RIGHT`. In the case where you do want to handle trackball events differently (such as to handle flings), you will do so in `onTrackballEvent(MotionEvent)`. Be sure to return `true` to consume the event.

Creating a Custom View

To better understand input and scrolling, we're going to make a custom view. We're going to make a view that takes an array of icons (`Drawables`) and draws them. It will assume they are all the same size and draw them from left to right. That doesn't sound too exciting, but we will see how to handle positioning each of the `Drawables` to be drawn, how to keep things efficient, how to handle scrolling and overscrolling, and how to detect when a `Drawable` is touched. This view actually requires a fairly significant amount of code, so don't be afraid to jump back to the beginning of this chapter or the previous chapter to remember the general concepts.

Creating the Initial Custom View Files

We'll get started with a new project, creating a `dimens.xml` file in `res/values` that has two dimensions. The first dimension is `icon_size` and represents the width and height of the icons; set it to 48dp. The second dimension is `icon_spacing` and represents the space between icons; set it to 16dp. The file should look like Listing 13.1.

Listing 13.1   The Simple `dimens.xml` File

```
<resources>
    <!-- Default screen margins, per the Android Design guidelines. -->
    <dimen name="activity_horizontal_margin">16dp</dimen>
    <dimen name="activity_vertical_margin">16dp</dimen>

    <dimen name="icon_size">48dp</dimen>
    <dimen name="icon_spacing">16dp</dimen>
</resources>
```

Next, we create the `HorizontalIconView` class that extends `View`. We implement all the constructors and each constructor should call through to `init(Context)`, which we'll be making shortly. There are also several class variables to create. See Listing 13.2 for how the class should initially look like with all the variables included. These are all the variables that will be used throughout the next few sections, so don't worry about understanding all of them just yet; they'll be explained as we build each method that requires them.

Listing 13.2   The Initial `HorizontalIconView`

```
public class HorizontalIconView extends View {
    private static final String TAG = "HorizontalIconView";

    private static final int INVALID_POINTER =
➥ MotionEvent.INVALID_POINTER_ID;

    /**
     * int to track the ID of the pointer that is being tracked
     */
```

```
private int mActivePointerId = INVALID_POINTER;

/**
 * The List of Drawables that will be shown
 */
private List<Drawable> mDrawables;

/**
 * EdgeEffect or "glow" when scrolled too far left
 */
private EdgeEffectCompat mEdgeEffectLeft;

/**
 * EdgeEffect or "glow" when scrolled too far right
 */
private EdgeEffectCompat mEdgeEffectRight;

/**
 * List of Rects for each visible icon to calculate touches
 */
private final List<Rect> mIconPositions = new ArrayList<>();

/**
 * Width and height of icons in pixels
 */
private int mIconSize;

/**
 * Space between each icon in pixels
 */
private int mIconSpacing;

/**
 * Whether a pointer/finger is currently on screen that is being
 tracked
 */
private boolean mIsBeingDragged;

/**
 * Maximum fling velocity in pixels per second
 */
private int mMaximumVelocity;

/**
 * Minimum fling velocity in pixels per second
 */
private int mMinimumVelocity;

/**
 * How far to fling beyond the bounds of the view
```

```
        */
       private int mOverflingDistance;

       /**
        * How far to scroll beyond the bounds of the view
        */
       private int mOverscrollDistance;

       /**
        * The X coordinate of the last down touch, used to determine when
➥ a drag starts
        */
       private float mPreviousX = 0;

       /**
        * Number of pixels this view can scroll (basically width - visible
➥ width)
        */
       private int mScrollRange;

       /**
        * Number of pixels of movement required before a touch is "moving"
        */
       private int mTouchSlop;

       /**
        * VelocityTracker to simplify tracking MotionEvents
        */
       private VelocityTracker mVelocityTracker;

       /**
        * Scroller to do the hard work of scrolling smoothly
        */
       private OverScroller mScroller;

       /**
        * The number of icons that are left of the view and therefore not
➥ drawn
        */
       private int mSkippedIconCount = 0;

       public HorizontalIconView(Context context) {
           super(context);
           init(context);
       }

       public HorizontalIconView(Context context, AttributeSet attrs) {
           super(context, attrs);
           init(context);
       }
```

```
        public HorizontalIconView(Context context, AttributeSet attrs, int
➥ defStyleAttr) {
            super(context, attrs, defStyleAttr);
            init(context);
        }

    @TargetApi(Build.VERSION_CODES.LOLLIPOP)
        public HorizontalIconView(Context context, AttributeSet attrs, int
➥ defStyleAttr, int defStyleRes) {
            super(context, attrs, defStyleAttr, defStyleRes);
            init(context);
        }
    }
```

Now it's time to create the `init(Context)` method. It's a private method that does not return anything and just sets up some values for the view. We need to get a reference to the `Resources` by calling `context.getResources()`. We'll use `getDimensionPixelSize(int)` to set both the `mIconSize` and the `mIconSpacing` using the two dimensions we previously created (`R.dimen.icon_size` and `R.dimen.icon_spacing`). Next, we get a `ViewConfiguration` reference by calling its static `get(Context)` method. The `ViewConfiguration` class can give us values to use in views to make sure custom views behave in the same way as all other views. For instance, set `mTouchSlop` to the value returned by `ViewConfiguration`'s `getScaledTouchSlop()` method. This value is the number of pixels a pointer/finger must travel on the screen before being considered "moving" and is scaled to the device's density. If we did not consider touch slop, it would be extremely hard to touch down on an exact pixel and lift your finger without moving to another pixel on accident. Once a pointer has moved the touch slop amount, it's moving, so it can become a gesture such as a drag or a fling. We also set `mMinimumVelocity` via `getScaledMinimumFlingVelocity()` (which represents the minimum pixels per second a pointer has to move to initiate a fling gesture), `mMaximumVelocity` via `getScaledMaximumFlingVelocity()` (which represents the maximum pixels per second that a fling can travel at), `mOverflingDistance` via `getScaledOverflingDistance()` (which represents the maximum distance to fling beyond the edge of the view; we'll convert that value into the glow at the edge of the view instead of scrolling beyond), and `mOverscrollDistance` via `getScaledOverscrollDistance()` (which represents the same thing as the overfling distance but when you are dragging or scrolling the view instead of flinging it).

To be explicit, we call `setWillNotDraw(false)` on our view to ensure that the `onDraw(Canvas)` method will be called. It's good to get into the habit of calling this method in an initialization method for all your custom views that draw so that you don't forget to do so when extending a view that will not draw unless you call this method; otherwise, you could be in for a few hours of frustrating troubleshooting.

We set up the `mEdgeEffectLeft` and `mEdgeEffectRight` by instantiating a new `EdgeEffectCompat` from the support library. This class is where you put all the extra "energy" when scrolling beyond the bounds of the view. The more that you scroll beyond the view, the brighter it glows. We also set `mScroller` as a new `OverScroller`. That will be used to do the hard work of animating flings.

When we're done with the `init(Context)` method, it should look like Listing 13.3.

Listing 13.3   The Complete `init` Method

```
/**
 * Perform one-time initialization
 *
 * @param context Context to load Resources and ViewConfiguration data
 */
private void init(Context context) {
    final Resources res = context.getResources();
    mIconSize = res.getDimensionPixelSize(R.dimen.icon_size);
    mIconSpacing = res.getDimensionPixelSize(R.dimen.icon_spacing);

    // Cache ViewConfiguration values
    final ViewConfiguration config = ViewConfiguration.get(context);
    mTouchSlop = config.getScaledTouchSlop();
    mMinimumVelocity = config.getScaledMinimumFlingVelocity();
    mMaximumVelocity = config.getScaledMaximumFlingVelocity();
    mOverflingDistance = config.getScaledOverflingDistance();
    mOverscrollDistance = config.getScaledOverscrollDistance();

    // Verify this View will be drawn
    setWillNotDraw(false);

    // Other setup
    mEdgeEffectLeft = new EdgeEffectCompat(context);
    mEdgeEffectRight = new EdgeEffectCompat(context);
    mScroller = new OverScroller(context);
    setFocusable(true);
}
```

Now that our view sets up all the basic values it will need, there's just one thing remaining before measuring and drawing the view: We need to be able to set the `Drawables`. For this, we create a public method called `setDrawables(List<Drawable>)`. It's not quite as straightforward as just updating `mDrawables`. First, we check if `mDrawables` is null; if it is, we check if the passed-in `List` is null. If both are null, we can just return because nothing needs to be updated. If `mDrawables` is null but the passed-in `List` is not, we call `requestLayout()` because there is a new `List` of `Drawables` to measure. If `mDrawables` is not null but the passed-in `List` is, we call `requestLayout()`, set `mDrawables` to null, and return. If `mDrawables` and the passed-in `List` of `Drawables` are the same size, the view simply needs to be redrawn (remember, all of the "icons" or `Drawables` are being drawn at the size specified in `dimens.xml`, so only the number of them has to be compared), so we call `invalidate()`. If the two `Lists` are a different size, we need to `requestLayout()`. Anything that didn't return needs to update `mDrawables`, so we create a new `List` containing the `Drawables`. The reason for creating a new `List` is because the view should not have to handle the case of the `List` being modified by external code that adds or removes `Drawables`. See Listing 13.4 for the complete method.

Listing 13.4   The Complete `setDrawables` Method

```
/**
 * Sets the List of Drawables to display
 *
 * @param drawables List of Drawables; can be null
 */
public void setDrawables(List<Drawable> drawables) {
    if (mDrawables == null) {
        if (drawables == null) {
            return;
        }
        requestLayout();
    } else if (drawables == null) {
        requestLayout();
        mDrawables = null;
        return;
    } else if (mDrawables.size() == drawables.size()) {
        invalidate();
    } else {
        requestLayout();
    }
    mDrawables = new ArrayList<>(drawables);
    mIconPositions.clear();
}
```

You could make this also check for empty `Lists` being passed in, if you believe that is a use case that will happen frequently. Without explicitly checking for empty lists, the view will just treat them like a nonempty `List`, but it will never draw anything.

Measuring

The first challenge of creating your custom view is to handle the measuring. Some custom views are extremely easy to measure; others take a bit of work. If your view is being used internally only (i.e., it's not going to be in a library or repository that other developers can use), you can take some shortcuts to simply make it support the layouts you will use it in; otherwise, you need to make sure your view handles whatever the parent asks of it.

It's very common to create private methods called `measureHeight(int)` and `measureWidth(int)` to split up measuring the two dimensions, so we'll do that now. Both should return an int that represents the measured size. The height is the easier of the two to measure, so we'll start there. We declare an int called `result` and set it to 0; it will be the measured size. We get the mode portion of the int that was passed in by using `MeasureSpec.getMode(int)` and get the size portion by calling `MeasureSpec.getSize(int)` just like we did in the previous chapter. If the mode is `MeasureSpec.EXACTLY`, we can set your result to the size and we're done. In all other cases, we want to determine our size. We add the top padding size and the bottom padding size (you can use `getPaddingTop()` and `getPaddingBottom()`, respectively) plus the `mIconSize` to set `result` to the desired height. Next, we check if the mode is `MeasureSpec.AT_MOST`. If it is, the parent view is saying your view needs to be no bigger than the passed size. We use `Math.min(int, int)` to set `result` to the smaller of the passed-in size and your calculated size and then return the result. You might notice that this is extremely similar to what we did in the previous chapter; in fact, this pattern of handling measurement is very common, so getting used to it will help with any custom views you make. Your method should look like Listing 13.5.

Listing 13.5   The Simple `measureHeight` Method

```
/**
 * Measures height according to the passed measure spec
 *
 * @param measureSpec
 *              int measure spec to use
 * @return int pixel size
 */
private int measureHeight(int measureSpec) {
    int specMode = MeasureSpec.getMode(measureSpec);
    int specSize = MeasureSpec.getSize(measureSpec);

    int result;
    if (specMode == MeasureSpec.EXACTLY) {
        result = specSize;
    } else {
        result = mIconSize + getPaddingTop() + getPaddingBottom();
        if (specMode == MeasureSpec.AT_MOST) {
            result = Math.min(result, specSize);
        }
    }

    return result;
}
```

Now we can copy and paste the method we just made and rename it to `measureWidth(int)`. We need to calculate the full size of the view with all drawables in place to know how much it needs to scroll regardless of the size of the visible portion of the view. Just after pulling the mode and size out of the passed int, we will calculate the maximum size. We retrieve the number of icons by getting the size of `mDrawables` (remember that it can be null) and multiply the icon count by the `mIconSize` to get the amount of space needed just for drawing the icons. Then we calculate the amount of space needed for the dividers (the space between the icons). If the icon count is one or less, there will be no divider space; otherwise, there will be `mIconSpacing` times one less than the icon count (e.g., if there are three icons, there are two spaces: one between the first and second item and one between the second and third). Now we add the divider space, the icon space, and the padding to get the maximum size needed for this view.

Down in the code we copied in, we need to adjust the `else` statement. If the spec mode is `AT_MOST`, we set the result to the smaller of the maximum size and the passed spec size. In all other cases, we set the result to the maximum size we calculated.

Finally, we need to determine how much scrolling should be possible. If the maximum size we calculated is greater than the result (i.e., there is more to draw than will fit in the allowed space), we set `mScrollRange` to the difference; otherwise, set it to 0. See Listing 13.6 for the complete method.

Listing 13.6 The Complete `measureWidth` Method

```
/**
 * Measures width according to the passed measure spec
 *
 * @param measureSpec
 *              int measure spec to use
 * @return int pixel size
 */
private int measureWidth(int measureSpec) {
    int specMode = MeasureSpec.getMode(measureSpec);
    int specSize = MeasureSpec.getSize(measureSpec);

    // Calculate maximum size
    final int icons = (mDrawables == null) ? 0 : mDrawables.size();
    final int iconSpace = mIconSize * icons;
    final int dividerSpace;
    if (icons <= 1) {
        dividerSpace = 0;
    } else {
        dividerSpace = (icons - 1) * mIconSpacing;
    }
    final int maxSize = dividerSpace + iconSpace + getPaddingLeft() +
➥ getPaddingRight();

    // Calculate actual size
    int result;
    if (specMode == MeasureSpec.EXACTLY) {
        result = specSize;
    } else {
        if (specMode == MeasureSpec.AT_MOST) {
```

```
            result = Math.min(maxSize, specSize);
        } else {
            result = maxSize;
        }
    }

    if (maxSize > result) {
        mScrollRange = maxSize - result;
    } else {
        mScrollRange = 0;
    }

    return result;
}
```

We can now implement the actual onMeasure(int, int) method with ease. We simply override the method to call setMeasuredDimension(int, int), passing in the values from the two methods we created. It should look like Listing 13.7.

Listing 13.7   The Complete onMeasure Method

```
@Override
protected void onMeasure(int widthMeasureSpec, int heightMeasureSpec) {
    setMeasuredDimension(measureWidth(widthMeasureSpec), measureHeight(
➥ heightMeasureSpec));
}
```

That's all there is for measuring. If you're making a view for a library, you should consider how you will handle undesirable sizes. For instance, obviously you only want to use this view where it fits the desired height (vertical padding plus the icon), but what if a user gives a different height? Should you adjust the measuring by seeing how much vertical room there actually is for the icon? Yes and no are both acceptable answers, as long as they are documented.

A ViewGroup would also implement onLayout at this point to position each of its children. The ViewGroup needs to simply call layout on each of the children, passing in the left, top, right, and bottom pixel positions. Because this custom view does not have any children, we do not need to implement that method and can move on to the drawing phase.

Drawing

Now that we have measured our view, we need to implement the drawing step. All of this will be done in the view's onDraw(Canvas) call, so we can start implementing that now. First, we check if we have anything to draw. If mDrawables is null or mDrawables is an empty list, we can immediately return for efficiency.

Next, we get the dimensions we need to work with. First, we get a local copy of the width by calling `getWidth()`. Then, we create a copy of the bottom, left, and top padding with the `getPadding` calls. We need to determine the portion of the overall view that is visible (this will be important once we handle scrolling). Although our view may be a few thousand pixels wide, it could just be showing 200 pixels, so we do not want to draw more than we need to (remember, it's important to be efficient while drawing). See Figure 13.1 for a visual explanation (and note that this example uses several alphabetic drawables to make it easy to see the scroll position). This shows the full view width, but the `onDraw(Canvas)` method should only draw the portion displayed by the device.

Scroll X

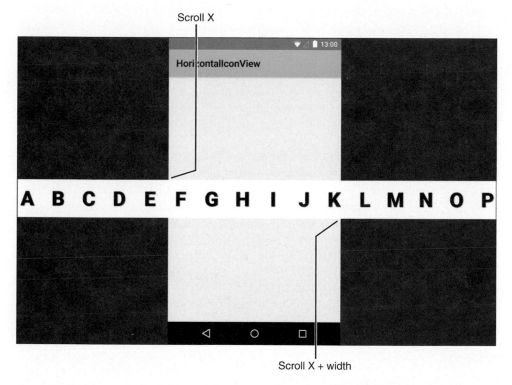

Scroll X + width

Figure 13.1 The full view is represented horizontally here, but the device is just a window into a portion of it

To get the left edge of the display, we call `getScrollX()`, which returns the horizontal offset caused by scrolling. For now, this will always be 0, but it will change once we've added in support for scrolling. To keep the code clear, we also determine the right edge of the display by adding the width to the left edge. Now we can easily check if our drawables are within these coordinates.

Now we create a `left` and a `top` nonfinal int. This is a common technique for tracking where you are drawing to next, so we set the `left` to `paddingLeft` and set the `top` to `paddingTop`.

In this example, everything is drawn in a straight line, so `top` won't change, but we will be increasing `left`. Keep in mind the `left` value is using the coordinate system for the view, not the currently shown portion of the view. In other words, it's based on the full horizontal image from Figure 13.1 and not just the portion shown on the screen.

We update the `mSkippedIconCount` to 0. This keeps track of how many icons we skipped before starting to draw. The value of tracking this will be more apparent soon. We loop through the `mDrawables` list, checking if the icon is onscreen. If the current `left` position plus the width of the icon (in other words, the rightmost pixel of the drawable) is less than the `leftEdge` of the screen, then we add the icon size and spacing to `left`, increment the skipped icon count, and continue—there is no need to draw it. If the current value for `left` is greater than the right edge, we have drawn everything that will go on the screen and we can break out of the loop and skip all the icons to the right of the screen.

For all icons that are actually displayed on the screen, we will get the drawable, set the bounds, and draw it with the canvas. The bounds will have the left and top set to the `left` and `top` variables, respectively. The right and bottom will be set to `left` plus icon size and `top` plus icon size, respectively.

Before continuing on with the next drawable, we want to store the bounds of the drawable as a `Rect` in `mIconPositions`. This can later be used to see if the user taps within the bounds of a given drawable. Note that we want to keep as few objects as possible, so we don't create a `Rect` for every single drawable; we create one for each drawable on the screen. Looking back at Figure 13.1, you can see that the F is the first drawable, so it would be the `Rect` at position 0. The K would be the `Rect` at position 5. If the `mIconPositions` list already contains a `Rect` for that position, the bounds can simply be copied from the drawable to that `Rect`; otherwise, a new `Rect` can be created by using the `Drawable`'s `copyBounds()` method without any arguments and added to the list.

Before continuing on with the next drawable, we don't want to forget to increase `left` by the icon width plus the icon spacing. At this point, our `onDraw(Canvas)` method should look like Listing 13.8.

Listing 13.8 The `onDraw` Method So Far

```
@Override
protected void onDraw(Canvas canvas) {
    if (mDrawables == null || mDrawables.isEmpty()) {
        return;
    }

    final int width = getWidth();
    final int height = getHeight();
    final int paddingLeft = getPaddingLeft();
    final int paddingTop = getPaddingTop();
```

```
// Determine edges of visible content
final int leftEdge = getScrollX();
final int rightEdge = leftEdge + width;

int left = paddingLeft;
final int top = paddingTop;
mSkippedIconCount = 0;

final int iconCount = mDrawables.size();
for (int i = 0; i < iconCount; i++) {
    if (left + mIconSize < leftEdge) {
        // Icon is too far left to be seen
        left = left + mIconSize + mIconSpacing;
        mSkippedIconCount++;
        continue;
    }

    if (left > rightEdge) {
        // All remaining icons are right of the view
        break;
    }

    // Get a reference to the icon to be drawn
    final Drawable icon = mDrawables.get(i);
    icon.setBounds(left, top, left + mIconSize, top + mIconSize);
    icon.draw(canvas);

    // Icon was drawn, so track position
    final int drawnPosition = i - mSkippedIconCount;
    if (drawnPosition + 1 > mIconPositions.size()) {
        final Rect rect = icon.copyBounds();
        mIconPositions.add(rect);
    } else {
        final Rect rect = mIconPositions.get(drawnPosition);
        icon.copyBounds(rect);
    }

    // Update left position
    left = left + mIconSize + mIconSpacing;
    }
}
```

Now that we've managed to create all this drawing code, it's a good idea to test it. For now, we just create a list of drawables in the activity, instantiate a new instance of our custom view, set the list of drawables, and then call setContentView(View) with our HorizontalIconView. See Listing 13.9 for a simple example of what our Activity's onCreate(Bundle) method can look like at this point, and see Figure 13.2 for what the output might look like.

Figure 13.2 This is the view so far

Listing 13.9   A Simple `onCreate` Method in an `Activity`

```
@Override
protected void onCreate(Bundle savedInstanceState) {
    super.onCreate(savedInstanceState);

    // Get a List of Drawables
    final Resources res = getResources();
    final List<Drawable> list = new ArrayList<>();
    list.add(res.getDrawable(R.drawable.a));
    list.add(res.getDrawable(R.drawable.b));
    list.add(res.getDrawable(R.drawable.c));
    list.add(res.getDrawable(R.drawable.d));
    list.add(res.getDrawable(R.drawable.e));
    list.add(res.getDrawable(R.drawable.f));
    list.add(res.getDrawable(R.drawable.g));
    list.add(res.getDrawable(R.drawable.h));
    list.add(res.getDrawable(R.drawable.i));
    list.add(res.getDrawable(R.drawable.j));
    list.add(res.getDrawable(R.drawable.k));
    list.add(res.getDrawable(R.drawable.l));
    list.add(res.getDrawable(R.drawable.m));
    list.add(res.getDrawable(R.drawable.n));
    list.add(res.getDrawable(R.drawable.o));
    list.add(res.getDrawable(R.drawable.p));
    list.add(res.getDrawable(R.drawable.q));
```

```
    list.add(res.getDrawable(R.drawable.r));
    list.add(res.getDrawable(R.drawable.s));
    list.add(res.getDrawable(R.drawable.t));
    list.add(res.getDrawable(R.drawable.u));
    list.add(res.getDrawable(R.drawable.v));
    list.add(res.getDrawable(R.drawable.w));
    list.add(res.getDrawable(R.drawable.x));
    list.add(res.getDrawable(R.drawable.y));
    list.add(res.getDrawable(R.drawable.z));

    final HorizontalIconView view = new HorizontalIconView(this);
    view.setDrawables(list);

    setContentView(view);
}
```

Preparing for Touch Input

Touch input can be one of the most challenging aspects of creating a view due to the many places you can make mistakes that cause bizarre behavior, missed interactions, or sluggishness. Also, a lot of interactions and considerations go into making touch behavior feel right. This custom view will give you the opportunity to see how to handle touches, drags, flings, overscrolling, and edge effects.

First, we start with some of the easier methods to get prepared for the heavy work. We will start with overriding and implementing `computeScroll()`, which updates scrolling during flings. We check if `mScroller`'s `computeScrollOffset` returns `true`. If it does, the `OverScroller` hasn't finished animating and we need to continue scrolling the view (if not, we don't need to do anything else in this method). We get the X position by calling `getScrollX()`. It represents the current X position but not what it should be after the scroll is complete, so it's commonly called `oldX`. We get what the X position should be by calling `mScroller`'s `getCurrX()` (just called `x`). If these are not the same, we call `overScrollBy(int, int, int, int, int, int, int, int, boolean)`. Yes, that method takes a ridiculous amount of ints. They are in pairs, starting with the change in X (`x` minus `oldX`) and the change in Y (0) position, then the current scroll positions for X (`oldX`) and Y (0), followed by the X scroll range (`mScrollRange`) and Y scroll range (0), and the last ints are the maximum overscroll distance for X (`mOverflingDistance`) and Y (0). The last value is a boolean that indicates if this is a touch event (pass `false` because this is triggered when the view is still scrolling after a fling).

Now we call `onScrollChanged(x, 0, oldX, 0)` to notify the view that you scrolled it. If `x` is less than zero and `oldX` is not, then the fling has gone beyond the left end, so `mEdgeEffectLeft` should react. We call its `onAbsorb(int)` method, passing in the current velocity (get it from the `mScroller`'s `getCurrVelocity()` method). Similarly, if `x` is greater than `mScrollRange` and `oldX` is not, then the fling went beyond the right edge, so `mEdgeEffectRight` should react. See Listing 13.10 for the full method.

Listing 13.10 The Complete `computeScroll` Method

```
@Override
public void computeScroll() {
    if (mScroller.computeScrollOffset()) {
        int oldX = getScrollX();
        int x = mScroller.getCurrX();

        if (oldX != x) {
            overScrollBy(x - oldX, 0, oldX, 0, mScrollRange, 0,
➥ mOverflingDistance, 0, false);
            onScrollChanged(x, 0, oldX, 0);

            if (x < 0 && oldX >= 0) {
                mEdgeEffectLeft.onAbsorb((int) mScroller.
➥ getCurrVelocity());
            } else if (x > mScrollRange && oldX <= mScrollRange) {
                mEdgeEffectRight.onAbsorb((int) mScroller.
➥ getCurrVelocity());
            }
        }
    }
}
```

Any time you create a view that calls the `overScrollBy` method, you should also override `onOverScrolled(int, int, boolean, boolean)`, so we will do that next. This one is actually very easy. If `mScroller`'s `isFinished()` method returns `true`, we just call through to the super method. If not, we call `setScrollX(scrollX)` to update the scroll position. If `clamped` is `true`, we need to call the `mScroller`'s `springBack(int, int, int, int, int, int)` method. This method brings the `OverScroller` back to a valid position and, more specifically, allows the glow at the edge of the view when you fling it. Be careful with this method; the ints are not quite in X/Y pairs. The first two are the start for X (`scrollX`) and Y (0), the next two are the minimum (0) and maximum (`mScrollRange`) values for X (*not* the minimum for X and Y), and the last two are the minimum and maximum values for Y. You are probably starting to notice how easy it can be to mix up one of these ints and end up with bugs and strange behavior; there isn't really a good solution to avoiding these bugs, so be extra careful any time you have to work with any of these crazy int-happy methods. See Listing 13.11 for the full method.

Listing 13.11 The Complete `onOverScrolled` Method

```
@Override
protected void onOverScrolled(int scrollX, int scrollY, boolean
➥ clampedX, boolean clampedY) {
```

```
    if (mScroller.isFinished()) {
        super.scrollTo(scrollX, scrollY);
    } else {
        setScrollX(scrollX);
        if (clampedX) {
            mScroller.springBack(scrollX, 0, 0, mScrollRange, 0, 0);
        }
    }
}
```

Another method to implement that's relatively short is `fling(int)`. We will use this internally to trigger a fling. If `mScrollRange` is 0, we just return because there is nowhere to fling. Otherwise, we calculate an int called `halfWidth` by subtracting the horizontal padding from the width of the view and dividing the result by 2. This value will be used for the "overfling" range. We call the `mScroller`'s `fling(int, int, int, int, int, int, int, int)` method. This is another one that's easy to make a mistake on. The first two ints are for the starting position for X (`getScrollX()`) and Y (0). The second pair is the velocity for X (`velocity`) and Y (0). After that, you have the min X position (0) and max X position (`mScrollRange`), followed by the min Y position (0) and max Y position (0). The last pair is the overfling range for X (`halfWidth`) and Y (0). See Listing 13.12 for the full method.

Listing 13.12   The Complete `fling` Method

```
/**
 * Flings the view horizontally with the specified velocity
 *
 * @param velocity int pixels per second along X axis
 */
private void fling(int velocity) {
    if (mScrollRange == 0) {
        return;
    }

    final int halfWidth = (getWidth() - getPaddingLeft() -
➥ getPaddingRight()) / 2;
    mScroller.fling(getScrollX(), 0, velocity, 0, 0, mScrollRange, 0,
➥ 0, halfWidth, 0);
    invalidate();
}
```

We need to update the `onDraw(Canvas)` method to draw the overscroll glow. At the end of the method, we check if `mEdgeEffectLeft` is not null (it shouldn't be, but at some point you might want the view to support disabling the edge glow). If `mEdgeEffectLeft.isFinished()` returns `false`, we need to rotate the canvas 270 degrees and then translate (move) it back by the height of the view so that we can draw the effect. When we call the `mEdgeEffectLeft`'s draw(Canvas) method, it returns true if the effect hasn't yet faded out (meaning we need to invalidate the view). We then restore the canvas to its state prior to your rotation and translation. The work is similar for mEdgeEffectRight. See Listing 13.13 for the detailed code. This code is taken from the HorizontalScrollView with minor modification.

Listing 13.13   The Code for Drawing the Edge Effects in onDraw(Canvas)

```
if (mEdgeEffectLeft != null) {
    if (!mEdgeEffectLeft.isFinished()) {
        final int restoreCount = canvas.save();
        canvas.rotate(270);
        canvas.translate(-height, Math.min(0, leftEdge));
        mEdgeEffectLeft.setSize(height, width);
        if (mEdgeEffectLeft.draw(canvas)) {
            postInvalidateOnAnimation();
        }
        canvas.restoreToCount(restoreCount);
    }
    if (!mEdgeEffectRight.isFinished()) {
        final int restoreCount = canvas.save();
        canvas.rotate(90);
        canvas.translate(0, -(Math.max(mScrollRange, leftEdge) +
    width));
        mEdgeEffectRight.setSize(height, width);
        if (mEdgeEffectRight.draw(canvas)) {
            postInvalidateOnAnimation();
        }
        canvas.restoreToCount(restoreCount);
    }
}
```

One final helper method to create before we can start diving into the gritty touch code is onSecondaryPointerUp(MotionEvent). This is called when the user has two (or more) fingers down on the view and lifts one of them up. The MotionEvent passed into this method was triggered by the finger that lifted, so we need to check to see if its pointer ID matches the one we are tracking (well, the one we will be tracking soon when we do the heavy touch code). If it does, we need to get another pointer to track. Although there can be many different pointers, it is good enough (for this view at least) to simply switch to the second pointer if the first was lifted or the first pointer if the second was lifted. You also need to clear the velocity because we're tracking a new pointer. See Listing 13.14 for the full method; this is another one that comes mostly from HorizontalScrollView.

Listing 13.14   The Complete onSecondaryPointerUp Method

```
private void onSecondaryPointerUp(MotionEvent ev) {
    final int pointerIndex = MotionEventCompat.getActionIndex(ev);
```

```
      final int pointerId = MotionEventCompat.getPointerId(ev,
➥ pointerIndex);
      if (pointerId == mActivePointerId) {
          final int newPointerIndex = pointerIndex == 0 ? 1 : 0;
          mPreviousX = ev.getX(newPointerIndex);
          mActivePointerId = ev.getPointerId(newPointerIndex);
          if (mVelocityTracker != null) {
              mVelocityTracker.clear();
          }
      }
   }
}
```

Handling Touch Input

We've done all the preparatory work for handling touch events, so now it's time to dive in and tackle the hard part. We need to override the `onTouchEvent(MotionEvent)` method. If `mVelocityTracker` is null, we get a new reference by calling `VelocityTracker.obtain()`. We add the movement represented in this `MotionEvent` to the tracker by calling `addMovement(MotionEvent)` on it. Then we get the action int, which tells us what this `MotionEvent` represents (was it a touch or a movement or something else), by calling `MotionEventCompat.getActionMasked(MotionEvent)`. The `MotionEventCompat` class comes in the support library and has a few static methods to help work with `MotionEvents`. Now, we switch on the action.

The first case to tackle is `MotionEvent.ACTION_DOWN`. This is only ever triggered by the first pointer (the pointer with index 0) touching the view; it will never be triggered by a second pointer touching the view when a pointer is already touching it. This means that if the `mScroller` has not finished animating (check `isFinished()`), we need to stop it (`mScroller.abortAnimation()`). In other words, if the view is flinging and the user touches the view, it should stop flinging as if grabbed. We store the X coordinate of the motion event in `mPreviousX` by calling `MotionEventCompat.getX(MotionEvent, 0)`. We also store the pointer ID in `mActivePointerId`. This is the identifier for the pointer we will be watching for movements. If another pointer touches the view and starts sliding around, we don't care about it.

The next case is the hardest one, and that's `MotionEvent.ACTION_MOVE`. First, we find the index of the pointer we care about (remember the difference between index and ID, as explained earlier in the chapter) and get its X coordinate. If `mIsBeingDragged` is not `true`, it means the user has touched the view but has not yet moved the finger enough to be considered a drag, so we need to check if the difference between this X coordinate and `mPreviousX` that you updated in the `ACTION_DOWN` case is greater than the touch slop. If it is, the user is now dragging the view, so we set `mIsBeingDragged` to `true` and remove the touch slop from the delta between the previous X position and the current one. This subtle change to the delta prevents the view from feeling like it suddenly skips the amount the pointer had moved. Think of sliding your finger across something slightly slick in real life, such as a magazine cover. Your finger might slide a little before there is enough friction to move that object, then the object continues to move from the point where there was enough friction as opposed to the object suddenly jumping as if your first point of contact had enough friction.

If the user is dragging the view, we need to call `overScrollBy` (and get all those ints just right). The return result indicates if it scrolls beyond the bounds, so we clear the velocity tracker if it does. If `mEdgeEffectLeft` is not null, we should check if the view is being scrolled beyond its bounds. For example, if the view is being scrolled beyond the left edge (0), we need to call the `onPull(float, float)` method of `mEdgeEffectLeft`. If that's the case, we should also call `abortAnimation()` on `mEdgeEffectRight` if it's not already finished because we're done pulling on that edge. We do the same for if the view is being scrolled beyond the right edge (pulled past `mScrollRange`). The `abortAnimation()` call will tell us if the view is still animating, so we can check it to see if we need to invalidate the view, but we're potentially dealing with two edge effects (one that might be starting to glow now and one that might have already been glowing), so it's easier to just check if either edge is not finished after doing everything else.

The next case to handle is `MotionEvent.ACTION_UP`, and it signifies that there are no more pointers touching the view. This means that we need to check whether this results in a fling of the view or a touch that didn't drag. If `mIsBeingDragged` is `true`, we need to calculate the velocity stored in `mVelocityTracker` by calling `computeCurrentVelocity(1000, mMaximumVelocity)`, where the first value is the units (1000 means velocity in pixels per second) and the second is the maximum velocity you care about. This actually calls through to a native method to calculate the velocity because it can be a complex calculation. After triggering that method, we can get the result by calling `getXVelocity(int)`. If the result is greater than `mMinimumVelocity`, we call `fling` with the inverse of our velocity. The reason we pass the inverse is because you're actually moving the displayed portion of the view in the opposite direction of the fling. For example, if your finger slides to the right very fast, you have a fling with a positive velocity; however, the view is supposed to look like it is scrolling left. If the velocity was not enough to be a fling, we call the `mScroller`'s `springBack` method to make sure we stay within the bounds of the view. We now recycle the `VelocityTracker` and remove our reference to it. By recycling it, we return it to the pool that can be handed out to another view, so we must not interact with it after that. If `mEdgeEffectLeft` is not null, we should call `onRelease()` on both `mEdgeEffectLeft` and `mEdgeEffectRight`.

Still in `ACTION_UP`, if `mIsBeingDragged` is `false`, we should check if it was just a touch of a `Drawable`. We get the X and Y coordinates for the pointer and then loop through `mIconPositions`, checking each `Rect`'s `contains(int, int)` method to see if the pointer is within that view. If it is, we use a `Toast` to indicate which position was touched and indicate how many `Rect`s are in the `mIconPositions` list (so we can see that it does not grow excessively). If we were really going to do something significant with the touch, we would want to check whether it was a regular touch or a long press and we would want to update the drawable states to let them know when they were being touched. We can determine the amount of time needed before a touch is a long press by comparing the time it has been touched with `ViewConfiguration.getLongPressTimeout()`, which will return the number of milliseconds (usually 500).

The case after that is `MotionEvent.ACTION_CANCEL`, and it's relatively easy because this indicates that the gesture has been aborted (e.g., if a parent view started to intercept the touch events). The general goal of this method is to do what you do when it's an `ACTION_UP`, but do not trigger any events (no flinging, no selecting, and so on). If the view wasn't being dragged, we do nothing. If it was, we spring back to valid coordinates, recycle the `VelocityTracker` and remove our reference to it, and call `onRelease()` on both of our `EdgeEffectCompat`s.

Finally, the last case to worry about: `MotionEvent.ACTION_POINTER_UP`. This indicates that a pointer other than the primary one went up. Now we can call that handy `onSecondaryPointerUp(MotionEvent)` method we created earlier. That's it! See Listing 13.15 for the complete class, including the full `onTouchEvent(MotionEvent)` method.

> **note**
>
> Listing 13.15 is quite lengthy because it contains the entire custom `Horizontal-IconView`. You should spend time reviewing it to make sure that it makes sense and consider re-reading any sections of this chapter that are not quite clear to you.
>
> Remember that the code examples for this book are all available at https://github.com/IanGClifton/auid2, so you can access all of the code from Chapter 13 to run it yourself and experiment. Sometimes changing existing code to see how it affects the resulting app is the best way to understand it.

Listing 13.15 The Complete `HorizontalIconView` Class

```
public class HorizontalIconView extends View {
    private static final String TAG = "HorizontalIconView";

    private static final int INVALID_POINTER =
➥ MotionEvent.INVALID_POINTER_ID;

    /**
     * int to track the ID of the pointer that is being tracked
     */
    private int mActivePointerId = INVALID_POINTER;

    /**
     * The List of Drawables that will be shown
     */
    private List<Drawable> mDrawables;
```

```java
/**
 * EdgeEffect or "glow" when scrolled too far left
 */
private EdgeEffectCompat mEdgeEffectLeft;

/**
 * EdgeEffect or "glow" when scrolled too far right
 */
private EdgeEffectCompat mEdgeEffectRight;

/**
 * List of Rects for each visible icon to calculate touches
 */
private final List<Rect> mIconPositions = new ArrayList<>();

/**
 * Width and height of icons in pixels
 */
private int mIconSize;

/**
 * Space between each icon in pixels
 */
private int mIconSpacing;

/**
 * Whether a pointer/finger is currently on screen that is being
 * tracked
 */
private boolean mIsBeingDragged;

/**
 * Maximum fling velocity in pixels per second
 */
private int mMaximumVelocity;

/**
 * Minimum fling velocity in pixels per second
 */
private int mMinimumVelocity;

/**
 * How far to fling beyond the bounds of the view
 */
private int mOverflingDistance;

/**
 * How far to scroll beyond the bounds of the view
 */
private int mOverscrollDistance;
```

```
    /**
     * The X coordinate of the last down touch, used to determine when
➥ a drag starts
     */
    private float mPreviousX = 0;

    /**
     * Number of pixels this view can scroll (basically width - visible
➥ width)
     */
    private int mScrollRange;

    /**
     * Number of pixels of movement required before a touch is "moving"
     */
    private int mTouchSlop;

    /**
     * VelocityTracker to simplify tracking MotionEvents
     */
    private VelocityTracker mVelocityTracker;

    /**
     * Scroller to do the hard work of scrolling smoothly
     */
    private OverScroller mScroller;

    /**
     * The number of icons that are left of the view and therefore not
➥ drawn
     */
    private int mSkippedIconCount = 0;

    public HorizontalIconView(Context context) {
        super(context);
        init(context);
    }

    public HorizontalIconView(Context context, AttributeSet attrs) {
        super(context, attrs);
        init(context);
    }

    public HorizontalIconView(Context context, AttributeSet attrs, int
➥ defStyleAttr) {
        super(context, attrs, defStyleAttr);
        init(context);
    }
```

```java
    @TargetApi(Build.VERSION_CODES.LOLLIPOP)
    public HorizontalIconView(Context context, AttributeSet attrs, int
➥ defStyleAttr, int defStyleRes) {
        super(context, attrs, defStyleAttr, defStyleRes);
        init(context);
    }

    @Override
    public void computeScroll() {
        if (mScroller.computeScrollOffset()) {
            int oldX = getScrollX();
            int x = mScroller.getCurrX();

            if (oldX != x) {
                overScrollBy(x - oldX, 0, oldX, 0, mScrollRange, 0,
➥ mOverflingDistance, 0, false);
                onScrollChanged(x, 0, oldX, 0);

                if (x < 0 && oldX >= 0) {
                    mEdgeEffectLeft.onAbsorb((int) mScroller.
➥ getCurrVelocity());
                } else if (x > mScrollRange && oldX <= mScrollRange) {
                    mEdgeEffectRight.onAbsorb((int) mScroller.
➥ getCurrVelocity());
                }
            }
        }
    }

    @Override
    public boolean onTouchEvent(@NonNull MotionEvent ev) {
        if (mVelocityTracker == null) {
            mVelocityTracker = VelocityTracker.obtain();
        }
        mVelocityTracker.addMovement(ev);

        final int action = MotionEventCompat.getActionMasked(ev);
        switch (action) {
            case MotionEvent.ACTION_DOWN: {
                if (!mScroller.isFinished()) {
                    mScroller.abortAnimation();
                }

                // Remember where the motion event started
                mPreviousX = (int) MotionEventCompat.getX(ev, 0);
                mActivePointerId = MotionEventCompat.getPointerId(ev, 0);
                break;
            }

            case MotionEvent.ACTION_MOVE: {
```

```
                final int activePointerIndex = MotionEventCompat.findPo
interIndex(ev, mActivePointerId);
                if (activePointerIndex == INVALID_POINTER) {
                    Log.e(TAG, "Invalid pointerId=" + mActivePointerId
+ " in onTouchEvent");
                    break;
                }

                final int x = (int) MotionEventCompat.getX(ev, 0);
                int deltaX = (int) (mPreviousX - x);
                if (!mIsBeingDragged && Math.abs(deltaX) > mTouchSlop) {
                    mIsBeingDragged = true;
                    if (deltaX > 0) {
                        deltaX -= mTouchSlop;
                    } else {
                        deltaX += mTouchSlop;
                    }
                }
                if (mIsBeingDragged) {
                    // Scroll to follow the motion event
                    mPreviousX = x;

                    final int oldX = getScrollX();
                    final int range = mScrollRange;

                    if (overScrollBy(deltaX, 0, oldX, 0, range, 0,
mOverscrollDistance, 0, true)) {
                        // Break our velocity if we hit a scroll barrier.
                        mVelocityTracker.clear();
                    }

                    if (mEdgeEffectLeft != null) {
                        final int pulledToX = oldX + deltaX;
                        final int y = (int) MotionEventCompat.getY(ev, 0);
                        final float yDisplacement = 1 - ((float) y /
getHeight());
                        if (pulledToX < 0) {
                            mEdgeEffectLeft.onPull((float) deltaX /
getWidth(), yDisplacement);
                            if (!mEdgeEffectRight.isFinished()) {
                                mEdgeEffectRight.onRelease();
                            }
                        } else if (pulledToX > range) {
                            mEdgeEffectRight.onPull((float) deltaX /
getWidth(), yDisplacement);
                            if (!mEdgeEffectLeft.isFinished()) {
                                mEdgeEffectLeft.onRelease();
                            }
                        }
                    }
```

```
                                if (!mEdgeEffectLeft.isFinished() ||
➡ !mEdgeEffectRight.isFinished()) {
                                    postInvalidateOnAnimation();
                                }

                            }

                        }
                        break;
                }
                case MotionEvent.ACTION_UP: {
                    if (mIsBeingDragged) {
                        mVelocityTracker.computeCurrentVelocity(1000,
➡ mMaximumVelocity);
                        int initialVelocity = (int) mVelocityTracker.getXVe
➡ locity(mActivePointerId);

                        if ((Math.abs(initialVelocity) > mMinimumVelocity)) {
                            fling(-initialVelocity);
                        } else {
                            if (mScroller.springBack(getScrollX(), 0, 0,
➡ mScrollRange, 0, 0)) {
                                postInvalidateOnAnimation();
                            }
                        }

                        mActivePointerId = INVALID_POINTER;
                        mIsBeingDragged = false;
                        mVelocityTracker.recycle();
                        mVelocityTracker = null;

                        if (mEdgeEffectLeft != null) {
                            mEdgeEffectLeft.onRelease();
                            mEdgeEffectRight.onRelease();
                        }
                    } else {
                        // Was not being dragged, was this a press on an
➡ icon?
                        final int activePointerIndex =
➡ ev.findPointerIndex(mActivePointerId);
                        if (activePointerIndex == INVALID_POINTER) {
                            return false;
                        }
                        final int x = (int) ev.getX(activePointerIndex) +
➡ getScrollX();
                        final int y = (int) ev.getY(activePointerIndex);
                        int i = 0;
                        for (Rect rect : mIconPositions) {
```

```
                            if (rect.contains(x, y)) {
                                final int position = i + mSkippedIconCount;
                                Toast.makeText(getContext(), "Pressed icon "
➥ + position + "; rect count: " + mIconPositions.size(), Toast.LENGTH_SHORT).
➥ show();
                                break;
                            }
                            i++;
                        }
                    }
                    break;
                }
                case MotionEvent.ACTION_CANCEL: {
                    if (mIsBeingDragged) {
                        if (mScroller.springBack(getScrollX(), 0, 0,
➥ mScrollRange, 0, 0)) {
                            postInvalidateOnAnimation();
                        }
                        mActivePointerId = INVALID_POINTER;
                        mIsBeingDragged = false;
                        if (mVelocityTracker != null) {
                            mVelocityTracker.recycle();
                            mVelocityTracker = null;
                        }

                        if (mEdgeEffectLeft != null) {
                            mEdgeEffectLeft.onRelease();
                            mEdgeEffectRight.onRelease();
                        }
                    }
                    break;
                }
                case MotionEvent.ACTION_POINTER_UP: {
                    onSecondaryPointerUp(ev);
                    break;
                }
            }
        return true;
    }

    /**
     * Sets the List of Drawables to display
     *
     * @param drawables List of Drawables; can be null
     */
    public void setDrawables(List<Drawable> drawables) {
        if (mDrawables == null) {
            if (drawables == null) {
                return;
            }
```

```
            requestLayout();
        } else if (drawables == null) {
            requestLayout();
            mDrawables = null;
            return;
        } else if (mDrawables.size() == drawables.size()) {
            invalidate();
        } else {
            requestLayout();
        }
        mDrawables = new ArrayList<>(drawables);
        mIconPositions.clear();
    }


    @Override
    protected void onDraw(Canvas canvas) {
        if (mDrawables == null || mDrawables.isEmpty()) {
            return;
        }

        final int width = getWidth();
        final int height = getHeight();
        final int paddingLeft = getPaddingLeft();
        final int paddingTop = getPaddingTop();

        // Determine edges of visible content
        final int leftEdge = getScrollX();
        final int rightEdge = leftEdge + width;

        int left = paddingLeft;
        final int top = paddingTop;
        mSkippedIconCount = 0;

        final int iconCount = mDrawables.size();
        for (int i = 0; i < iconCount; i++) {
            if (left + mIconSize < leftEdge) {
                // Icon is too far left to be seen
                left = left + mIconSize + mIconSpacing;
                mSkippedIconCount++;
                continue;
            }

            if (left > rightEdge) {
                // All remaining icons are right of the view
                break;
            }

            // Get a reference to the icon to be drawn
            final Drawable icon = mDrawables.get(i);
```

```
            icon.setBounds(left, top, left + mIconSize, top + mIconSize);
            icon.draw(canvas);

            // Icon was drawn, so track position
            final int drawnPosition = i - mSkippedIconCount;
            if (drawnPosition + 1 > mIconPositions.size()) {
                final Rect rect = icon.copyBounds();
                mIconPositions.add(rect);
            } else {
                final Rect rect = mIconPositions.get(drawnPosition);
                icon.copyBounds(rect);
            }

            // Update left position
            left = left + mIconSize + mIconSpacing;
        }

        if (mEdgeEffectLeft != null) {
            if (!mEdgeEffectLeft.isFinished()) {
                final int restoreCount = canvas.save();
                canvas.rotate(270);
                canvas.translate(-height, Math.min(0, leftEdge));
                mEdgeEffectLeft.setSize(height, width);
                if (mEdgeEffectLeft.draw(canvas)) {
                    postInvalidateOnAnimation();
                }
                canvas.restoreToCount(restoreCount);
            }
            if (!mEdgeEffectRight.isFinished()) {
                final int restoreCount = canvas.save();
                canvas.rotate(90);
                canvas.translate(0, -(Math.max(mScrollRange, leftEdge)
➥ + width));
                mEdgeEffectRight.setSize(height, width);
                if (mEdgeEffectRight.draw(canvas)) {
                    postInvalidateOnAnimation();
                }
                canvas.restoreToCount(restoreCount);
            }
        }
    }

    @Override
    protected void onMeasure(int widthMeasureSpec, int
➥ heightMeasureSpec) {
        setMeasuredDimension(measureWidth(widthMeasureSpec), measureHei
➥ ght(heightMeasureSpec));
    }
```

```java
    @Override
    protected void onOverScrolled(int scrollX, int scrollY, boolean
➥ clampedX, boolean clampedY) {
        if (mScroller.isFinished()) {
            super.scrollTo(scrollX, scrollY);
        } else {
            setScrollX(scrollX);
            if (clampedX) {
                mScroller.springBack(scrollX, 0, 0, mScrollRange, 0, 0);
            }
        }
    }

    /**
     * Flings the view horizontally with the specified velocity
     *
     * @param velocity int pixels per second along X axis
     */
    private void fling(int velocity) {
        if (mScrollRange == 0) {
            return;
        }

        final int halfWidth = (getWidth() - getPaddingLeft() -
➥ getPaddingRight()) / 2;
        mScroller.fling(getScrollX(), 0, velocity, 0, 0, mScrollRange,
➥ 0, 0, halfWidth, 0);
        invalidate();
    }

    /**
     * Perform one-time initialization
     *
     * @param context Context to load Resources and ViewConfiguration
➥ data
     */
    private void init(Context context) {
        final Resources res = context.getResources();
        mIconSize = res.getDimensionPixelSize(R.dimen.icon_size);
        mIconSpacing = res.getDimensionPixelSize(R.dimen.icon_spacing);

        // Cache ViewConfiguration values
        final ViewConfiguration config = ViewConfiguration.get(context);
        mTouchSlop = config.getScaledTouchSlop();
        mMinimumVelocity = config.getScaledMinimumFlingVelocity();
        mMaximumVelocity = config.getScaledMaximumFlingVelocity();
        mOverflingDistance = config.getScaledOverflingDistance();
        mOverscrollDistance = config.getScaledOverscrollDistance();
```

```java
        // Verify this View will be drawn
        setWillNotDraw(false);

        // Other setup
        mEdgeEffectLeft = new EdgeEffectCompat(context);
        mEdgeEffectRight = new EdgeEffectCompat(context);
        mScroller = new OverScroller(context);
        setFocusable(true);
    }

    /**
     * Measures height according to the passed measure spec
     *
     * @param measureSpec
     *            int measure spec to use
     * @return int pixel size
     */
    private int measureHeight(int measureSpec) {
        int specMode = MeasureSpec.getMode(measureSpec);
        int specSize = MeasureSpec.getSize(measureSpec);

        int result;
        if (specMode == MeasureSpec.EXACTLY) {
            result = specSize;
        } else {
            result = mIconSize + getPaddingTop() + getPaddingBottom();
            if (specMode == MeasureSpec.AT_MOST) {
                result = Math.min(result, specSize);
            }
        }

        return result;
    }

    /**
     * Measures width according to the passed measure spec
     *
     * @param measureSpec
     *            int measure spec to use
     * @return int pixel size
     */
    private int measureWidth(int measureSpec) {
        int specMode = MeasureSpec.getMode(measureSpec);
        int specSize = MeasureSpec.getSize(measureSpec);

        // Calculate maximum size
        final int icons = (mDrawables == null) ? 0 : mDrawables.size();
        final int iconSpace = mIconSize * icons;
        final int dividerSpace;
```

```java
        if (icons <= 1) {
            dividerSpace = 0;
        } else {
            dividerSpace = (icons - 1) * mIconSpacing;
        }
        final int maxSize = dividerSpace + iconSpace + getPaddingLeft()
 ➥ + getPaddingRight();

        // Calculate actual size
        int result;
        if (specMode == MeasureSpec.EXACTLY) {
            result = specSize;
        } else {
            if (specMode == MeasureSpec.AT_MOST) {
                result = Math.min(maxSize, specSize);
            } else {
                result = maxSize;
            }
        }

        if (maxSize > result) {
            mScrollRange = maxSize - result;
        } else {
            mScrollRange = 0;
        }

        return result;
    }

    private void onSecondaryPointerUp(MotionEvent ev) {
        final int pointerIndex = MotionEventCompat.getActionIndex(ev);
        final int pointerId = MotionEventCompat.getPointerId(ev,
 ➥ pointerIndex);
        if (pointerId == mActivePointerId) {
            final int newPointerIndex = pointerIndex == 0 ? 1 : 0;
            mPreviousX = ev.getX(newPointerIndex);
            mActivePointerId = ev.getPointerId(newPointerIndex);
            if (mVelocityTracker != null) {
                mVelocityTracker.clear();
            }
        }
    }
}
```

Now we can test out our new view. We should make sure it can scroll (see Figure 13.3) through the full range of drawables, left and right. Also, we should make sure the overscroll visuals on the left work (see Figure 13.4) and the overscroll visuals on the right work.

Figure 13.3 The `HorizontalIconView` being scrolled

Figure 13.4 The `HorizontalIconView`'s edge effect being tested

You might be wondering why the overscroll glow appears over the entire activity area. That's because the custom view was passed in with `setContentView(View)`. To verify it really works how it should, we should try putting it in a layout. You might also consider adding padding or other attributes that may affect the way it draws. See Listing 13.16 for a sample layout.

Listing 13.16   A Simple Layout for Testing the Custom View

```
<LinearLayout xmlns:android="http://schemas.android.com/apk/res/android"
              xmlns:tools="http://schemas.android.com/tools"
              android:layout_width="match_parent"
              android:layout_height="match_parent"
              android:orientation="vertical"
              android:background="#FFEEEEEE"
              tools:context=".MainActivity">

    <android.support.v7.widget.Toolbar
        android:id="@+id/toolbar"
        android:layout_width="match_parent"
        android:layout_height="?attr/actionBarSize"
        android:elevation="4dp"
        android:background="?attr/colorPrimary"/>

    <Space
        android:layout_width="match_parent"
        android:layout_height="0dp"
        android:layout_weight="1"/>

    <com.auidbook.horizontaliconview.HorizontalIconView
        android:id="@+id/horizontal_icon_view"
        android:layout_width="match_parent"
        android:layout_height="wrap_content"
        android:background="@android:color/white"
        android:padding="16dp" />

    <Space
        android:layout_width="match_parent"
        android:layout_height="0dp"
        android:layout_weight="1"/>

</LinearLayout>
```

Updating the activity to use that layout and running it on a device gives the result in Figure 13.5. Notice that the glow on the left side is contained within the view itself. The view is correctly centered and has the correct background.

Now is a great time to go back through the code and make sure you understand each method. Don't be afraid to experiment. See what happens if you comment out certain lines or change the values. That's one of the best ways to understand what is really happening with the code and why you pass certain values to methods. For example, if touch slop still seems like a weird concept, see what happens when you multiply it by 10.

Figure 13.5 The custom view being tested within a layout

Other Considerations

This view is far from perfect, but it does demonstrate the challenging parts of creating a custom view. It also has a potential bug in that the number of `Rects` that are kept for hit detection can actually be one greater than the number of views on the screen. It's not a major problem, but it's something that would be worth fixing before making this part of some library. Of course, if you were to make this part of a library, you would want to finish the hit handling for the icons and use a custom listener interface to report touches instead of directly handling them.

Another problem with this view is that it only works on Android 4.2 and above (API level 16) because of the use of `postInvalidateOnAnimation()`, which causes `invalidate` to happen on the next frame. To improve compatibility with older versions of Android, you can use reflection to see if this method exists. If not, the standard `invalidate()` method will work. The `OverScroller`'s `getCurrVelocity()` method is used, which was added in Android 4.0 (API level 14). You can instead use the velocity from your `mVelocityTracker`'s last report, calculate the velocity yourself, use reflection, use a fixed value, or even just comment out those lines (in which case a fling just won't cause the glow).

Summary

This is definitely the most challenging and detailed chapter of the book. If you feel like you don't quite understand all of it, that's okay. The important part is understanding the concepts so that you can start to work on custom views yourself. The first few views you make on your own are likely to have bugs or cause some frustration. There are a lot of places to mix up an int or forget to call a method, so don't be surprised if you have to spend effort troubleshooting. That's a great way to learn. Hopefully by reading this book, you've learned to avoid some of the common pitfalls, such as not calling `setWillNotDraw(false)` and wondering for hours why your drawing code isn't working.

When you're ready to learn more about custom views, the Android developer site has some good documentation on additional ways to work with touch input at http://developer.android .com/training/gestures/index.html. Of course, there's rarely a better place to learn than the code itself, so don't be afraid to pull up the source for one of the built-in views. You'll start to see many repeating patterns, and that's when your understanding really starts to come together.

GOOGLE PLAY ASSETS

Google Play is the primary method for distributing Android apps, and it has the largest world-wide reach of any Android app store. Although there is no lengthy review process, you should have all of your assets ready for the store before you launch the app, even if you're doing a "soft" launch (i.e., a launch with no explicit publicity). Having the right assets ensures that you reach the maximum number of users by showing them what is great about your app and by enabling it to be featured by Google Play.

Application Description

Although this book is focused on design and the impact of design on the user experience, not emphasizing the importance of a good app description would be a major failing. The app description not only lets you tell the users what your app is about and why they must download it now, but also gives you the opportunity to set their expectations.

Use concise, clear language that explains what your app is and what need it fulfills. Many users will only read the first portion of your description, so make sure you get the most important pieces across right away. If there are any problems with the app, be upfront about them. For instance, if the app is a prototype that demonstrates functionality but drains battery quickly, say so. If the app is intended for a specific audience, make that clear upfront (e.g., "This demo for Android app developers does X, Y, and Z"). If you created a weather app that only supports forecasts for one country, be explicit about that right away (and, in this specific case, consider limiting it geographically to those in that country). Setting expectations not only allows users to filter themselves (e.g., "Oh, it doesn't work in my country, so I won't try it"), it makes them far less likely to leave negative feedback. By not setting the expectations right away, you run the risk of negative reviews from users who had their own expectations (e.g., "Why doesn't this stupid app provide weather forecasts in my country?"). A few negative reviews can influence many future would-be users to avoid your app.

Do not make your app description sound "market-y." In other words, this is not the place to brag excessively about your app or talk about how it was downloaded a million times in the first week. Focus on what the user gets out of it. What makes it different from the competition? Is it faster, better presented, or easier to use?

If your app fulfills a new need or an uncommon one, you have to explain what that need is. For instance, you might make an app for pilots to track their flight details, automatically populating time and distance based on the device sensors. You can declare the audience immediately (e.g., "This app allows pilots to…"). Because pilots know the importance of keeping maintenance and flight records, you can instead emphasize what your app does to make that record keeping easier and what records it actually keeps. If your app is a new take on an existing and common app type (e.g., a new Twitter client), you have to put the emphasis on what makes your app special. You can assume that people looking at your app know what Twitter is and what they want to do with your app, so your description needs to state what makes your app different from the other Twitter apps out there.

Do not use automatic translation for your application description. It may be tempting to use Google Translate or a similar service to automatically translate your description into other languages, but you should avoid doing so. In most cases, doing so will get the gist of your app's meaning across, but it will often be riddled with minor errors or awkward phrasing that will not convey a sense of professionalism. You don't want a user's first experience to be with a grammatically flawed description; otherwise, it could be the last.

The Change Log

Whenever you update the app, update the change log. No exceptions. Many people are afraid to put anything there for fear that they risk sounding like the app was flawed; however, no app is perfect. How did the update make it better? Did you fix a crash bug? Did you fix some silly typos? Is there new content for users? This is your chance to show existing users that they are not forgotten, and it's your chance to show potential users that the app is constantly improving. Existing users want to know whether the change is worth downloading now, later, or ever. When you don't update the change log or you put something generic, such as "fixes," you're telling the users that the update isn't important.

Be specific. "Fixed rare crash on launch for Nexus 4 users" is good, but "Fixed bugs" is not. Be concise. "Added support for Hungarian" is good, but "Updated the whole app to support users who have their device set to Hungarian" is excessive. This is not the place to fully explain new features; instead, you can briefly introduce them ("Added swiping for faster navigation") and then explain them on first launch of the app, if needed. It can be helpful to look back through your commit messages in your version control software such as Git to recall what has changed.

Application Icon

The application icon for Google Play must be 512×512. Only PNG images are supported, so you should upload a 32-bit PNG that matches your default launcher icon. Whenever possible, it's ideal to create assets such as your application icon as vector graphics so that they can be scaled (and sharpened or otherwise adjusted) to match a variety of sizes.

The application icon is one of the most important parts of your app. It is often the first graphic a user sees related to your app, and it's the one users search for when launching your app. It needs to convey what your app is about in a simple but recognizable way. This means that it needs to follow all the standard conventions.

A good icon . . .

- **Uses the majority of the space available to it**. This means the touch target is obvious and you don't have an overly thin icon. Icons that are too thin don't look touchable and they can often be lost against certain backgrounds.

- **Has a notable shape**. Android does not force all app icons into the same shape, so this is one of the best ways to make your icon stand out. Is it an analog clock? Perhaps you should consider a round icon. Is it for tracking stars in the sky? Maybe you could try a star or constellation shape. Look at the variety of shapes in the default apps. There aren't just circles and rounded rectangles but mail-shaped icons and icons that look like headphones.

- **Sticks to a simple color scheme**. Look at the apps that come on an Android device and you should notice a very common pattern among the default icons. Most of them stick to a simple but distinct color scheme. Gmail is red and white. Play Music is orange and yellow. Calendar is blue and white. Where shapes are similar, colors are different. The color of your icon should reflect the colors of your app, when possible. This helps the user associate your icon with your app.

■ **Applies the core themes of Material Design**. The same clean concepts, simple shadows, bold colors, and geometry apply to icons. The top of the icon can be slightly lighter and the bottom slightly darker. You want to have a soft shadow, just like a paper element from Material Design, but you can also add a 45 degree shadow for any raised elements, a score across the icon for depth, or other visual embellishments.

Take a look at both the Google Maps icon and the Google Music icon in Figure A.1. Notice the bright, playful colors and the shapes. Both of these types of apps typically have very simple icons. The Google Maps icon uses a location pin to break away from a simple rounded square that another mapping app might use for its icon. Music applications are another example where people typically do something simple such as a rounded rectangle with a music note or CD on it. Google used the unique shape of headphones to ensure the icon stands out and chose a vibrant orange color to make it more distinct. Consider how bland the icon would have been with a standard black headband instead of orange.

Figure A.1 The Google Music and Google Maps icons

Creating an Icon the Easy Way

Learning how to design an icon effectively is deceptively hard. Despite that it's relatively small, a lot of thought should go into a good icon. In most cases, developers either don't have time to learn all the details or simply don't want to. If that describes you, consider using the Android Asset Studio to create the launcher icon (https://romannurik.github.io/AndroidAssetStudio/icons-launcher.html). You can supply an image, use some clipart, or even just type some text to create the icon. You'll specify colors, shapes, and visual effects and all the work is done for you. Figure A.2 shows a few simple icons for the woodworking app, created using Android Asset Studio, that just use "WW" as the content.

Figure A.2 Icons created with Android Asset Studio demonstrating long shadow (left), score (center), and dog-ear (right) effects

Creating an Icon Manually

Although Android Asset Studio is amazing, there are times when you want to create an icon yourself. The Material Design guidelines for icons (https://www.google.com/design/spec/style/icons.html#icons-product-icons) are quite detailed; you should definitely read through them in detail before starting on an icon. Once you're ready to begin, you should grab the "Product Icons sticker sheet" (https://www.google.com/design/spec/resources/sticker-sheets-icons .html), which provides templates for Adobe Illustrator that simplifies the process. Figure A.3 shows the template.

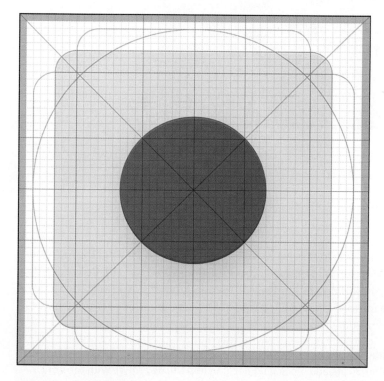

Figure A.3 Icon template

After opening the template, you'll see several layers that will help guide the creation of a new icon. You should choose a background shape that will work well with the content of the icon. For instance, the woodworking tools app might use a hammer as the central part of the icon. Although a literal hammer isn't one of the emphasized tools in the app, it is a simple shape that evokes the sense of "construction" and "tools," both of which go well with the app. Placing that hammer at an angle is more interesting than simply having it vertical or horizontal, so using the wider rounded rectangle might be a good idea. The color can often be the app's primary color. Figure A.4 shows the background created with the template.

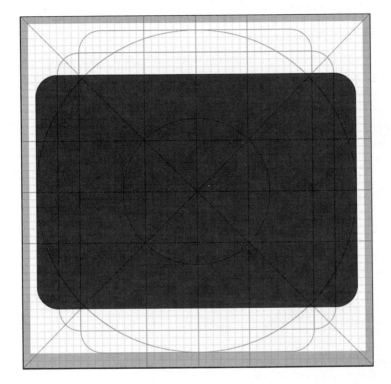

Figure A.4 Icon with the background created

A subtle but important addition to the background is the lighting and shading. The top of the icon has a tinted edge (1dp, 20% opacity, pure white) and the bottom has a shaded edge (1dp, 20% opacity, pure black), creating a hint of shape to the background instead of making it too flat. If you're using a shape for the background other than what was included in the template, you'll need to make these edges yourself.

An easy way to create the shaded edge is to select the background shape, copy it, and paste it twice. Click the front duplicate and move it up one unit (tap the up arrow). With the front duplicate still selected, hold Shift and click the duplicate behind it (it is sticking out one unit at the bottom) to select both shapes. Open the Pathfinder window and click the "Minus Front" option. This basically cuts the front shape out of the other shape, leaving just that slim offset. Make that edge black and set the opacity to 20% then make sure it is positioned in front of the very bottom of the background.

Creating the top tinted edge is the same process, but the duplicate is moved down one unit and the edge is set to white and 20% opacity. Make sure it's in front of the very top of the background. Figure A.5 shows the updated icon, though the edges are extremely subtle, so they may be difficult to see.

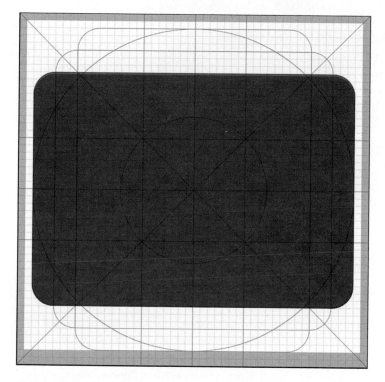

Figure A.5 Background with very subtle edge effects added to the top and bottom

With the background ready, it's time to create the content of the icon. This is the part that is most difficult to provide directions for because it depends entirely on what makes sense on your icon. In some cases, a letter or two can work well. In other cases, you want some kind of shape or logo. Try to keep it relatively simple (remember, the icon will usually be displayed at about the size of the user's thumb). If necessary, you can find a real photo of the type of object you'd like, bringing it into Illustrator and drawing over it with the pen tool. Once you've created the shape, you can delete the photo and tweak your shape until it looks right.

Ensure that the content of the icon has sufficient contrast with the background. Sometimes you can use your accent color, but other times you may need to change it. If the content is meant to appear floating or needs more character, you can use the same tinted/shaded edge trick that was used on the background. Figure A.6 shows the icon so far.

Figure A.6 Icon with the content added

If you want to create a long shadow for the content of the icon, create two new copies of it and drag one of them off the bottom-right edge of the background while holding shift (which constrains the movement to 45 degrees). Make both copies black with the opacity set to 0% on the bottom-right one. Open the Object menu, pick Blend, and open Blend Options. The dropdown should have Specified Distance selected and the unit should be 1. Select both copies and blend them (Object, Blend, Blend).

At this point, the shadow will be very harsh and it will extend beyond the background. To lighten the shadow, select the blended object and open the Transparency window. Set the blend mode to Multiply and the opacity to 25%. Now the shadow won't be as harsh, but it still extends too far, so select the icon background and make a copy of it in front of the long shadow (make sure it lines up with the original background). Select both the shadow and the copied background and then open the Object menu, select Clipping Mask, and choose Make. This will clip your shadow to the background. Figure A.7 shows what this looks like.

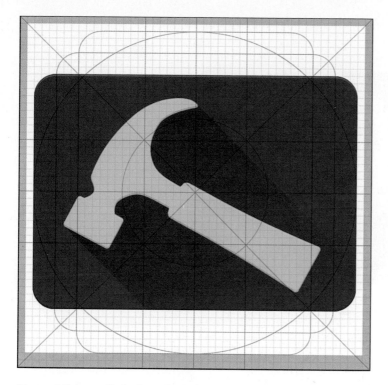

Figure A.7 Icon with the long shadow added

Now the icon needs the "finish," which is simply a radial gradient centered on the top left of the canvas. The gradient goes from white with 10% opacity to 0% opacity. There is also a layer in the template that provides an example. Note that the effect is very subtle (it will look like the icon is just a little lighter).

The final thing to do is add a drop shadow to the icon background. Select the background shape and open the Effect menu, click Stylize, and select Drop Shadow. The mode should be Normal, opacity 20%, X offset 0, Y offset 4, and blur 4. Figure A.8 shows the final icon.

Screenshots

Screenshots can be a wide range of sizes now from the original 320×480 resolution on up to 2160×3840. They should be 24-bit PNGs to keep the graphics crisp, but JPEGs are also acceptable. As new resolutions become more common on Android devices, support for new screenshot sizes is added, so be sure to double-check what sizes you can upload in the developer console when you are submitting your app (https://play.google.com/apps/publish).

A lot of users will look at the screenshots before they've even begun to read your app description. Screenshots provide the first glimpse into what your app is really like, so they're absolutely

Figure A.8 The completed icon

vital to include. Google Play requires two screenshots, but you should provide more. Ideally, you should provide one screenshot for each primary section of the app. For instance, an email app could show a screenshot of the inbox, a full email, replying to an email, and any other core functionality, such as searching.

Screenshots are an excellent way to show off support for alternate form factors. If you support tablets, include a few tablet screenshots. This is often one of the first places users look to see if their tablet is supported, and seeing only phone screenshots will be perceived as an indication that tablets are not supported. Some users will even back out of an app's details in Google Play without reading the description or downloading the app to give it a try because they're using a tablet and the screenshots don't indicate support for tablets.

Do not use Google Play screenshots for promotional material. Some people make the mistake of using them to advertise for other apps, but they are meant to be specific to the app they are for and shouldn't have added text on them that doesn't reflect the user experience. Do not show screenshots of unimportant screens just to have more screenshots available. For instance, it does not make sense to include a screenshot of the settings screen for most apps (an exception being for apps that are intended for power users or focused on customizability). Settings screens generally have a lot to look at and interpret and don't reflect the primary user experience of the app.

Exclude distracting pieces from the screenshots; you should remove any status bar notifications from each screenshot. Android 6.0 supports this through the developer options, but you can also use the Clean Status Bar app, which will allow you to replace the status bar with a clean one on the device itself, so you can just grab the screenshots without extra work (https://play.google.com/store/apps/details?id=com.emmaguy.cleanstatusbar). Some people like to include the frame of a real device around the screenshot, but you shouldn't do that. Doing so decreases the size of the actual screenshot (which is what the users care about) and it also means your screenshots will look dated faster since devices change so frequently. Be sure to review each screenshot. It's easy to make the mistake of taking a screenshot of an app that includes user-generated content that might not be appropriate. If your screenshots are taken on a device that's customized (e.g., one that has a custom style for the status bar), modify them to look like what the user will see to keep the focus on your app and not the trim.

Feature Graphic

The feature graphic must be 1024×500 (although it will be resized for use in a variety of places). Ideally, it should be a PNG, but a JPEG with minimal compression works well, too. In either case, it must be a 24-bit image (no alpha channel).

Your feature graphic is an important part of marketing your app and is currently included at the top of your app's page in the Google Play app. It's also often scaled down to be used in the Google Play app and on the website at a variety of sizes. Many designers are very tempted to put a lot of detail into this image because it is fairly large, but it should be clean and clear so that it can scale effectively. Think of it like a book cover; the goal is to entice viewers with strong visuals that emphasize the characteristics of your app.

Consider incorporating your logo or other visual representing your app into the design of your feature graphic. It is a good idea to include the name of your app in a very large font because this graphic can be used to represent your app on its own. If you scale this image down to one-tenth the normal size and you cannot read the app name, your text is not big enough. Another common piece of this image is a tagline of some sort. This is a brief bit of text that gives the user some sense of what your app does, preferably in a memorable way. The tagline is especially helpful for apps that have a name that doesn't necessarily explain what they are. If your app is called "Image Cleaner" and it is an app that takes images and automatically processes them in ways to improve their appearance, your tagline might be something like "Automatically makes your images beautiful" or "Bad images in; good images out." Sometimes simplicity can be powerful, but you have to be careful to make sure you are telling enough. For instance, your tagline might be "Your images. Beautiful." That in itself might not be clear enough, but your graphic might depict a blurry image turning into a sharp one or something similar to convey the rest of the meaning. Whatever the tagline is, it needs to reflect the voice of your app (is your app playful, sophisticated, or snarky?) and give some feel for its purpose.

You should not include small text in this image. It's far too tempting to include some bullet points or even a brief intro into what your app is, but these small bits of text just become blurry, unprofessional lines once the graphic is scaled down. You should also avoid including screenshots in the feature graphic for the same reason. Once the image is scaled down, the screenshots are not useful and can detract from the message (besides, there's already a spot specifically for screenshots). Further, people are often tempted to put their screenshots into device mockups to make them look like the devices are really running the app. That can look really nice at large size, but again it's terrible at a smaller size and, perhaps worse, it becomes outdated extremely fast. Android devices change very rapidly, adjusting constantly to consumer demand, new technologies, and growing trends.

You should also avoid having anything too important in the bottom third of the feature graphic, because it can be covered by content, or at the very top, which can be covered by the app bar. Figure A.9 shows the top of the Google Maps page in Google Play in portrait orientation, with the app bar removed. Figure A.10 shows the same page in landscape orientation. Notice that the bottom third is mostly covered in landscape orientation. Also note that the app name is large and with sufficient contrast to be clear at different sizes and that a play button is added because the app has a video.

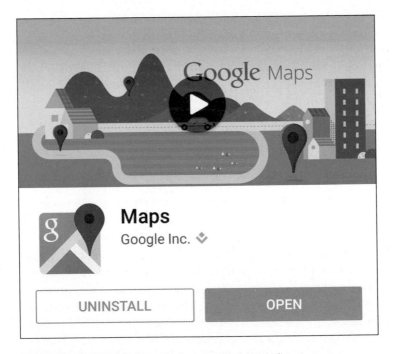

Figure A.9 The Google Maps feature graphic in portrait

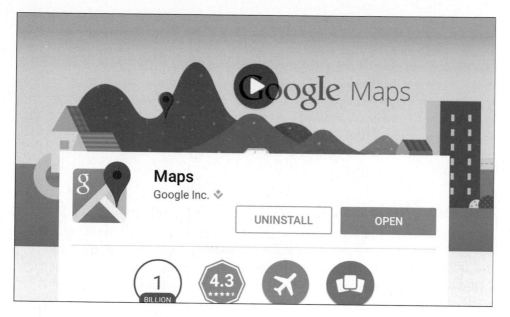

Figure A.10 The Google Map feature graphic in landscape

> **tip**
>
> Although you might hope that just making an amazing app is enough to get it
> noticed by the world, the reality is that preparing proper Google Play assets makes
> a significant difference. The obvious required pieces, such as the screenshots and
> description, are extremely important, but now you also know how important the
> feature graphic is. If you're still looking for some help understanding what good
> assets look like, consider visiting Google Play (https://play.google.com/store/apps)
> and viewing some of the featured apps.

Promotional Graphic

The promotional graphic has to be 180×120. It should be a PNG to avoid JPEG artifacts at such
a small size, but you can upload a JPEG image. There is no support for an alpha channel, so it
should be a 24-bit image.

This graphic is probably the least important asset. It originally served a purpose similar to the
feature graphic in the Android Market (before the rebranding to Google Play) for phones. Apps
that were being promoted in the Android Market would have the promotional graphic shown
at the top and in a few other places. Neither the current Google Play app for devices nor the

Google Play website show the promotional graphic anywhere, so it wouldn't be surprising if this asset went away completely.

All of this does not mean that the promotional graphic has no value; it just means it has less value than some of the other assets. If you do not have the time (or want to spend the time) creating a promotional graphic, a good option is to use a resized version of your feature graphic. If you have done the feature graphic well, scaling it to the size of the promotional graphic should give you something reasonable. You may choose to remove some text or to sharpen other text to ensure it is readable, but the purpose of the two images is very similar.

Video (YouTube)

Adding a video for your application is a great way to demonstrate the app in action. You can give the user a quick view of what the app looks like and how usable it is. Video has the advantage of being able to better demonstrate the app in use and take advantage of audio, but it is a supplement (not replacement) for screenshots. Screenshots must be to-the-point, faithful depictions of the actual app experience. The video, however, is open to a full range of options. It can be as simple as a user demonstrating the app with a voiceover explaining each screen, or it can be as involved as a comedic movie short meant to entertain and delight the user.

The type of movie should be reflective of the type of app and its personality. Is your app cool, to the point, and entirely utilitarian, or is your app bright, playful, and exciting? The former would lend itself to a video that demonstrates the key features of the app, and the latter is more open to entertainment. Regardless of the type of app, be sure to keep your video short (30 seconds to 3 minutes).

Paper Camera (https://play.google.com/store/apps/details?id=com.dama.papercamera) is an app that allows you to take photos and videos using various effects that make the media look like pastels, sketches, and so on. Their demo video is beautiful in its ability to accurately portray the app in the real world with a simplicity that makes it understandable and accessible to all levels of users. The app itself is also a great example of how to use a fully UI that is still intuitive. You can see the video on YouTube at https://www.youtube.com/watch?v=_Aw6jEVnE2o.

Promoting Your App

Once you have your app listed in Google Play with the assets specified in this appendix, you might consider promoting your app elsewhere. For instance, you might write to various blogs and ask them to cover your app. Be sure to include the Google Play link and a brief blurb about what the app is right away (you do want to include more details, but you are emailing people who are dealing with a significant volume of emails that are just like yours, so you have to get to the point in the first paragraph). Do not include any attachments in the email; instead, provide a link to download promotional photos, videos, and so on. Unlike for the screenshots for Google Play, you can use device mockups for the screenshots in this case (take a look at the official Device Art Generator, which allows you to just drag and drop images to put them in a device: http://developer.android.com/distribute/promote/device-art.html). Provide a point of contact for any questions. Never send the email multiple times; otherwise, your app quickly goes from being a potentially interesting new app to one that has to be spammed to be noticed. Finally, be willing to accept that your app won't be covered by everyone you email and that most of these people won't have the time to respond to you.

Amazon Appstore

The Amazon Appstore is an alternative to Google Play and reaches a fair number of users. The process for submitting an app is detailed on the website (https://developer.amazon.com/public/support/submitting-your-app/tech-docs/submitting-your-app), but it's worth calling out a few differences in the assets used when submitting to the Amazon Appstore. The application icon needs to be available in two sizes, 512×512 (just like you need for Google Play) and 114×114. You also have to submit at least three screenshots and a variety of sizes are acceptable (800×480, 1024×600, 1280×720, 1280×800, 1920×1200, and 2560×1600). The Amazon Appstore allows you to upload an optional "promotional image" that is very similar in purpose to the promotional graphic used for Google Play. Amazon requires a 1024×500 image, so you may be able to use the version you create for Google Play with a bit of cropping.

The Amazon Appstore listing can support up to five videos. They must be 720px to 1080px wide (both 4:3 and 16:9 ratios are supported). They should be 1200kbps or higher and will generally look best using the H.264 codec.

COMMON TASK REFERENCE

While working on Android apps, you are likely to learn certain tasks well. You will know the Activity and Fragment lifecycles without needing a reference. You will know how to execute code on a background thread. You will know how to do many tasks because you will have to do them all the time; however, some tasks you only need to do every now and then. You need to do them just often enough that you wish you could easily remember how to accomplish them, but not often enough to necessarily memorize them. Appendix B is meant to show you how to do some of these tasks and serve as a future reference.

Dismissing the Software Keyboard

Generally, Android does a good job of showing and hiding the Android keyboard as needed, but there are times when you need to dismiss the software keyboard manually. Perhaps you've made your own custom view that needs to dismiss the keyboard at certain times, or maybe the user has entered enough text into an `EditText` that you're able to show results but the keyboard would otherwise obscure them. Whatever the reason, dismissing the software keyboard is actually very easy to do. You just need to get a window token (`IBinder`) from an onscreen view such as your custom view or the `EditText` that the user was typing into and use the `InputMethodManager`'s `hideSoftInputFromWindow` method. See Listing B.1 for a simple example.

Listing B.1   Using the `InputMethodManager` to Dismiss the Software Keyboard

```
InputMethodManager imm = (InputMethodManager)
➥ getSystemService(Context.INPUT_METHOD_SERVICE);imm.
➥ hideSoftInputFromWindow(view.getWindowToken(), 0);
```

Using Full Screen Mode

Most apps should not use full screen mode. Generally users are jumping into and out of apps in seconds or minutes and are not engrossed enough in an app to warrant hiding the status bar at the top of the screen. There are a few exceptions, such as for a noncasual game (most casual games, such as Solitaire, do not have a need to take the full screen) and temporary full screen use for video playback, for example. When in doubt, don't make your app full screen.

If your activity should always be full screen, such as for a game, then it should specify a theme in the `AndroidManifest.xml` file that extends from one of the existing full screen themes. As of Android 4.0, device manufacturers are required to include the device default theme and the Holo themes as part of the compatibility test suite (any manufacturer that wants to include Google's apps such as the Play Store must ensure their devices pass the compatibility suite, which ensures platform consistency across devices). This means that the easiest way to have an `Activity` appear full screen is to include `android:theme="@android:style/Theme.DeviceDefault.NoActionBar.Fullscreen"` in the activity tag of the manifest (if your app extends Holo, then replace `DeviceDefault` with `Holo`). The theme prior to Holo that was full screen was `Theme.NoTitleBar.Fullscreen`, so apps that support older versions of Android can use that. If you are implementing a custom theme and cannot extend those or if you are using one of the AppCompat themes, you can specify `android:windowFullscreen` as `true` and `android:windowContentOverlay` as `@null`. Listing B.2 shows an example theme.

Listing B.2   A Custom Full Screen Theme

```
<style name="FullScreen" parent="Theme.AppCompat.Light.NoActionBar">
    <item name="android:windowFullscreen">true</item>
    <item name="android:windowContentOverlay">@null</item>
</style>
```

Back in Honeycomb (API level 11), Android added support for software system buttons (that is, the back, home, and recents/overview buttons could be shown on the screen). This means that the concept of "full screen" changed slightly because being truly full screen on a device with software buttons prevents the user from pressing any of those buttons. To handle that issue, the `View` class was given a method called `setSystemUiVisibility(int)` that allows you to hide that system navigation or to dim it. For example, if the user taps a view that is displaying a video to play it full screen, the view can call `setSystemUiVisibility(View.SYSTEM_UI_FLAG_HIDE_NAVIGATION)` to become full screen. For situations where you don't want to hide the system navigation because the user still needs it, you can instead dim the navigation (making the buttons appear like faint dots) by passing `View.SYSTEM_UI_FLAG_LOW_PRO-FILE int` instead.

Keeping the Screen On

Sometimes you need to keep the screen on while your app is in the foreground. For instance, you might be showing a video and you don't expect the user to interact with the device for a few minutes. Because the user isn't interacting with the device, it may time out and turn off the screen. Many developers mistakenly use the `WakeLock` class for this simple task. Not only does `WakeLock` require an extra permission, it has to be manually released to avoid excessive battery drain.

The easy way to accomplish this is to get a reference to the `Window` and set the `FLAG_KEEP_SCREEN_ON` flag. The call looks like this: `getWindow().addFlags(WindowManager.LayoutParams.FLAG_KEEP_SCREEN_ON)`. The nice thing about using this method is that it doesn't require a special permission. It will also only be enabled while your app is in the foreground. This means that you don't have to worry about your app keeping the system on even after the user has pressed the home button and moved on to something else. When you no longer need to keep the screen on, you call `getWindow().clearFlags(WindowManager.LayoutParams.FLAG_KEEP_SCREEN_ON)`. Although this method of keeping the screen on when you need it is much better than using a `WakeLock`, keep in mind that the screen is typically a device's biggest battery drain, so keeping the screen on more than necessary will adversely affect battery life no matter which method you use. The vast majority of apps do not need to keep the screen on artificially since the user's interactions will keep the screen on, so consider heavily whether keeping the screen on is beneficial to the user experience.

Determining the Device's Physical Screen Size

In the past, devices were broken up into broad size categories of small, normal, large, and extra large. Although the recommendation now is to use density-independent pixels and the various resource qualifiers covered in Chapter 4, "Adding App Graphics and Resources," there are still times when you need to know which size "bucket" the app falls into at runtime. You do this by getting the Configuration object from Resources and checking the screenLayout field. The screenLayout contains more information about the display, such as when it's "long" and in which direction the text is laid out, so you need to use the SCREENLAYOUT_SIZE_MASK to pull out the specific int you're looking for. See Listing B.3 for an example.

Listing B.3   Determining a Device's Size at Runtime

```
switch (getResources().getConfiguration().screenLayout &
➥ Configuration.SCREENLAYOUT_SIZE_MASK) {
    case Configuration.SCREENLAYOUT_SIZE_XLARGE:
        // Extra large (most 10" tablets)
        break;
    case Configuration.SCREENLAYOUT_SIZE_LARGE:
        // Large (most 7" tablets)
        break;
    case Configuration.SCREENLAYOUT_SIZE_NORMAL:
        // Normal (most phones)
        break;
    case Configuration.SCREENLAYOUT_SIZE_SMALL:
        // Small (very uncommon)
        break;
}
```

Determining the Device's Screen Size in Pixels

Sometimes you simply need to know how many pixels wide or high the display is. You can do this by getting a reference to the WindowManager to get a reference to the Display and then get the size from it. Prior to Android 3.0 (API level 13), you would use the getWidth and getHeight methods; since then, the getSize method has been available. If you're in an activity, you can get the WindowManager by simply calling getWindowManager. If not, you can get it as a system service as shown in Listing B.4.

Listing B.4   Getting the Screen Width and Height

```
WindowManager wm = (WindowManager) context.
➥ getSystemService(Context.WINDOW_SERVICE);
```

```
Display display = wm.getDefaultDisplay();
Point size = new Point();
display.getSize(size);
int screenWidth = size.x;
int screenHeight = size.y;
```

Determining the Device DPI

For the most part, you never have to directly consider converting to/from pixels and density-independent pixels. When you get dimensions from `Resources`, the work is done for you. When you specify sizes in your layouts, the conversion happens automatically. However, sometimes you do need to know the device DPI, such as when implementing a custom view that handles density-specific drawing. You know that one pixel on an MDPI device is two pixels on an XHDPI device, but how do you know the density of a given device? From the DisplayMetrics object, you can see the density, which will be an int that represents the dots per inch (dpi). Listing B.5 shows how you can use this, but you should note that there are additional possible values. For instance, a device can be 560 dpi, which has a constant of `DENSITY_560`. You should use the density for comparison in most cases rather than looking for exact values.

Listing B.5   Determining a Device's Density at Runtime

```
final int density = getResources().getDisplayMetrics().densityDpi;
if (density > DisplayMetrics.DENSITY_XXXHIGH) {
    // Display is more than 560 dots per inch
} else if (density > DisplayMetrics.DENSITY_XXHIGH) {
    // Display is more than 480 dots per inch
} else if (density > DisplayMetrics.DENSITY_XHIGH) {
    // Density is more than 320 dots per inch
} else if (density > DisplayMetrics.DENSITY_HIGH) {
    // Density is more than 240 dots per inch
} else if (density > DisplayMetrics.DENSITY_MEDIUM) {
    // Density is more than 160 dots per inch
} else if (density > DisplayMetrics.DENSITY_LOW) {
    // Density is more than 120 dots per inch
}
```

If you instead have a pixel value for MDPI and need to scale it for the current screen density, you can use the `density` property of `DisplayMetrics` (as opposed to the `densityDpi` property). This will be a float that you can multiply the MDPI value by to scale it properly. For instance, on an XXXHDPI device, the `density` property will be 4.0.

Checking for a Network Connection

The majority of apps use a network connection, so checking whether there is a connection or not can be very useful. If your app needs some assets on startup or fetches new data, you should check if there is a network connection to notify the user when one is not available. Being proactive gives a much better user experience than just waiting for a failed network attempt and showing an error. By actually telling the user that the device does not have a network connection (preferably in an unobtrusive inline UI element), you enable the user to possibly fix the problem (e.g., if the user has accidently left the device in airplane mode or has not yet connected to an available Wi-Fi network) and you also take some of the blame off your app. Instead of your app showing failed connection errors or having unexplained missing assets everywhere, you inform the user right away that something is wrong. See Listing B.6 for an example of a static method you might want to put in a utility class (keep in mind that this just determines if there is an active network connection, not if the device is connected to the Internet).

Listing B.6   A Static Method for Determining if a Device Has a Connection

```
/**
 * Returns true if the device has a network connection
 *
 * @param context Context to access the ConnectivityManager
 * @return true if the device has a network connection
 */
public static boolean isConnectedToNetwork(Context context) {
    boolean connected = false;
    ConnectivityManager cm = (ConnectivityManager) context.
➥ getSystemService(Context.CONNECTIVITY_SERVICE);
    if (cm != null) {
        NetworkInfo ni = cm.getActiveNetworkInfo();
        if (ni != null) {
            connected = ni.isConnected();
        }
    }
    return connected;
}
```

Checking if the Current Thread Is the UI Thread

You should never modify views from a background thread, but there are times when a piece of code can run on the main (UI) thread or a background thread, so it's necessary to determine whether or not it's the UI thread. Fortunately, this is really easy. The Looper class has a static method called myLooper() that returns the Looper for the current thread. It also has a getMainLooper() method that returns the Looper for the UI thread. If these objects are the same, your code is running on the UI thread. See Listing B.7 for an example.

Listing B.7   How to Check if the Current Thread Is the UI Thread

```
if (Looper.myLooper() == Looper.getMainLooper()) {
    // UI Thread
} else {
    // Other Thread
}
```

Custom View Attributes

Although custom view attributes were partly covered in the chapters of this book, some additional attributes are available. Unfortunately, the Android site does not currently provide a list of these, and it can be tough to interpret them when reading through the ones in the Android source.

By convention, custom attributes go in an attrs.xml file in res/values. This file will specify which XML attributes are available for the view. For a complete example, see Listing B.8.

Listing B.8   A Sample attrs.xml File That Specifies Many Custom Attributes

```
<?xml version="1.0" encoding="utf-8"?>
<resources>
    <declare-styleable name="CustomAttributesView">

        <!-- boolean -->
        <attr name="booleanExample" format="boolean" />

        <!-- integer -->
        <attr name="integerExample" format="integer" />

        <!-- float -->
        <attr name="floatExample" format="float" />

        <!-- fraction (actually a percentage like "50%") -->
        <attr name="fractionExample" format="fraction" />

        <!-- string -->
        <attr name="stringExample" format="string" />

        <!-- dimension -->
        <attr name="colorExample" format="color" />
```

```xml
        <!-- dimension -->
        <attr name="dimensionExample" format="dimension" />

        <!-- reference -->
        <attr name="referenceExample" format="reference" />

        <!-- enum -->
        <attr name="enumExample">
            <enum name="zero_enum" value="0"/>
            <enum name="one_enum" value="1"/>
        </attr>

        <!-- flag - the user can use multiple flags -->
        <attr name="flagExample">
            <flag name="oneFlag" value="1"/>
            <flag name="twoFlag" value="2"/>
            <flag name="fourFlag" value="4"/>
        </attr>

        <!-- reference OR color -->
        <attr name="referenceOrColorExample" format="reference|color" />

        <!-- existing attribute -->
        <attr name="android:textColor" />
    </declare-styleable>
</resources>
```

To use these values, the layout file they'll be used in needs to specify the namespace for the app's package and then each attribute needs the namespace prefix. Typically, you'll specify the namespace as "app," but that's a convention. In most cases you will use this: `xmlns:app="http://schemas.android.com/apk/res-auto"`. See Listing B.9 for a simple layout that specifies each of the custom values.

Listing B.9 Simple Layout Using a Custom View with Custom Attributes

```xml
<RelativeLayout
    xmlns:android="http://schemas.android.com/apk/res/android"
    xmlns:app="http://schemas.android.com/apk/res-auto"
    xmlns:tools="http://schemas.android.com/tools"
    android:layout_width="match_parent"
    android:layout_height="match_parent"
    tools:context=".MainActivity" >

    <com.auidbook.appendixb.MyCustomView
        android:layout_width="match_parent"
        android:layout_height="match_parent"
        android:textColor="#FFFF0000"
        app:booleanExample="true"
```

```
                    app:colorExample="#FFFF0000"
                    app:dimensionExample="100dp"
                    app:enumExample="one_enum"
                    app:flagExample="oneFlag|fourFlag"
                    app:floatExample="5.5"
                    app:fractionExample="10%"
                    app:integerExample="42"
                    app:referenceExample="@string/app_name"
                    app:referenceOrColorExample="#FF00FF00"
                    app:stringExample="My String" />
    </RelativeLayout>
```

The custom view needs to use `Context`'s `obtainStyledAttributes` method to retrieve a `TypedArray` of the attributes that were specified in the XML layout. The various attributes are available from that `TypedArray`. Most of these are pretty simple, but a few need a little bit of explanation. The enum type does not return an actual `enum`; it just ensures that only one of the possible choices is selected. It's up to you to make use of the int to decide what to do. The flag type needs to use "bitwise and" operations to determine which values are set. The reference in this example isn't actually used to do anything other than print its int, but you can get the value the reference points to with the `Resources` object. When a value can be multiple types, and those types are different (e.g., color or reference), you can use the `peekValue` method to get a `TypedValue` object and determine the type from there. See Listing B.10 for a simple custom view that reads all these attributes and then creates a string to display that shows which ones were passed. Figure B.1 shows what this view can look like on a device. This complete example is available in the `appendixb` folder of the book's source code.

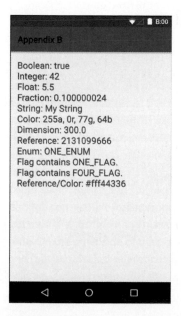

Figure B.1 Sample output of the custom view showing the attributes that were passed

Listing B.10 A Custom View that Utilizes a Variety of Custom Attributes

```java
public class CustomAttributesView extends View {

    // Enum values
    private static final int ZERO_ENUM = 0;
    private static final int ONE_ENUM = 1;

    // Flag values
    private static final int ONE_FLAG = 1;
    private static final int TWO_FLAG = 2;
    private static final int FOUR_FLAG = 4;

    private String mDisplayString;
    private final Paint mPaint = new Paint(Paint.ANTI_ALIAS_FLAG);
    private StaticLayout mLayout;
    private TextPaint mTextPaint;

    public CustomAttributesView(Context context) {
        super(context);
        mDisplayString = "No custom attributes";
        mPaint.setColor(Color.BLACK);
        mTextPaint = new TextPaint(mPaint);

        mTextPaint.setTextSize(context.getResources().getDimension
        (R.dimen.customViewTextSize));
    }

    public CustomAttributesView(Context context, AttributeSet attrs) {
        super(context, attrs);
        init(context, attrs);
    }

    public CustomAttributesView(Context context, AttributeSet attrs,
    int defStyleAttr) {
        super(context, attrs, defStyleAttr);
        init(context, attrs);
    }

    @TargetApi(Build.VERSION_CODES.LOLLIPOP)
    public CustomAttributesView(Context context, AttributeSet attrs,
    int defStyleAttr, int defStyleRes) {
        super(context, attrs, defStyleAttr, defStyleRes);
        init(context, attrs);
    }

    @Override
    public void onDraw(Canvas canvas) {
        canvas.save();
```

```
        canvas.clipRect(getPaddingLeft(), getPaddingTop(), getWidth() -
➡ getPaddingRight(), getHeight() - getPaddingBottom());
        canvas.translate(getPaddingLeft(), getPaddingTop());
        mLayout.draw(canvas);
        canvas.restore();
    }
    @Override
    protected void onLayout(boolean changed, int left, int top, int
➡ right, int bottom) {
        super.onLayout(changed, left, top, right, bottom);
        if (mLayout == null || changed) {
            mLayout = new StaticLayout(mDisplayString, mTextPaint,
➡ right - left, Layout.Alignment.ALIGN_NORMAL, 1, 0, true);
        }
    }

    private void init(Context context, AttributeSet attrs) {
        final TypedArray customAttrs = context.
➡ obtainStyledAttributes(attrs, R.styleable.CustomAttributesView);
        final StringBuilder sb = new StringBuilder();
        int currentAttribute;

        // boolean
        currentAttribute = R.styleable.
➡ CustomAttributesView_booleanExample;
        boolean booleanExample = customAttrs.
➡ getBoolean(currentAttribute, false);
        sb.append("Boolean:").append(booleanExample).append('\n');

        // integer
        currentAttribute = R.styleable.
➡ CustomAttributesView_integerExample;
        int integerExample = customAttrs.getInt(currentAttribute, 0);
        sb.append("Integer:").append(integerExample).append('\n');

        // float
        currentAttribute = R.styleable.
➡ CustomAttributesView_floatExample;
        float floatExample = customAttrs.getFloat(currentAttribute, 0f);
        sb.append("Float:").append(floatExample).append('\n');

        // fraction
        currentAttribute = R.styleable.
➡ CustomAttributesView_fractionExample;
        float fractionExample = customAttrs.
➡ getFraction(currentAttribute, 1, 1, -1);
        sb.append("Fraction:").append(fractionExample).append('\n');
```

```
        // string
        currentAttribute = R.styleable.
➥ CustomAttributesView_stringExample;
        String stringExample = customAttrs.getString(currentAttribute);
        sb.append("String:").append(stringExample).append('\n');

        // color
        currentAttribute = R.styleable.
➥ CustomAttributesView_colorExample;
        int colorExample = customAttrs.getColor(currentAttribute,
➥ Color.BLACK);
        sb.append("Color:")
          .append(Color.alpha(colorExample))
          .append("a,")
          .append(Color.red(colorExample))
          .append("r,")
          .append(Color.green(colorExample))
          .append("g,")
          .append(Color.blue(colorExample))
          .append("b")
          .append('\n');

        // dimension
        currentAttribute = R.styleable.
➥ CustomAttributesView_dimensionExample;
        float dimensionExample = customAttrs.
➥ getDimension(currentAttribute, 0);
        sb.append("Dimension:").append(dimensionExample).append('\n');

        // reference
        currentAttribute = R.styleable.
➥ CustomAttributesView_referenceExample;
        int referenceExample = customAttrs.
➥ getResourceId(currentAttribute, 0);
        sb.append("Reference:").append(referenceExample).append('\n');

        // enum
        currentAttribute = R.styleable.CustomAttributesView_enumExample;
        int enumExample = customAttrs.getInt(currentAttribute, -1);
        if (enumExample == ZERO_ENUM) {
            sb.append("Enum: ZERO_ENUM\n");
        } else if (enumExample == ONE_ENUM) {
            sb.append("Enum: ONE_ENUM\n");
        } else {
            sb.append("Enum not specified.\n");
        }
```

```
        // flag
        currentAttribute = R.styleable.CustomAttributesView_flagExample;
        int flagExample = customAttrs.getInt(currentAttribute, -1);
        if (flagExample == -1) {
            sb.append("Flag not specified.\n");
        } else {
            if ((flagExample & ONE_FLAG) != 0) {
                sb.append("Flag contains ONE_FLAG.\n");
            }
            if ((flagExample & TWO_FLAG) != 0) {
                sb.append("Flag contains TWO_FLAG.\n");
            }
            if ((flagExample & FOUR_FLAG) != 0) {
                sb.append("Flag contains FOUR_FLAG.\n");
            }
        }

        // reference OR color
        currentAttribute = R.styleable.
➥ CustomAttributesView_referenceOrColorExample;
        TypedValue tv = customAttrs.peekValue(currentAttribute);
        if (tv == null) {
            sb.append("Did not contain reference or color.\n");
        } else {
            sb.append("Reference/Color:").append(tv.coerceToString()).
➥ append('\n');
        }

        // android:textColor
        currentAttribute = R.styleable.
➥ CustomAttributesView_android_textColor;
        tv = customAttrs.peekValue(currentAttribute);
        if (tv == null) {
            mPaint.setColor(Color.BLACK);
        } else {
            mPaint.setColor(tv.data);
        }

        customAttrs.recycle();
        mDisplayString = sb.toString();
        mTextPaint = new TextPaint(mPaint);
        mTextPaint.setTextSize(context.getResources().getDimension
➥ (R.dimen.customViewTextSize));
    }
}
```

> **note**
>
> Although you may have read straight through this appendix to see what it offers, it's largely intended to be a reference. There are those times when you can't quite remember things such as how to specify a custom attribute that is an enum, and trying to figure it out by racking your brain, looking at the source, or even browsing the Web can be a slow process. That's when this appendix is meant to be helpful. Hopefully you will reference it when needed, so you can focus on the important parts of your code.

INDEX

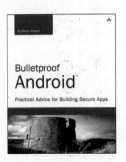